Cooking Light®

SUPERfast

suppers

SPEEDY SOLUTIONS FOR DINNER DILEMMAS

Oxmoor House®

White Bean and Pepper Soup, page 55

Cooking Light®

SUPERfast

suppers

SPEEDY SOLUTIONS FOR DINNER DILEMMAS

compiled and edited by
Anne C. Cain, M.S., M.P.H., R.D.

Oxmoor House®

ISBN: 0-8487-2628-6

Printed in the United States of America
Tenth printing 2006

Be sure to check with your health-care provider before making any changes in your diet.

Oxmoor House, Inc.

Editor-in-Chief: Nancy Fitzpatrick Wyatt
Executive Editor: Katherine M. Eakin
Art Director: Cynthia R. Cooper
Copy Chief: Catherine Ritter Scholl

Cooking Light Superfast Suppers

Editor: Anne C. Cain, M.S., M.P.H., R.D.
Assistant Editor: Holley C. Johnson, R. D.
Copy Editor: Jacqueline B. Giovanelli
Editorial Assistant: Megan Graves
Director, Test Kitchens: Elizabeth Tyler Luckett
Assistant Director, Test Kitchens: Julie Christopher
Recipe Editor: Gayle Hays Sadler
Test Kitchens Staff: Kristi Carter, Nicole L. Faber,
    Jan A. Smith, Elise Weis, and Kelley Self Wilton
Senior Photographer: Jim Bathie
Photographer: Brit Huckabay
Senior Photo Sylist: Kay Clarke
Photo Stylist: Ashley J. Wyatt
Publishing Systems Administrator: Rick Tucker
Director, Production and Distribution: Phillip Lee
Books Production Manager: Greg Amason
Production Coordinator: Leslie Johnson
Production Assistant: Faye Porter Bonner

Contributors:
Designer: Rita Yerby
Indexer: Mary Ann Laurens
Editorial Intern: Terri Laschober
Photographers: Ralph Anderson, Keith Harrelson
Photo Stylists: Missie Neville Crawford, Connie Formby,
    Katie Stoddard
Proofreader: Barzella Papa
Recipe Developers: Rebecca M. Boggan,
    Maureen Callahan, M.S., R.D., Jennifer Cofield,
    Nancy Hughes, Ana Kelly, Jean Kressy, Kathleen Phillips

Cover: Seared Chicken with Avocado (page 300)

IT'S ALL ABOUT time

· · · · · · · · · · · · · · · · · · · ·

To help you fit these recipes and menus into your busy schedule, *each recipe gives you the prep and cook times; each menu lists the total time.*

Prep time is what's needed for tasks such as chopping, slicing, stirring, and assembling. Cook time includes all cooking procedures in the recipe. If the recipe involves cooking two things at once (cooking the pasta while you sauté the vegetables), those times aren't counted separately.

Total menu time is the time it will take you to get the entire meal on the table, start to finish, and also takes into account overlapping tasks.

To order additional copies of this book or others, call 1-800-765-6400.

For more books to enrich your life, visit
oxmoorhouse.com

contents

"Not a night goes by at my house that I don't get asked about what we're having for supper or when we'll eat. Sometimes it really tries my patience because I'm running out of ideas."

what's for
SUPPER?

Superfast Suppers offers real solutions to help you creatively solve your dinnertime dilemmas. We start by giving you the basic guidelines for healthy eating and by helping you plan quick and easy menus. Then we take you to the grocery store, show you what to buy, and how to get it on the table fast.

So the next time you hear, "What's for supper?", you'll have the answers. Here are some of our favorite meals:

- **Black Bean and Poblano Tortilla Wraps** (page 42)

- **Burgundy Beef Stew** (page 130)

- **Slow-Cooker Lasagna** (page 152)

- **Creamy Seafood Parmesan Pasta** (page 260)

- **Spicy Pork au Jus** (page 288)

- **Seared Chicken with Avocado** (page 300)

"I want to make nutritious meals for my family, but with two of us working full-time, and two kids involved in soccer, piano lessons, and scouting—having the time to cook a healthy meal is just a dream."

the healthy meal challenge

Scan our shortcut version of the Dietary Guidelines on the next four pages to see how simple healthy eating can be.

good news! Sitting down with your family for a nutritious meal isn't an illusive dream. Make it a reality by transforming the basic principles of healthy eating into shortcut strategies.

The USDA Dietary Guidelines give you a basic framework for healthy eating based on 10 general guidelines. Their premise is that eating is one of life's great pleasures and that there are many ways to build a healthy diet. The following guidelines simply point the way:

1. Aim for a healthy weight.
2. Be physically active each day.
3. Let the Pyramid guide your food choices.
4. Choose a variety of grains daily.
5. Choose a variety of fruits and vegetables daily.
6. Keep food safe to eat.
7. Choose a diet that is low in saturated fat and cholesterol and moderate in total fat.
8. Choose beverages and foods to moderate your intake of sugars.
9. Choose and prepare foods with less salt.
10. If you drink alcoholic beverages, do so in moderation.

The following shortcut solutions help you follow the guidelines without spending time fretting about what you should eat. Each time you make one positive change in your eating habits, you're one step closer to better health.

10 Steps to Health—the SUPER**fast** way

1

Aim for a healthy weight.
Determine your healthy weight (talk to your doctor or a registered dietitian if you need to), and choose a lifestyle that combines sensible eating with regular physical activity.

SUPER**fast** Solution:

Every menu in *Superfast Suppers* is designed to provide the right mix of foods so that you'll get the nutrients you need without extra calories. The nutrient values at the end of each recipe will help you see what you're getting. For more information, see Nutritional Analysis on page 356.

2

Be physically active each day.
Everybody needs to move, and there is more and more evidence supporting the importance of exercise in terms of health and disease prevention.

SUPER**fast** Solution:

No time to exercise? By spending less time in the kitchen preparing meals, you'll have a few more minutes in your day for physical activity. Start with the meals in the following chapters.

• **No-Cook Meals:** You'll be in and out of the kitchen in minutes because these meals require no cooking and very little preparation.

• **Slow Cooker Suppers:** Put the ingredients in the cooker in the morning, and supper is ready whenever you get home.

3

Let the Pyramid guide your food choices.
Different foods contain different nutrients and other healthful substances. No single food can supply all the nutrients in the amounts you need. Build a healthy base by using the variety of foods in the pyramid as a starting point. (See the Food Guide Pyramid below.)

SUPER**fast** Solution:

Don't get stressed about variety in your diet. Use the 7-Day Menu Planner (page 16) to help you eat a lot of different foods without spending a lot of time cooking.

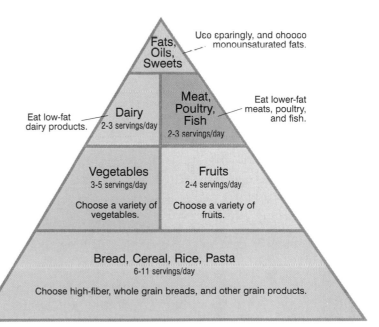

THE FOOD GUIDE PYRAMID

4 Choose a variety of grains daily, especially whole grains.

Foods made from grains (such as wheat, rice, and oats) help form the foundation of a nutritious diet. Eating plenty of whole grains such as whole wheat bread or oatmeal may help protect against heart disease, type 2 diabetes, and certain cancers. Try for at least 6 servings of grains per day, with as many as possible being whole grain.

SUPER**fast** Solution:

Focus on the following fast whole grains:

- whole grain breads
- whole grain dry cereals
- instant oatmeal
- quick-cooking barley
- quick-cooking brown rice
- whole wheat pastas

5 Choose a variety of fruits and vegetables daily.

If you're like most Americans, you may fall far short of the recommended 2 fruits and 3 vegetables a day. And that's just the minimum requirement! So add more fruits and vegetables to your day to protect yourself against type 2 diabetes, heart disease, and certain types of cancer.

SUPER**fast** Solution:

With so many convenient options available, it's easy to incorporate fruits and vegetables into your diet. Some require no prep at all, other than rinsing and eating. And the market is now full of shortcut produce so that all you have to do is open a bag or a container.

Check out your local supermarket for some of the items on the right and see how easy eating fruits and veggies can be.

10 Ways to Sneak Fruits and Veggies Into Your Day

- Order lettuce and tomato on your sandwich.

- Add a chopped apple to tuna salad.

- Purée ripe berries or a banana in fat-free milk, and add a little vanilla extract. Drink as a shake, or pour over fruit salad for a sweet, creamy treat.

- Jazz up plain brown rice by adding mushrooms, chopped tomato, broccoli, diced carrots, or raisins.

- Serve raw vegetable sticks instead of chips with salsa. Try zucchini, snow peas, and cucumbers in addition to carrots and celery.

- Eat a cluster of grapes instead of chips with your sandwich.

- Leave out the meat in your spaghetti sauce and use diced tomatoes, grated carrots, or chopped zucchini for fat-free texture and flavor.

- Top your pizza with pineapple chunks.

- Add cubed cantaloupe to a chicken or lamb kabob before grilling.

- Add color, texture, flavor, and nutrients to pasta salad with red, green, or yellow peppers; broccoli florets; sliced carrots; cucumbers; cubed squash; and diced celery.

- bagged salad greens
- salad bars
- premade salads
- refrigerated fresh fruit
- precut fresh fruit
- precut fresh vegetables
- canned fruits and vegetables
- frozen fruits and vegetables

6 Keep food safe to eat.

Everyone wants to eat food that tastes good, but making sure the food is safe to eat is even more crucial.

SUPERfast Solution:

When you need information about food safety, here's where to turn.

- USDA/Food Safety and Inspection Services, www.fsis.usda.gov or 800-535-4555
- FightBAC! ™, www.fightbac.org
- American Dietetic Association, www.eatright.org or 800-877-1600
- FDA/Center for Food Safety and Applied Nutrition, www.cfsan.fda.gov or 888-SAFEFOOD

7 Choose a diet that is low in saturated fat and cholesterol and moderate in total fat.

High-fat meats are often the reason that a diet is high in saturated fats. When you take steps to replace high-fat meats with lean cuts, the decrease in saturated fat will be significant.

SUPERfast Solution:

The recipes in the Easy Entrées chapter (page 240) feature quick-cooking cuts of lean beef, pork, poultry and fish. Meatless Main Dishes (page 190) offers over 30 meat-free meals.

Garlic Turkey-Broccoli
Stir-Fry, page 306

Fresh Berries with Maple
Cream, page 337

8 Choose beverages and foods to moderate your intake of sugars.

It's not that sugar itself is bad for you, but if you eat too much sugar (or foods containing excess sugars), you may be missing out on important nutrients and/or getting more calories than you need. You can add sweetness (and nutrients) to foods by using less sugar and maximizing the natural sweetness of fruits and fruit juices.

SUPERfast Solution:

Satisfy your sweet tooth with low-sugar desserts in Deadline Desserts (page 332). Here are some that you can make in 10 minutes or less:

- Strawberries with Orange Custard Sauce (page 335)
- Fresh Berries with Maple Cream (page 337)
- Cookies and Cream Parfaits (page 339)
- Chocolate-Peanut Butter Sundaes (page 339)
- Pineapple Sundaes (page 340)
- Chocolate-Banana Cream Tarts (page 346)
- Pear Custard Tarts (page 347)

9 Choose and prepare foods with less salt.

The recommended intake of sodium is no more than 2,400 milligrams per day—that's about 1 teaspoon of salt per day.

Convenience foods are often higher in sodium than their fresh counterparts, so cutting back on salt when you're using these products can be a challenge.

SUPER**fast** Solution:
Add flavor to your foods with a variety of herbs and spices instead of salt. To make that an easy option, keep spice blends on hand. With one little shake, you can take your taste buds on a trip around the world. Some of our favorites include:
- Creole
- Moroccan
- Greek
- Lemon Pepper
- Italian
- Thai
- Southwestern
- Mesquite
- Mexican

10 If you drink alcoholic beverages, do so in moderation.

Moderate intake of alcohol, especially wine, has been associated with a reduced risk of heart disease.

SUPER**fast** Solution: Slow down and enjoy your meals with a glass of wine—your heart might thank you. With the 20-minute meals in *Superfast Suppers*, you'll be able to spend less time in the kitchen and more time at the table enjoying good wine, conversation, and friends.

If you choose to have a glass of wine with dinner, here are some ideas for wine pairings.
- Peppered Beef Tenderloin (page 176) with cabernet sauvignon
- Maple-Glazed Salmon (page 169) with pinot noir
- Creamy Seafood-Parmesan Pasta (page 260) with chardonnay
- Roasted Tomato-Cannellini Pasta (page 211) with Chianti

Food in the Fast Lane

Think fast food is the only way? **Homecooked can be better** in terms of nutrition and time, especially if you have to sit in the drive-thru line for a while! Compare the differences in nutrients and time between fast food and Superfast recipes.

BURGERS AND FRIES

Nutrients/ Time	Superfast **Basic Veggie Burgers** (page 77) Steak fries, broiled Bottled water (12 ounces)	Fast Food McDonald's Quarter Pounder with Cheese French fries (small) Cola (12 ounces)
Calories	459	880
Fat	10.2g	40g
Saturated Fat	2.8g	14g
Sodium	1,141mg	1,235mg
Time	13 minutes	15 minutes

Although there's only a slight difference in the sodium, there is a big savings in calories and fat with the veggie burger.

PIZZA

Nutrients/ Time	Superfast **Roasted Red Pepper and Arugula Pizza,** 2 slices (page 212)	Fast Food Pizza Hut Veggie Lover's Hand Tossed Pizza, 2 slices
Calories	333	444
Fat	11.6g	14g
Saturated Fat	4.8g	6g
Sodium	903mg	1,282mg
Time	21 minutes	30 minutes (delivery)

You save about 110 calories, 379 milligrams of sodium, and a minimum of 7 minutes with the Superfast veggie pizza. If you order a meat pizza instead of a Veggie Lover's, the fat and calories will be much higher than the values listed here.

CHINESE TAKEOUT

Nutrients/ Time	Superfast **Cashew Broccoli and Tofu,** 1¼ cups and 1 cup rice (page 236)	Fast Food Cashew Chicken, 1¼ cups and 1 cup rice
Calories	424	744
Fat	16.2g	38.7g
Saturated Fat	3g	6.6g
Sodium	806mg	1,135mg
Time	16 minutes	30 minutes (takeout)

Takeout portions are much larger than the Superfast portion, but for the same serving size, the savings in calories, fat, and sodium are significant.

"_If someone would just give me a list of what to eat, I'd be happy._**"**

mastering menus

Meal planning is easy with our 7-Day Superfast Menu Plan and Grocery List.

We've set up a week of menus for breakfast, lunch, dinner, and a snack. The recipes in bold are from this book, with page numbers provided for easy reference. The other items—fresh fruits, vegetables, breads, and grains—are simple ways to round out the meals.

Our menu plan isn't meant to be an exact prescription, but an example of how to mix and match the menus in _Superfast Suppers_ to suit your busy schedule. Since this menu plan is guaranteed to be superfast, every meal can be prepared in 20 minutes or less. (The Slow-Cooker Lasagna cooks all day, but requires only 12 minutes of prep time.)

Each daily menu provides approximately 1,600 calories. If you need to cut back from that, choose smaller portions, or trim a few of the snacks from the menu. We don't advise eating less than 1,500 calories, especially if you're moderately active. To add calories, include more than one serving of a particular recipe on the menu, or add more nutrient-rich snacks.

Following the current dietary guidelines for total fat intake, each daily menu provides less than 30 percent calories from fat.

"_Call me a nerd,_ **but I make out weekly menus** _so I know exactly what we're having when I walk in the door. That saves me from standing in front of the pantry door trying to figure out what to make. I try to go to the grocery store just once a week and buy the things I need for that week. Of course, if my husband suggests that we go out for dinner, I never argue!_**"**

Alyson Haynes,
Foods Editor

Use the grocery list below to ensure that you have everything you need for this one week of meals. The menu plan lists amounts and calories for single servings. When you're using the grocery list, be sure to buy enough of the non-recipe items for the number in your household. Refer to the menus to determine the amount to buy for each recipe.

"Simplify. *I don't try to make a 5-course meal—one or two items, three at the most, is plenty to fill us up.***"**

Kelley Wilton,
Test Kitchens staff

7-Day Superfast Menu Plan Grocery List

fresh produce

- ❑ asparagus
- ❑ avocado
- ❑ bell pepper, green
- ❑ bell pepper, red
- ❑ carrots, baby
- ❑ carrots, matchstick-cut
- ❑ celery
- ❑ cucumbers
- ❑ garlic cloves
- ❑ green beans
- ❑ herbs: cilantro, mint, basil, parsley
- ❑ lettuce, curly
- ❑ lettuce, romaine
- ❑ mushrooms, presliced
- ❑ onions, green
- ❑ onion, red
- ❑ pecan pieces
- ❑ salad greens, mixed
- ❑ spinach leaves, baby
- ❑ tomato
- ❑ tomatoes, grape

fruits and juices

- ❑ apples
- ❑ bananas
- ❑ blueberries
- ❑ cranberries, dried
- ❑ grapes, green and red
- ❑ lemons
- ❑ molon ouboo
- ❑ oranges
- ❑ pineapple-orange juice
- ❑ strawberries

deli/bakery

- ❑ bagels, whole wheat
- ❑ boboli pizza crust
- ❑ buttermilk bread
- ❑ English muffins
- ❑ French bread/rolls
- ❑ pita bread
- ❑ pizza crust dough
- ❑ wheat berry bread, sliced

refrigerated meats

- ❑ chicken breast halves
- ❑ chicken breast strips, grilled
- ❑ chicken breast tenders
- ❑ ground round
- ❑ lean ham/lower-sodium ham
- ❑ turkey breast, roasted

canned goods

- ❑ black beans
- ❑ chicken broth, less-sodium
- ❑ chickpeas (garbanzo beans)
- ❑ mushrooms, sliced
- ❑ olives, ripe and kalamata
- ❑ pasta sauce
- ❑ tomato paste, flavored
- ❑ tuna
- ❑ water chestnuts

pasta/rice

- ❑ pasta: angel hair, fusilli, lasagna noodles, penne
- ❑ rice, boil-in-bag long-grain

cereals/snacks/chips

- ❑ gingersnaps
- ❑ rye crackers
- ❑ vegetable chips
- ❑ whole oats cereal

dairy

- ❑ Amaretto-flavored creamer
- ❑ cream cheese, fat-free
- ❑ Cheddar cheese, reduced-fat
- ❑ feta cheese with black pepper
- ❑ feta cheese, reduced-fat
- ❑ Havarti cheese, reduced-fat
- ❑ Monterey Jack cheese with jalapeños
- ❑ mozzarella cheese, part-skim
- ❑ ricotta cheese, part-skim
- ❑ milk, fat-free
- ❑ sour cream, reduced-fat
- ❑ yogurt, fat-free plain
- ❑ yogurt, low-fat lemon/vanilla
- ❑ eggs

freezer

- ❑ chicken, chopped cooked
- ❑ fruit sorbet
- ❑ green peas
- ❑ ice cream sandwiches, low-fat
- ❑ lime pops
- ❑ strawberries

staples

- ❑ butter, light
- ❑ capers
- ❑ cooking spray
- ❑ fruit spread
- ❑ garlic, bottled minced
- ❑ maple syrup, reduced-calorie
- ❑ mayonnaise, light
- ❑ olive oil
- ❑ olive oil vinaigrette, reduced-fat
- ❑ peanut butter
- ❑ pesto
- ❑ ranch dressing, fat-free
- ❑ salt
- ❑ sugar
- ❑ black pepper
- ❑ cinnamon
- ❑ cumin
- ❑ curry powder
- ❑ crushed red pepper
- ❑ dried Italian seasoning

7-Day Superfast Menu Plan

	DAY 1	DAY 2	DAY 3	
BREAKFAST	Whole wheat bagel, 1 (3.4 oz.) Fat-free cream cheese, 2 T. Strawberries, 1c. Pineapple-orange juice, ½ c.	English muffin, 2 halves Light butter, 2 T. Fruit spread, 2 T. Orange sections, 1c. Fat-free milk, 1 c.	Cheese toast, 2 slices (2 slices wheat berry bread, 2 oz. reduced-fat Cheddar cheese) Apple, 1 sliced Fat-free milk, 1 c.	
LUNCH	**Sweet Curry-Tuna Salad Sandwiches, page 47,** 1 sandwich **Minted Melon, page 47,** 1 serving Vegetable chips, 10 (1 oz.)	**Ham and Pea Salad, page 27,** 1 serving Baby carrots, 1 c. Rye crackers, 2 Red grapes, ½ c.	**Mushroom-Spinach Pizza, page 215** 1 serving Baby carrots, 1 c. Low-fat ice cream sandwich, 1	
DINNER	**Greek Grilled Chicken Salad, page 32,** 1 serving **Blueberries with Lemon Yogurt, page 32,** 1 serving Whole wheat pita wedges, 4 (1 pita) Fruit sorbet, ½ c.	**Slow Cooker Lasagna, page 152,** 1 serving Tossed green salad, 1½ c. Reduced-fat olive oil vinaigrette, 2 T. French bread, 2 slices	**Buttery Herbed Chicken, page 64,** 1 serving Steamed asparagus, 1c. Strawberries, 1 c.	
SNACK	Reduced-fat Cheddar cheese, 1 oz. Apple, 1, sliced	Whole wheat bagel, 1 Fat-free cream cheese, 2 T.	Gingersnaps, 6 Apple, 1 Fat-free milk, 1 c.	
	Total calories: 1594	**Total calories: 1673**	**Total calories: 1630**	

page 50

page 164

c. = cup, oz. = ounce, T. = tablespoon, tsp. = teaspoon

DAY 4	DAY 5	DAY 6	DAY 7	
Toasted ham and cheese English muffins (2 muffin halves, 1 oz. ham, 1 oz. reduced-fat Cheddar cheese) Strawberries, 1 c. Fat-free milk, 1c.	Whole oats cereal, 2 c. Blueberries, ½ c. Fat-free milk, 1c.	**Amaretto French Toast, page 162,** 1 serving **Strawberry-Banana Smoothie, page 162,** 1 serving	Toast with peanut butter (2 slices wheat berry bread, 2 T. peanut butter) Fresh melon, 1 c. Fat-free milk, 1c.	BREAKFAST
Turkey-Apple Salad Sandwiches, page 49, 1 sandwich Vegetable chips, 10 (1 oz.) Gingersnaps, 6	**Chicken Pesto Pizza, page 59,** 1 serving Baby carrots and celery sticks, 2 c. Fat-free ranch dressing, 2 T. Fruit sorbet, ½ c	**Black Bean Soup, page 164,** 1 serving **Pepper Cheese Toasts, page 164,** 1 serving Frozen lime pop, 1	**Smoked Turkey-Cream Cheese Bagel Sandwiches, page 50,** 1 sandwich Baby carrots, 1 c. Green grapes, ½ c.	LUNCH
Chicken-Garbanzo Salad, page 31 1 serving Whole wheat pita wedges, 4 (1 pita) Red grapes, 1 c.	**Beefy Skillet Pasta, page 69,** 1 serving Spinach salad with red onion, 1 c. Reduced-fat olive oil vinaigrette, 2 T. Fresh melon cubes, 1 c.	**Chicken Piccata, page 188,** 1 serving **Garlic-Basil Pasta, page 188,** 1 serving Steamed green beans, ½ c.	**Pesto Chicken with Penne, page 62,** 1 serving Sliced tomatoes drizzled with reduced-fat olive oil vinaigrette (4 tomato slices, 1 T. vinaigrette) French bread, 1 slice	DINNER
Low-fat ice cream sandwich, 1	Peanut butter sandwich, ½ (1 slice wheat berry bread, 1 T. peanut butter,)	Reduced-fat Cheddar cheese, 1 oz. Rye crackers, 2	Whole oats cereal, 1 c. Fat-free milk, 1c.	SNACK
Total calories: 1636	**Total calories: 1655**	**Total calories: 1595**	**Total calories: 1668**	

> **"** *I have to do my shopping while the babysitter has the kids, so there's no time to go up and down every aisle looking for unusual ingredients.* **"**

speed shopping

If you want to be a true speed shopper, determine your shopping style and plan accordingly using our supermarket strategic plan.

What kind of grocery shopper are you? Read the descriptions below to find out.*

• **Dasher:** Runs into the store on the way home every night to pick up something for that night's dinner. Frequents the deli and frozen food sections, and grabs whatever looks good. Opts for a basket rather than a cart. Generally has less than 8 items; uses the express aisle.

• **Gatherer:** Travels up and down every aisle grabbing items that might be thrown together for a meal. Subject to impulse buys and advertised specials. Sometimes ends up with a cart full of groceries, but still can't figure out what to cook for supper.

• **Hunter:** Enters a detailed weekly grocery list into the palm pilot and meticulously searches for each and every item on the list. Not uncommon for this shopper to visit several stores on the quest for one item. Often seen with coupons.

Whatever your shopping style, you can make your selections quickly and move on if you know where to find the most nutritious fast foods in each section of the store. Our plan on the next page will help you simplify your shopping whether you're shopping for the month, week, or just for the night.

This is more than a grocery list—its' a strategic plan for shopping. We've identified the key areas of the store where you'll find healthy convenience products. Although the specific layouts will be different, most stores will have these same areas. Look on the next page to see how it works.

> **"Be creative.** *You don't have to go out and buy a lot of ingredients to make a quick supper that tastes good. Use your leftovers to make something new and different.* **"**

Nicole Faber,
Test Kitchens staff

Based on research done for the national Cattleman's Beef Association.

Ready, Set, Go!

below is a sample layout of a grocery store highlighting key sections containing foods you need for quick, healthy meals. Start in the bottom left and work your way through the store. In each section, there is a list of the products you'll find in that section—these are the items that you'll need to keep on hand to be a superfast chef extraordinaire.

The order in which you move through the sections isn't crucial, except that we do recommend that you add frozen foods and dairy products to your cart last.

The **Hunters** and **Gatherers** will probably go to each section. The **Dashers** may only hit a few. Either way, you've saved yourself the time of going up and down every aisle.

One key point to keep in mind for this strategy to work: stock up on staples. If you shop once for the staples and condiments that you use frequently, you won't have to spend time doing that each time you visit the store. See the staples list on the page 15 or the one on page 54 for items you need to keep on hand for *Superfast Suppers.*

Superfast Sections of Supermarket

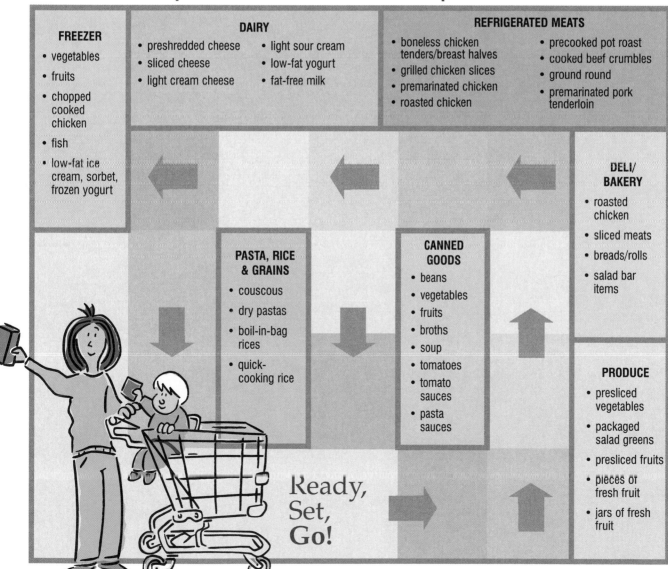

FREEZER
- vegetables
- fruits
- chopped cooked chicken
- fish
- low-fat ice cream, sorbet, frozen yogurt

DAIRY
- preshredded cheese
- sliced cheese
- light cream cheese
- light sour cream
- low-fat yogurt
- fat-free milk

REFRIGERATED MEATS
- boneless chicken tenders/breast halves
- grilled chicken slices
- premarinated chicken
- roasted chicken
- precooked pot roast
- cooked beef crumbles
- ground round
- premarinated pork tenderloin

DELI/ BAKERY
- roasted chicken
- sliced meats
- breads/rolls
- salad bar items

PASTA, RICE & GRAINS
- couscous
- dry pastas
- boil-in-bag rices
- quick-cooking rice

CANNED GOODS
- beans
- vegetables
- fruits
- broths
- soup
- tomatoes
- tomato sauces
- pasta sauces

PRODUCE
- presliced vegetables
- packaged salad greens
- presliced fruits
- pieces of fresh fruit
- jars of fresh fruit

Ready, Set, Go!

66I want to eat healthfully, but I just don't know that much about cooking and don't really have time to learn.99

NO-COOK
meals

Getting supper on the table isn't always about cooking. Some nights all you have time for

is assembly. With the enormous selection of fruits and vegetables, breads, cheeses, and

deli meats available in supermarkets, you can

get a meal on the table in minutes without

feeling the heat.

Asian Spinach Salad, page 35

feta-couscous salad
with bagel chips and fresh pear slices   serves 4 · total time 20 minutes

Even though you do boil the water for the couscous in the microwave, the salad is classified as a no-cook meal because you don't have to heat up the kitchen.

SUPPER plan

1. Prepare couscous, and let it cool.

2. While couscous stands and cools:
- Chop parsley and halve tomatoes.
- Combine remaining salad ingredients.
- Slice pears.

3. Assemble salads on plates.

Feta-Couscous Salad

prep: 20 minutes

For a unique presentation, pack the couscous mixture in a 1-cup dry measuring cup, and invert onto the spinach leaves. The couscous will take on the shape of the measuring cup.

1	cup water
⅔	cup uncooked couscous
1	cup grape tomatoes, halved
¾	cup (3 ounces) crumbled feta cheese with basil and sun-dried tomatoes
¾	cup chopped fresh parsley
¼	cup pine nuts
1	tablespoon dried basil
½	teaspoon salt
½	cup fat-free Italian dressing, divided
4	cups spinach leaves (about half of a 10-ounce package)

Place water in a small microwave-safe bowl. Microwave at HIGH 1½ minutes or until water boils. Remove from heat, and stir in couscous. Cover and let stand 5 minutes or until liquid is absorbed; fluff with a fork. Spoon onto a baking sheet, and spread in a thin layer; let stand 7 minutes or until cool.

Combine tomato, next 5 ingredients, and ¼ cup dressing in a bowl. Add cooled couscous to parsley mixture, and toss well.

Combine spinach and ¼ cup dressing; toss gently. Place spinach mixture on each of 4 individual plates. Top with couscous mixture. Yield: 4 servings (serving size: 1 cup spinach mixture and 1 cup couscous mixture).

CALORIES 258 (34% from fat); FAT 9.7g (sat 4.1g, mono 2.7g, poly 2.1g); PROTEIN 11.3g; CARB 32.5g; FIBER 4.4g; CHOL 20mg; IRON 3.9mg; SODIUM 857mg; CALC 219mg
EXCHANGES: 2 Starch, 1 High-Fat Meat

FINDit

● ● ● ● ● ● ● ● ● ● ● ● ● ● ● ● ● ●

You'll find boxes of couscous *on the grocery shelves next to the rice and the other grains. Technically, couscous is a pasta because it's made from semolina wheat (durum wheat that's more coarsely ground than other wheat flour), but the texture is more like that of fluffy rice.*

The couscous sold in supermarkets today is pre-cooked, so all you have to do is stir it into boiling water, and let it stand, covered, for 5 minutes.

romaine and greek vegetable salad
with turkey roll-ups   serves 4 · total time 20 minutes

If you think a salad supper is light and delicate, think again. This Greek salad features bold Mediterranean flavors and is served with savory turkey-packed pitas.

SUPPER plan

1. Prepare roll-ups; cover and chill, if desired.

2. Rinse and drain chickpeas for salad.

3. Halve tomatoes; peel and chop cucumber; slice onion; pit and chop olives.

4. Combine salad ingredients; toss salad with dressing and feta cheese.

Turkey Roll-Ups

prep: 5 minutes

If the pitas are difficult to roll, cover them with paper towels, and microwave at HIGH 20 seconds.

2   tablespoons light cream cheese with chives and onion
4   (6-inch) pitas
4   (1-ounce) slices deli turkey
1   small red bell pepper, thinly sliced

Spread 2 tablespoons cream cheese over each pita. Top each with 1 turkey slice and pepper strips. Roll up, and secure with wooden picks. Yield: 4 servings (serving size: 1 roll-up).

CALORIES 212 (10% from fat); FAT 2.4g (sat 1.1g, mono 0.2g, poly 0.4g);
PROTEIN 11g; CARB 36g; FIBER 1.7g; CHOL 15mg; IRON 2.2mg;
SODIUM 697mg; CALC 68mg
EXCHANGES: 2 Starch, 1 Lean Meat

Romaine and Greek Vegetable Salad

prep: 15 minutes

Toss this salad together just before serving so the lettuce stays crisp.

4   cups packaged torn romaine lettuce
1   (15½-ounce) can chickpeas (garbanzo beans), rinsed and drained
16   grape tomatoes, halved
1   cucumber, chopped and peeled
4   ounces presliced mushrooms
¼   cup thinly sliced red onion
12   coarsely chopped pitted kalamata olives
1   to 2 tablespoons dried oregano
¼   cup low-fat Italian dressing
4   ounces crumbled feta cheese with basil and sun-dried tomatoes

Combine first 8 ingredients in a large bowl; toss gently. Add dressing and cheese just before serving; toss gently. Yield: 4 servings (serving size: 2 cups).

CALORIES 226 (36% from fat); FAT 9g (sat 4.7g, mono 2.6g, poly 0.9g);
PROTEIN 10.7g; CARB 28.1g; FIBER 6.6g; CHOL 26mg; IRON 3.5mg;
SODIUM 872mg; CALC 232mg
EXCHANGES: 1 Starch, 1 Vegetable, 1 High-Fat Meat

crunchy picante salad
with tropical smoothies — serves 4 • total time 20 minutes

Meat-free and easy, this all-veggie version of taco salad is a terrific option for a quick Mexican fiesta. A Mexican beer such as Corona or Dos Equis pairs nicely with this salad. Think of the smoothie as a drinkable dessert.

SUPPER plan

1. Peel and slice bananas into 1-inch slices; place on baking sheet or plate. Place baking sheet and open can of pineapple in freezer.

2. Rinse and drain beans for salad; drain olives.

3. Peel and cut avocado; quarter lime; chop cilantro.

4. Assemble salads.

5. Blend smoothies.

Crunchy Picante Salad

prep: 15 minutes

6	cups preshredded lettuce
5	cups baked tortilla chips, broken into bite-sized pieces (about 3 ounces)
1	cup mild picante sauce
½	cup (2 ounces) shredded reduced-fat sharp Cheddar cheese
1	(15-ounce) can pinto beans, rinsed and drained
1	(2.25-ounce) can sliced ripe olives, drained
1	ripe avocado, peeled and cut into bite-sized pieces
1	large lime, quartered
½	cup reduced-fat sour cream
½	cup chopped fresh cilantro

Place 1½ cups lettuce on each of 4 plates; top evenly with chips. Spoon picante sauce evenly over chips; top evenly with cheese, beans, olives, and avocado. Squeeze a lime quarter over each salad. Top each salad with 2 tablespoons each of sour cream and cilantro. Yield: 4 servings.

CALORIES 345 (39% from fat); FAT 14.8g (sat 5.1g, mono 4.9g, poly 1.7g); PROTEIN 12.9g; CARB 45.3g; FIBER 9g; CHOL 26mg; IRON 3.5mg; SODIUM 1,019mg; CALC 315mg
EXCHANGES: 3 Starch, 1 Medium-Fat Meat, 1 Fat

Tropical Smoothies

prep: 5 minutes   freeze: 10 minutes

Keep banana slices in the freezer in a heavy duty, zip-top plastic bag to have on hand for smoothies.

1	(15-ounce) can pineapple tidbits in juice, undrained
2	bananas, sliced and chilled
1	cup vanilla fat-free frozen yogurt

Place opened can of pineapple tidbits in freezer 10 minutes.

Combine pineapple tidbits, banana, and frozen yogurt in a blender; process until smooth. Yield: 4 servings (serving size: 1 cup).

CALORIES 163 (2% from fat); FAT 0.4g (sat 0.2g, mono 0g, poly 0.1g); PROTEIN 3g; CARB 38.1g; FIBER 2.3g; CHOL 1mg; IRON 0.5mg; SODIUM 41mg; CALC 87mg
EXCHANGES: 1 Starch, 1½ Fruit

Crunchy Picante Salad

shrimp and caper salad

with sliced melon and crisp breadsticks   serves 4 • total time 15 minutes

Cool, sweet melon balances the tangy, hot flavors of the shrimp salad.

SUPPER plan

1. Drain capers; mince garlic; chop parsley.

2. Combine all ingredients except greens and let stand.

3. While shrimp mixture stands, slice melon (honeydew or cantaloupe).

4. Assemble salads.

Shrimp and Caper Salad

prep: 10 minutes   stand: 5 minutes

1	pound peeled and deveined cooked shrimp
2	tablespoons capers, drained
6	tablespoons fresh lemon juice (about 2 lemons)
2	tablespoons extravirgin olive oil
2	garlic cloves, minced
1	teaspoon dried oregano
1	teaspoon hot sauce
½	teaspoon salt
½	cup chopped fresh parsley
8	cups gourmet salad greens

Combine first 9 ingredients in a medium bowl. Let stand 5 minutes.

Place salad greens on each of 4 plates. Spoon shrimp mixture on top of greens. Yield: 4 servings (serving size: 2 cups greens and about ¾ cup shrimp mixture).

CALORIES 172 (42% from fat); FAT 8.1g (sat 1.2g, mono 5.2g, poly 1.1g); PROTEIN 19.7g; CARB 6.2g; FIBER 3g; CHOL 161mg; IRON 4.8mg; SODIUM 504mg; CALC 116mg
EXCHANGES: 1 Vegetable, 3 Very Lean Meat, 1 Fat

QUICKtips

• • • • • • • • • • • • • • • • • •

Buy precooked shrimp *at the seafood market or in the seafood department of the grocery store.*

If you want to buy shrimp in the shell, you'll need to get 2 pounds. To cook, place the unpeeled shrimp in about 6 cups of boiling water for 3 minutes or until shrimp are done. Drain, and peel.

Deveining *the shrimp is a personal choice rather than a necessity. The black sand vein line that runs down the back of shrimp is its intestinal tract. In small shrimp it's not really noticeable, but in large shrimp the vein is unappealing and can add a gritty, muddy taste.*

There's no harm in eating shrimp that aren't deveined, but if you prefer to remove it, you can use a special deveining tool or a knife. Slit the shrimp lengthwise down its back, and pull away the vein with the tip of the knife.

ham and pea salad
with baby carrots, rye crackers, and frozen seedless grapes · serves 4 · total time 20 minutes

You can make the ham and pea mixture a day or two ahead, and keep it in the refrigerator. Just before serving, spoon it onto the greens.

SUPPER plan

1. Place grapes in a single layer on a baking sheet, and freeze for at least 20 minutes.

2. Cube ham; slice cucumber; chop onion.

3. Combine salad ingredients.

Ham and Pea Salad

prep: 20 minutes

Keep resealable 1-pound packages of cubed ham on hand in the refrigerator.

¾	pound extralean ham, cubed (about 3 cups)
1	medium red or green bell pepper, chopped
1⅓	cups frozen green peas, rinsed
½	cup finely chopped red onion
1	cup sliced pickling cucumber (about 2 small)
⅓	cup light mayonnaise
1	teaspoon sugar
¼	teaspoon black pepper
1	(10-ounce) package torn hearts of romaine

Combine all ingredients, except romaine, in a bowl. Toss gently to coat.

Divide lettuce evenly among 4 plates; top with ham mixture. Yield: 4 servings (serving size: 1½ cups ham mixture and about 1¼ cups romaine).

CALORIES 242 (42% from fat); FAT 11.5g (sat 1.1g, mono 0g, poly 0.2g); PROTEIN 19.9g; CARB 16.5g; FIBER 5.4g; CHOL 52mg; IRON 2.7mg; SODIUM 1,092mg; CALC 51mg
EXCHANGES: 1 Starch, 2 Lean Meat, 1 Fat

FINDit

Pickling cucumbers *are small cucumbers that are generally used for making pickles. You'll also see them in the produce department labeled as "salad cucumbers." The skins are usually not as tough and bitter as larger cucumbers, so you don't have to peel them.*

One medium pickling cucumber (about 5 inches in length) will yield about ⅔ cup sliced or chopped cucumber.

dijon beef and spring greens
with chilled strawberry soup   serves 4 · total time 20 minutes

Fill up on a hearty salad that has the robust flavors of roast beef, Dijon mustard, balsamic vinegar, and blue cheese.

SUPPER plan

1. Thaw strawberries in microwave for soup.

2. Make soup, and chill.

3. Seed bell pepper, and cut into strips.

4. Make vinaigrette.

5. Assemble salads.

Dijon Beef and Spring Greens

prep: 15 minutes

¼	cup Dijon mustard
1½	tablespoons balsamic vinegar
1	garlic clove, minced
2	teaspoons sugar
1	(12-ounce) package spring greens or 6 cups fresh mesclun mix
9	ounces deli roast beef, diagonally sliced
1	small red bell pepper, seeded and cut into thin strips
2	ounces blue cheese, crumbled
½	cup alfalfa sprouts

Combine first 4 ingredients in a small bowl; stir with a wire whisk.

Arrange greens evenly on 4 serving plates; top evenly with beef, red bell pepper strips, cheese, and sprouts.

Drizzle salads with mustard dressing. Yield: 4 servings.

CALORIES 209 (44% from fat); FAT 10.3g (sat 4.8g, mono 0.5g, poly 0.5g); PROTEIN 20.9g; CARB 9.7g; FIBER 2.3g; CHOL 57mg; IRON 3mg; SODIUM 918mg; CALC 148mg
EXCHANGES: 2 Vegetable, 2 Medium-Fat Meat

Chilled Strawberry Soup

prep: 5 minutes

Serve this sweet soup as a starter or as a light dessert.

2	(10-ounce) packages frozen strawberries in lite syrup, thawed
½	cup fat-free half-and-half
¼	cup unsweetened white grape juice
¼	cup reduced-fat sour cream

Place first 3 ingredients in a blender or food processor; process until smooth. Cover and chill.

Ladle soup into serving bowls, and top each serving with 1 tablespoon sour cream. Yield: 4 servings (serving size: ¾ cup).

CALORIES 160 (11% from fat); FAT 2g (sat 1.2g, mono 0g, poly 0g); PROTEIN 1.4g; CARB 33.8g; FIBER 0g; CHOL 8mg; IRON 0.8mg; SODIUM 42mg; CALC 63mg
EXCHANGES: 1 Starch, 1 Fruit

QUICKtip

• • • • • • • • • • • • • • • • • •

We tested this recipe using deli roast beef, *but there are other quick beef options available:*
- *frozen cooked beef strips (such as Tyson), thawed*
- *packaged roast beef slices*
- *refrigerated, fully cooked roast beef (such as Hormel)*
- *leftover roast beef*

Chilled Strawberry Soup

Chicken-
Garbanzo Salad

chicken-garbanzo salad
with pita wedges and red grapes   serves 4 · total time 18 minutes

If you need a make-ahead salad, combine everything but the spinach, cheese, and lemon wedges. Cover and chill overnight. Fold the spinach and cheese into the chicken mixture just before serving, and garnish with lemon wedges.

SUPPER plan

1. Thaw chicken in microwave or skillet.

2. Rinse and drain chickpeas.

3. Seed and chop cucumber; chop onions and mint or basil; mince garlic; slice lemon.

4. Assemble salads.

5. Cut pita wedges.

Chicken-Garbanzo Salad

prep: 18 minutes

Instead of serving this Mediterranean-style salad with pita wedges, make sandwiches. Spoon about ½ cup into pita halves lined with extra spinach leaves.

  1 (9-ounce) package frozen cooked chopped chicken breast, thawed
  1 (15-ounce) can chickpeas (garbanzo beans), rinsed and drained
  1 cup chopped seeded cucumber (about 1 small)
  ½ cup chopped green onions (about 4 small)
  ¼ cup chopped fresh mint or basil
  ½ cup plain fat-free yogurt
  2 garlic cloves, minced
  ¼ teaspoon salt
  2 cups prepackaged baby spinach leaves
  ⅓ cup (1.3 ounces) feta cheese with cracked pepper, crumbled
  4 lemon wedges

Combine first 8 ingredients; toss gently. Gently fold in spinach leaves and feta cheese. Serve salad with lemon wedges. Yield: 4 servings (serving size: 1¾ cups).

CALORIES 258 (21% from fat); FAT 6.0g (sat 2.7g, mono 1.6g, poly 1g); PROTEIN 27.8g; CARB 22.9g; FIBER 4.9g; CHOL 66mg; IRON 2.9mg; SODIUM 675mg; CALC 190mg
EXCHANGES: 1 Starch, 1 Vegetable, 3 Lean Meat

QUICKtip

· · · · · · · · · · · · · · · · · · ·

To quickly thaw *frozen cooked chicken, place the chicken in a microwave-safe dish, and heat at HIGH for 2 to 3 minutes. Or heat the frozen chicken in a skillet over medium heat for 3 to 4 minutes, stirring often.*

greek grilled chicken salad
with whole wheat pita wedges and
blueberries with lemon yogurt

serves 4 • total time 19 minutes

Enjoy a generous portion of this zesty Greek-style salad with a glass of white wine and a bowl of lemony berries.

SUPPER plan

1. Chop lettuce, chicken, and cucumber; slice onion; halve tomatoes; squeeze lemon juice.

2. Prepare dressing, and toss with salad.

3. Cut pitas into wedges.

4. Rinse and drain blueberries; top with yogurt.

Greek Grilled Chicken Salad

prep: 14 minutes

For a quick Greek dressing with made-from-scratch-flavor, we stirred a bit of fresh lemon juice into a commercial olive oil vinaigrette.

  1 (12-ounce) package romaine lettuce, chopped
  2 (6-ounce) packages refrigerated grilled chicken breast strips, coarsely chopped
  2 cups grape tomatoes, halved
  ¾ cup chopped seeded cucumber (about 1 small)
  ⅓ cup reduced-fat feta cheese
  2 tablespoons sliced ripe olives
  ¼ cup thinly sliced red onion
  ¼ teaspoon freshly ground black pepper
  ¼ cup reduced-fat olive oil vinaigrette
  1 tablespoon fresh lemon juice (½ lemon)

  Combine first 8 ingredients; toss gently. Combine vinaigrette and lemon juice in a small bowl; stir with a whisk. Pour dressing over lettuce mixture; toss gently. Yield: 4 servings (serving size: about 3⅓ cups).

CALORIES 200 (37% from fat); FAT 8.3g (sat 2.2g, mono 0.4g, poly 0.2g); PROTEIN 23.2g; CARB 10.2g; FIBER 2.7g; CHOL 59mg; IRON 2.2mg; SODIUM 1,072mg; CALC 59mg
EXCHANGES: 2 Vegetable, 3 Lean Meat

Blueberries with Lemon Yogurt

prep: 5 minutes

  2 cups fresh blueberries
  ¾ cup low-fat lemon yogurt

  Place ½ cup blueberries in each of 4 small bowls. Top each with 3 tablespoons yogurt. Yield: 4 servings.

CALORIES 80 (10% from fat); FAT 0.9g (sat 0.4g, mono 0.2g, poly 0.1g); PROTEIN 2.8g; CARB 16.6g; FIBER 2g; CHOL 2mg; IRON 0.2mg; SODIUM 35mg; CALC 83mg
EXCHANGE: 1 Fruit

QUICKtip

• • • • • • • • • • • • • • • • •

To seed a cucumber quickly, *cut it in half lengthwise and use the tip of a spoon or a melon baller to scoop out the seeds.*

Greek Grilled
Chicken Salad

Asian Spinach Salad

asian spinach salad
with rice crackers and lemon sorbet   serves 4 • total time 13 minutes

The ramen noodles in this salad aren't cooked so they provide crunch to the slightly sweet chicken and greens mixture.

SUPPER plan

1. Thaw chicken and snow peas in the microwave.

2. Chop bell pepper; peel and grate ginger.

3. Prepare dressing.

4. Assemble salads.

Asian Spinach Salad

prep: 13 minutes

1	(3-ounce) package ramen noodles
1	(7-ounce) package baby spinach (about 8 cups)
1	(9-ounce) package frozen cooked chopped chicken breast, thawed
1	red bell pepper, seeded and chopped
1	(6-ounce) package frozen snow peas, thawed and drained
½	cup golden raisins
¼	cup honey
3	tablespoons cider vinegar
1½	tablespoons low-sodium soy sauce
1½	tablespoons grated peeled fresh ginger

Discard seasoning packet in package of noodles. Crumble noodles.

Place 2 cups spinach on each of 4 plates. Top evenly with of noodles, chicken, and next 3 ingredients.

Combine honey and remaining 3 ingredients, stirring with a whisk. Spoon about 2½ tablespoons honey mixture over each salad. Yield: 4 servings.

CALORIES 373 (14% from fat); FAT 5.7g (sat 1.5g, mono 2g, poly 1.3g); PROTEIN 26.6g; CARB 57g; FIBER 4.8g; CHOL 54mg; IRON 4.6mg; SODIUM 656mg; CALC 111mg
EXCHANGES: 2 Starch, 1 Fruit, 1 Vegetable, 3 Very Lean Meat, ½ Fat

QUICKtips

• • • • • • • • • • • • • • • • • •

Thaw chicken *in the refrigerator overnight, or in the microwave at HIGH for 2 to 3 minutes. You can also use refrigerated grilled chicken breast strips, deli roasted chicken (skin removed), or left-over cooked chicken.*

To measure honey *without mess, spray the measuring cup with cooking spray before measuring. The honey will come out of the cup easily, and the cup will be easy to clean.*

orange-ginger-chicken slaw
and citrus fruit with cilantro

serves 4 • total time 13 minutes

Slaw isn't just a side for barbecue. This main-dish slaw takes its cue from gingery Asian-style dishes and is chock-full of tender diced chicken. Fresh lime juice and honey transform an ordinary fruit salad into a complementary and refreshing quick dessert.

SUPPER plan

1. Thaw chicken in microwave.

2. Grate ginger and chop peanuts for slaw; chop cilantro for fruit salad.

3. Make dressing for slaw.

4. Prepare Citrus Fruit with Cilantro.

Orange-Ginger-Chicken Slaw

prep: 9 minutes

1	(10-ounce) package angel hair slaw (about 6 cups)
1	(9-ounce) package frozen cooked chopped chicken breast, thawed
1	cup matchstick-cut carrots
¾	cup orange juice
¼	cup low-sodium soy sauce
2	tablespoons honey
2	teaspoons grated peeled fresh ginger or 2 teaspoons ground ginger
1½	teaspoons sesame oil
¼	teaspoon crushed red pepper
¼	teaspoon salt
6	tablespoons honey-roasted peanuts, coarsely chopped

Combine first 3 ingredients in a large bowl.
Combine orange juice and next 6 ingredients in a small bowl, stirring with a whisk. Add orange juice mixture to slaw mixture; toss gently. Spoon salad into individual shallow bowls.

Sprinkle evenly with peanuts. Yield: 4 servings (serving size: 1½ cups).

CALORIES 242 (25% from fat); FAT 6.6g (sat 1.3g, mono 2.6g, poly 2.1g); PROTEIN 23.7g; CARB 23.4g; FIBER 3.4g; CHOL 54mg; IRON 1.9mg; SODIUM 904mg; CALC 64mg
EXCHANGES: 1 Starch, 1 Vegetable, 3 Very Lean Meat, 1 Fat

Citrus Fruit with Cilantro

prep: 4 minutes

1	(24-ounce) jar refrigerated citrus fruit salad, drained
2	tablespoons fresh lime juice (about 1 lime)
1	tablespoon honey
2	tablespoons chopped fresh cilantro

Combine all ingredients, stirring gently. Yield: 4 servings (serving size: ½ cup).

CALORIES 57 (2% from fat); FAT 0.1g (sat 0g, mono 0g, poly 0g); PROTEIN 0.8g; CARB 14.8g; FIBER 1.9g; CHOL 0mg; IRON 0.2mg; SODIUM 0mg; CALC 26mg
EXCHANGE: 1 Fruit

FINDit

• • • • • • • • • • • • • • • • • • •

Look for citrus fruit salad *in the produce department next to the fresh cut melon and fresh squeezed orange juice. Packages of matchstick-cut carrots are in the vegetable produce section.*

turkey and gorgonzola salad
with cracked pepper crackers   serves 4 • total time 18 minutes

Take a break from sandwiches and use your leftover holiday turkey in this chunky, crisp salad.

SUPPER plan

1. Cube turkey; slice apple; chop onion.

2. Toast pecans.

3. Prepare dressing.

4. Assemble salads.

Turkey and Gorgonzola Salad

prep: 18 minutes

8	ounces deli-style turkey, cubed
1	Gala apple, cored and thinly sliced
½	cup chopped red onion
1	(5-ounce) package spring greens salad mix
¼	cup pecans, toasted
⅓	cup (1.3 ounces) crumbled Gorgonzola cheese
¼	teaspoon freshly ground black pepper
½	cup frozen apple juice concentrate, thawed
¼	cup balsamic vinegar
1½	teaspoons dark sesame oil

Combine first 3 ingredients in a medium bowl; toss well.

Place 1½ cups spring greens on each of 4 plates. Top evenly with turkey mixture; sprinkle with pecans, cheese, and pepper.

Combine apple juice concentrate, vinegar, and oil; stir well with a whisk. Spoon about 3 tablespoons dressing over each serving. Yield: 4 servings.

CALORIES 251 (39% from fat); FAT 10.9g (sat 3.2g, mono 3.8g, poly 2.5g); PROTEIN 13g; CARB 28g; FIBER 2.6g; CHOL 31mg; IRON 2.3mg; SODIUM 816mg; CALC 101mg
EXCHANGES: 2 Fruit, 2 Lean Meat, 1 Fat

SIMPLEsubstitutions

• • • • • • • • • • • • • • • • • •

If you're unable *to find the spring greens salad mix, use 6 cups of any type of salad greens. You can also use blue cheese instead of the Gorgonzola.*

We preferred the sweet flavor *and crisp texture of the Gala apple for this salad. Braeburn or Fuji apples would be good substitutes.*

❝Using precut vegetables and fruits,
especially bagged salad greens, is my big time saver. Not having to spend a lot of time peeling and chopping really helps me get things ready quicker.❞

Holley Johnson,
Assistant Foods Editor

pepperoni and white bean salad
with roasted red pepper spread
and crisp breadsticks · serves 4 · total time 18 minutes

Savor the flavors of Tuscany with this beans and greens main-dish salad accented with the sweet, pungent flavors of pepperoncini peppers and balsamic vinegar.

SUPPER plan

1. Make Roasted Red Pepper Spread.

2. Rinse and drain beans for salad; drain pepperoncini peppers; drain olives.

3. Halve tomatoes; chop parsley; cut pepperoni into strips.

4. Make vinaigrette.

5. Combine salad ingredients.

Roasted Red Pepper Spread

prep: 7 minutes

  1 (7-ounce) bottle roasted red bell peppers, drained and finely chopped
 ⅓ cup tub light cream cheese, softened
  2 teaspoons bottled minced garlic
  2 teaspoons white balsamic vinegar
 ¼ teaspoon salt
 ¼ teaspoon freshly ground black pepper

   Combine all ingredients, stirring well. Serve with breadsticks, Melba toast, or celery sticks. Yield: 1 cup (serving size: 1 tablespoon).

CALORIES 16 (51% from fat); FAT 0.9g (sat 0.6g, mono 0g, poly 0.1g); PROTEIN 0.7g; CARB 1.1g; FIBER 0.1g; CHOL 2mg; IRON 0.1mg; SODIUM 105mg; CALC 9mg
EXCHANGE: Free (up to ¼ cup)

Pepperoni and White Bean Salad

prep: 11 minutes

  6 cups baby spinach
  2 cups grape tomatoes, halved
 24 turkey pepperoni slices, cut into thin strips
  1 (15-ounce) can navy beans, rinsed and drained
 ⅓ cup sliced pepperoncini peppers, drained
  1 (2.25-ounce) can sliced ripe olives, drained
 ½ cup chopped fresh parsley
 ⅓ cup white balsamic vinegar
  1 tablespoon extravirgin olive oil
 ½ cup (2 ounces) preshredded fresh Parmesan cheese

   Combine first 7 ingredients in a large bowl.
   Combine vinegar and oil in a small bowl, stirring with a whisk. Pour dressing over spinach mixture, tossing well. Spoon salad onto individual plates. Sprinkle evenly with cheese. Yield: 4 servings (serving size: 2½ cups).

CALORIES 255 (38% from fat); FAT 10.7g (sat 3.6g, mono 5.4g, poly 1.1g); PROTEIN 16.2g; CARB 25.9g; FIBER 6.5g; CHOL 22mg; IRON 4.4mg; SODIUM 854mg; CALC 292mg
EXCHANGES: 1 Starch, 2 Vegetable, 2 Medium-Fat Meat

NUTRITIONnote

• • • • • • • • • • • • • • • •

Turkey pepperoni *has about 75 percent less fat than beef or pork pepperoni, but the sodium is approximately the same.*

chicken-parmesan-romaine salad
with **grand marnier strawberries**
and crisp breadsticks   serves 4 • total time 14 minutes

With its grilled chicken strips and creamy buttermilk dressing, this satisfying salad may remind you of a grilled chicken Caesar salad.

SUPPER plan

1. Prepare dressing; cover and chill.

2. Mince garlic, and chop chicken and onion for salad.

3. Slice strawberries, and grate orange rind. Combine with liqueur.

4. Prepare salad.

Chicken-Parmesan-Romaine Salad

prep: 8 minutes   chill: 5 minutes

⅓	cup low-fat buttermilk
3	tablespoons light mayonnaise
1	teaspoon anchovy paste
2	teaspoons Dijon mustard
1	tablespoon red wine vinegar
1	garlic clove, minced
1	(10-ounce) package torn hearts of romaine
2	(6-ounce) packages refrigerated grilled chicken strips, coarsely chopped
¼	cup chopped red onion
¼	cup (1 ounce) preshredded fresh Parmesan cheese
¼	teaspoon cracked black pepper (optional)

Combine first 6 ingredients in a small bowl; stir with a whisk. Cover and chill 5 minutes.

Combine romaine lettuce, chicken, onion, and dressing in a large bowl, toss gently. Place salad on 4 plates. Top each with 1 tablespoon Parmesan cheese, and sprinkle with cracked pepper, if desired. Yield: 4 servings (serving size: about 2⅓ cups).

CALORIES 200 (39% from fat); FAT 8.7g (sat 2.6g, mono 0.6g, poly 0.2g); PROTEIN 23.7g; CARB 6.6g; FIBER 1.5g; CHOL 66mg; IRON 1.9mg; SODIUM 1,314mg; CALC 128mg
EXCHANGES: 2 Vegetable, 3 Very Lean Meat, 1 Fat

Grand Marnier Strawberries

prep: 6 minutes

1	quart strawberries, sliced
¼	cup grand Marnier (orange-flavored liqueur)
2	teaspoons grated fresh orange rind

Combine all ingredients in a medium bowl; toss gently.

Spoon 1 cup strawberries into each of 4 dessert dishes. Yield: 4 servings.

CALORIES 101 (6% from fat); FAT 0.7g (sat 0g, mono 0.1g, poly 0.3g); PROTEIN 1g; CARB 18.2g; FIBER 3.9g; CHOL 0mg; IRON 0.7mg; SODIUM 3mg; CALC 25mg
EXCHANGE: 1 Fruit

NUTRITION**note**

• • • • • • • • • • • • • • • •

Packaged cooked chicken *strips offer quick convenience, but contain additional sodium (780 milligrams per 3-ounce serving of packaged grilled chicken). If you need to reduce the sodium in the salad, grill your own chicken without adding salt or use leftover cooked chicken without salt. (Both have about 60 milligrams of sodium for 3 ounces.)*

summer tomato sandwiches
with fresh peach slices
and low-fat vanilla ice cream

serves 4 • total time 15 minutes

There's just nothing better on a summer day than a tomato sandwich made with red, juicy, fresh-from-the-garden tomatoes, unless it's fresh peaches and ice cream for dessert.

SUPPER plan

1. Slice tomatoes, and chop onion for sandwiches.

2. Slice peaches.

3. Toast bread.

4. Assemble sandwiches.

Summer Tomato Sandwiches

prep: 15 minutes

Use half of a 16-ounce loaf of sliced French bread, or slice the loaf yourself into ¾-inch-thick slices.

3	tablespoons pesto
¼	cup fat-free mayonnaise
2	teaspoons balsamic vinegar
1	teaspoon bottled minced garlic
¼	teaspoon dry mustard
1	green onion, chopped
⅛	teaspoon freshly ground black pepper
8	(1-ounce) slices French bread, toasted
1	cup spinach leaves or gourmet salad greens
8	(¼-inch-thick) slices tomato

Combine first 7 ingredients in a small bowl; stir with a whisk.

Spread mayonnaise mixture evenly on 4 slices of bread (about 2 tablespoons per slice).

Place ¼ cup spinach leaves on each bread slice; top each with 2 slices tomato. Top with remaining bread slices. Yield: 4 servings.

CALORIES 242 (29% from fat); FAT 7.8g (sat 1.7g, mono 4.6g, poly 0.9g); PROTEIN 7.2g; CARB 36.3g; FIBER 2.6g; CHOL 3mg; IRON 2mg; SODIUM 556mg; CALC 102mg
EXCHANGES: 2 Starch, 1 Vegetable, 1 Fat

NUTRITIONnote

• • • • • • • • • • • • • • • • • •

Sure tomatoes taste great on sandwiches. *Now researchers are telling us that tomatoes can reduce the risk of prostate cancer.*

The cancer-fighting compound in tomatoes is lycopene—the substance that gives tomatoes their vibrant color. In addition to the antioxidant lycopene, tomatoes also provide vitamins A and C, both of which can help reduce the risk of cancer and heart disease. One study in Italy showed that eating seven or more servings of tomatoes a week reduced the risk of colon, rectal, and stomach cancer by 60 percent.

Summer Tomato
Sandwiches

black bean and poblano tortilla wraps
with jícama salad
and mango slices   serves 4 • total time 19 minutes

When you're tired of the same old sandwich routine, try this wrap packed with a spicy bean mixture.

SUPPER plan

1. Peel and dice jícama; chop poblano chile; prepare Jícama Salad.

2. Rinse and drain beans; peel and dice avocado; chop onion, chile, and cilantro for wraps.

3. Assemble wraps.

Black Bean and Poblano Tortilla Wraps

prep: 12 minutes

½	cup reduced-fat sour cream
½	teaspoon ground cumin
1	(15-ounce) can black beans, rinsed and drained
1	cup ripe diced peeled avocado (about 1)
½	poblano chile, finely chopped (about ⅓ cup)
¼	cup finely chopped red onion
¼	cup chopped fresh cilantro leaves
3	tablespoons fresh lime juice (about 1 large lime)
¼	teaspoon salt
4	(8-inch) flour tortillas

Combine sour cream and cumin in a small bowl; stir with a whisk.

Combine beans and next 6 ingredients in a bowl. Spoon equal amounts of black bean mixture down center of each tortilla. Roll up, cut in half, and secure with wooden picks if necessary. Serve with sour cream mixture. Yield: 4 servings (serving size: 1 wrap and 2 tablespoons sour cream mixture).

CALORIES 298 (38% from fat); FAT 12.6g (sat 3.9g, mono 5g, poly 1.2g); PROTEIN 9.2g; CARB 40.3g; FIBER 5.1g; CHOL 16mg; IRON 2.4mg; SODIUM 606mg; CALC 177mg
EXCHANGES: 2 Starch, 2 Vegetable, 2 Fat

Jícama Salad

prep: 7 minutes

Go ahead and chop all the poblano chile, and squeeze extra lime juice. You'll need them both for the black bean mixture in the wraps.

2	cups diced peeled jícama (about 1 small)
2	tablespoons fresh lime juice (about 1 lime)
2	tablespoons orange juice
2	teaspoons olive oil
⅛	teaspoon salt
½	poblano chile, finely chopped (about ⅓ cup)

Combine all ingredients in a bowl. Yield: 4 servings (serving size: 1½ cups).

CALORIES 60 (38% from fat); FAT 2.5g (sat 0.4g, mono 1.7g, poly 0.3g); PROTEIN 0.9g; CARB 9.4g; FIBER 4.1g; CHOL 0mg; IRON 0.6mg; SODIUM 78mg; CALC 11mg
EXCHANGES: 2 Vegetable

FINDit

• • • • • • • • • • • • • • • •

Look for presliced mango *in the produce department near the fresh squeezed orange juice.*

Black Bean and Poblano Tortilla Wraps
with Jícama Salad

black bean salsa pitas with fresh grapefruit sections and frozen lime juice bars serves 4 · total time 18 minutes

If you're not in the mood for a sandwich, serve the black bean mixture over shredded lettuce with low-fat tortilla chips on the side.

SUPPER plan

1. Rinse and drain beans.

2. Chop tomatoes, onion, cilantro, and jalapeños for bean mixture; dice cheese.

3. Prepare bean mixture.

4. Stuff pitas.

Black Bean Salsa Pitas

prep: 18 minutes

1 (15-ounce) can black beans, rinsed and drained
2 cups finely chopped tomatoes (about 2)
1 cup (4 ounces) diced part-skim mozzarella cheese
½ cup chopped onion (about ½ onion)
½ cup chopped fresh cilantro
¼ cup fresh lime juice (about 2 limes)
2 tablespoons finely chopped pickled jalapeños
½ teaspoon salt
4 (6-inch) whole wheat pitas, cut in half
½ cup reduced-fat sour cream
1 lime, cut into 4 wedges

Combine first 8 ingredients in a bowl. Spoon bean mixture evenly into pita halves (about ½ cup per half). Top each with 2 tablespoons sour cream, and serve with lime wedges. Yield: 4 servings (serving size: 2 pita halves).

CALORIES 349 (27% from fat); FAT 10.4g (sat 5.7g, mono 1.6g, poly 0.9g); PROTEIN 18.3g; CARB 51.8g; FIBER 9.1g; CHOL 31mg; IRON 3.2mg; SODIUM 960mg; CALC 298mg
EXCHANGES: 3 Starch, 1 Vegetable, 1 Lean Meat, 1 Fat

FINDit

• • • • • • • • • • • • • • • •

Purchase precut orange *and grapefruit sections in jars in the produce department. This fruit doesn't contain added sugar or syrup—it's packed in its own juice. So you're getting the same calories and nutrients as you would if you peeled your own citrus fruit. Store these jars of fruit in the refrigerator.*

Frozen lime juice bars *(such as Edy's) are in the frozen section near the ice cream and sorbets. These bars contain real fruit, but do have some added sugar. One bar has 80 calories and 20 grams of carbohydrate but no fat, cholesterol, or fiber. Edy's brand fruit bars are available in lime and strawberry.*

open-faced mediterranean sandwiches

with seedless grapes and fruit sorbet serves 4 • total time 11 minutes

Spread a savory cream cheese mixture on a bread shell, and top it with basil, tomatoes, and olives for this cross between a sandwich and a pizza.

SUPPER plan

1. Prepare cream cheese mixture.

2. Slice tomatoes; pit and chop olives; mince garlic.

3. Assemble sandwiches.

Open-Faced Mediterranean Sandwiches

prep: 11 minutes

A 10-ounce package of personal size Italian bread shells contains 2 shells.

¼ cup reduced-fat tub-style cream cheese
3 tablespoons reduced-fat sour cream
1 garlic clove, minced
⅛ teaspoon salt
⅛ teaspoon freshly ground black pepper
1 (10-ounce) package personal size Italian bread shells (such as Boboli)
½ cup fresh basil leaves
7 ounces plum tomatoes, sliced lengthwise
10 kalamata olives, pitted and chopped
¼ cup (1½-ounces) sun-dried tomato and basil feta cheese, crumbled

Combine cream cheese and next 4 ingredients in a small bowl; stir until smooth.

Spread half of cream cheese mixture onto top of each bread shell. Sprinkle ¼ cup fresh basil leaves on each shell; top each with half of sliced tomatoes, olives, and feta cheese. Cut each bread shell into 4 wedges. Yield: 4 servings (servings size: 2 wedges).

CALORIES 294 (35% from fat); FAT 11.5g (sat 5.3g, mono 1.9g, poly 0.4g); PROTEIN 11.3g; CARB 35.3g; FIBER 0.8g; CHOL 19mg; IRON 2.3mg; SODIUM 755mg; CALC 276mg
EXCHANGES: 2 Starch, 1 Vegetable, 1 Medium-Fat Meat, 1 Fat

SIMPLEsubstitutions

• • • • • • • • • • • • • • • • • • • •

If you can't find *the personal size bread shells, use one large shell in a 10-ounce package. After sandwich is assembled, cut it into 4 wedges (one wedge per serving).*

You can also make this sandwich using a focaccia round from the deli or with a small loaf of French bread, cut in half lengthwise.

open-faced tarragon-shrimp salad sandwiches
with tomato wedges and strawberry sorbet

serves 4 • total time 15 minutes

Cajun-style shrimp salad is a spicy alternative to chicken salad when you're looking for a zesty sandwich filling.

SUPPER plan

1. Slice celery, and chop onions for salad.

2. Cut tomatoes into wedges.

3. Toast bread.

4. Assemble sandwiches.

Open-Faced Tarragon-Shrimp Salad Sandwiches

prep: 15 minutes

Buy precooked shrimp at the seafood market or in the seafood department of the grocery store.

⅓	cup light mayonnaise
1	teaspoon dried tarragon
1	teaspoon Cajun seasoning
2	tablespoons fresh lemon juice (1 lemon)
1	pound peeled and deveined cooked shrimp
1	cup thinly sliced celery (about 3 large ribs)
½	cup finely chopped green onions (about 2)
4	(1-ounce) slices sourdough bread, toasted
2	cups preshredded iceberg lettuce

Combine first 4 ingredients in a medium bowl, stirring with a whisk. Add shrimp, celery, and green onions.

Top each bread slice with ½ cup lettuce. Top lettuce with about 1 cup shrimp mixture. Yield: 4 servings.

CALORIES 244 (31% from fat); FAT 8.4g (sat 1.4g, mono 0.5g, poly 0.6g); PROTEIN 20.6g; CARB 20.2g; FIBER 2.4g; CHOL 168mg; IRON 3.7mg; SODIUM 666mg; CALC 77mg
EXCHANGES: 1 Starch, 3 Very Lean Meat, 1 Fat

NUTRITIONnote

• • • • • • • • • • • • • • • • • •

For a quick and easy sweet treat *to end a meal, you can't beat frozen desserts. But check the labels for calorie and fat content before you scoop to make sure you're not getting more than you bargained for. Some frozen treats are clearly better for you than others. Keep the following definitions in mind when buying frozen treats.*

Sorbet: *a frozen mixture of fruit and sweetened fruit juice that doesn't contain milk and is usually a softer consistency than sherbet.*

Sherbet: *a frozen mixture of sweetened fruit juice and water which usually also contains milk, egg whites, and/or gelatin.*

Ice: *a frozen mixture of water, sugar, and flavored liquid such as fruit juice, wine, or coffee. An ice has a more granular texture than a sorbet or sherbet. The Italian word for an ice is* granita.

Ice Cream: *a frozen combination of milk products, sugar or artificial sweeteners, and often other ingredients such as fruit, chocolate, and nuts. Calorie, fat, and sugar contents vary greatly between premium custard-based ice creams and fat-free, no-sugar-added versions, so read the labels carefully to get one that meets your nutrient needs.*

sweet curry-tuna salad sandwiches
with **minted melon**   serves 4 • total time 18 minutes

On a sultry summer night when it's too hot to think about cooking, chill out with a curried tuna salad sandwich and a frosty fruit salad.

SUPPER plan

1. Place melon in freezer.

2. Chop water chestnuts and bell pepper, and slice celery for salad; chop mint for melon.

3. Prepare tuna salad.

4. Prepare Minted Melon.

5. Toast bread and assemble sandwiches.

Sweet Curry-Tuna Salad Sandwiches

prep: 15 minutes

Instead of tuna, you can use a 10-ounce can of chunk white chicken in water.

⅓   cup light mayonnaise
1½ tablespoons sugar
¾   teaspoon curry powder
1   (9-ounce) can chunk light tuna in water, drained
1   (8-ounce) can sliced water chestnuts, drained and coarsely chopped
½   cup matchstick-cut carrots
½   cup thinly sliced celery (about 2 ribs)
½   cup chopped red bell pepper (½ large)
8   (1.3-ounce) slices wheat berry bread (such as Branola), toasted

Combine first 3 ingredients in a medium bowl. Stir well. Stir in tuna, water chestnuts, carrots, celery, and pepper.

Spoon ¾ cup tuna mixture onto each of 4 bread slices. Top with remaining bread slices. Yield: 4 servings.

CALORIES 360 (26% from fat); FAT 10.3g (sat 2.1g, mono 1.4g, poly 0.9g); PROTEIN 18.8g; CARB 48.6g; FIBER 6.9g; CHOL 20mg; IRON 13mg; SODIUM 722mg; CALC 97mg
EXCHANGES: 3 Starch, 1 Vegetable, 1 Lean Meat, 1 Fat

Minted Melon

prep: 3 minutes

The melon will get frosty if you let it freeze while you make the rest of the meal, but you can let it stay in the freezer for up to an hour.

4   cups refrigerated cantaloupe, honeydew, or watermelon cubes
½   cup pineapple-orange juice
2   tablespoons chopped fresh mint

Place melon cubes in freezer until frosty. Combine melon cubes and juice; stir well. Sprinkle with mint. Serve immediately. Yield: 4 servings (serving size: 1 cup).

CALORIES 74 (5% from fat); FAT 0.4g (sat 0.1g, mono 0.1g, poly 0.2g); PROTEIN 1.4g; CARB 17.9g; FIBER 1.3g; CHOL 0mg; IRON 0.6mg; SODIUM 17mg; CALC 19mg
EXCHANGE: 1 Fruit

FINDit

• • • • • • • • • • • • • • • • • • • •

Look for cubed melon *in the prepared fruit section of the produce department—usually near the prepackaged salads. Any combination of fruit will work.*

ham and cheese spirals

with raw vegetables, low-fat ranch dressing, and watermelon slices   serves 4 • total time 13 minutes

Kids will love these roly-poly ham and cheese sandwiches, with or without the green stuff (spinach). Let them help arrange the vegetables on a platter and pour the ranch dressing in a bowl.

SUPPER plan

1. Prepare mayonnaise mixture.

2. Slice onion.

3. Assemble sandwiches.

4. Arrange raw vegetables, such as baby carrots, broccoli florets, cauliflower florets, and cherry tomatoes, on a platter.

5. Slice watermelon.

Ham and Cheese Spirals

prep: 8 minutes

If it's hard to roll up the tortillas, cover them with paper towels, and microwave at HIGH for 10 seconds to soften them.

¼	cup light mayonnaise
1½	tablespoons honey
2	teaspoons prepared mustard
¼	teaspoon ground allspice (optional)
4	(8-inch) low-fat flour tortillas (such as Mission)
8	ounces thinly sliced lean ham
3	ounces thinly sliced reduced-fat Swiss cheese
2	cups baby spinach
⅓	cup thinly sliced red onion

Combine first 3 ingredients and allspice, if desired, in a small bowl. Spread mayonnaise mixture evenly over tortillas, leaving a 1-inch border. Top tortillas evenly with ham, cheese, spinach, and onion. Roll up, and secure with wooden picks. Yield: 4 servings.

CALORIES 343 (32% from fat); FAT 12.1g (sat 3.1g, mono 3.1g, poly 0.8g); PROTEIN 22.3g; CARB 36.3g; FIBER 0.8g; CHOL 39mg; IRON 2mg; SODIUM 1,276mg; CALC 327mg
EXCHANGES: 2 Starch, 2 Vegetable, 2 Lean Meat, 1 Fat

NUTRITIONnote

• • • • • • • • • • • • • • • • • • •

The sodium value for these sandwiches *is higher than that of some of the other sandwiches in this chapter because of ingredients such as ham and cheese. Surprisingly, tortillas have a good bit of sodium as well. The other items in the menu—veggies and melon—are very low in sodium, so you should be able to have a reasonable intake for the day.*

Although there is no Recommended Dietary Allowance (RDA) for sodium, 2,400 milligrams or less per day for healthy adults is the amount used to calculate the % Daily Value for the Nutrition Facts panel of food labels. That's equivalent to about 1 teaspoon of table salt. The American Heart Association currently recommends 3,000 milligrams or less of sodium per day.

turkey-apple salad sandwiches

with vegetable chips and gingersnaps

serves 4 • total time 12 minutes

Have a holiday-flavored sandwich meal when you don't have the energy or time to cook a holiday-style dinner.

SUPPER plan

1. Toast nuts, if desired.
2. Chop turkey, apple, and vegetables, and grate orange rind for salad mixture.
3. Make salad, and assemble sandwiches.

Turkey-Apple Salad Sandwiches

prep: 12 minutes

This sweet and crunchy turkey-fruit salad is also good stuffed in a pita half or served on a lettuce leaf.

¼	cup pecan pieces, toasted, if desired
4	ounces oven-roasted turkey breast, chopped
1	small Gala apple, cored and chopped
½	cup sweetened dried cranberries (such as Craisins)
¼	cup chopped green bell pepper
¼	cup chopped celery (about 1 rib)
1	tablespoon finely chopped red onion
1	teaspoon grated fresh orange rind
6	tablespoons plain fat-free yogurt
8	(1.3-ounce) slices wheat berry bread (such as Branola)

Combine first 9 ingredients in a medium bowl. Spread about ¾ cup turkey salad on each of 4 bread slices; top with remaining bread slices. Yield: 4 servings.

CALORIES 353 (23% from fat); FAT 9.1g (sat 0.5g, mono 4g, poly 3.6g); PROTEIN 12.6g; CARB 56.1g; FIBER 7.1g; CHOL 11mg; IRON 2mg; SODIUM 724mg; CALC 82mg
EXCHANGES: 2 Starch, 1 Fruit, 1 Vegetable, 1 Very Lean Meat, 1 Fat

HOWto

• • • • • • • • • • • • • • • • • • • •

Toasting enhances the flavor *of most nuts. If you want to use toasted pecans in the turkey salad, put them in a dry skillet, and cook over medium heat for about 3 minutes, stirring often.*

While you're at it, go ahead and toast extra nuts to keep on hand for other recipes. Store them in an airtight container, and freeze them for up to 6 months.

Because nuts contain a lot of oil, they can go rancid and develop a stale taste fairly quickly, so be sure to store them in an airtight container.

smoked turkey-cream cheese bagel sandwiches

with baby carrots and green grapes serves 4 • total time 8 minutes

Bagels aren't just for breakfast—pile on meat, cheese, and veggies for an extraordinary sandwich supper.

SUPPER plan

1. Pit and chop olives; slice onion, tomato, and avocado.

2. Prepare cream cheese mixture.

3. Assemble sandwiches.

Smoked Turkey-Cream Cheese Bagel Sandwiches

prep: 8 minutes

2	tablespoons (1 ounce) tub-style fat-free cream cheese
4	large pitted kalamata olives, chopped
4	(3.4-ounce) whole wheat bagels, sliced
4	curly leaf lettuce leaves
4	(0.3-ounce) slices smoked deli ham
4	ounces thinly sliced smoked deli turkey
2	ounces reduced-fat Havarti cheese, thinly sliced
2	thin slices red onion
4	slices ripe tomato (about 1 small)
¼	ripe avocado, cut into 4 very thin slices

Combine cream cheese and olives.

Split each bagel in half; spread bottom halves with olive spread.

Place lettuce leaves over spread; layer ham, turkey, and cheese on lettuce. Separate onion slices into rings, and divide evenly among sandwiches. Add tomato and avocado slices. Cover with remaining bagel halves. Yield: 4 servings.

CALORIES 380 (18% from fat); FAT 7.7g (sat 1g, mono 1.8g, poly 0.9g); PROTEIN 22.7g; CARB 60.5g; FIBER 10.5g; CHOL 20mg; IRON 3.8mg; SODIUM 1,029mg; CALC 159mg
EXCHANGES: 4 Starch, 1 Medium-Fat Meat

SIMPLEsubstitutions

• • • • • • • • • • • • • • • • • • • •

The possibilities are endless *for this big bagel sandwich. Use your favorite flavor of bagel: plain, onion, sesame seed, pumpernickel. As long as the weight of the bagels are the same, the calories in all of these flavor variations will be about the same.*

Use any type of reduced-fat cheese. Cheddar, Swiss, and American are all good choices.

Substitute lean roast beef for the ham or turkey, or use only one kind of meat.

❝Seasonal fruits and vegetables, fresh herbs, and good cheese are my mainstays.

The recipes and ingredients are simple, but the combinations of flavors are satisfying. And what little slicing or dicing is required is a good stress reliever at the end of a long day.❞

Kathy Eakin,
Executive Editor

Smoked Turkey-Cream
Cheese Bagel Sandwiches

❝I live 30 minutes from the nearest grocery store, so I can't just run by the store to pick up something for dinner.❞

on
HAND

If you stock your kitchen and fridge with 20 versatile ingredients (see list on page 54), you'll always be able to create a meal. It's amazing what you can come up with when you use the same ingredients in a variety of combinations.

Deep-Dish Taco Pizza, page 69

Chicken-Pepper
Tostadas

3 Chicken-Pepper Tostadas

prep: 10 minutes   cook: 11 minutes

    4   (6-inch) corn tortillas
Cooking spray
   12   ounces frozen pepper stir-fry
   12   ounces chicken breast tenders, cut into
         bite-sized pieces
  2½   teaspoons salt-free Mexican seasoning
    ½   teaspoon salt
    ¼   teaspoon crushed red pepper
    1   cup (4 ounces) shredded reduced-fat sharp
         Cheddar or part-skim mozzarella cheese

Preheat broiler.

Place tortillas on a baking sheet; lightly coat each tortilla with cooking spray. Broil 4 to 5 minutes or until crisp, turning once; set aside.

Place pepper stir-fry in a colander. Rinse in cold running water 30 seconds or until peppers thaw; drain well, and pat dry.

Coat a large skillet with cooking spray; place over medium-high heat until hot. Add pepper stir-fry; sauté 4 minutes. Add chicken, seasoning, salt, and red pepper. Sauté 2 to 3 minutes or until chicken is done.

Top each tortilla with ½ cup chicken mixture and ¼ cup cheese. Broil 1 minute or until cheese melts. Yield: 4 servings (serving size: 1 tostada).

CALORIES 256 (25% from fat); FAT 7.1g (sat 3.9g, mono 0.4g, poly 0.5g); PROTEIN 31g; CARB 17.3g; FIBER 2.9g; CHOL 70mg; IRON 1.2mg; SODIUM 627mg; CALC 314mg
EXCHANGES: 1 Starch, 3 Lean Meat

SERVE**with**

• • • • • • • • • • • • • • • • • •

Balance the spiciness of the tostadas *with refreshing mango slices and a pitcher of cool lemonade.*

4 Chicken Quesadillas

prep: 4 minutes   cook: 19 minutes

Cook the chicken and the tortillas in the same skillet so you'll have only one pan to clean.

    1   pound chicken breast tenders, chopped
    2   teaspoons salt-free Mexican seasoning
Cooking spray
    1   teaspoon olive oil
    ½   cup frozen chopped onion
    4   (8-inch) flour tortillas
    1   cup (4 ounces) shredded reduced-fat
         Cheddar or part-skim mozzarella cheese
    ½   cup salsa

Sprinkle chicken with seasoning. Heat oil in a large nonstick skillet coated with cooking spray over medium-high heat. Add chicken and onion; sauté 7 to 8 minutes or until chicken is done. Remove chicken and onion from pan; wipe pan dry with paper towels.

Coat pan with cooking spray; place over medium-high heat until hot. Place 2 tortillas in pan. Sprinkle ¼ of chicken mixture and cheese over 1 side of each tortilla. Fold tortillas in half. Cook 3 minutes on each side or until golden. Repeat procedure with remaining tortillas, chicken mixture, and cheese. Cut each folded tortilla into 2 wedges. Serve with salsa. Yield: 4 servings (serving size: 2 quesadilla wedges and 2 tablespoons salsa).

CALORIES 379 (26% from fat); FAT 10.8g (sat 4.8g, mono 2.6g, poly 0.9g); PROTEIN 40.4g; CARB 29.6g; FIBER 0.9g; CHOL 86mg; IRON 2.2mg; SODIUM 786mg; CALC 377mg
EXCHANGES: 2 Starch, 4 Lean Meat

SERVE**with**

• • • • • • • • • • • • • • • • • •

Serve these chicken-and-cheese-filled *tortillas with shredded lettuce and diced tomatoes.*

5 Chicken and Pepper Fajitas

prep: 6 minutes   cook: 15 minutes

- 2 teaspoons olive oil
- 1 pound chicken breast tenders, cut into ¼-inch strips
- 1 (16-ounce) package frozen pepper stir-fry
- 2 tablespoons bottled minced garlic
- 2 teaspoons salt-free Mexican seasoning
- 8 (8-inch) fat-free flour tortillas
- ½ cup shredded Monterey Jack cheese

Reduced-fat sour cream (optional)

Salsa (optional)

Heat oil in a large nonstick skillet over medium-high heat. Add chicken, and cook, stirring occasionally, 6 minutes. Remove chicken, and set aside.

Add pepper stir-fry, garlic, and Mexican seasoning to pan. Sauté 6 minutes or until vegetables are tender and most of water has evaporated. Add chicken, and cook 2 to 3 minutes or until thoroughly heated.

Warm tortillas according to package directions. Spoon about ½ cup chicken mixture onto each tortilla; sprinkle each with 1 tablespoon cheese. Fold bottom and sides of tortillas to center. Serve with reduced-fat sour cream and salsa, if desired. Yield: 4 servings (serving size: 2 fajitas).

CALORIES 474 (18% from fat); FAT 9.3g (sat 3.4g, mono 3.2g, poly 0.6g); PROTEIN 38.9g; CARB 55.7g; FIBER 6.2g; CHOL 78mg; IRON 4.1mg; SODIUM 849mg; CALC 212mg
EXCHANGES: 3 Starch, 2 Vegetable, 3 Lean Meat

SERVE**with**

● ● ● ● ● ● ● ● ● ● ● ● ● ● ● ● ●

Celebrate Cinco de Mayo *with these easy fajitas, refrigerated citrus sections, and Mexican beer.*

6 Mexican-Style Chicken

prep: 5 minutes   cook: 12 minutes

Prepare 3 cups cooked rice using 1 extra-large bag of boil-in-bag long-grain rice. Start the rice, and let it cook while you prepare the chicken mixture.

- 1 tablespoon chili powder
- 1 tablespoon sugar
- 2 tablespoons salt-free Mexican seasoning
- 1 cup salsa
- 1 (14.5-ounce) can stewed tomatoes, coarsely chopped

Cooking spray

- 1 pound chicken breast tenders
- ½ (16-ounce) package frozen pepper stir-fry (about 2½ cups)
- 1 cup frozen chopped onion
- 3 cups hot cooked long-grain rice

Combine first 3 ingredients in a small bowl. Combine salsa and tomatoes.

Place a large nonstick skillet coated with cooking spray over medium-high heat until hot. Add chicken, and sprinkle evenly with chili powder mixture. Top with pepper stir-fry and onion. Pour salsa mixture evenly over top. Bring to a boil; cover and reduce heat. Simmer 10 minutes or until chicken is done. Serve over cooked rice. Yield: 4 servings (serving size: 1½ cups chicken mixture and ¾ cup rice).

CALORIES 349 (6% from fat); FAT 2.3g (sat 0.5g, mono 0.5g, poly 0.6g); PROTEIN 32.8g; CARB 49g; FIBER 6g; CHOL 66mg; IRON 2.8mg; SODIUM 854mg; CALC 71mg
EXCHANGES: 3 Starch, 3 Very Lean Meat

SERVE**with**

● ● ● ● ● ● ● ● ● ● ● ● ● ● ● ● ●

Balance the heat *of this spicy chicken dish with fresh pineapple slices.*

7 Mexican Chicken Pizza

prep: 3 minutes   cook: 18 minutes

While the crust bakes, thaw the chicken in the microwave according to package directions.

  1 (10-ounce) can refrigerated pizza crust dough
Cooking spray
  ¾ cup chunky salsa
  ½ teaspoon salt-free Mexican seasoning
  ¼ teaspoon black pepper
  2 cups frozen chopped cooked chicken, thawed
  1 cup canned black beans, rinsed and drained
1½ cups (6 ounces) shredded part-skim mozzarella or reduced-fat Cheddar cheese

Preheat oven to 450°.

Unroll pizza dough onto a baking sheet coated with cooking spray; pat dough into a 12-inch square. Bake at 450° for 9 minutes.

Spread salsa over crust, leaving a ½-inch border. Sprinkle seasoning and pepper over salsa. Arrange chicken evenly over salsa; sprinkle black beans evenly over chicken, and top with cheese. Bake at 450° for 9 minutes or until crust is lightly browned. Cut into 4 squares. Yield: 4 servings (serving size: 1 [6 x 6-inch] square).

CALORIES 415 (22% from fat); FAT 10g (sat 4.3g, mono 1.9g, poly 0.2g); PROTEIN 35.9g; CARB 45g; FIBER 4.1g; CHOL 62mg; IRON 2.8mg; SODIUM 1,255mg; CALC 302mg
EXCHANGES: 3 Starch, 3 Lean Meat

SERVEwith

● ● ● ● ● ● ● ● ● ● ● ● ● ● ● ● ● ●

Chocolate has traditionally *been a delicacy associated with Mexican cuisine, so end your meal with a scoop of low-fat chocolate ice cream.*

8 Chicken-Pesto Pizza

prep: 2 minutes   cook: 17 minutes

Sauté the chicken while the crust bakes so your whole meal will be ready in under 20 minutes.

  1 (10-ounce) can refrigerated pizza crust dough
Olive oil-flavored cooking spray
  1 pound chicken breast tenders, chopped
  1 teaspoon dried Italian seasoning
  3 tablespoons commercial pesto
  1 cup (4 ounces) shredded part-skim mozzarella or reduced-fat Cheddar cheese

Preheat oven to 450°.

Unroll pizza crust dough onto a baking sheet coated with cooking spray; pat into a 12 x 8-inch rectangle. Bake at 450° for 9 minutes.

Sprinkle chicken with Italian seasoning. Heat a large nonstick skillet over medium-high heat until hot. Add chicken, and sauté 3 to 4 minutes or until done.

Spread pesto evenly over pizza crust; top with chicken, and sprinkle with cheese. Bake at 450° for 5 minutes or until cheese melts. Cut into 8 pieces. Yield: 4 servings (serving size: 2 [4 x 3-inch] pieces).

CALORIES 442 (28% from fat); FAT 13.7g (sat 4.7g, mono 4.9g, poly 0.8g); PROTEIN 41.4g; CARB 35.4g; FIBER 1.4g; CHOL 86mg; IRON 3.2mg; SODIUM 767mg; CALC 284mg
EXCHANGES: 2 Starch, 1 Vegetable, 4 Very Lean Meat, 2 Fat

SERVEwith

● ● ● ● ● ● ● ● ● ● ● ● ● ● ● ● ● ●

Munch on fresh raw vegetables *(carrots, celery, broccoli florets) along with the pizza, and scoop up low-fat sorbet for dessert.*

White Bean-Chicken
Chili

9
White Bean-Chicken Chili

prep: 4 minutes   cook: 22 minutes

To get 3 cups of frozen chopped cooked chicken, buy a 20-ounce package. You'll have about 2 cups of chicken left over for another use.

  1   teaspoon olive oil
  1   cup frozen chopped onion
  2   teaspoons bottled minced garlic
  2   (15.5-ounce) cans cannellini beans, undrained
  3   cups frozen chopped cooked chicken
  1   (14.5-ounce) can fat-free, less-sodium chicken broth
1½   teaspoons salt-free Mexican seasoning
  ¼   teaspoon salt
  1   cup (4 ounces) shredded Monterey Jack cheese with jalapeño peppers

Heat oil in a Dutch oven over medium-high heat. Add onion and garlic; sauté 2 minutes.

Mash one can of beans in a small bowl with a fork. Add mashed beans, remaining can beans, and next 4 ingredients to pan; bring to a boil. Reduce heat, and simmer 15 minutes.

Add cheese; simmer 5 minutes, stirring constantly. Yield: 6 servings (serving size: 1½ cups).

CALORIES 284 (26% from fat); FAT 8.3g (sat 4.2g, mono 0.6g, poly 0.7g); PROTEIN 28.3g; CARB 23.5g; FIBER 6.1g; CHOL 58mg; IRON 2.1mg; SODIUM 920mg; CALC 187mg
EXCHANGES: 1½ Starch, 3 Lean Meat

ADD**ons**

• • • • • • • • • • • • • • • • • •

Top the chili *with any of these tasty toppings:*
• *additional Monterey Jack cheese*
• *low-fat sour cream or plain fat-free yogurt*
• *chopped green onions*
• *chopped fresh cilantro*
• *salsa*
• *crumbled low-fat tortilla chips*

10
Chicken Cacciatore

prep: 5 minutes   cook: 10 minutes

A 26-ounce jar of pasta sauce contains about 3 cups. If you've got pasta sauce left over, keep it refrigerated in the jar, and use it in another recipe.

  1   (3½-ounce) bag boil-in-bag long-grain rice
  1   cup frozen pepper stir-fry, chopped
  2   teaspoons olive oil
  1   pound chicken breast tenders, cut into bite-sized pieces
  ½   cup frozen chopped onion
  2   teaspoons Creole seasoning
  2   cups chunky pasta sauce
  ½   cup water

Cook rice according to package directions, omitting salt and fat.

Place frozen peppers in a colander, and rinse with cold water 30 seconds; drain well.

Heat oil in a large nonstick skillet over medium-high heat. Add chicken, onion, and Creole seasoning; sauté 4 minutes or until chicken is browned and onion is tender. Add peppers, pasta sauce, and water. Bring to a boil; cover, reduce heat, and simmer 5 minutes or until thoroughly heated.

Combine rice and chicken mixture. Yield: 4 servings (serving size: 1½ cups).

CALORIES 299 (11% from fat); FAT 3.8g (sat 0.7g, mono 2g, poly 0.5g); PROTEIN 30.6g; CARB 33g; FIBER 2.9g; CHOL 66mg; IRON 2.4mg; SODIUM 775mg; CALC 59mg
EXCHANGES: 2 Starch, 4 Very Lean Meat

SERVE**with**

• • • • • • • • • • • • • • • • • •

Round out the meal *with garlic toast: slice a garlic clove in half, rub cut sides over pieces of Italian bread, and toast in the toaster, toaster oven, or conventional oven until lightly browned.*

11

Pesto Chicken with Penne

prep: 2 minutes   cook: 15 minutes

*If you need to thaw the chicken tenders, place
them on a microwave-safe plate, and microwave
at MEDIUM-LOW (30% power) 8 minutes or
until thawed.*

2¼ cups (8 ounces) uncooked penne pasta
     (tube-shaped pasta)
1   pound chicken breast tenders
½   teaspoon salt
¼   teaspoon freshly ground black pepper
Cooking spray
⅓   cup commercial pesto

Cook pasta according to package directions,
omitting salt and fat.

Sprinkle chicken with salt and pepper. Place
a large nonstick skillet coated with cooking
spray over medium-high heat until hot. Add
chicken to pan, and sauté until done.

Drain pasta. Add pesto and chicken to
warm pasta; toss lightly. Yield: 4 servings
(serving size: about 1⅓ cups).

CALORIES 428 (23% from fat); FAT 10.8g (sat 2.8g, mono 5.7g, poly 1.3g);
PROTEIN 36.8g; CARB 43.7g; FIBER 1.9g; CHOL 72mg; IRON 3.7mg;
SODIUM 514mg; CALC 156mg
EXCHANGES: 3 Starch, 4 Very Lean Meat, 1 Fat

SERVE**with**

● ● ● ● ● ● ● ● ● ● ● ● ● ● ● ● ● ●

Serve this flavorful pasta *with sliced fresh
tomatoes drizzled with balsamic vinegar and
sprinkled with freshly ground black pepper.*

12

Cheesy Chicken Spaghetti

prep: 5 minutes   cook: 31 minutes

*You can cover and refrigerate the casserole
overnight, and sprinkle with cheese before baking. Bake at 350° for 25 minutes until bubbly.*

9   ounces uncooked spaghetti
Cooking spray
1   cup frozen chopped onion
1   tablespoon bottled minced garlic
2   (14.5-ounce) cans stewed tomatoes,
     undrained and chopped
1   tablespoon low-sodium Worcestershire sauce
2   teaspoons dried Italian seasoning
¼   teaspoon salt
2   cups (8 ounces) shredded reduced-fat
     Cheddar cheese, divided
3   cups frozen chopped cooked chicken,
     thawed

Preheat oven to 350°.

Cook pasta according to package directions,
omitting salt and fat. Drain.

Coat a nonstick skillet with cooking spray;
place over medium-high heat until hot. Add
onion and garlic; sauté 5 minutes. Add tomatoes, Worcestershire sauce, seasoning, and salt;
bring to a boil. Reduce heat, and simmer,
uncovered, 10 minutes. Stir in 1 cup cheese,
cooked spaghetti, and chicken. Spoon into a
3-quart casserole coated with cooking spray.
Sprinkle with remaining 1 cup cheese. Bake at
350° for 15 minutes. Yield: 6 servings (serving
size: 1⅓ cups).

CALORIES 395 (19% from fat); FAT 8.5g (sat 4.9g, mono 0.1g, poly 0.4g);
PROTEIN 36g; CARB 45.3g; FIBER 3.1g; CHOL 65mg; IRON 1.9mg;
SODIUM 934mg; CALC 417mg
EXCHANGES: 3 Starch, 3 Lean Meat

SERVE**with**

● ● ● ● ● ● ● ● ● ● ● ● ● ● ● ● ● ●

While the spaghetti casserole bakes, *toss a
green salad using a package of mixed salad greens
and reduced-fat olive oil vinaigrette.*

Cheesy Chicken
Spaghetti

13

Buttery Herbed Chicken

prep: 2 minutes   cook: 10 minutes

Prepare 3 cups cooked rice by using 1 extra-large bag boil-in-bag rice, and cook according to package directions using fat-free, less-sodium chicken broth instead of water. Start the rice first, and let it cook while you prepare the chicken.

2 tablespoons light butter, softened
¼ teaspoon dried Italian seasoning
¼ teaspoon salt
¼ teaspoon freshly ground black pepper
2 teaspoons olive oil
1 pound chicken breast tenders
3 cups hot cooked long-grain rice

Combine butter and next 3 ingredients in a small bowl.

Heat oil in a large nonstick skillet over medium-high heat. Add chicken, and cook 4 to 5 minutes on each side or until done.

Remove pan from heat, add butter mixture, and toss to coat chicken evenly. Serve immediately over rice. Yield: 4 servings (serving size: about 3 ounces chicken and ¾ cup rice).

CALORIES 292 (21% from fat); FAT 6.9g (sat 2.7g, mono 2.1g, poly 0.6g); PROTEIN 29.3g; CARB 26.5g; FIBER 0.8g; CHOL 76mg; IRON 1.7mg; SODIUM 259mg; CALC 25mg
EXCHANGES: 1½ Starch, 3 Lean Meat

SERVE**with**

• • • • • • • • • • • • • • • • • • •

Steam 2 cups fresh or frozen sugar snap peas *in the microwave to round out the meal. Steam on HIGH 5 to 7 minutes or until tender.*

14

Creole Baked Shrimp

prep: 3 minutes   cook: 8 minutes

For an extraspicy shrimp dish, add hot sauce to taste.

2 tablespoons low-sodium Worcestershire sauce
2 tablespoons light butter, melted
2 teaspoons Creole seasoning
2 teaspoons olive oil
Olive oil-flavored cooking spray
1 pound frozen peeled shrimp

Preheat oven to 450°.

Combine first 4 ingredients in a small bowl. Place shrimp in an 11 x 7-inch baking dish coated with cooking spray. Pour butter mixture over shrimp, stirring to coat. Bake at 450° for 8 minutes or until shrimp are done. Yield: 3 servings (serving size: about 5 ounces shrimp).

CALORIES 223 (39% from fat); FAT 9.6g (sat 3.6g, mono 2.6g, poly 1.3g); PROTEIN 31.4g; CARB 2g; FIBER 0g; CHOL 243mg; IRON 3.7mg; SODIUM 684mg; CALC 81mg
EXCHANGES: 4 Lean Meat

SERVE**with**

• • • • • • • • • • • • • • • • • • •

Serve this spicy shrimp *in shallow bowls along with crusty French bread to sop up the sauce. Or if you prefer, serve the shrimp mixture over fettuccine or angel hair pasta.*

15

Spicy Shrimp and Pepper Skillet

prep: 2 minutes   cook: 10 minutes

Start cooking the rice before you sauté the shrimp and pepper mixture. Use 1 extra-large bag boil-in-bag rice to get 3 cups of cooked rice.

  3   cups (about 10 ounces) frozen pepper stir-fry, thawed
Cooking spray
  1   tablespoon olive oil
  1   tablespoon bottled minced garlic
1½   pounds frozen peeled shrimp, thawed
  1   tablespoon low-sodium Worcestershire sauce
  2   teaspoons Creole seasoning
 ¼   teaspoon freshly ground black pepper
  3   cups hot cooked long-grain rice

Place peppers in a colander, and rinse under running water; drain well. Set aside.

Heat oil in large nonstick skillet coated with cooking spray over medium-high heat. Add garlic and pepper stir-fry; sauté 5 minutes or until peppers are tender.

Add shrimp and next 3 ingredients to pan; sauté 5 minutes or until shrimp are done and mixture is thoroughly heated. Serve shrimp mixture over rice. Yield: 6 servings (serving size: ⅔ cup shrimp mixture and ½ cup rice).

CALORIES 222 (14% from fat); FAT 3.5g (sat 0.6g, mono 1.9g, poly 0.6g); PROTEIN 20g; CARB 25.9g; FIBER 1.2g; CHOL 161mg; IRON 3.7mg; SODIUM 401mg; CALC 46mg
EXCHANGES: 1 Starch, 2 Vegetable, 2 Very Lean Meat

HOWto

• • • • • • • • • • • • • • • • • •

It's important to rinse the pepper mixture *in this recipe before you add it to the skillet. Otherwise, the mixture will be too watery. Rinsing helps get rid of some of the liquid in the frozen peppers. If you just let the mixture cook down to evaporate the water, the shrimp will be overcooked and tough.*

16

Pesto-Shrimp Pizza

prep: 7 minutes   cook: 15 minutes

Sauté the onions and shrimp while the crust bakes.

  1   (10-ounce) can refrigerated pizza crust dough
Cooking spray
  3   cups frozen chopped onion
4½   tablespoons water
  1   pound frozen peeled shrimp
  2   tablespoons balsamic vinegar
 ⅓   cup commercial pesto
  1   cup preshredded fresh Parmesan cheese

Preheat oven to 450°.

Unroll dough onto a baking sheet coated with cooking spray; pat into a 12 x 8-inch rectangle. Bake at 450° for 9 minutes.

Place a large nonstick skillet over medium-high heat until hot; coat with cooking spray. Add onion, and sauté 4 minutes or until golden brown, adding 1 tablespoon water every minute. Add shrimp, remaining water, and balsamic vinegar. Sauté 3 minutes or until shrimp are done and onion is golden.

Coat prepared pizza crust with cooking spray. Spread pesto evenly over top of crust, leaving a ½-inch border. Top with onion mixture and cheese. Bake at 450° for 6 minutes or until cheese melts and crust is golden. Cut into 6 squares. Yield: 6 servings (serving size: 1 [4-inch] square).

CALORIES 348 (35% from fat); FAT 13.6g (sat 5.0g, mono 5.4g, poly 0.8g); PROTEIN 25.8g; CARB 29.6g; FIBER 2g; CHOL 125mg; IRON 3.7mg; SODIUM 857mg; CALC 361mg
EXCHANGES: 2 Starch, 3 Lean Meat, 1 Fat

VEGETARIANoption

• • • • • • • • • • • • • • • • • •

For a quick vegetarian version *of this pizza, substitute 1 (8-ounce) package sliced mushrooms for the shrimp, and top the onion mixture with blue cheese, mozzarella, or Parmesan.*

17

Beef and Black Bean Soup

prep: 1 minute   cook: 18 minutes

1   pound ground round
2   teaspoons salt-free Mexican seasoning
2   (15-ounce) cans black beans, rinsed and
     drained
2   cups frozen pepper stir-fry, slightly thawed
1   (14-ounce) can low-salt beef broth
1   cup chunky salsa

Cook beef in a large saucepan over
medium-high heat until beef is browned, stirring to crumble; drain. Return beef to pan; stir
in seasoning.

Mash 1 can beans with a fork. Add mashed
beans and remaining can beans to beef mixture.
Stir in peppers and broth; bring to a boil.
Reduce heat, stir in salsa, and simmer, uncovered, 5 minutes. Yield: 4 servings (serving size:
1¾ cups).

CALORIES 280 (23% from fat); FAT 7.2g (sat 2.6g, mono 2.9g, poly 0.3g);
PROTEIN 32g; CARB 25.3g; FIBER 6.8g; CHOL 65mg; IRON 4.2mg;
SODIUM 914mg; CALC 45mg
EXCHANGES: 1 Starch, 2 Vegetable, 3 Very Lean Meat

ADD**ons**

• • • • • • • • • • • • • • • • • •

Top the soup with your choice *of low-fat*
toppers: low-fat sour cream, additional salsa,
cilantro, chopped green onions, lime slices, or
crumbled low-fat tortilla chips.

18

Meaty Calzones

prep: 7 minutes   cook: 21 minutes

Prepare the pizza dough rectangles while the
beef mixture cooks so that you can spoon hot
beef directly from the skillet onto the dough.

½   pound ground round
¾   cup frozen chopped onion
1   teaspoon bottled minced garlic
½   teaspoon dried Italian seasoning
¼   teaspoon salt
⅛   teaspoon freshly ground black pepper
1   (10-ounce) can refrigerated pizza crust dough
¾   cup (3 ounces) shredded part-skim
     mozzarella or reduced-fat Cheddar cheese
Cooking spray
1⅓   cups pasta sauce

Preheat oven to 400°.

Cook beef, onion, and garlic in a large nonstick skillet over medium-high heat until beef is
browned, stirring to crumble. Drain. Return to
pan, and add Italian seasoning, salt, and pepper.

Unroll pizza crust onto an ungreased baking
sheet. Cut dough into 4 squares. Press each
square into a 6 x 5-inch rectangle. Spoon beef
mixture evenly into center of each rectangle;
sprinkle evenly with cheese. Bring opposite
corners of rectangles together, pinching seams
together to seal. Coat tops of calzones with
cooking spray.

Bake at 400° for 11 minutes or until lightly
browned. Place pasta sauce in a microwave-
safe dish; microwave at HIGH 2 minutes or
until thoroughly heated. Serve calzones with
warm pasta sauce. Yield: 4 servings (serving
size: 1 calzone and ⅓ cup pasta sauce).

CALORIES 374 (23% from fat); FAT 9.5g (sat 3.4g, mono 2.4g, poly 0.3g);
PROTEIN 26g; CARB 43.8g; FIBER 2.9g; CHOL 45mg; IRON 3.9mg;
SODIUM 994mg; CALC 176mg
EXCHANGES: 2 Starch, 2 Vegetable, 3 Lean Meat

Meaty Calzones

Deep-Dish Taco Pizza

19

Deep-Dish Taco Pizza

prep: 2 minutes   cook: 22 minutes
stand: 5 minutes

This family-pleasing dish is a cross between a pizza and a casserole, and guaranteed to please even the pickiest of eaters.

  1 pound ground round
 ½ cup frozen chopped onion
  1 (15-ounce) can diced tomatoes with green chiles, drained
  1 teaspoon salt-free Mexican seasoning
  1 (10-ounce) can refrigerated pizza crust dough
Cooking spray
  1 cup (4 ounces) shredded reduced-fat sharp Cheddar or part-skim mozzarella cheese
Salsa (optional)
Reduced-fat sour cream (optional)

Preheat oven to 425°.

Cook beef and onion in a large nonstick skillet over medium-high heat until beef is browned, stirring to crumble. Drain well, and return beef mixture to pan. Stir in tomatoes and seasoning; cook over medium-high heat 1 minute or until thoroughly heated; set aside.

Unroll pizza crust dough. Press into bottom and halfway up sides of a 13 x 9-inch baking dish coated with cooking spray. Spoon beef mixture over pizza crust dough.

Bake at 425° for 12 minutes. Top with cheese, and bake 5 minutes or until cheese melts and edges of crust are browned. Let stand 5 minutes before slicing. Serve warm. Top with salsa and sour cream, if desired. Yield: 6 servings (serving size: 1 slice).

CALORIES 306 (29% from fat); FAT 9.8g (sat 4.1g, mono 1.9g, poly 0.2g); PROTEIN 27.9g; CARB 25.6g; FIBER 1.3g; CHOL 57mg; IRON 2.9mg; SODIUM 693mg; CALC 183mg
EXCHANGES: 1 Starch, 2 Vegetable, 3 Lean Meat

20

Beefy Skillet Pasta

prep: 2 minutes   cook: 15 minutes

Bring the water for the pasta to a boil, and let the pasta cook while you brown the beef.

  1 pound ground round
  2 cups pasta sauce
 ¼ teaspoon salt
 ¼ teaspoon pepper
  3 cups hot cooked fusilli (about 6 ounces uncooked pasta)
 ½ cup (2 ounces) shredded part-skim mozzarella or reduced-fat Cheddar cheese

Cook beef in a large nonstick skillet over medium-high heat until browned, stirring to crumble. Drain and return beef to pan.

Add pasta sauce, salt, and pepper; cook 2 minutes, stirring occasionally. Add pasta; cook 2 minutes. Sprinkle with cheese; cook 1 minute or until cheese melts. Yield: 4 servings (serving size: about 1⅓ cups).

CALORIES 418 (22% from fat); FAT 10g (sat 4.1g, mono 3.6g, poly 0.7g); PROTEIN 30.7g, CARB 42.2g, FIBER 3.1g, CHOL 73mg; IRON 5.2mg; SODIUM 644mg; CALC 143mg
EXCHANGES: 3 Starch, 3 Lean Meat

SIMPLE**substitutions**

• • • • • • • • • • • • • • • • • • • •

Use macaroni or any other short pasta *you have on hand in place of the fusilli.*

66Everybody in my family wants something different for supper. I'm trying to lose weight, my husband can't stand "diet" food, my 15-year-old daughter is a vegetarian, and my four-year-old will eat only chicken fingers! Help!99

have it
YOUR WAY

Serve your family the food they want, just the way they want it! Prepare one base recipe, then modify it with a variety of ingredients to fit everyone's individual tastes. Everyone will be happy. You'll be a hero.

Vegetable Fried Rice, page 90

build a blintz
serve with lemon pepper asparagus

serves 4 • total time 25 to 30 minutes

A fun idea for light supper fare is a blintz blitz. (A blintz is a thin pancake that holds a cheese mixture and either a savory or sweet filling.) Make one recipe of Basic Blintzes, then choose one of the savory toppings and one of the dessert toppings. Or if you can't make up your mind, make all four, and let each person pick a favorite.

Choose from the following:

- SMOKED SALMON BLINTZES
- MONTE CRISTO BLINTZES
- VERY BERRY BLINTZES
- CARAMEL-BANANA BLINTZES

Basic Blintzes

prep: 8 minutes   cook: 3 minutes

- 1 (8-ounce) package ⅓-less-fat cream cheese
- ½ cup fat-free cottage cheese
- 3 tablespoons egg substitute
- 8 prepackaged crêpes (such as Melissa's)

Place first 3 ingredients in a microwave-safe bowl. Microwave at MEDIUM-LOW (30% power) 3 minutes, stirring every minute or until cheese is softened; whisk until smooth. Place about 2 tablespoons cheese mixture in center of each crêpe; fold opposite sides of each crêpe in toward center, forming a square. Yield: 8 blintzes.

CALORIES 128 (50% from fat); FAT 7.1g (sat 4.7g, mono 0.3g, poly 0.1g); PROTEIN 6.2g; CARB 9.2g; FIBER 0g; CHOL 26mg; IRON 0.5mg; SODIUM 277mg; CALC 47mg
EXCHANGES: 1 Starch, ½ High-Fat Meat

SUPPER plan

1. Prepare Basic Blintzes.

2. Prepare ingredients for all desired toppings.

3. Bake Monte Cristo Blintzes.

4. While blintzes bake:
   - Prepare Lemon Pepper Asparagus.
   - Heat toppings for desired dessert sauces.
   - Top blintzes with desired toppings.

FINDit

• • • • • • • • • • • • • • • • • • •

Look for prepackaged crêpes *in the section of the grocery store where you find tortillas and prepackaged pizza crusts.*

The crêpe brand we used, Melissa's, is available in a resealable package, and there are 10 crêpes per package. Store unused crêpes in the refrigerator.

The crêpes are ready to use, so all you have to do is heat them, if desired. Each 9-inch crêpe contains 37 calories, 1 gram of fat, and 60 milligrams of sodium.

Very Berry Blintzes, page 75

Smoked Salmon Blintzes, page 74

Smoked Salmon Blintzes

prep: 8 minutes

½ cup finely chopped cucumber
½ cup low-fat sour cream
2 teaspoons chopped fresh dill
1 teaspoon bottled minced garlic
4 BASIC BLINTZES (page 72)
1 (4-ounce) package smoked salmon, cut into thin strips
Dill sprigs (optional)

Combine cucumber, sour cream, dill, and garlic in a small bowl. Top each blintz with salmon; spoon sauce over salmon. Garnish with dill sprigs, if desired. Yield: 4 servings (serving size: 1 blintz, 1 ounce salmon, and ¼ cup sauce).

CALORIES 212 (51% from fat); FAT 12g (sat 7.3g, mono 0.9g, poly 0.4g); PROTEIN 13g; CARB 12g; FIBER 0.2g; CHOL 49mg; IRON 0.8mg; SODIUM 862mg; CALC 105mg
EXCHANGES: 1 Starch, 1 Medium-Fat Meat, 1 Fat

FIND**it**

Look for packages *of thinly sliced smoked salmon in the seafood department of the grocery store. Smoked salmon is fresh salmon that has been cured by either hot smoking (6 to 12 hours at 120° to 180°) or cold smoking (1 day to 3 weeks at 70° to 90°). Smoked salmon doesn't taste quite as salty as kippered salmon or lox, which are soaked in brine, then smoked. One ounce of salmon has 33 calories, 1.2 grams of fat, and 222 milligrams of sodium and contains the same heart-healthy omega-3 fats as fresh salmon.*

Monte Cristo Blintzes

prep: 3 minutes   cook: 12 minutes

The inspiration for this sweet and savory blintz is a Monte Cristo sandwich: cooked ham or turkey and Swiss cheese on bread that has been dipped in egg and cooked in butter. The sandwich is usually topped with powdered sugar and jam.

4 BASIC BLINTZES (page 72)
2 ounces thinly sliced deli ham
¼ cup (1 ounce) shredded reduced-fat Swiss cheese
¼ cup strawberry spread (such as Polaner All Fruit)
1 teaspoon powdered sugar

Preheat oven to 400°.
Place 4 blintzes in an 11 x 7-inch baking dish. Top with ham and cheese. Bake at 400° for 12 minutes. Top each with strawberry spread, and sprinkle with powdered sugar. Yield: 4 servings (serving size: 1 blintz, ½ ounce ham, 1 tablespoon cheese, 1 tablespoon strawberry spread, and ¼ teaspoon sugar).

CALORIES 203 (36% from fat); FAT 8.2g (sat 5.1g, mono 0.8g, poly 0.2g); PROTEIN 11.1g; CARB 20.3g; FIBER 0g; CHOL 36mg; IRON 0.6mg; SODIUM 501mg; CALC 116mg
EXCHANGES: 1½ Starch, 1 Lean Meat, 1 Fat

SIMPLE**substitution**

Use turkey or chicken *slices instead of ham—it's still a Monte Cristo. And if you don't care for strawberry spread, use raspberry.*

Very Berry Blintzes

prep: 2 minutes   cook: 1 minute

½   cup fresh blackberries
½   cup fresh raspberries
¼   cup strawberry spread (such as Polaner All Fruit)
4   BASIC BLINTZES (page 72)

Combine berries and strawberry spread in a microwave-safe dish; cover and vent. Microwave at HIGH 1 minute or until thoroughly heated. Spoon berry mixture over blintzes. Yield: 4 servings (serving size: 1 blintz and ¼ cup berry mixture).

CALORIES 187 (35% from fat); FAT 7.3g (sat 4.7g, mono 0.4g, poly 0.2g); PROTEIN 6.6g; CARB 23.5g; FIBER 2g; CHOL 26mg; IRON 0.6mg; SODIUM 280mg; CALC 57mg
EXCHANGES: 1 Starch, ½ Fruit, ½ Medium-Fat Meat, 1 Fat

Caramel-Banana Blintzes

prep: 2 minutes   cook: 6 minutes

½   cup light brown sugar
¼   cup water
2   small bananas, sliced
1   teaspoon vanilla extract
4   BASIC BLINTZES (page 72)

Combine sugar and water in a small skillet; bring to a boil, stirring until sugar dissolves. Add banana and vanilla; cook 4 minutes or until thickened. Spoon banana mixture over blintzes. Yield: 4 servings (serving size: 1 blintz and ⅓ cup banana mixture).

CALORIES 244 (27% from fat); FAT 7.4g (sat 4.8g, mono 0.4g, poly 0.2g); PROTEIN 6.7g; CARB 38.8g; FIBER 1.2g; CHOL 27mg; IRON 1mg; SODIUM 284mg; CALC 66mg
EXCHANGES: 2 Starch, ½ Fruit, 1 Fat

Lemon Pepper Asparagus

prep: 2 minutes   cook: 3 minutes

For a satisfying meal, serve tender spears of asparagus with Smoked Salmon Blintzes or Monte Cristo Blintzes.

1   pound asparagus, trimmed
¼   cup water
1   tablespoon light butter
½   teaspoon lemon pepper

Spread asparagus in a shallow microwave-safe dish; add water. Microwave at HIGH 3 to 5 minutes or until tender; drain in a colander. Return asparagus to dish; top with butter and lemon pepper. Toss well. Yield: 4 servings.

CALORIES 38 (43% from fat); FAT 1.8g (sat 1g, mono 0g, poly 0g); PROTEIN 3.7g; CARB 4.2g; FIBER 1g; CHOL 5mg; IRON 0.8mg; SODIUM 77mg; CALC 25mg
EXCHANGE: 1 Vegetable

QUICKtip

● ● ● ● ● ● ● ● ● ● ● ● ● ● ● ● ● ●

Bunches of fresh asparagus *are usually sold bound with wide rubber bands. Keep the rubber band around the spears, and trim them where they begin to turn white.*

Basic Veggie Burger

burgers your way

serve with baked steak fries · serves 4 · total time 16 to 28 minutes

You'll have everybody at your house singing "Have It Your Way," when you start with soy protein burger patties and offer toppings to suit a variety of eating styles. It might be cumbersome to prepare all five variations, so we suggest trying two or three at a time. The recipe for each burger is for four servings, so adjust the ingredients based on the number of servings of each that you need.

Choose from the following:

- BASIC VEGGIE BURGERS
- VERY VEGGIE BURGERS
- BLUE CHEESE-BACON BURGERS
- SANTA FE BURGERS
- MUSHROOM-SWISS PATTY MELTS

SUPPER plan

1. Broil frozen steak fries according to package directions.

2. While steak fries broil:
   - Prepare ingredients for desired burgers.
   - Cook burgers.

3. Assemble burgers and toppings.

Basic Veggie Burgers

prep: 7 minutes   cook: 6 minutes

If you're watching your sodium intake, leave off the pickles. Since pickles are an optional ingredient, they're not included in the analysis.

- 4 (2.8-ounce) frozen meatless soy protein burgers (such as Boca Burgers or Morningstar Farms)
- 4 (2.8-ounce) whole grain hamburger buns
- 4 teaspoons creamy mustard blend (such as Dijonnaise)
- 4 teaspoons ketchup
- 4 lettuce leaves
- 4 (¾-ounce) slices 2% American cheese
- 4 (¼-inch) slices tomato
- 8 dill pickle slices (optional)

Cook burgers in a nonstick skillet according to package directions.

Spread creamy mustard blend on cut side of bottom half of each bun and ketchup over cut side of top half. Line bottom halves of hamburger buns with a lettuce leaf, and top each with 1 burger patty, 1 cheese slice, 1 tomato slice, pickle slices, if desired, and top half of bun. Yield: 4 servings (serving size: 1 burger).

CALORIES 326 (14% from fat); FAT 5.2g (sat 2g, mono 0g, poly 0g); PROTEIN 22.6g; CARB 54.5g; FIBER 8.3g; CHOL 10mg; IRON 4mg; SODIUM 1,063mg; CALC 250mg
EXCHANGES: 3 Starch, 1 Vegetable, 1 Lean Meat

HOWto

· ·

If you prefer to make your own meatless burger patties, *here's a simple recipe: Rinse and drain 1 (15-ounce) can black beans, and partially mash beans with a fork. Stir in ½ cup dry breadcrumbs, ¼ cup minced red onion, ½ teaspoon dried oregano, ¼ teaspoon ground cumin, ¼ teaspoon hot sauce, ⅛ teaspoon pepper, and 1 large egg. Shape mixture into 4 (4-inch-diameter) patties. Place patties in a skillet coated with cooking spray, and cook over medium heat 4 minutes on each side or until thoroughly heated. Yield: 4 patties.*

Very Veggie Burgers

prep: 7 minutes   cook: 6 minutes

Vary the veggie toppings with whatever you happen to have on hand. Zucchini, yellow squash, cucumbers, and onions are all good options.

- 4   (2.8-ounce) frozen meatless soy protein burgers
- 8   thinly sliced green bell pepper rings
- ½   cup alfalfa sprouts
- 4   lettuce leaves
- 4   (¼-inch) slices tomato
- 4   (2.8-ounce) whole grain hamburger buns
- ¼   cup light ranch dressing

Cook burgers in a nonstick skillet according to package directions.

Place 2 bell pepper rings, 2 tablespoons sprouts, 1 lettuce leaf, and 1 tomato slice on bottom half of each hamburger bun. Top with 1 burger; drizzle each with 1 tablespoon dressing. Cover with top halves of buns. Serve immediately. Yield: 4 servings (serving size: 1 burger).

CALORIES 311 (16% from fat); FAT 5.7g (sat 0.3g, mono 0g, poly 0.1g); PROTEIN 18g; CARB 53.1g; FIBER 8.8g; CHOL 4mg; IRON 4.2mg; SODIUM 751mg; CALC 108mg
EXCHANGES: 3 Starch, 1 Vegetable, 1 Lean Meat

Blue Cheese-Bacon Burgers

prep: 3 minutes   cook: 6 minutes

Just add bacon and blue cheese to the veggie burgers, and the meat lovers will be as happy as can be. If you want to keep the burgers meat-free, use veggie bacon slices.

- 4   (2.8-ounce) frozen meatless soy protein burgers
- ½   cup crumbled blue cheese
- ¼   cup fat-free mayonnaise
- 4   (2.8-ounce) whole grain hamburger buns, toasted
- 4   reduced-fat bacon slices, cooked and cut in half crosswise

Cook burgers in a nonstick skillet according to package directions.

Combine blue cheese and mayonnaise; stir with a whisk. Place 1 burger patty on bottom half of each bun. Spread about 2 tablespoons blue cheese mixture over each burger. Top each with 2 half-slices bacon and top half of bun. Serve immediately. Yield: 4 servings (serving size: 1 burger).

CALORIES 355 (21% from fat); FAT 8.4g (sat 3.7g, mono 1.3g, poly 0.1g); PROTEIN 23.3g; CARB 52.2g; FIBER 7.9g; CHOL 18mg; IRON 4.1mg; SODIUM 1,081mg; CALC 182mg
EXCHANGES: 3 Starch, 1 Vegetable, 1 Lean Meat, 1 Fat

NUTRITION**note**

All of the burger variations *can be made using ground round patties instead of soy protein burgers. Use 4 ounces ground round per serving, and broil 5 to 6 minutes on each side or until desired degree of doneness.*

TYPE OF BURGER PATTY	CALORIES	FAT (g)	FIBER (g)
Ground round patty	191	9	0
Soy protein patty	70	0	4
Black bean patty*	113	1.8	3.8

*To make your own black bean burger patties, see the instructions on page 77.

Santa Fe Burgers

prep: 4 minutes   cook: 6 minutes

Serve this south-of-the-border burger with low-fat tortilla chips instead of steak fries.

  4 (2.8-ounce) frozen meatless soy protein
     burgers
  4 (2.8-ounce) whole grain hamburger buns
  4 (¾-ounce) slices 2% Monterey Jack cheese
     with peppers
  8 thin slices avocado
  ½ cup chunky salsa

Cook burgers in a nonstick skillet according to package directions.

Place 1 burger on bottom half of each bun; top with 1 cheese slice, 2 avocado slices, and 2 tablespoons salsa. Cover with top half of bun. Serve immediately. Yield: 4 servings (serving size: 1 burger).

CALORIES 367 (23% from fat); FAT 9.4g (sat 2.8g, mono 2.2g, poly 0.5g); PROTEIN 24.2g; CARB 52.5g; FIBER 9.6g; CHOL 11mg; IRON 4.4mg; SODIUM 872mg; CALC 314mg
EXCHANGES: 3 Starch, 1 Vegetable, 1 Lean Meat, 1 Fat

Mushroom-Swiss Patty Melts

prep: 8 minutes   cook: 17 minutes

For those who aren't big burger fans, this patty melt is an easy alternative.

  4 (2.8-ounce) frozen meatless soy protein
     burgers
  1 cup sliced mushrooms
  1 cup chopped onion
  ¼ teaspoon freshly ground black pepper
  8 (1-ounce) slices rye bread
  4 ounces reduced-fat Jarlsberg cheese, grated
Cooking spray

Cook burgers in a nonstick skillet according to package directions. Set aside, and keep warm.

Add mushrooms, onion, and pepper to pan, and cook over medium-high heat 5 minutes or until tender, stirring occasionally.

Divide mushroom mixture evenly over 4 bread slices; top each with 1 burger and one-fourth of cheese. Cover with remaining bread slices. Coat 1 side of each sandwich with cooking spray. Cook, coated side down, in batches, in pan over medium heat 3 minutes or until golden. Coat top side of sandwiches; turn, and cook 3 additional minutes or until golden. Repeat procedure with remaining sandwiches. Serve immediately. Yield: 4 servings (serving size: 1 sandwich).

CALORIES 285 (11% from fat); FAT 3.5g (sat 1.3g, mono 1.1g, poly 0.6g); PROTEIN 21.5g; CARB 44.1g; FIBER 8.1g; CHOL 10mg; IRON 3.4mg; SODIUM 740mg; CALC 361mg
EXCHANGES: 2 Starch, 2 Vegetable, 1 Lean Meat

pasta bar
serve with breadsticks and mixed green salad

serves 5 • total time 25 minutes

Please everyone with one basic pasta and four different sauces. Each sauce recipe makes enough for one serving, so if you want more, just multiply the ingredients by the number of servings needed. To keep things simple, we recommend choosing one or two sauces, but you know best how to satisfy your crew.

Choose from the following:

- CHEESY PASTA
- ROASTED RED PEPPER PASTA
- CHICKEN CACCIATORE PASTA
- ASIAN-STYLE PASTA

Basic Pasta

prep: 1 minute   cook: 8 minutes

3	cups ditalini (tiny, very short tubes of pasta)
3	tablespoons light butter
2	teaspoons dried minced onion
1	teaspoon dried basil
¼	teaspoon salt
¼	teaspoon freshly ground black pepper

Cook pasta according to package directions; omitting salt and fat. Drain. Toss with butter and remaining ingredients. Yield: 5 servings (serving size: 1 cup).

CALORIES 317 (14% from fat); FAT 4.8g (sat 2.6g, mono 0.1g, poly 0.5g); PROTEIN 10.5g; CARB 57.8g; FIBER 2.1g; CHOL 12mg; IRON 3.2mg; SODIUM 164mg; CALC 25mg
EXCHANGES: 4 Starch

SUPPER plan

1. Chop and slice fresh ingredients for desired toppings.

2. Cook pasta.

3. While pasta cooks, prepare sauce(s) of choice:
   - Cook cheese sauce in microwave.
   - Prepare roasted red pepper sauce.
   - Cook cacciatore sauce in skillet.
   - Cook peanut sauce in microwave.
   - Bake breadsticks, if desired, or open package of crisp breadsticks.

4. Prepare salad with packaged salad greens and reduced-fat olive oil vinaigrette.

SIMPLEsubstitutions

Use any short pasta you have on hand *for your pasta bar. Other good choices include seashell pasta, elbow macaroni, rotini, fusilli, or radiatore. We've used a short pasta for all these variations because the short types work well with all the sauces. The rule of thumb for pastas and sauces is: the thinner the sauce, the longer the pasta. So, if you prefer to use a long pasta such as spaghetti, use the sauces for Cheesy Pasta and Asian-Style Pasta because they're creamy.*

Cheesy Pasta, page 82

Asian-Style Pasta, page 83

Roasted Red Pepper Pasta, page 82

Cheesy Pasta

prep: 1 minute   cook: 1 minute

This cheesy pasta is always a kid-pleaser.

¼ cup refrigerated reduced-fat Alfredo sauce
¼ cup (1 ounce) shredded reduced-fat Cheddar
    cheese
1   cup hot cooked BASIC PASTA (page 80)

Place Alfredo sauce in a small microwave-safe bowl. Cover and microwave at HIGH 1 minute, stirring after 30 seconds or until thoroughly heated. Remove from microwave, and stir in cheese. Combine cheese sauce and hot pasta; stir well. Serve immediately. Yield: 1 serving (serving size: 1 cup pasta and ¼ cup sauce).

CALORIES 478 (28% from fat); FAT 14.9g (sat 9.1g, mono 0.1g, poly 0.5g);
PROTEIN 23.7g; CARB 63.3g; FIBER 2.1g; CHOL 52mg; IRON 3.2mg;
SODIUM 717mg; CALC 379mg
EXCHANGES: 4 Starch, 1 Lean Meat, 2 Fat

SERVEwith

● ● ● ● ● ● ● ● ● ● ● ● ● ● ● ● ● ● ● ●

You have several options *when it comes to breadsticks. Bake refrigerated soft breadstick dough or brown-and-serve soft breadsticks; open a package of crisp sesame breadsticks or thin onion breadsticks. Compare the calories, fat, and sodium in the different varieties.*

BREADSTICK	CALORIES	FAT (g)	SODIUM (mg)
Refrigerated dough (1)	110	2.0	290
Brown-and-serve (1)	150	1.5	290
Sesame (1 ounce)	119	3.9	223
Thin onion (1 ounce)	124	3.5	203

Roasted Red Pepper Pasta

prep: 3 minutes

There's no need to get out another saucepan if you make this no-cook sauce.

1   bottled roasted red bell pepper (about
    ½ cup)
¼ teaspoon bottled minced garlic
1   teaspoon balsamic vinegar
¼ teaspoon freshly ground black pepper
1   cup hot cooked BASIC PASTA (page 80)
1   tablespoon preshredded Parmesan cheese
1   tablespoon chopped fresh basil
1   tablespoon pine nuts

Place first 4 ingredients in a food processor. Pulse 15 to 20 seconds or until mixture is almost smooth. Toss with hot pasta. Top with Parmesan cheese, basil, and pine nuts. Yield: 1 serving (serving size: 1 cup pasta and ⅓ cup sauce).

CALORIES 376 (16% from fat); FAT 6.8g (sat 3.6g, mono 0.6g, poly 0.9g);
PROTEIN 13.9g; CARB 64.7g; FIBER 3g; CHOL 16mg; IRON 4.1mg;
SODIUM 612mg; CALC 108mg
EXCHANGES: 4 Starch, 1 Vegetable, 1 Fat

Chicken Cacciatore Pasta

prep: 3 minutes   cook: 3 minutes

Add this chunky chicken-tomato sauce to hot pasta for a quick-fix version of an Italian classic.

½	teaspoon olive oil
¼	teaspoon bottled minced garlic
2	tablespoons sliced green bell pepper
2	tablespoons chopped onion
2	tablespoons sliced mushrooms
¼	cup low-fat pasta sauce
¼	cup chopped cooked chicken breast
1	cup hot cooked BASIC PASTA (page 80)
1	teaspoon preshredded fresh Parmesan cheese

Heat olive oil in a small nonstick skillet over medium-high heat. Add garlic and next 3 ingredients; cook 2 to 3 minutes or just until tender. Add sauce and chicken, and cook 1 to 2 minutes or until thoroughly heated. Pour over hot cooked pasta, and top with Parmesan cheese. Yield: 1 serving (serving size: 1 cup pasta and ½ cup sauce).

CALORIES 454 (21% from fat); FAT 10.4g (sat 4g, mono 3g, poly 1.3g); PROTEIN 23.4g; CARB 66.9g; FIBER 3.9g; CHOL 43mg; IRON 4.4mg; SODIUM 414mg; CALC 79mg
EXCHANGES: 4 Starch, 1 Vegetable, 1 Lean Meat, 1 Fat

Asian-Style Pasta

prep: 6 minutes   cook: 1 minute

Add Asian flair to plain pasta with creamy peanut butter, crisp snow peas, and peppery ginger.

1½	tablespoons reduced-fat creamy peanut butter
1½	tablespoons hot water
2	teaspoons low-sodium soy sauce
¼	teaspoon grated peeled fresh ginger
⅛	teaspoon crushed red pepper
1	cup hot cooked BASIC PASTA (page 80)
¼	cup matchstick-cut carrots
¼	cup coarsely chopped snow peas
2	tablespoons chopped green onions

Combine peanut butter and water in a small microwave-safe dish. Microwave at HIGH 1 minute, stirring after 30 seconds. Add soy sauce, ginger, and red pepper; stir until smooth. Microwave at HIGH 30 seconds or until thoroughly heated. Combine hot cooked pasta, sauce, carrots, and snow peas; toss well. Top with green onions. Yield: 1 serving (serving size: 1 cup pasta and 3 tablespoons sauce).

CALORIES 471 (25% from fat); FAT 13g (sat 4g, mono 4.3g, poly 3g); PROTEIN 18.5g; CARB 72.2g; FIBER 5.6g; CHOL 12mg; IRON 4.4mg; SODIUM 667mg; CALC 53mg
EXCHANGES: 4 Starch, 2 Vegetable, 2 Fat

Maui Pizza, page 86

pick a pizza
serve with low-fat chocolate ice cream

serves 4 • total time 19 minutes

Make this versatile basic French bread pizza, then let each person top theirs as they want before baking. There are enough choices to please even the pickiest eater. To keep it really simple, just serve the basic version.

Choose from the following

- BASIC FRENCH BREAD PIZZAS
- MAUI PIZZA
- MEAT AND MUSHROOM PIZZA
- MEDITERRANEAN VEGETABLE PIZZA
- ARTICHOKE-MUSHROOM PIZZA

SUPPER plan

1. Prepare ingredients for desired toppings: green onions, pineapple, ham, mushrooms, spinach, and artichokes.
2. Bake bread.
3. Top bread with marinara sauce, and then with desired toppings and cheese.
4. Bake pizzas.

Basic French Bread Pizzas

prep: 2 minutes   cook: 8 minutes

Finicky eaters just might like the simple flavors of this basic pizza.

    1   (16-ounce) loaf French bread, cut in half
         horizontally and vertically to form 4 pieces
Cooking spray
    1   cup marinara sauce
    1   cup (4 ounces) shredded part-skim
         mozzarella cheese

Preheat oven to 450°.

Coat cut sides of bread with cooking spray; place bread, cut sides up, on a baking sheet. Bake at 450° for 3 to 5 minutes or until lightly browned.

Spread ¼ cup marinara sauce on each bread quarter; top each with ¼ cup cheese. Bake at 450° for 5 minutes or until cheese melts. Yield: 4 servings (serving size: 1 pizza).

CALORIES 413 (18% from fat); FAT 8.3g (sat 3.8g, mono 2.8g, poly 0.9g); PROTEIN 18.7g; CARB 64.3g; FIBER 4.3g; CHOL 15mg; IRON 3mg; SODIUM 840mg; CALC 338mg
EXCHANGES: 4 Starch, 1 Vegetable, 1 Medium-Fat Meat

NUTRITIONnote

• • • • • • • • • • • • • • • • • • • •

Compare the nutrient values for BASIC FRENCH BREAD PIZZAS with *those of commercial frozen French bread pizzas.*

PIZZA	CALORIES	FAT (g)	SODIUM (mg)
SuperFAST Basic French Bread Pizza	413	8.3	840
Stouffer's French Bread White Pizza	460	28.0	760
Stouffer's French Bread Deluxe Pizza	857	41.3	1,880
Stouffer's Sausage and Pepperoni French Bread Pizza	895	45.0	1,720

pick a pizza

To make any of these variations, prepare **Basic French Bread Pizzas** (page 85) but hold the cheese. Add your choice of the other ingredients, then top with the cheese, and bake until the cheese melts. The amounts in each recipe are for 1 serving. Double, triple or quadruple the ingredients for the desired number of servings.

Maui Pizza

prep: 2 minutes   cook: 5 minutes

Go Hawaiian by adding a little ham and pineapple to your pizza.

1	piece prepared BASIC FRENCH BREAD PIZZAS (page 85)
2	tablespoons pineapple tidbits in juice, drained
1	tablespoon diced deli ham
¼	teaspoon bottled minced garlic
1	tablespoon sliced green onion

Preheat oven to 450°.

Sprinkle all ingredients on 1 piece prepared pizza. Top with ¼ cup cheese, and bake at 450° for 5 minutes or until cheese melts. Yield: 1 serving.

CALORIES 443 (18% from fat); FAT 8.7g (sat 4g, mono 3g, poly 1g); PROTEIN 20.6g; CARB 68.7g; FIBER 5.1g; CHOL 19mg; IRON 3.2mg; SODIUM 965mg; CALC 345mg
EXCHANGES: 4 Starch, ½ Fruit, 1 Vegetable, 1 Medium-Fat Meat

Meat and Mushroom Pizza

prep: 2 minutes   cook: 5 minutes

Here's the version for those who prefer a traditional meaty pizza.

1	piece prepared BASIC FRENCH BREAD PIZZAS (page 85)
2	tablespoons diced deli ham
5	slices turkey pepperoni (such as Hormel)
1	mushroom, thinly sliced

Preheat oven to 450°.

Sprinkle all ingredients on 1 piece prepared pizza. Top with ¼ cup cheese, and bake at 450° for 5 minutes or until cheese melts. Yield: 1 serving.

CALORIES 461 (20% from fat); FAT 10g (sat 4.4g, mono 3.5g, poly 1.3g); PROTEIN 25.2g; CARB 65.8g; FIBER 4.6g; CHOL 33mg; IRON 3.6mg; SODIUM 1,235mg; CALC 343mg
EXCHANGES: 4 Starch, 1 Vegetable, 2 Medium-Fat Meat

Mediterranean Vegetable Pizza

prep: 2 minutes   cook: 5 minutes

Eggplant, spinach, and mushrooms contribute to this pizza's earthy, rustic flavor.

  1   piece prepared BASIC FRENCH BREAD
      PIZZAS (page 85)
  2   tablespoons commercial caponata (such as
      Alessi)
  ½   cup prepackaged baby spinach
  1   mushroom, thinly sliced
  ¼   teaspoon bottled minced garlic

  Preheat oven to 450°.
  Sprinkle all ingredients on 1 piece prepared pizza. Top with ¼ cup cheese, and bake at 450° for 5 minutes or until cheese melts. Yield: 1 serving.

CALORIES 451 (21% from fat); FAT 10.4g (sat 3.8g, mono 2.8g, poly 1g);
PROTEIN 20.2g; CARB 68.5g; FIBER 5.9g; CHOL 15mg; IRON 4mg;
SODIUM 993mg; CALC 368mg
EXCHANGES: 4 Starch, 2 Vegetable, 1 Medium Fat Meat

FIND**it**

• • • • • • • • • • • • • • • • • • • •

Look for a can of caponata *on the grocery store shelves near the salsas, relishes, and condiments. Caponata is a relish-type mixture made of eggplant, tomatoes, anchovies, olives, pine nuts, capers, vinegar, and olive oil. It's often served as an appetizer with crackers or on baguette slices. One tablespoon has about 26 calories, 1.3 grams of fat, and 58 milligrams of sodium.*

Artichoke-Mushroom Pizza

prep: 2 minutes   cook: 6 minutes

The bold flavor of this meat-free pizza comes from the garlic and artichoke hearts.

  ½   teaspoon olive oil
  ¼   cup artichoke hearts, drained and chopped
  2   tablespoons sliced mushrooms
  ½   teaspoon bottled minced garlic
  ⅛   teaspoon Italian seasoning
  1   piece prepared BASIC FRENCH BREAD
      PIZZAS (page 85)

  Preheat oven to 450°.
  Heat olive oil in a nonstick skillet over medium-high heat. Add artichokes, mushrooms, garlic, and Italian seasoning; sauté 1 minute or until mushrooms are tender.
  Sprinkle artichoke mixture over 1 piece prepared pizza. Top with ¼ cup cheese, and bake at 450° for 5 minutes or until cheese melts. Yield: 1 serving.

CALORIES 468 (19% from fat); FAT 9.9g (sat 4.1g, mono 3.6g, poly 1.3g);
PROTEIN 22g; CARB 73.3g; FIBER 8.6g; CHOL 15mg; IRON 3.8mg;
SODIUM 886mg; CALC 364mg
EXCHANGES: 4 Starch, 2 Vegetable, 1 Medium-Fat Meat

favorite fried rice

serve with sliced pineapple **serves 4 • total time 34 minutes**

For an easy skillet supper, stir your favorite ingredients into chilled rice. The basic fried rice recipe is essentially the same for each variation—so if you want to make two variations, just prepare the basic recipe, divide it according to the number of variations you want, then add the additional ingredients.

Choose from the following:

- BASIC FRIED RICE
- VEGETABLE FRIED RICE
- SHRIMP FRIED RICE
- PORK FRIED RICE
- CHICKEN FRIED RICE

SUPPER plan

1. Cook and chill brown rice. Divide into portions to use in variations, if desired.

2. Slice green onions; prepare and assemble remaining ingredients for desired variations.

3. Prepare desired fried rice variations using same skillet for each.

Basic Fried Rice

prep: 3 minutes   cook: 6 minutes (plus 10 minutes for rice)

The best way to make fried rice is with chilled rice, so if you have leftover brown rice, use it in these recipes. Or go ahead and cook some rice the night before, and refrigerate it in an airtight container.

2	teaspoons dark sesame oil
½	cup matchstick-cut carrots
½	cup sliced green onions
2	teaspoons bottled minced garlic
¼	teaspoon pepper
4	cups chilled cooked brown rice
1	large egg, lightly beaten
2	tablespoons low-sodium soy sauce
1	tablespoon water

Heat sesame oil in large nonstick skillet over high heat. Add carrot and next 3 ingredients, and stir-fry until tender. Add cooked rice; stir-fry 2 minutes. Push rice mixture to sides of pan, forming a well in center. Add egg to center of pan, and let cook 30 seconds; toss with rice, and stir-fry until egg is cooked. Stir in soy sauce and water; cook until thoroughly heated. Yield: 4 servings (serving size: 1 cup).

CALORIES 234 (20% from fat); FAT 5.1g (sat 0.7g, mono 1.4g, poly 1.1g); PROTEIN 7.6g; CARB 38.4g; FIBER 3.1g; CHOL 53mg; IRON 0.8mg; SODIUM 572mg; CALC 15mg
EXCHANGES: 2 Starch, 2 Vegetable, 1 Fat

HOWto

• • • • • • • • • • • • • • • • • • • •

Cooked Brown Rice
To get 4 cups of cooked brown rice, cook 2 cups uncooked instant brown rice in 1¾ cups water or fat-free, less-sodium chicken broth according to package directions, omitting the salt and fat. Cover and chill.

Chicken Fried Rice, page 91

Vegetable Fried Rice, page 90

favorite fried rice

Each of these four recipes is a variation of **BASIC FRIED RICE** on page 88. The added ingredients (spices, veggies, shrimp, pork, and chicken) give each a unique flavor.

Vegetable Fried Rice

prep: 5 minutes   cook: 7 minutes (plus 10 minutes for rice)

When you're making brown rice for this recipe (see page 88), add extra flavor by cooking the rice in vegetable broth (a 14-ounce can) instead of 1¾ cups water.

- 2 teaspoons dark sesame oil
- ¾ cup sliced shiitake mushrooms
- ½ cup matchstick-cut carrots
- ½ cup sliced green onions
- 2 teaspoons bottled minced garlic
- ¼ teaspoon pepper
- 4 cups chilled cooked brown rice (page 88)
- 1 large egg, lightly beaten
- 2 tablespoons low-sodium soy sauce
- 1 tablespoon water
- 3 tablespoons dry white wine
- ⅓ cup frozen green peas

Heat sesame oil in a large nonstick skillet over high heat. Add mushrooms and next 4 ingredients; stir-fry until tender. Add cooked rice; stir-fry 2 minutes. Push rice mixture to sides of pan, forming a well in center. Add egg to center of pan, and let cook 30 seconds; toss with rice, and stir-fry until egg is cooked. Stir in soy sauce and remaining ingredients; cook until thoroughly heated. Yield: 4 servings (serving size: 1 cup).

CALORIES 262 (20% from fat); FAT 5.7g (sat 0.8g, mono 1.4g, poly 1.2g); PROTEIN 8.2g; CARB 45.1g; FIBER 4.4g; CHOL 53mg; IRON 1.2mg; SODIUM 736mg; CALC 20mg
EXCHANGES: 2 Starch, 2 Vegetable, 1 Fat

Shrimp Fried Rice

prep: 7 minutes   stand: 5 minutes
cook: 9 minutes (plus 10 minutes for rice)

Add chopped red bell pepper instead of carrots to Basic Fried Rice, and omit the black pepper. Stir in shrimp, ginger, and red pepper.

- ½ pound peeled and deveined shrimp
- 1 teaspoon grated peeled fresh ginger
- ¼ teaspoon crushed red pepper
- 2 teaspoons dark sesame oil
- ⅓ cup chopped red bell pepper
- ½ cup sliced green onions
- 1 tablespoon bottled minced garlic
- 4 cups chilled cooked brown rice (page 88)
- 1 large egg, lightly beaten
- 2 tablespoons low-sodium soy sauce
- 1 tablespoon water

Combine shrimp, ginger, and crushed red pepper in a small bowl; let stand 5 minutes.

Heat oil in a large nonstick skillet over high heat. Add bell pepper, green onions, and garlic; stir-fry 1 to 2 minutes or until tender. Add shrimp mixture to pan; stir-fry 4 to 5 minutes or until shrimp are done. Add cooked rice; stir-fry 2 minutes or until thoroughly heated. Push rice mixture to sides of pan, forming a well in center. Add egg to center of pan, and cook 30 seconds; toss with rice mixture, and stir-fry until egg is cooked. Stir in soy sauce and water; cook until thoroughly heated. Yield: 4 servings (serving size: about 1 cup).

CALORIES 274 (18% from fat); FAT 5.6g (sat 0.9g, mono 1.5g, poly 1.3g); PROTEIN 16.2g; CARB 38g; FIBER 2.9g; CHOL 134mg; IRON 2.1mg; SODIUM 659mg; CALC 29mg
EXCHANGES: 2 Starch, 1 Vegetable, 1 Very Lean Meat, 1 Fat

Pork Fried Rice

prep: 7 minutes   cook: 9 minutes (plus 10 minutes for rice)

Add pre-marinated teriyaki pork tenderloin to Basic Fried Rice.

- 2 teaspoons dark sesame oil
- ½ pound pre-marinated teriyaki pork tenderloin, cut into thin strips
- ½ cup matchstick-cut carrots
- ½ cup sliced green onions
- 2 teaspoons bottled minced garlic
- ¼ teaspoon black pepper
- ¼ teaspoon crushed red pepper
- 4 cups chilled cooked brown rice (page 88)
- 1 large egg, lightly beaten
- 2 tablespoons low-sodium soy sauce
- 1 tablespoon water

Heat oil in a large nonstick skillet over high heat. Add pork, and stir-fry 3 to 4 minutes or just until done. Add carrot and next 4 ingredients; stir-fry 2 minutes. Add cooked rice; stir-fry 2 minutes or until thoroughly heated. Push rice mixture to sides of pan, forming a well in center. Add egg to center of pan, and cook 30 seconds; toss with rice mixture, and stir-fry until egg is cooked. Stir in soy sauce and water; cook until thoroughly heated. Yield: 4 servings (serving size: 1¼ cups).

CALORIES 302 (21% from fat); FAT 6.9g (sat 1.3g, mono 2.1g, poly 1.5g); PROTEIN 17.9g; CARB 41.1g; FIBER 3.1g; CHOL 79mg; IRON 1.4mg; SODIUM 806mg; CALC 19mg
EXCHANGES: 2 Starch, 2 Vegetable, 1 Lean Meat, 1 Fat

Chicken Fried Rice

prep: 5 minutes   cook: 10 minutes (plus 10 minutes for rice)

Add pre-marinated teriyaki chicken to Basic Fried Rice, and sprinkle with chopped cashews.

- 2 teaspoons dark sesame oil
- 8 ounces pre-marinated teriyaki skinless, boneless chicken breasts, cut into strips
- ½ cup matchstick-cut carrots
- ½ cup sliced green onions
- 2 teaspoons bottled minced garlic
- ¼ teaspoon black pepper
- 4 cups chilled cooked brown rice (page 88)
- 1 large egg, lightly beaten
- 2 tablespoons low-sodium soy sauce
- 1 tablespoon water
- ¼ cup chopped cashews

Heat oil in a large nonstick skillet over high heat. Add chicken, and stir-fry 4 to 5 minutes or just until done. Add carrot, green onions, garlic, and pepper; stir-fry 2 minutes. Add cooked rice; stir-fry 2 minutes or until thoroughly heated. Push rice mixture to sides of pan, forming a well in center. Add egg to center of pan, and cook 30 seconds; toss with rice mixture. Stir-fry until egg is cooked. Stir in soy sauce and water, and cook until thoroughly heated. Sprinkle with cashews. Yield: 4 servings (serving size: 1¼ cups).

CALORIES 353 (29% from fat); FAT 11.4g (sat 2.1g, mono 2g, poly 1.4g); PROTEIN 20.9g; CARB 40.8g; FIBER 3.4g; CHOL 87mg; IRON 1.5mg; SODIUM 771mg; CALC 18mg
EXCHANGES: 2 Starch, 2 Vegetable, 2 Lean Meat, 1 Fat

Veggie Tostadas, page 94

top a tostada
serve with sliced mango   **serves 4 · total time 20 minutes**

Offer a tostada for every taste with this easy south-of-the-border menu. All you have to do is assemble the Basic Tostadas and let each person top their own with either pork barbecue, chicken, or extra veggies. Serve the tostadas with refrigerated mango slices from the produce department.

Choose from the following:

- BASIC TOSTADAS
- BARBECUE PORK TOSTADAS
- SOUTHWESTERN CHICKEN TOSTADAS
- VEGGIE TOSTADAS

SUPPER plan

1. Bake tortillas.

2. While tortillas bake:
- Rinse and drain black beans.
- Chop ingredients for desired toppings.
- Heat barbecue, cook chicken, and/or sauté vegetables.

3. Assemble tostadas.

Basic Tostadas

prep: 5 minutes   cook: 15 minutes

- 4   (6-inch) corn tortillas
- Cooking spray
- 1   (15-ounce) can no-salt-added black beans, rinsed and drained
- ½   (1.25-ounce) package 40%-less-sodium taco seasoning (about 2 tablespoons)
- ¼   cup water
- 1   cup pre shredded lettuce
- 1   cup refrigerated salsa
- ¼   cup (1 ounce) shredded reduced-fat Cheddar cheese

Preheat oven to 400°.

Place tortillas on a baking sheet. Coat tortillas on both sides with cooking spray. Bake at 400° for 12 minutes or until crisp; set aside.

Combine black beans, taco seasoning, and water in a medium saucepan; mash with a potato masher. Cook over medium heat 3 minutes or until thoroughly heated, stirring often.

Place tortillas on individual serving plates; spread black bean mixture evenly over tortillas. Top each serving with ¼ cup lettuce, ¼ cup salsa, and 1 tablespoon cheese. Yield: 4 servings (serving size: 1 tostada).

CALORIES 189 (11% from fat); FAT 2.4g (sat 1.1g, mono 0.2g, poly 0.5g); PROTEIN 10.1g; CARB 34.2g; FIBER 8g; CHOL 5mg; IRON 2.3mg; SODIUM 646mg; CALC 151mg
EXCHANGES: 2 Starch, 1 Vegetable

NUTRITION**note**

Corn tortillas are very low in fat—*it's only when they're fried in oil that the fat and calories escalate. One (6-inch) tortilla has about 60 calories, 0.5 grams of fat, 1 gram of fiber, and 40 milligrams of sodium, depending on the brand.*

top a tostada

For all of the variations, prepare **BASIC TOSTADAS** as directed. After you spread the black bean mixture on the tortillas, top with desired topping before adding lettuce, salsa, and cheese.

Barbecue Pork Tostadas

prep: 5 minutes   cook: 16 minutes

- 1   cup shredded pork barbecue (such as Lloyd's)
- 4   BASIC TOSTADAS (page 93)

Place barbecue in a microwave-safe dish. Cook on HIGH 1 to 2 minutes or until thoroughly heated. Spoon ¼ cup over black bean mixture on each tostada. Top with lettuce, salsa, and cheese. Yield: 4 servings (serving size: 1 tostada).

CALORIES 269 (14% from fat); FAT 4.4g (sat 1.6g, mono 0.2g, poly 0.5g); PROTEIN 17.1g; CARB 42.2g; FIBER 8g; CHOL 20mg; IRON 3mg; SODIUM 1,056mg; CALC 151mg
EXCHANGES: 2½ Starch, 1 Vegetable, 1 Lean Meat

Southwestern Chicken Tostadas

prep: 5 minutes   cook: 17 minutes

- 1⅓   cups Southwestern-seasoned cooked chicken breast strips
- 4   BASIC TOSTADAS (page 93)

Place a medium nonstick skillet over medium-high heat until hot. Add chicken, and cook 2 to 3 minutes or until thoroughly heated. Spoon ⅓ cup chicken over black bean mixture on each tostada. Top with lettuce, salsa, and cheese. Yield: 4 servings (serving size: 1 tostada).

Note: This tostada is higher in sodium than the other variations because of the seasoned chicken strips. If you need to decrease the sodium, use unseasoned cooked chicken and add ½ teaspoon salt-free Mexican seasoning.

CALORIES 285 (16% from fat); FAT 5g (sat 1.9g, mono 0.2g, poly 0.5g); PROTEIN 26.6g; CARB 35.1g; FIBER 8g; CHOL 53mg; IRON 2.9mg; SODIUM 1,313mg; CALC 151mg
EXCHANGES: 2 Starch, 1 Vegetable, 2 Lean Meat

Veggie Tostadas

prep: 10 minutes   cook: 18 minutes

Cooking spray
- 2   cups sliced mushrooms
- 2   small zucchini, sliced
- 1   large red bell pepper, chopped
- 4   BASIC TOSTADAS (page 93)

Place a medium nonstick skillet coated with cooking spray over medium-high heat until hot. Add mushrooms, zucchini, and bell pepper to pan. Sauté 3 to 5 minutes or until vegetables are tender. Spoon about ¾ cup vegetable mixture over black bean mixture on each tostada. Top with lettuce, salsa, and cheese. Yield 4 servings (serving size: 1 tostada).

CALORIES 215 (12% from fat); FAT 2.8g (sat 1.1g, mono 0.2g, poly 0.7g); PROTEIN 13g; CARB 38.7g; FIBER 10.5g; CHOL 5mg; IRON 3.4mg; SODIUM 404mg; CALC 172mg
EXCHANGES: 2 Starch, 2 Vegetable

Greek-Style Tortellini
Soup, page 96
Pita Crisps, page 97 (left)

souper soup
serve with **pita crisps**   **serves 5 • total time 22 to 30 minutes**

You can make this hearty pasta-packed soup three different ways: pasta-only, chicken vegetable, or vegetarian. If you're trying to satisfy a variety of eating styles, ladle the basic soup into individual bowls, then stir in the desired toppings.

Choose from the following:

- BASIC TORTELLINI SOUP
- GREEK-STYLE TORTELLINI SOUP
- WHITE BEAN-TORTELLINI SOUP

SUPPER plan

1. Bring ingredients for Basic Tortellini Soup to a boil.

2. While liquid comes to a boil, prepare ingredients for desired variations.

3. Add tortellini to soup, and cook.

4. While soup cooks, prepare Pita Crisps.

5. Add ingredients for variations.

Basic Tortellini Soup

prep: 5 minutes   cook: 17 minutes

Instead of 2 (9-ounce) packages of tortellini, you can use a (20-ounce) family-size package with only a slight increase in yield.

    4   cups fat-free, less-sodium chicken broth
    2   cups water
    ½   cup dry white wine
    ¼   cup fresh lemon juice (2 lemons)
    ½   teaspoon freshly ground black pepper
    2   (9-ounce) packages 3-cheese tortellini (such
        as Di Giorno)
Crumbled feta cheese (optional)
Plain fat-free yogurt (optional)

Combine first 5 ingredients in a Dutch oven; bring to a boil. Add tortellini; cook, uncovered, 8 minutes. If desired, top with feta cheese or yogurt. Yield: 4 servings (serving size: 1¾ cups).

CALORIES 431 (20% from fat); FAT 9.5g (sat 5.5g, mono 0g, poly 0g); PROTEIN 22g; CARB 61.2g; FIBER 1.7g; CHOL 47mg; IRON 1.9mg; SODIUM 985mg; CALC 319mg
EXCHANGES: 4 Starch, 1 Medium-Fat Meat, 1 Fat

Greek-Style Tortellini Soup

prep: 8 minutes   cook: 22 minutes

BASIC TORTELLINI SOUP (left)
    1   cup diced roasted skinless boneless chicken
        breast halves
    1   (14-ounce) can quartered artichoke hearts,
        drained and chopped
    1   (7-ounce) package fresh baby spinach
    1   tablespoon chopped fresh oregano

Prepare Basic Tortellini Soup as directed in recipe on the left. Stir in chicken, artichoke hearts, spinach, and oregano. Cook over medium heat 5 minutes or until thoroughly heated. Yield: 6 servings (serving size: 1½ cups).

CALORIES 363 (21% from fat); FAT 8.3g (sat 4.2g, mono 0.7g, poly 0.4g); PROTEIN 24.1g; CARB 46.4g; FIBER 3.5g; CHOL 51mg; IRON 2.4mg; SODIUM 943mg; CALC 252mg
EXCHANGES: 3 Starch, 2 Lean Meat

❝I'm not sure what I ate before deli roasted chicken *was around. I chop it up and use it in salads, sandwiches, soups, enchiladas, burritos, and white chili. Sometimes I just slice it and eat with some steamed vegetables. I also use packages of grilled chicken strips if I don't want to buy a whole chicken.*❞

Elizabeth Luckett,
Director, Test Kitchens

White Bean-Tortellini Soup

prep: 7 minutes   cook: 20 minutes

BASIC TORTELLINI SOUP (page 96)
- 4 cups vegetable broth
- 1 (15.8-ounce) can Great Northern beans, rinsed and drained
- 1 tablespoon chopped fresh parsley

Prepare Tortellini Soup, as directed in recipe on page 96, but substitute 4 cups vegetable broth for chicken broth. Stir in beans. Cook over medium-high heat 3 minutes or until thoroughly heated. Sprinkle with 1 tablespoon chopped fresh parsley. Yield: 4 servings (serving size: about 2 cups).

CALORIES 473 (20% from fat); FAT 10.5g (sat 5.5g, mono 0g, poly 0g); PROTEIN 24.3g; CARB 72.3g; FIBER 4.9g; CHOL 47mg; IRON 2.7mg; SODIUM 1,521mg; CALC 342mg
EXCHANGES: 4 Starch, 2 Vegetable, 1 Lean Meat, 1 Fat

Pita Crisps

prep: 4 minutes   cook: 4 minutes

- ¼ teaspoon garlic powder
- ¼ teaspoon onion powder
- ⅛ teaspoon ground red pepper
- ¼ teaspoon salt
- 2 whole wheat pitas, each cut into 8 wedges

Cooking spray

Preheat oven to 450°.
Combine first 4 ingredients. Coat pita wedges with cooking spray; sprinkle evenly with spice mixture. Bake at 450° for 4 minutes or until crisp. Yield: 4 servings (serving size: 4 crisps).

CALORIES 86 (9% from fat); FAT 0.8g (sat 0.1g, mono 0.1g, poly 0.3g); PROTEIN 3.2g; CARB 17.9g; FIBER 2.4g; CHOL 0mg; IRON 1mg; SODIUM 316mg; CALC 6mg
EXCHANGE: 1 Starch

SERVE**with**

• •

If you need ideas for toppings *and serving suggestions, here's a guide to a few key Greek ingredients.*

Aleppo peppers: *These dried crushed red peppers from the Middle East are milder than Mexican chile peppers. You can substitute a smaller amount of crushed red pepper.*

Feta cheese: *Feta is a slightly pungent, crumbly cheese made primarily from sheep's milk, with the addition of goat's milk.*

Kalamata olives: *Kalamata olives are almond-shaped with a pointy tip, black and firm yet juicy. Authentic kalamata olives are cured in brine, which contains high-quality local red wine vinegar.*

Lemon: *Freshly squeezed lemon juice is commonly used in savory and many sweet dishes.*

Olive oil: *Greek olive oils are a great bargain in American markets. Many small olive groves, mainly on Crete and in the Peloponnese, now produce excellent organic olive oils.*

Oregano: *Typically, dried oregano is used in traditional Greek cooking. Densely fragrant, imported Greek oregano is often mixed with domestic varieties when packaged in the United States because it's considered too potent for unaccustomed users. Look for Spice Hunter's Greek oregano in the spice section.*

Yogurt: *Greeks love sweet, creamy yogurt made from sheep's milk. Unfortunately, it isn't available in most American markets, so you can substitute drained plain low-fat yogurt.*

Chicken Enchilada Casserole, page 102

Chili Pie, page 103

> **“**_I love to cook, but the only day I have to spend time in the kitchen is Saturday. Am I doomed to only eating healthy stuff on the weekends?_ **”**

jump-start
SUPPERS

Make one big batch of a recipe (such as chili) when you have time. Store it in the refrigerator or freezer, and use it to create four more easy main-dish recipes. It's the best way we've found to get a jump start on supper during the week.

Turkey Chili Mac,
page 103

Chili Cheeseburger,
page 102

start with one pot of
chipotle black bean chili,
and make:

- CHILI CHEESEBURGERS
- CHICKEN ENCHILADA CASSEROLE
- TURKEY CHILI MAC
- CHILI PIE

Chipotle Black Bean Chili

prep: 6 minutes   cook: 17 minutes

Warm up with a bowl of this hearty chili on a wintry night. Or use it as the key ingredient in the recipes on the next two pages.

Chipotle Black Bean Chili

2   teaspoons olive oil
1   (10-ounce) package frozen chopped onion
3   tablespoons bottled minced garlic
3   tablespoons chili powder
1   tablespoon minced drained canned chipotle chile in adobo sauce
½   teaspoon black pepper
¼   teaspoon salt
4   (15-ounce) cans black beans, rinsed and drained
4   (14.5-ounce) cans no-salt-added diced tomatoes, undrained
2   (4.5-ounce) cans chopped green chiles, undrained

Heat olive oil in a 4-quart Dutch oven over medium-high heat. Add onion and garlic; sauté 2 minutes or until tender.

Add chili powder and next 6 ingredients; bring to a boil. Reduce heat; cover and simmer 15 minutes, stirring occasionally. Yield: 6 servings (serving size: about 2 cups).

CALORIES 250 (13% from fat); FAT 3.6g (sat 0.3g, mono 1.3g, poly 1.7g); PROTEIN 12.4g; CARB 43.8g; FIBER 15.9g; CHOL 0mg; IRON 5.2mg; SODIUM 1,086mg; CALC 126mg
EXCHANGES: 2 Starch, 3 Vegetable, ½ Fat

TOstore

• • • • • • • • • • • • • • • • • • • •

Place the chili in heavy-duty zip-top plastic bags *in 1- or 2-cup portions. Label and freeze up to 1 month. Or store in the refrigerator up to 3 days.*

TOreheat

• • • • • • • • • • • • • • • • • • • •

Thaw chili in the refrigerator *or in the microwave. Place in a saucepan, and cook over medium heat 5 to 8 minutes or until thoroughly heated.*

Chili Cheeseburgers, page 102

Chili Cheeseburgers

prep: 5 minutes   cook: 8 minutes

For extra heat, top the burgers with shredded Monterey Jack cheese with jalapeño peppers.

1	pound ground round
¼	cup minced red onion
¼	teaspoon salt, divided
1	cup CHIPOTLE BLACK BEAN CHILI (page 100)
4	sesame seed hamburger buns, toasted
¼	cup shredded reduced-fat sharp Cheddar cheese

Combine beef, onion, and ⅛ teaspoon salt in a large bowl. Divide mixture into 4 equal portions, shaping each into a ½-inch-thick patty. Heat a large nonstick skillet over medium-high heat until hot. Add patties, and cook 3 to 4 minutes on each side or until done.

Combine chili and remaining ⅛ teaspoon salt in a microwave-safe dish; cover and vent. Microwave at HIGH 2 minutes or until thoroughly heated.

Place patties on bottom halves of buns. Spoon ¼ cup chili over patties; sprinkle 1 tablespoon cheese over each patty. Top with top halves of buns. Yield: 4 servings (serving size: 1 cheeseburger).

CALORIES 375 (27% from fat); FAT 11.4g (sat 4.1g, mono 3.5g, poly 1.8g); PROTEIN 34.1g; CARB 32.1g; FIBER 3.5g; CHOL 70mg; IRON 4.7mg; SODIUM 644mg; CALC 156mg
EXCHANGES: 2 Starch, 4 Lean Meat

SERVE**with**

· · · · · · · · · · · · · · · · · ·

Serve these hearty burgers *with baked steak fries sprinkled with Mexican seasoning.*

Chicken Enchilada Casserole

prep: 12 minutes   cook: 10 minutes

Use a package of frozen chopped cooked chicken breast if you don't have any leftover chicken. One 9-ounce package contains about 1⅔ cups.

2	cups chopped cooked chicken breast
1	(10-ounce) can diced tomatoes and green chiles, drained (such as Rotel)
1	(10¾-ounce) can condensed reduced-fat, reduced-sodium cream of chicken soup, undiluted (such as Campbell's Healthy Request)
2½	cups CHIPOTLE BLACK BEAN CHILI (page 100)
6	(6-inch) corn tortillas, torn into large pieces
	Cooking spray
½	cup (2 ounces) shredded reduced-fat sharp Cheddar cheese, divided

Preheat oven to 450°.

Combine first 4 ingredients in a large saucepan. Cook 4 minutes over medium-high heat or until thoroughly heated, stirring occasionally; set aside.

Layer half of tortillas in an 8-inch square baking dish coated with cooking spray. Spoon half of chicken mixture onto tortillas. Repeat layers once. Top evenly with cheese. Bake at 450° for 6 minutes or until cheese melts. Yield: 4 servings (serving size: about 1½ cups).

CALORIES 334 (18% from fat); FAT 6.7g (sat 2.6g, mono 0.7g, poly 1g); PROTEIN 28.8g; CARB 40.7g; FIBER 7.3g; CHOL 54mg; IRON 2.3mg; SODIUM 1,054mg; CALC 241mg
EXCHANGES: 2 Starch, 2 Vegetable, 2 Lean Meat

SERVE**with**

· · · · · · · · · · · · · · · · · ·

Top the enchilada casserole *with salsa, and serve with shredded lettuce.*

Turkey Chili Mac

prep: 3 minutes   cook: 14 minutes

Even though it's called "chili mac," you can make this recipe with any type of short pasta you have on hand.

  1 cup uncooked medium elbow macaroni
  1 pound ground turkey
Cooking spray
  1 cup chopped green bell pepper (about
     1 large)
  1 (14-ounce) can petite diced tomatoes,
     undrained
  3 cups CHIPOTLE BLACK BEAN CHILI
     (page 100)
  ½ teaspoon salt
  ½ cup (2 ounces) shredded reduced-fat sharp
     Cheddar cheese

Cook pasta according to package directions, omitting salt and fat; drain well.

Cook turkey in a large nonstick skillet coated with cooking spray over medium-high heat until browned, stirring to crumble. Remove turkey from pan, and drain well.

Add bell pepper to pan; sauté 4 minutes or until tender. Return turkey to pan. Add tomatoes, chili, and salt; cook over medium heat until hot. Stir pasta into turkey mixture. Sprinkle with cheese. Yield: 6 servings (serving size: 1½ cups).

CALORIES 287 (29% from fat); FAT 9.2g (sat 3g, mono 2.7g, poly 2.1g); PROTEIN 22.3g; CARB 28.9g; FIBER 5.9g; CHOL 66mg; IRON 3.2mg; SODIUM 619mg; CALC 142mg
EXCHANGES: 2 Starch, 3 Lean Meat

SERVE**with**

• •

Top Turkey Chili Mac with oyster crackers, *and toss a mixed green salad using packaged salad greens and a commercial reduced-fat dressing.*

Chili Pie

prep: 4 minutes   cook: 18 minutes

Be sure to use a package of corn bread mix that requires the addition of water or buttermilk only, and use the water.

Cooking spray
  1 cup chopped zucchini
  1 (14.5-ounce) can no-salt-added diced
     tomatoes, drained
  1 (15.25-ounce) can no-salt-added whole-
     kernel corn, drained
  ½ teaspoon salt
  2 cups CHIPOTLE BLACK BEAN CHILI
     (page 100)
  1 (6-ounce) package buttermilk corn bread mix
     (such as Martha White)
  ⅔ cup water

Preheat oven to 450°.

Place a 10-inch cast-iron skillet over high heat until hot; coat with cooking spray. Add zucchini; sauté 2 minutes. Add tomatoes and next 3 ingredients; cook 1 minute or until thoroughly heated.

Prepare corn bread according to package directions using ⅔ cup water. Spread corn bread mixture evenly over chili mixture. Bake on top rack of oven at 450° for 15 minutes or until topping is golden brown. Cut pie into sections. Yield: 4 servings (serving size: ¼ of pie).

CALORIES 306 (13% from fat); FAT 4.4g (sat 0.7g, mono 0.3g, poly 0.4g); PROTEIN 9.6g; CARB 59g; FIBER 8.4g; CHOL 0mg; IRON 3.3mg; SODIUM 1,041mg; CALC 93mg
EXCHANGES: 3 Starch, 2 Vegetable, 1 Fat

SERVE**with**

• •

Steam green beans *in the microwave to serve with this one-skillet corn bread pie.*

Grilled Vegetables with
Potato Cakes, page 107

potato cakes,

- VEAL MARSALA AND POTATO CAKES

- SALMON AND GREENS WITH POTATO CAKES

- GRILLED VEGETABLES WITH POTATO CAKES

- POACHED EGGS AND POTATO CAKES WITH TOMATO HOLLANDAISE

Potato Cakes

Potato Cakes

prep: 8 minutes   cook: 10 minutes

These versatile mashed potato patties comple-ment an array of toppings from veggies to veal. And they're a unique alternative to noodles, rice, and bread.

2   (1-pound, 4-ounce) packages refrigerated mashed potatoes (such as Simply Potatoes)
1   tablespoon dried minced onion
½   teaspoon pepper
1   cup matzo meal
Cooking spray

Combine first 4 ingredients in a large bowl. Divide mixture into 16 portions, using about ⅓ cup in each portion. Pat each portion into a 4-inch diameter cake; place on wax paper.

Heat a large nonstick skillet over medium-high heat. Coat both sides of each cake with cooking spray; place in batches in pan. Reduce heat to medium; cook 1 to 2 minutes on each side or until browned. Remove from pan, and place on wax paper. Cool completely. Yield: 16 potato cakes (serving size: 1 potato cake).

CALORIES 80 (9% from fat); FAT 0.8g (sat 0g mono 0g, poly 0g); PROTEIN 1.8g; CARB 17g; FIBER 1.3g; CHOL 0mg; IRON 0.3mg; SODIUM 187mg; CALC 11mg
EXCHANGE: 1 Starch

TOstore

• • • • • • • • • • • • • • • • • •

Layer potato cakes *in an airtight container between sheets of wax paper or nonstick aluminum foil. Refrigerate or freeze.*

TOreheat

• • • • • • • • • • • • • • • • • •

Place frozen or chilled potato cakes *on a baking sheet coated with cooking spray or lined with nonstick aluminum foil. Bake frozen cakes at 350° for 17 minutes. Bake chilled cakes at 350° for 14 minutes.*

Veal Marsala and Potato Cakes

prep: 3 minutes   cook: 14 to 17 minutes

The secret to tender veal is to cook it quickly over high heat, and be careful not to overcook it. Don't worry if it's a little pink inside after 1 minute; it will continue to cook after it's removed from the pan. Cook the veal and mushrooms while the potato cakes reheat.

 2 POTATO CAKES (page 105)
 ¼ cup fat-free, less-sodium chicken broth
 ¼ cup dry Marsala
 1 teaspoon cornstarch
 ½ teaspoon salt
 1 teaspoon olive oil
 ½ pound veal scaloppine, cut into 3-inch pieces
 ½ teaspoon freshly ground black pepper
 1 cup sliced mushrooms
 1 teaspoon bottled minced garlic

Preheat oven to 350°. Reheat Potato Cakes according to recipe instructions on page 105.

Combine broth and next 3 ingredients.

Heat oil in a large nonstick skillet over high heat. Sprinkle veal with pepper; add to pan. Cook over high heat 30 seconds on each side. Remove from pan; set aside. Reduce heat to medium. Add mushrooms and garlic; sauté 4 minutes. Stir broth mixture with a whisk; add to mushroom mixture. Cook, stirring constantly with a whisk, 1 minute or until thickened. Pour sauce over veal. Spoon veal mixture evenly over potato cakes. Yield: 2 servings (serving size: 3 ounces veal, about ½ cup mushroom mixture, and 1 potato cake).

CALORIES 248 (24% from fat); FAT 6.5g (sat 1.3g, mono 2.7g, poly 0.6g); PROTEIN 26.3g; CARB 21g; FIBER 1.9g; CHOL 94mg; IRON 1.9mg; SODIUM 952mg; CALC 37mg
EXCHANGES: 1 Starch, 1 Vegetable, 3 Lean Meat

Salmon and Greens with Potato Cakes

prep: 5 minutes   cook: 14 to 17 minutes

Pair salmon and salad greens with a potato cake for a sophisticated light supper. Cook the salmon while the potato cakes reheat.

 4 POTATO CAKES (page 105)
 ½ teaspoon freshly ground black pepper, divided
 2 tablespoons fresh lemon juice (1 lemon)
 2 tablespoons dry white wine
 1 tablespoon extravirgin olive oil
 1 tablespoon water
 1 tablespoon Dijon mustard
 1 tablespoon drained capers, minced
 ⅛ teaspoon salt
 4 (6-ounce) skinless salmon fillets
Olive oil-flavored cooking spray
 4 cups gourmet salad greens

Preheat oven to 350°. Reheat Potato Cakes according to recipe instructions on page 105.

Combine ¼ teaspoon pepper and next 7 ingredients; stir well.

Sprinkle salmon with ¼ teaspoon pepper; coat with cooking spray. Place a large nonstick skillet over medium-high heat until hot. Add salmon; cook 4 minutes on each side or until fish flakes easily when tested with a fork. Remove salmon from pan; flake into large chunks.

Place greens on serving plates; top with potato cakes. Place salmon on potato cakes; drizzle with vinaigrette. Yield: 4 servings (serving size: 1 cup greens, 1 potato cake, 6 ounces salmon, and 2 tablespoons vinaigrette).

CALORIES 325 (29% from fat); FAT 10.6g (sat 1.5g, mono 4.2g, poly 2.8g); PROTEIN 37g; CARB 20.1g; FIBER 2.7g; CHOL 88mg; IRON 2.6mg; SODIUM 547mg; CALC 72mg
EXCHANGES: 1 Starch, 1 Vegetable, 4 Lean Meat

Grilled Vegetables with Potato Cakes

prep: 3 minutes   cook: 14 to 17 minutes

Use any combination of yellow squash and zucchini to get 3 cups of chopped squash. Grill the squash and mushroom caps while the potato cakes reheat.

    4 POTATO CAKES (page 105)
    2 small zucchini
    1 small yellow squash
    4 small portobello mushroom caps
    ½ teaspoon pepper
Cooking spray
    2 cups fire-roasted tomato and garlic pasta
       sauce (such as Classico)
    ½ cup preshredded fresh Parmesan cheese

Preheat oven to 350°. Reheat Potato Cakes according to recipe instructions on page 105.

Prepare grill.

Cut squash lengthwise into 4 slices each. Sprinkle squash and mushrooms with pepper, and coat with cooking spray. Place on grill rack coated with cooking spray; grill 3 minutes on each side or until tender. Remove from heat. Chop squash; set aside.

Pour pasta sauce into a 2-cup glass measure. Cover and microwave at HIGH 2 minutes or until thoroughly heated, stirring after 1 minute.

Place mushroom caps on plates; top each with a potato cake. Spoon squash over potato cakes. Top each with pasta sauce, and sprinkle with cheese. Yield: 4 servings (serving size: 1 portobello cap, 1 potato cake, ¾ cup squash, ½ cup pasta sauce, and 2 tablespoons cheese).

CALORIES 225 (19% from fat); FAT 4.7g (sat 1.8g, mono 0.9g, poly 0.1g); PROTEIN 10.7g; CARB 36.1g; FIBER 6.8g; CHOL 7mg; IRON 2.1mg; SODIUM 751mg; CALC 226mg
EXCHANGES: 2 Starch, 1 Vegetable, ½ High-Fat Meat

Poached Eggs and Potato Cakes with Tomato Hollandaise

prep: 3 minutes   cook: 14 to 17 minutes

This rich-tasting dish is a meatless variation of Eggs Benedict. Instead of placing the eggs on English muffins, you serve them on crispy potato cakes.

    4 POTATO CAKES (page 105)
    2 tablespoons white vinegar
    4 large eggs
    1 (0.9-ounce) package Hollandaise sauce mix
    ¾ cup 1% low-fat milk
    1 tablespoon light butter
    1 tablespoon sun-dried tomato sprinkles

Preheat oven to 350°. Reheat Potato Cakes according to recipe instructions on page 105.

Add water to a depth of 2 inches in a large nonstick skillet. Add vinegar. Bring to a boil; reduce heat, and maintain at a light simmer. Break eggs, 1 at a time, into a measuring cup or saucer; slip eggs, 1 at a time, into water, holding cup as close as possible to surface of water. Simmer 5 minutes or until done. Remove eggs with a slotted spoon.

Combine sauce mix and milk in a small saucepan; stir with a whisk until smooth. Add butter. Bring to a simmer over medium heat, stirring constantly with a whisk, 2 minutes or until thickened; stir in tomato sprinkles.

Place potato cakes on plates; top with eggs. Spoon sauce over eggs. Yield: 4 servings (serving size: 1 potato cake, 1 egg, and about ¼ cup sauce).

CALORIES 238 (29% from fat); FAT 7.8g (sat 2.9g, mono 2.1g, poly 0.7g); PROTEIN 9.9g; CARB 31.4g; FIBER 1.4g; CHOL 219mg; IRON 1.2mg; SODIUM 576mg; CALC 95mg
EXCHANGES: 2 Starch, 1 Medium-Fat Meat

simmer a pot of

tomato chutney,

and use it as the key ingredient in:

- BLACKENED CHICKEN SALAD WITH TOMATO CHUTNEY
- CHICKEN-TOMATO CHUTNEY PIZZA
- ITALIAN BEEF SUBS
- BOMBAY CURRIED SHRIMP AND RICE

Tomato Chutney

Tomato Chutney

prep: 6 minutes   cook: 30 minutes

Keep this sweet and savory condiment on hand to use in the recipes on the next two pages or as an alternative to salsa or ketchup on sandwiches, vegetables, and appetizers.

4	(14.5-ounce) cans diced tomatoes, drained
1½	cups chopped onion (about 1 large)
½	cup sugar
½	cup white wine vinegar
½	teaspoon crushed red pepper
½	teaspoon ground allspice

Combine all ingredients in a large saucepan. Bring to a boil over medium-high heat. Cook, uncovered, 30 minutes or until mixture is reduced to 3 cups, stirring often. Yield: 3 cups (serving size: 1 tablespoon).

CALORIES 14 (1% from fat); FAT 0g (sat 0g, mono 0g, poly 0g); PROTEIN 0.2g; CARB 3.6g; FIBER 0.4g; CHOL 0mg; IRON 0.1mg; SODIUM 27mg; CALC 5mg
EXCHANGE: Free (up to 2 tablespoons)

TOstore

• • • • • • • • • • • • • • • • • • • •

Spoon chutney into hot sterilized jars, *filling to ¼-inch from top; wipe jar rims. Cover at once with metal lids, and screw on bands; cool. Store in refrigerator. Use within 2 weeks.*

Blackened Chicken Salad with
Tomato Chutney, page 110

Blackened Chicken Salad with Tomato Chutney

prep: 5 minutes   cook: 12 minutes

    4   (4-ounce) skinless, boneless chicken breast
        halves
    2   teaspoons blackened steak seasoning (such
        as Paul Prudhomme's)
Cooking spray
    1   (10-ounce) package romaine salad greens
    1   cup sliced salad cucumber (about 1 small)
    1   cup chopped yellow bell pepper (about 1
        small)
   ⅓   cup reduced-fat olive oil vinaigrette
    1   cup TOMATO CHUTNEY (page 108)

   Sprinkle chicken with blackened steak
seasoning. Heat a large nonstick skillet over
medium-high heat. Coat chicken with cooking
spray; add to pan. Cook 6 minutes on each side
or until done.
   Combine salad greens and next 3 ingredients; toss well. Spoon greens mixture onto each
of 4 plates. Slice chicken diagonally into thin
strips. Arrange chicken over salads. Spoon
chutney over chicken. Yield: 4 servings (serving
size: 2 cups greens, 3 ounces chicken, and ¼
cup chutney).

CALORIES 247 (21% from fat); FAT 5.8g (sat 0.8g, mono 0.4g, poly 0.5g);
PROTEIN 28.8g; CARB 21.4g; FIBER 4.3g; CHOL 66mg; IRON 2.3mg;
SODIUM 553mg; CALC 78mg
EXCHANGES: 1 Starch, 2 Vegetable, 3 Very Lean Meat

SERVE**with**

• • • • • • • • • • • • • • • • • •

Balance the spiciness *of the chicken with crisp breadsticks or French bread baguette slices.*

Chicken-Tomato Chutney Pizza

prep: 8 minutes   cook: 10 minutes

The spicy sweetness of the tomato chutney adds a whole new taste dimension to pizza.

    1   (10-ounce) Italian cheese-flavored pizza crust
   ¼   cup TOMATO CHUTNEY (page 108)
    2   (6-ounce) packages grilled chicken strips
        (such as Louis Rich), chopped
   ¼   teaspoon pepper
    1   cup chopped yellow squash (about 1)
   ¼   cup chopped fresh cilantro
    1   cup (4 ounces) shredded part-skim
        mozzarella cheese

   Preheat oven to 450°.
   Place pizza crust on a baking sheet. Spread
chutney over pizza crust; sprinkle chopped
chicken, pepper, and squash over chutney. Top
with cilantro and shredded cheese. Bake at 450°
for 10 minutes. Cut into slices. Yield: 6 servings
(serving size: 1 slice).

CALORIES 261 (26% from fat); FAT 7.6g (sat 3.4g, mono 0.9g, poly 0.1g);
PROTEIN 22.8g; CARB 24.5g; FIBER 1.2g; CHOL 48mg; IRON 1.9mg;
SODIUM 876mg; CALC 255mg
EXCHANGES: 1 Starch, 2 Vegetable, 2 Lean Meat

SERVE**with**

• • • • • • • • • • • • • • • • • •

Serve slices of this upscale pizza *with a mixed green salad of gourmet greens and fat-free balsamic vinaigrette.*

Italian Beef Subs

prep: 5 minutes   cook: 14 minutes

Because of the deli roast beef, this sandwich has over 1,000mg of sodium. If you need to reduce the sodium, make the sandwich with thinly sliced leftover roast beef.

2	teaspoons olive oil
1	green bell pepper, seeded and cut into strips (about 1 cup)
2	teaspoons bottled minced garlic
1	teaspoon Italian seasoning
1	(14-ounce) can low-sodium beef broth
¾	pound thinly sliced deli roast beef
4	(3-ounce) whole wheat submarine rolls
½	cup TOMATO CHUTNEY (page 108)

Heat oil in a large nonstick skillet over medium-high heat. Add bell pepper and garlic; sauté 2 minutes. Stir in Italian seasoning and broth. Bring mixture to a boil; reduce heat, and simmer, uncovered, 10 minutes. Add beef to pepper mixture, and cook 45 seconds or until thoroughly heated, tossing to coat.

Divide beef evenly among submarine roll bottoms; top with bell pepper mixture. Spoon remaining broth mixture evenly over beef and bell pepper; top each with 2 tablespoons chutney. Cover with roll tops; cut sandwiches in half diagonally. Serve immediately. Yield: 4 servings (serving size: 1 sandwich).

CALORIES 389 (23% from fat); FAT 10g (sat 3.1g, mono 4.3g, poly 1.2g); PROTEIN 25.8g; CARB 50.8g; FIBER 5g; CHOL 38mg; IRON 5.2mg; SODIUM 1,241mg; CALC 172mg
EXCHANGES: 3 Starch, 1 Vegetable, 2 Medium-Fat Meat

SERVE**with**

• • • • • • • • • • • • • • • • • • • •

This hearty sandwich *is a meal in itself. For dessert, serve lemon sorbet or a bunch of grapes.*

Bombay Curried Shrimp and Rice

prep: 5 minutes   cook: 20 minutes

To save time, buy peeled and deveined shrimp from the grocery store seafood department.

1	cup uncooked basmati rice
1	(14-ounce) can fat-free, less-sodium chicken broth
¼	cup water
Cooking spray	
1½	pounds peeled and deveined medium shrimp
1¼	cups quartered and sliced zucchini (about 1 small)
1½	teaspoons curry powder
½	teaspoon salt
1	cup TOMATO CHUTNEY (page 108)

Cook rice according to package directions, using chicken broth and ¼ cup water.

Heat a large nonstick skillet coated with cooking spray over medium-high heat. Add shrimp and next 3 ingredients. Coat shrimp mixture with cooking spray. Sauté 4 minutes or until shrimp are done. Add chutney; cook 1 minute.

Spoon rice onto plates; top with shrimp mixture. Yield: 4 servings (serving size: 1¼ cups shrimp mixture and about ¾ cup rice).

CALORIES 432 (7% from fat); FAT 3.2g (sat 0.6g, mono 0.5g, poly 1.2g); PROTEIN 40g; CARB 63.1g; FIBER 3.9g; CHOL 259mg; IRON 6.3mg; SODIUM 919mg; CALC 118mg
EXCHANGES: 3 Starch, 2 Vegetable, 4 Very Lean Meat

SERVE**with**

• • • • • • • • • • • • • • • • • • • •

Fresh pineapple *is a refreshing accompaniment to this sweet and savory curry dish.*

Portuguese Frittata, page 114

sauté a big skillet of
chicken-vegetable toss,
then use it to create:

- PORTUGUESE FRITTATA
- CHICKEN AND BLACK BEAN BURRITOS
- CHICKEN AND POTATO HASH
- CHICKEN AND SHELLS WITH CHEESE SAUCE

Chicken-Vegetable Toss

prep: 7 minutes   cook: 9 minutes

Enjoy this chicken and vegetable medley as a one-dish skillet supper, or use it in the recipes on the next two pages.

Chicken-Vegetable Toss

Cooking spray
- 1 onion, finely chopped
- 1 large yellow bell pepper, finely chopped
- 1 small eggplant, finely chopped
- 3 garlic cloves, minced
- ¼ teaspoon freshly ground black pepper
- ¼ cup fat-free, less sodium chicken broth
- 2 tablespoons dry white wine
- 1 (4-ounce) jar diced pimiento, drained
- 3 (6-ounce) packages Italian-style chopped cooked chicken breast (about 4 cups)

Heat a large nonstick skillet coated with cooking spray over medium-high heat. Add onion and next 4 ingredients; sauté 8 minutes or until vegetables are tender.

Add chicken broth and wine; cook 1 minute. Remove from heat; stir in pimiento and chicken. Yield: 7 cups (serving size: 1 cup).

CALORIES 133 (20% from fat); FAT 3g (sat 1g, mono 0g, poly 0.1g); PROTEIN 19.5g; CARB 6.9g; FIBER 1.4g; CHOL 53mg; IRON 1.1mg; SODIUM 796mg; CALC 14mg
EXCHANGES: 1 Vegetable, 2 Lean Meat

TOstore

● ● ● ● ● ● ● ● ● ● ● ● ● ● ● ● ● ● ●

Place the cooked chicken mixture in heavy-duty *zip-top plastic bags in 1- or 2-cup portions. Label and freeze up to 6 months. Or store in the refrigerator up to 4 days.*

TOreheat

● ● ● ● ● ● ● ● ● ● ● ● ● ● ● ● ● ● ●

Thaw in the refrigerator or in the microwave. *Place in a saucepan, and cook over medium heat 5 to 8 minutes or until thoroughly heated.*

Portuguese Frittata

prep: 4 minutes   cook: 18 minutes

A cast-iron skillet is ideal to use for this recipe. To ovenproof another type of skillet, (preferably one without a plastic handle) wrap the handle tightly in heavy-duty aluminum foil.

Olive oil-flavored cooking spray
 1   cup CHICKEN-VEGETABLE TOSS (page 113)
 1   (14.5-ounce) can no-salt-added diced tomatoes, drained
 1   (8-ounce) carton egg substitute
 2   large eggs, lightly beaten
 1   tablespoon chopped fresh oregano
 ¼   teaspoon salt
 ¼   teaspoon freshly ground black pepper
 ½   cup shredded part-skim mozzarella cheese

Preheat oven to 450°.

Heat a medium (10-inch) ovenproof skillet coated with cooking spray over medium-high heat. Add Chicken-Vegetable Toss and tomatoes; sauté 2 minutes.

Combine egg substitute, eggs, oregano, salt, and pepper. Add egg mixture to pan; reduce heat to medium, and cook, uncovered, 5 minutes (do not stir). Sprinkle cheese over egg mixture, and place pan in oven. Bake at 450° for 10 minutes or until set. Broil 1 minute or until lightly browned. Cut into 4 wedges; serve immediately. Yield: 4 servings (serving size: 1 wedge).

CALORIES 149 (34% from fat); FAT 5.6g (sat 2.5g, mono 1.6g, poly 0.4g); PROTEIN 17.6g; CARB 6.8g; FIBER 1.4g; CHOL 128mg; IRON 1.9mg; SODIUM 586mg; CALC 142mg
EXCHANGES: 1 Vegetable, 2 Lean Meat

SERVE**with**

· · · · · · · · · · · · · · · · · ·

Serve the frittata with *steamed asparagus, crusty French bread, and fresh nectarines.*

Chicken and Black Bean Burritos

prep: 12 minutes   cook: 3 minutes

 1   (15-ounce) can no-salt-added black beans, rinsed and drained
 ¼   cup water
 2   cups CHICKEN-VEGETABLE TOSS (page 113)
 ¼   teaspoon salt
 6   (8-inch) flour tortillas
 1½   cups shredded iceberg lettuce
 6   tablespoons salsa
 6   tablespoons shredded reduced-fat sharp Cheddar cheese

Combine black beans and water in a medium skillet; mash black beans with back of a fork. Place pan over medium-high heat; stir in Chicken-Vegetable Toss and salt. Cook 3 minutes, stirring occasionally, or until thoroughly heated.

Heat tortillas according to package directions. Spread about ½ cup chicken mixture down center of each tortilla; top each with ¼ cup shredded lettuce, 1 tablespoon salsa, and 1 tablespoon cheese. Roll up tortillas. Yield: 6 servings (serving size: 1 burrito).

CALORIES 270 (19% from fat); FAT 5.6g (sat 2g, mono 1.4g, poly 0.6g); PROTEIN 17.1g; CARB 38.6g; FIBER 4.4g; CHOL 23mg; IRON 2.5mg; SODIUM 740mg; CALC 184mg
EXCHANGES: 2½ Starch, 2 Lean Meat

SERVE**with**

· · · · · · · · · · · · · · · · · ·

Serve the burritos with a fresh fruit duo *of mango and pineapple.*

Chicken and Potato Hash

prep: 6 minutes   cook: 12 minutes

Nothing says "comfort" like a hearty skillet dinner of pan-fried potatoes, vegetables, and meat.

    2   teaspoons butter
    1   (20-ounce) package refrigerated new potato
        wedges, coarsely chopped (such as Simply
        Potatoes)
    ¼   teaspoon pepper
    ½   teaspoon salt
    2   teaspoons chopped fresh sage
    2   cups CHICKEN-VEGETABLE TOSS
        (page 113)

Melt butter in a large nonstick skillet over medium-high heat. Add potatoes; cook, stirring occasionally, 10 minutes or until lightly browned.

Stir in pepper and remaining ingredients, and cook 2 minutes, stirring occasionally, or until thoroughly heated. Yield: 3 servings (serving size: about 1½ cups).

CALORIES 229 (18% from fat); FAT 4.6g (sat 2.3g, mono 0.8g, poly 0.1g); PROTEIN 17.7g; CARB 28.2g; FIBER 5.6g; CHOL 42mg; IRON 1.6mg; SODIUM 1,146mg; CALC 14mg
EXCHANGES: 2 Starch, 2 Very Lean Meat

SERVE**with**

• • • • • • • • • • • • • • • • • •

Make a salad with red leaf lettuce *and reduced-fat honey mustard dressing, and warm some whole wheat rolls.*

Chicken and Shells with Cheese Sauce

prep: 2 minutes   cook: 11 minutes

Use any small pasta you have on hand, and cook it while you make the cheese sauce.

    2   cups uncooked small seashell pasta
    1   tablespoon butter
    3   tablespoons all-purpose flour
    ¼   teaspoon salt
    ¼   teaspoon ground red pepper
  1½   cups low-fat 1% milk
    ½   cup (2 ounces) shredded reduced-fat sharp
        Cheddar cheese
    3   cups CHICKEN-VEGETABLE TOSS
        (page 113)

Cook pasta according to package directions, omitting salt and fat. Drain well.

Melt butter in a small saucepan over medium heat. Stir in flour, salt, and red pepper; gradually add milk, stirring with a whisk until blended. Cook 5 minutes or until thick, stirring constantly. Add cheese; stir until cheese melts. Add pasta and Chicken-Vegetable Toss; cook 3 minutes or until thoroughly heated. Serve immediately. Yield: 4 servings (serving size: 1½ cups).

CALORIES 427 (21% from fat); FAT 10g (sat 5.2g, mono 1.4g, poly 1g); PROTEIN 30.3g; CARB 55.1g; FIBER 3.1g; CHOL 61mg; IRON 2.8mg; SODIUM 934mg; CALC 264mg
EXCHANGES: 3 Starch, 2 Vegetable, 2 Lean Meat, 1 Fat

SERVE**with**

• • • • • • • • • • • • • • • • • •

Serve this cheesy pasta dish *with steamed broccoli and a simple fruit salad such as Apple-Yogurt Salad (page 310) or Pear Waldorf Salad (page 312).*

heat a saucepan of
asian barbecue sauce
to keep on hand for:

- BARBECUE TOFU STIR-FRY
- BARBECUE TUNA TACOS
- ASIAN BARBECUE FLANK STEAK
- ASIAN PORK BARBECUE SANDWICHES

Asian Barbecue Sauce

prep: 1 minute   cook: 9 minutes

With Asian-style ingredients such as hot chili sauce, sesame oil, soy sauce, and ginger, this sweet-hot sauce is a cut above a bottled barbecue sauce.

Asian Barbecue Sauce

2	teaspoons sesame oil
½	onion, finely chopped (about ¾ cup)
½	cup cider vinegar
1	cup ketchup
¾	cup lightly packed light brown sugar
½	cup low-sodium soy sauce
2	tablespoons hot chili sauce with garlic (such as A Taste of Thai)
2	tablespoons dry sherry
1	teaspoon ground ginger

Heat sesame oil in a medium saucepan over medium-high heat. Add onion; cook 2 minutes or until tender. Add vinegar and remaining ingredients; combine with a whisk. Bring to a boil; reduce heat, and simmer 7 minutes. Yield: 2½ cups (serving size: 1 tablespoon).

CALORIES 28 (8% from fat); FAT 0.3g (sat 0g, mono 0.1g, poly 0.1g); PROTEIN 0.3g; CARB 6.5g; FIBER 0.2g; CHOL 0mg; IRON 0.3mg; SODIUM 213mg; CALC 6mg
EXCHANGE: ½ Starch

TOstore

• • • • • • • • • • • • • • • • • • •

Place the barbecue sauce *in an airtight container, and store in the refrigerator up to 1 month.*

TOreheat

• • • • • • • • • • • • • • • • • • •

Place in a saucepan, *bring to a boil, reduce heat, and simmer for 5 to 7 minutes or until thoroughly heated.*

Barbecue Tofu Stir-Fry, page 118

Barbecue Tofu Stir-Fry

prep: 12 minutes   cook: 6 minutes

Use one extra-large bag of boil-in-bag rice to get 3 cups of cooked rice. Start cooking the rice while the tofu is being pressed.

 1   (15-ounce) package extra-firm tofu, drained
 2   teaspoons peanut or vegetable oil
 1   head bok choy, trimmed and thinly sliced (about 7 cups)
 1   (4-ounce) package gourmet mushroom blend or ½ (8-ounce) package presliced mushrooms
 1   cup packaged shredded carrots
 ¾   cup ASIAN BARBECUE SAUCE (page 116)
 3   cups hot cooked long-grain rice

Wrap tofu in several layers of paper towels; place in a shallow dish. Place a weight over tofu. Let stand 10 minutes. Cut tofu into cubes.

Heat a wok or large skillet over high heat until hot; add oil. Add tofu; stir-fry 2 minutes or until lightly browned. Remove from pan using a slotted spoon; set aside. Add bok choy, mushrooms, and carrots to pan; stir-fry 2 minutes. Return tofu to pan; add barbecue sauce. Stir-fry 30 seconds or until thoroughly heated. Serve over rice. Yield: 4 servings (serving size: 1¼ cups tofu mixture and ¾ cup rice).

CALORIES 407 (22% from fat); FAT 10g (sat 1.9g, mono 2.7g, poly 5.1g); PROTEIN 17.1g; CARB 63.6g; FIBER 3.5g; CHOL 0mg; IRON 5mg; SODIUM 731mg; CALC 243mg
EXCHANGES: 3 Starch, 3 Vegetable, 2 Fat

Barbecue Tuna Tacos

prep: 1 minute   cook: 12 minutes

Take a break from Tex-Mex tacos—fill flour tortillas with a mixture of tuna and mango in a sweet-hot Asian sauce.

 1½   pounds tuna steaks
Cooking spray
 ¾   cup ASIAN BARBECUE SAUCE (page 116), divided
 1   ripe mango, peeled and thinly sliced
 ¼   cup slivered red onion
 ¼   cup chopped fresh cilantro
 8   (6-inch) flour tortillas

Preheat broiler.

Place tuna steaks on a broiler pan coated with cooking spray; brush 2 tablespoons barbecue sauce over steaks. Broil 6 minutes. Turn steaks; brush with 2 tablespoons barbecue sauce. Broil 6 minutes or until fish is done. Transfer steaks to work surface; coarsely chop.

Combine mango, onion, and cilantro; toss.

Heat tortillas in microwave according to package directions.

Spoon tuna evenly over tortillas; drizzle remaining barbecue sauce evenly over tuna (about 1 tablespoon each). Top evenly with mango mixture, and fold tortilla over mixture. Yield: 4 servings (serving size: 2 tacos).

CALORIES 481 (13% from fat); FAT 6.8g (sat 1.4g, mono 0.6g, poly 0.8g); PROTEIN 45.1g; CARB 59.5g; FIBER 3.5g; CHOL 77mg; IRON 2.7mg; SODIUM 1,122mg; CALC 92mg
EXCHANGES: 3 Starch, 1 Fruit, 5 Very Lean Meat

HOW**to**

• • • • • • • • • • • • • • • • •

Press the tofu *to remove excess moisture, or it will release water during cooking, and your dish will be too liquidy. Items you can use for a weight include a gallon jug of water, a heavy skillet, or heavy cans.*

Asian Barbecue Flank Steak

prep: 5 minutes   marinate: 30 minutes
cook: 12 minutes   stand: 2 to 5 minutes

Marinate the meat at least 30 minutes so it will absorb the flavor of the marinade.

    1   pound flank steak, trimmed
    ¾   cup ASIAN BARBECUE SAUCE (page 116)
Cooking spray
    ¼   cup sliced green onions

Place flank steak in a heavy-duty zip-top plastic bag; pour barbecue sauce over meat, turning to coat. Cover and marinate at least 30 minutes.

Remove meat from marinade. Place marinade in a small saucepan; bring to a boil, and cook 1 minute. Remove from heat, and set aside.

Prepare grill.

Place meat on grill rack coated with cooking spray; cover and grill 6 to 8 minutes on each side or until a thermometer registers 145° (medium-rare). Transfer to a serving platter; let stand 2 to 5 minutes. Cut diagonally across grain into thin slices. Sprinkle with green onions. Serve with reserved marinade. Yield: 4 servings (serving size: 3 ounces steak and 3 tablespoons marinade).

CALORIES 267 (32% from fat); FAT 9.6g (sat 3.9g, mono 3.8g, poly 0.7g); PROTEIN 24.7g; CARB 20g; FIBER 0.7g; CHOL 59mg; IRON 3.1mg; SODIUM 712mg; CALC 29mg
EXCHANGES: 1 Starch, 3 Lean Meat

SERVE**with**

• • • • • • • • • • • • • • • • • •

While you're grilling the steak, *grill some fresh pineapple slices to accompany the meat. Slice cored fresh pineapple into ½-inch slices. Place on the grill, and cook 1 to 2 minutes on each side. Serve warm.*

Asian Pork Barbecue Sandwiches

prep: 11 minutes   cook: 2 minutes

Perk up the flavor of a "tired ol' " barbecue sandwich by using a tasty new sauce.

Cooking spray
    3   (4-ounce) boneless center-cut loin pork
        chops, trimmed and thinly sliced crosswise
    ½   cup ASIAN BARBECUE SAUCE (page 116)
    4   (1.9-ounce) onion buns, toasted (such as
        Earth Grains)
    1   cup packaged shredded red cabbage
        (such as Fresh Express) or about ¼ of 1
        small cabbage
    12 sandwich-cut bread-and-butter pickles
        (optional)

Heat a 10-inch nonstick skillet coated with cooking spray over medium-high heat. Add pork, and sauté 2 minutes or until pork is done. Add barbecue sauce to pan; toss pork with sauce.

Spoon pork mixture evenly onto bottom halves of buns; top each with ¼ cup red cabbage and, if desired, pickle slices. Top with top halves of buns. Yield: 4 servings (serving size: 1 sandwich).

CALORIES 320 (20% from fat); FAT 7.2g (sat 2.8g, mono 2.3g, poly 1.6g); PROTEIN 23.8g; CARB 40.1g; FIBER 1.7g; CHOL 54mg; IRON 2.8mg; SODIUM 741mg; CALC 92mg
EXCHANGES: 2 Starch, 2 Vegetable, 2 Lean Meat

SERVE**with**

• • • • • • • • • • • • • • • • • •

Make a bowl of *Coleslaw with Pineapple (page 316) to serve with these sweet and tangy sandwiches.*

"I have only a short amount of time to spend with my 3-year-old daughter in the evenings, so I sure don't want to be in the kitchen all night cooking or washing pots and pans."

ONE-DISH
wonders

Simplify supper by using only one dish to prepare one dish. Whether it's a skillet, saucepan, or Dutch oven, you'll have just one pan to clean. Each meal is complete with a protein source, a starch or grain food, and a vegetable; add a bread or quick salad if you like.

Thai Tofu and Spicy Asian Noodles, page 122

thai tofu and spicy asian noodles with fresh fruit salad
and chai tea   serves 4 · total time 18 minutes

If you're hungry for Thai food, satisfy your craving in a hurry with these spicy noodles smothered in an authentic Thai-style peanut sauce.

SUPPER plan

1. Cook pasta.

2. While pasta cooks:
  • Prepare peanut sauce.
  • Prepare fresh fruit salad using 4 cups of desired cubed fruit; drizzle with 2 teaspoons each of lime juice and honey.
  • Chop cilantro.

3. Combine pasta mixture, peanut sauce, and cilantro.

Thai Tofu and Spicy Asian Noodles

prep: 9 minutes   cook: 9 minutes

  1   (8-ounce) package uncooked linguine
  1   (8-ounce) package fresh sugar snap peas
  2   tablespoons peanut oil
  2   tablespoons low-sodium tamari sauce
      or low-sodium soy sauce
  1   tablespoon smooth peanut butter
  1   tablespoon fresh lime juice or rice wine
      vinegar
  1   teaspoon chili garlic sauce
  1   garlic clove, crushed
  1   (8-ounce) package Thai-flavored or plain
      baked tofu, cut into cubes
  ⅓   cup chopped fresh cilantro

Bring 2 quarts water to a boil in a saucepan. Place linguine in boiling water 5 minutes; add peas, and cook 2 minutes.

Combine peanut oil and next 5 ingredients. Drain pasta mixture, and return to pan. Stir in peanut sauce and tofu. Sprinkle with chopped cilantro. Serve immediately. Yield: 4 servings (serving size: 1¾ cups).

CALORIES 338 (36% from fat); FAT 13.4g (sat 2.2g, mono 4.8g, poly 4.7g); PROTEIN 14.5g; CARB 42.3g; FIBER 3.9g; CHOL 0mg; IRON 2.8mg; SODIUM 628mg; CALC 83mg
EXCHANGES: 2 Starch, 2 Vegetable, 1 High-Fat Meat, 1 Fat

FINDit

• • • • • • • • • • • • • • • • • • • •

Look for baked or grilled tofu *in the produce section of the grocery store along with other soy products. One slice of baked tofu (about 2 ounces) has approximately 56 calories, 7 grams of protein, 120 milligrams of sodium, and 3 grams of fat. It has no saturated fat and no cholesterol.*

Cut the slices into cubes or strips, or leave in slices, depending on the recipe.

"I always make a pasta dish *at least once or twice a week. My kids will eat it, and I always have some kind of pasta in the pantry. My sauces are never fancy (usually from a jar) or I chop up whatever veggies I have left in the refrigerator to make the sauce while the pasta is cooking—so it never takes much longer than 20 minutes to get supper on the table.***"**

Elise Weiss,
Test Kitchens staff

Thai Tofu and Spicy
Asian Noodles

greek artichoke-spinach frittata
with minted fresh fruit salad   serves 4 · total time 21 minutes

A fresh veggie frittata is just right for the nights when you need a light dinner.

SUPPER plan

1. Slice tomatoes; drain and chop artichokes.

2. Prepare Greek Artichoke-Spinach Frittata.

3. While frittata broils, make fruit salad:
  - Stir together any combination of precut fresh fruit (melon, pineapple, strawberries).
  - Sprinkle fruit with lime juice.
  - Toss fruit with chopped fresh mint.

Greek Artichoke-Spinach Frittata

prep: 6 minutes   cook: 15 minutes

If you don't have an iron skillet, ovenproof a skillet by wrapping the handle tightly with aluminum foil.

1½	teaspoons olive oil
2	cups refrigerated hash brown potatoes (such as Simply Fresh)
1	tablespoon Greek seasoning
½	cup coarsely chopped drained water-packed artichoke hearts
1	cup tightly packed prewashed baby spinach leaves (about 1½ ounces)
6	large eggs
⅓	cup fat-free milk
¼	teaspoon freshly ground black pepper
2	ounces feta cheese, crumbled
2	Roma tomatoes, thinly sliced

Preheat broiler.

Heat oil in a 10-inch cast-iron skillet over medium heat. Add hash browns; sprinkle with Greek seasoning, and sauté 4 to 5 minutes or until lightly browned. Add chopped artichokes, and cook 2 minutes or until thoroughly heated. Stir in spinach, and cook 2 minutes or until spinach wilts, stirring frequently.

Separate eggs, reserving 4 egg yolks for another use. Combine remaining 2 egg yolks, whites, and milk, stirring with a whisk. Pour egg mixture over potato mixture. Sprinkle with pepper and feta cheese. Arrange tomato slices over feta. Cook over medium heat 3 to 4 minutes or until edges are set. Place frittata under broiler, and cook 4 to 5 minutes or until center is set and top begins to brown. Cut into 8 wedges. Yield: 4 servings (serving size: 2 wedges).

CALORIES 271 (41% from fat); FAT 12.2g (sat 4.9g, mono 4g, poly 1.6g); PROTEIN 15.6g; CARB 25.7g; FIBER 3.3g; CHOL 332mg; IRON 3.2mg; SODIUM 405mg; CALC 176mg
EXCHANGES: 1 Starch, 2 Vegetable, 1 High-Fat Meat, 1 Fat

STOREit

• • • • • • • • • • • • • • • • • •

Refrigerate unbroken raw egg yolks, *covered with water, for up to 2 days in an airtight container. If you can't use the yolks in 2 days, hard cook them just as you would cook whole eggs in the shell, drain, and store in the refrigerator in an airtight container for up to 4 or 5 days.*

It's not a good idea to freeze raw egg yolks because they tend to thicken or gel, getting so gelatinous that you can't use them.

shrimp-edamame salad with crisp sesame breadsticks and fresh pineapple   serves 4 • total time 22 minutes

When you use steamed shrimp from the seafood counter, this warm salad requires only 6 minutes of cooking time.

SUPPER plan

1. Bring water to a boil to pour over noodles.

2. Chop bell pepper; dice and peel avocado; chop cilantro; crush garlic.

3. Pour boiling water over noodles, and let stand.

4. Thaw soybeans by rinsing in cold, running water.

5. Sauté shrimp and soybean mixture.

6. Combine all ingredients for salad.

Shrimp-Edamame Salad

prep: 11 minutes   stand: 5 minutes

cook: 6 minutes

For a slightly tangier salad, use 2 tablespoons of lemon juice in place of the rice vinegar.

3½ ounces Chinese noodles (⅓ of a 10-ounce package)
7   teaspoons extravirgin olive oil, divided
1   (16-ounce) package frozen shelled edamame (soybeans), thawed
½   teaspoon salt, divided
2   garlic cloves, crushed
1   pound steamed peeled shrimp
¾   cup chopped red bell pepper
½   cup diced peeled avocado (about ½ small)
¼   cup chopped fresh cilantro
2   tablespoons seasoned rice vinegar
2   tablespoons lemon juice
2   teaspoons low-sodium soy sauce

Break noodles into large pieces. Place noodles in a large nonstick skillet, and cover with boiling water. Cover and let stand 5 minutes. Drain. Cut noodles into small pieces.

Wipe pan dry with paper towels. Heat 1 teaspoon oil in pan over medium-high heat. Add cooked noodles, soybeans, and ¼ teaspoon salt; sauté 3 minutes or until thoroughly heated. Stir in garlic and shrimp; cook 3 minutes or until thoroughly heated. Remove from heat, and stir in remaining 2 tablespoons oil, remaining ¼ teaspoon salt, bell pepper, and remaining ingredients. Toss gently. Yield: 4 servings (serving size: 1¾ cups).

CALORIES 460 (40% from fat); FAT 20.3g (sat 2.6g, mono 9.2g, poly 4.7g); PROTEIN 42.1g; CARB 31.6g; FIBER 6.8g; CHOL 243mg; IRON 7.9mg; SODIUM 659mg; CALC 209mg
EXCHANGES: 2 Starch, 5 Lean Meat, 1 Fat

NUTRITIONnote

• • • • • • • • • • • • • • • • • • •

Soy products are in the spotlight *because they contain estrogen-like substances called isoflavones, which may reduce the risk of heart disease and breast cancer, strengthen bones, and ease symptoms of menopause. To benefit from soy products, you need about 30-35 milligrams of isoflavones each day (but not more than 200 milligrams). A ½-cup serving of shelled edamame (Japanese for soybeans) has 35 milligrams.*

In addition to providing isoflavones, soybeans are low in fat and sodium, are cholesterol free, and provide protein and fiber.

Fresh soybeans are available in Asian markets from late spring to early fall. Frozen soybeans are available year-round; you can buy them in the pods or shelled.

creamy shrimp and pea pasta with french bread
and balsamic strawberries serves 4 · total time 18 minutes

Pause for a while and savor a plate of creamy, rich pasta, a slice of fresh French bread, and a glass of chilled white wine.

SUPPER plan

1. Cook pasta.

2. While pasta cooks:
• Chop basil.
• Slice strawberries.
• Sauté shrimp mixture.

3. Combine pasta, peas, and shrimp mixture.

4. Just before serving, drizzle strawberries with balsamic vinegar (2 teaspoons vinegar per 2 cups berries).

Creamy Shrimp and Pea Pasta

prep: 5 minutes   cook: 13 minutes

Ask for peeled and deveined shrimp in the seafood market or at the seafood counter at the grocery store. If you prefer to buy it in the shell, you'll need to get about 1⅓ pounds.

8	ounces uncooked angel hair pasta, broken into pieces
2	tablespoons butter
1	pound peeled and deveined shrimp
1	garlic clove, crushed
¾	cup fat-free half-and-half
⅓	cup chopped fresh basil, divided
¾	teaspoon salt
¼	teaspoon freshly ground black pepper
⅓	cup preshredded fresh Parmesan cheese
1½	cups frozen green peas

Cook pasta according to package directions, omitting salt and fat.

Melt butter in a large nonstick skillet over medium heat. Add shrimp and garlic; sauté 4 minutes or until done. Add half-and-half, 3 tablespoons chopped basil, salt, and pepper; bring to a simmer, and cook, uncovered, 4 minutes. Add cheese, and cook 1 minute or until cheese melts.

Place peas in a colander. Drain pasta over peas in colander.

Add pasta and peas to shrimp mixture, and toss gently. Cook over low heat 2 minutes. Stir in remaining chopped basil. Serve immediately. Yield: 4 servings (serving size: 1¾ cups).

CALORIES 409 (24% from fat); FAT 10.9g (sat 5.9g, mono 1.9g, poly 0.7g); PROTEIN 31.4g; CARB 43.8g; FIBER 3.7g; CHOL 182mg; IRON 5mg; SODIUM 982mg; CALC 163mg
EXCHANGES: 3 Starch, 3 Lean Meat

QUICKtip

• • • • • • • • • • • • • • • • • • • •

There's no need to cook the frozen green peas *before adding them to the the pasta. When you drain the hot pasta water over the peas, it thaws them. Then they cook just slightly when you combine them with the shrimp and pasta in the saucepan.*

shrimp and feta scampi
and crisp breadsticks serves 4 · total time 15 minutes

When you toss peas into a scampi-style dish, you have starch, vegetable, and protein servings all in one bowl.

SUPPER plan

1. Boil water for pasta.

2. Slice green onions.

3. Cook pasta.

4. Combine ingredients for pasta dish.

Shrimp and Feta Scampi

prep: 3 minutes   cook: 12 minutes

1	(8-ounce) package spaghetti
1½	pounds peeled and deveined shrimp
1	(10-ounce) package frozen snow peas or 10 ounces fresh sugar snap peas
4	green onions, sliced
⅓	cup reduced-fat olive oil vinaigrette
¼	teaspoon freshly ground black pepper
½	cup crumbled reduced-fat feta cheese

Bring 2 quarts water to a boil in a large saucepan. Add pasta, and cook, uncovered, 9 minutes. Add shrimp; cook, uncovered, 3 minutes or until shrimp turn pink. Place pea pods in a colander. Drain pasta over pea pods.

Transfer mixture to a large serving bowl. Add onions, vinaigrette, and pepper; toss lightly. Sprinkle with crumbled feta cheese. Yield: 4 servings (serving size: 2 cups).

CALORIES 430 (17% from fat); FAT 8.3g (sat 2.1g, mono 0.4g, poly 0.9g); PROTEIN 36.9g; CARB 50g; FIBER 6.1g; CHOL 247mg; IRON 6.4mg; SODIUM 630mg; CALC 138mg
EXCHANGES: 3 Starch, 1 Vegetable, 3 Lean Meat

QUICKtip

· ·

To save prep time, *we call for peeled deveined shrimp in our superfast recipes. If you want to start with unpeeled fresh shrimp, you'll need 2 pounds in order to end up with 1½ pounds of peeled shrimp.*

The chart below shows how much unpeeled raw shrimp to buy when your recipe calls for peeled and deveined raw shrimp.

UNPEELED RAW SHRIMP	PEELED AND DEVEINED RAW SHRIMP
⅔ pound	½ pound
1 pound	¾ pound
1⅓ pounds	1 pound
2 pounds	1½ pounds
2⅔ pounds	2 pounds
4 pounds	3 pounds

smoky bacon-clam chowder with mixed green salad and oyster crackers   serves 4 • total time 26 minutes

Warm up on a wintery night with a steaming bowl of chowder.

SUPPER plan

1. Cook bacon.

2. While bacon cooks:
   • Chop onion and parsley.
   • Rinse and chop smoked clams.

3. Prepare chowder.

4. While chowder simmers, prepare salad using packaged salad greens and low-fat vinaigrette.

Smoky Bacon-Clam Chowder

prep: 5 minutes   cook: 26 minutes

   3   40%-less-fat bacon slices
   ½   cup chopped onion
   2   cups refrigerated shredded hash brown potatoes
   ⅓   cup all-purpose flour
   ¾   teaspoon freshly ground black pepper, divided
   1   (8-ounce) bottle clam juice
   4   cups 2% reduced-fat milk
   3   (6½-ounce) cans chopped clams, undrained
   1   (3-ounce) can smoked baby clams in oil, drained, rinsed, and chopped
   3   tablespoons chopped fresh parsley

   Cook bacon in a Dutch oven over medium heat until crisp. Remove bacon from pan, and crumble.

   Add onion to drippings in pan; sauté 3 minutes or until tender. Add potatoes, and sauté 3 minutes or until lightly browned. Stir in flour and ½ teaspoon pepper; cook 1 minute. Add clam juice, stirring just until thickened (about 1 minute). Stir in milk. Bring mixture to a boil;

cover, reduce heat, and simmer 6 minutes or until potatoes are tender.

   Uncover and add clams. Cook 2 minutes or until thoroughly heated. Stir in parsley and remaining ¼ teaspoon pepper. Spoon chowder into bowls, and sprinkle evenly with crumbled bacon. Yield: 4 servings (serving size: 2 cups).

CALORIES 376 (38% from fat); FAT 15.9g (sat 8g, mono 3.5g, poly 0.8g); PROTEIN 27.6g; CARB 41.8g; FIBER 2g; CHOL 64mg; IRON 13.6mg; SODIUM 990mg; CALC 378mg
EXCHANGES: 2 Starch, 1 Low-Fat Milk, 2 Lean Meat

NUTRITIONnote

• • • • • • • • • • • • • • • • • • •

Compare the calories, fat, and sodium *in the following types of bacon.*

BACON (1 SLICE)	CALORIES	FAT (g)	SODIUM (mg)
40%-less-fat	25	1.5	145
Precooked bacon	23	1.7	73
Turkey bacon	34	2.7	184
Pork bacon	36	3.1	101

skillet lasagna with fennel salad
and focaccia   serves 4 • total time 37 minutes

This easy lasagna requires only 5 minutes of preparation and one skillet.

SUPPER plan

1. Chop roasted peppers.

2. Prepare Skillet Lasagna.

3. While lasagna simmers, prepare Fennel Salad.

Skillet Lasagna

prep: 5 minutes   cook: 30 minutes
stand: 2 minutes

½	pound ground round
2	tablespoons balsamic vinegar
2	teaspoons dried Italian seasoning, divided
1	cup part-skim ricotta cheese
4	uncooked lasagna noodles, broken into large pieces
1	(14.5-ounce) can diced tomatoes with onions, undrained
1	cup bottled roasted red bell peppers, chopped
¾	cup water
5	teaspoons commercial pesto
½	cup (2 ounces) mozzarella-Parmesan cheese blend

Cook beef in a large nonstick skillet over medium-high heat until browned, stirring to crumble. Add vinegar and 1 teaspoon Italian seasoning. Dollop ricotta cheese, by rounded tablespoons, over meat. Top with broken noodles, making one flat layer (noodles will overlap a little bit).

Pour tomatoes and peppers over noodles, making sure that noodles are completely covered. Add water, and sprinkle with remaining 1 teaspoon Italian seasoning. Dollop pesto by half teaspoons over top. Bring mixture to a boil.

Cover, reduce heat, and simmer 30 minutes or until noodles are fully cooked. Uncover and sprinkle with cheese. Cover and let stand 2 minutes or until cheese melts. Cut into wedges. Remove from pan with a slotted spatula. Yield: 4 servings (serving size: 1 wedge).

CALORIES 407 (33% from fat); FAT 14.9g (sat 7.1g, mono 5.7g, poly 0.8g); PROTEIN 29.7g; CARB 38.1g; FIBER 1.9g; CHOL 63mg; IRON 3.7mg; SODIUM 676mg; CALC 418mg
EXCHANGES: 2 Starch, 2 Vegetable, 2 Medium-Fat Meat, 1 Fat

Fennel Salad

prep: 5 minutes

2	cups thinly sliced fennel bulbs (about 4 small bulbs)
1	small red onion, thinly sliced
1	cup bottled citrus sections or fresh orange sections
2	teaspoons olive oil
½	teaspoon kosher salt
¼	teaspoon freshly ground black pepper
1	tablespoon fennel fronds

Combine first 3 ingredients in a large bowl. Add oil and remaining ingredients, tossing gently to coat. Yield: 4 cups (serving size: 1 cup).

CALORIES 66 (33% from fat); FAT 2.4g (sat 0.3g, mono 1.7g, poly 0.2g); PROTEIN 1.3g; CARB 11g; FIBER 3g; CHOL 0mg; IRON 0.5mg; SODIUM 259mg; CALC 46mg
EXCHANGES: ½ Fruit, 1 Vegetable

burgundy beef stew
and sourdough rolls   serves 4 • total time 18 minutes

Here's a homestyle beef stew almost too good to be true—3 minutes to prepare and only about 15 minutes to cook.

SUPPER plan

1. Cook stew.

2. While stew simmers, chop parsley.

Burgundy Beef Stew

prep: 3 minutes   cook: 15 minutes

Thaw pot roast in the refrigerator overnight or in the microwave for 6 to 7 minutes or until thawed.

 1 (24-ounce) package frozen Yankee Pot Roast dinner (such as Stouffer's), thawed
 1 (14.5-ounce) can roasted garlic diced tomatoes, undrained
 1 (10½-ounce) can beef consommé
 ½ cup dry red wine
 ½ teaspoon freshly ground black pepper
 1 (10-ounce) package frozen green peas and pearl onions
 2 tablespoons chopped fresh parsley

Combine first 5 ingredients in a Dutch oven; bring to a boil. Reduce heat and simmer, uncovered, 12 minutes. Stir in peas and onions; cook 3 to 4 minutes or until peas and onions are thoroughly heated. Sprinkle with parsley. Yield: 4 servings (serving size: 1¾ cups).

CALORIES 261 (17% from fat); FAT 4.8g (sat 2.1g, mono 0g, poly 0.1g); PROTEIN 15.2g; CARB 39.4g; FIBER 5g; CHOL 26mg; IRON 3.1mg; SODIUM 1,551mg; CALC 103mg
EXCHANGES: 2 Starch, 2 Vegetable, 1 Medium-Fat Meat

NUTRITIONnote

• • • • • • • • • • • • • • • • • •

Because this recipe relies on convenience products *such as frozen pot roast, canned tomatoes, and canned soup, the sodium content is higher than some of the other recipes in this chapter.*

If you need to reduce the sodium, use either a low-sodium or no-salt-added canned beef broth. A 10.5-ounce can of beef consommé has 1,969 milligrams of sodium; the same amount of low-sodium beef broth has 89 milligrams of sodium. The broth won't provide as rich a flavor as the consommé, but the sodium reduction is significant.

HOWto

• • • • • • • • • • • • • • • • • •

Wrap fresh parsley *loosely in a wet paper towel, and store in a zip-top plastic bag.*

Burgundy Beef Stew

Chipotle Red and White
Bean Chili

chipotle red and white bean chili
with corn bread crackers   serves 4 • total time 19 minutes

Two beans are better than one in this hot and hearty chili that's full of sausage, two kinds of beans, and three kinds of peppers.

SUPPER plan

1. Chop bell peppers; seed and chop chipotle peppers.

2. Rinse and drain beans.

3. Prepare chili.

Chipotle Red and White Bean Chili

prep: 7 minutes   cook: 12 minutes

- 1   cup frozen chopped onion
- ½   pound reduced-fat pork sausage
- 1   green bell pepper, chopped
- 1   red bell pepper, chopped
- 1   (1.25-ounce) package 30%-less-sodium taco seasoning mix (such as McCormick's)
- 1   (14.5-ounce) can Mexican-style diced tomatoes, drained
- 1   (8-ounce) can no-salt-added tomato sauce
- 1   (15-ounce) can no-salt-added light red kidney beans, rinsed and drained
- 1   (19-ounce) can cannellini beans, rinsed and drained
- 2   chipotle peppers in adobo sauce, seeded and chopped plus 2 teaspoons adobo sauce
- ¼   cup chopped fresh cilantro

Cook onion, sausage, and peppers in a non-stick skillet over medium-high heat until sausage is browned and vegetables are tender, stirring to crumble sausage.

Drain sausage mixture, and return to pan. Add seasoning mix and next 5 ingredients.

Bring mixture to a boil; cover and simmer 5 minutes. Stir in cilantro just before serving. Yield: 4 servings (serving size: 1¾ cups).

CALORIES 432 (24% from fat); FAT 11.4g (sat 3.7g, mono 0.1g, poly 0.4g); PROTEIN 23.2g; CARB 57.4g; FIBER 12.3g; CHOL 40mg; IRON 6.5mg; SODIUM 1,151mg; CALC 116mg
EXCHANGES: 3 Starch, 2 Vegetable, 2 Medium-Fat Meat

QUICKtip

• •

When there's no time to make a pan of corn bread *to serve with your chili, try corn bread crackers (we used Keebler). They're crisp with a hint of sweetness and have only 2.5 grams of fat per serving (serving size: 2 crackers). You may never make corn bread again!*

Or try some other reduced-fat crackers with your soups and chilis. Here are some of our favorites.

CRACKER (serving size)	FAT (grams)
Thin Rye-Crisp (2)	0.1
Saltines (2)	0.7
Oyster Crackers (10)	1.2
100% Stoned Wheat (2)	1.4
Harvester's Multi-Grain (2)	1.4
Triscuits (2)	1.7
Snackwell's Wheat (2)	3.0
Snackwell's Cracked Pepper (2)	3.1

sausage-wild rice casserole
with mandarin orange salad
and pumpernickel rolls   **serves 4 • total time 17 minutes**

Simmer a savory sausage casserole in a skillet instead of baking it in a casserole dish.

SUPPER plan

1. Thaw peas in microwave.

2. Slice onion into wedges.

3. Prepare Sausage-Wild Rice Casserole.

4. While rice mixture simmers, prepare Mandarin Orange Salad.

Sausage-Wild Rice Casserole

prep: 5 minutes   cook: 12 minutes

Cooking spray
- ½   pound reduced-fat sausage
- 2   small onions, cut into 8 wedges
- 2   cups water
- 1   (6.2-ounce) package fast-cooking recipe long-grain and wild rice (such as Uncle Ben's)
- ½   teaspoon dried oregano
- ¼   teaspoon crushed red pepper
- 1   cup frozen petite green peas, thawed

Heat a large nonstick skillet coated with cooking spray over medium heat. Add sausage, and cook 3 minutes or until browned, stirring often. Remove sausage from pan, and keep warm.

Separate onion wedges into layers. Recoat pan with cooking spray. Add onion; and cook 3 minutes or until browned, stirring frequently. Increase heat to high, and add water to pan; bring to a boil. Add rice, seasoning packet, oregano, and red pepper. Return to a boil; cover, reduce heat, and simmer 4 minutes or

until liquid is almost absorbed. Stir in reserved sausage and peas. Yield: 4 servings (serving size: 1¾ cups).

CALORIES 332 (31% from fat); FAT 11.4g (sat 4g, mono 0g, poly 0.1g); PROTEIN 16.5g; CARB 41.3g; FIBER 3g; CHOL 40mg; IRON 3mg; SODIUM 979mg; CALC 48mg
EXCHANGES: 2½ Starch, 1 Vegetable, 1 Medium-Fat Meat, 1 Fat

Mandarin Orange Salad

prep: 4 minutes

- 1   (5-ounce) package mixed salad greens
- 1   (11-ounce) can mandarin oranges, drained
- ¼   red onion, sliced
- ½   cup low-fat balsamic vinaigrette

Combine all ingredients in a large serving bowl; toss gently to coat. Yield: 4 servings (serving size: 1½ cups).

CALORIES 73 (1% from fat); FAT 0.1g (sat 0g, mono 0g, poly 0.1g); PROTEIN 0.7g; CARB 16.6g; FIBER 0.9g; CHOL 0mg; IRON 0.7mg; SODIUM 473mg; CALC 21mg
EXCHANGE: 1 Fruit

VEGETARIANoption

• • • • • • • • • • • • • • • • • • •

To make the Sausage-Wild Rice Skillet Casserole meat-free, *use 1 (8-ounce) package of veggie breakfast patties, chopped, instead of the reduced-fat sausage.*

mustard-braised sausage and potato skillet
with pumpernickel bread   **serves 4 • total time 24 minutes**

It doesn't have to be Oktoberfest for you to enjoy a robust German-style supper. With only one skillet to clean, you'll have time to do the polka.

SUPPER plan

1. Quarter and slice onion; chop cabbage.

2. Brown sausage.

3. Cook onion, potato, and cabbage; add remaining ingredients and complete cooking.

Mustard-Braised Sausage and Potato Skillet

prep: 6 minutes   cook: 18 minutes

The strong flavors of mustard, caraway seeds, and cabbage will please fans of German food.

Cooking spray
- 1 (14-ounce) package low-fat smoked sausage, sliced into ½-inch pieces
- 1 onion, quartered and sliced
- 1 (20-ounce) package refrigerated new potato wedges (such as Simply Potatoes)
- 2 cups coarsely chopped green cabbage
- 1 cup beer
- ½ teaspoon freshly ground black pepper
- 1 tablespoon stone-ground mustard
- ½ teaspoon caraway seeds

Coat a large nonstick skillet with cooking spray; add sausage, and cook over medium-high heat 5 minutes or until sausage is browned, stirring often. Remove sausage from pan, and set aside.

Add onion, potato, and cabbage to pan. Cook 10 to 12 minutes or until lightly browned, stirring often. Return sausage to pan; add beer and remaining ingredients. Increase heat to high, and cook 3 to 5 minutes or until liquid is almost evaporated. Yield: 4 servings (serving size: 1¾ cups).

CALORIES 240 (11% from fat); FAT 2.9g (sat 0.9g, mono 0g, poly 0.1g); PROTEIN 18.8g; CARB 33.9g; FIBER 5.1g; CHOL 35mg; IRON 1.7mg; SODIUM 1,071mg; CALC 31mg
EXCHANGES: 2 Starch, 1 Vegetable, 1 Lean Meat

SERVE**with**

• • • • • • • • • • • • • • • • • • • •

If you have time to prepare another dish *to go with this menu, we suggest the Caramel Apple-Cranberry Crisp on page 348 in the Deadline Desserts chapter.*

Or prepare baked apples in the microwave. Melt 2 tablespoons light butter in a microwave-safe dish on HIGH. Stir in 2 tablespoons orange or apple juice. Slice 2 cooking apples into ½-inch-thick rings, and add to butter mixture, turning to coat. Cover and microwave at HIGH 4 to 5 minutes or until tender, rearranging apples after 2 minutes. Serve warm.

red curry pork and noodles
with fresh snow peas   serves 4 • total time 24 minutes

Add to the Asian-style theme of this meal and eat with chopsticks. It's always nice to slow down and take a little time for dinner.

SUPPER plan

1. Trim and slice pork.

2. Slice green onions; sqeeze lime juice.

3. Prepare Red Curry Pork and Noodles.

4. While noodles simmer, steam fresh snow peas in microwave for 1 minute, if desired, or serve raw.

Red Curry Pork and Noodles

prep: 7 minutes   cook: 17 minutes

- 1   (1-pound) pork tenderloin
- 1   teaspoon vegetable oil
- 2   teaspoons bottled minced garlic
- 1   teaspoon bottled red curry paste (such as Thai Kitchen)
- 1   (14-ounce) can fat-free, less-sodium chicken broth
- 1   (13.5-ounce) can light coconut milk
- 2   tablespoons fish sauce
- 1   (8-ounce) package dried Chinese egg noodles, broken into small pieces
- 2   teaspoons fresh lime juice (about ½ lime)
- 5   green onions, cut into thin strips

Trim fat from pork; cut pork in half lengthwise and then diagonally across grain into thin strips.

Heat oil in a large nonstick skillet over medium heat. Add garlic; sauté 1 minute. Stir in curry paste and pork; stir-fry 3 minutes or until pork is browned. Add broth, coconut milk, and fish sauce; bring to a boil. Stir in noodles; cover and simmer 7 minutes or until noodles are tender. Remove from heat; stir in lime juice and green onions. Yield: 4 servings (serving size: 1½ cups).

CALORIES 411 (26% from fat); FAT 11.8g (sat 5g, mono 3g, poly 1.3g); PROTEIN 32.2g; CARB 41.8g; FIBER 2.8g; CHOL 119mg; IRON 4.3mg; SODIUM 1,086mg; CALC 29mg
EXCHANGES: 3 Starch, 3 Lean Meat

QUICKtip

• • • • • • • • • • • • • • • • • • • •

Snow peas have bright green pods *that are thin, crisp, and entirely edible. They're the ultimate fast food—just pinch off the tips, and eat them raw. If you cook them, steam them for only about a minute so they'll stay crisp.*

tuscan chickpea stew
and olive bread   **serves 7 • total time 15 minutes**

This simple stew is typical of the rustic Italian dishes served in Tuscany. For a true Tuscan touch, place a slice of crusty bread in a shallow bowl, and spoon the stew over the bread.

SUPPER plan

1. Crush garlic; chop rosemary.

2. Sauté sausage.

3. Prepare Tuscan Chickpea Stew.

4. Serve stew over bread slices, if desired.

Tuscan Chickpea Stew

prep: 5 minutes   cook: 10 minutes

2	tablespoons olive oil, divided
3	garlic cloves, crushed
3	(2-ounce) links chicken, basil, and sun-dried tomato sausage, coarsely chopped (such as Gerhard's)
1	tablespoon chopped fresh rosemary
¼	teaspoon pepper
1	(14.5-ounce) can diced tomatoes with green pepper, celery, and onions, undrained
3	(15½-ounce) cans chickpeas (garbanzo beans), undrained
2	cups prepackaged fresh baby spinach
¼	cup preshredded fresh Parmesan cheese

Heat 1 tablespoon oil in a large saucepan over medium-high heat. Add garlic and next 3 ingredients. Sauté 4 minutes or until sausage is browned, stirring constantly. Add tomatoes and 2 cans chickpeas, scraping pan to loosen brown bits.

Drain remaining can chickpeas. Add chickpeas to pan. Bring to a boil; cover, reduce heat, and simmer 2 minutes. Uncover and stir in spinach; cook 2 minutes or until spinach wilts. Spoon into bowls over bread, if desired. Drizzle evenly with remaining 1 tablespoon olive oil. Sprinkle evenly with Parmesan cheese. Yield: 7 servings (serving size: 1 cup).

CALORIES 331 (25% from fat); FAT 9.2g (sat 1.9g, mono 3.6g, poly 1.3g); PROTEIN 14.4g; CARB 49.3g; FIBER 10.1g; CHOL 20mg; IRON 3.5mg; SODIUM 968mg; CALC 127mg
EXCHANGES: 3 Starch, 1 High-Fat Meat

NUTRITIONnote

• • • • • • • • • • • • • • • • • • •

Chicken sausage is a lower-fat alternative *to pork sausage with only 7 grams of fat per 2-ounce serving. The same amount of Italian pork sausage has about 14 grams of fat. The chicken sausage is made from skinless, boneless chicken plus herbs and spices. Most brands come fully cooked, so all you have to do is reheat.*

microwave green chile-chicken risotto

and sliced tomatoes   serves 4 · total time 33 minutes

Cooking risotto in the microwave is a real time-saver, compared to the traditional method of standing and stirring.

SUPPER plan

1. Chop onion; chop chicken; chop cilantro.

2. Prepare Microwave Green Chile-Chicken Risotto.

3. While risotto cooks, slice tomatoes, and drizzle with balsamic vinegar. Sprinkle with freshly ground black pepper, if desired.

Microwave Green Chile-Chicken Risotto

prep: 5 minutes   cook: 23 minutes
stand: 5 minutes

2	tablespoons butter
½	cup chopped red onion, divided
1	cup uncooked arborio rice
1	(14-ounce) can fat-free, less-sodium chicken broth
1½	cups water, divided
1	(4.5-ounce) can whole green chiles, drained
1½	cups chopped roasted chicken breast
1	cup (4 ounces) shredded reduced-fat sharp Cheddar cheese
2	tablespoons water
¼	teaspoon salt
¼	cup chopped fresh cilantro

Combine butter, onion, rice, broth, and ¾ cup water in a 2-quart microwave-safe dish. Cover with heavy-duty plastic wrap, and vent. Microwave at HIGH 15 minutes, rotating dish a half-turn after 7½ minutes. Stir in remaining ¾ cup water; cover and microwave at HIGH 5 minutes.

Stir green chiles and chicken into rice; cover and let stand 5 minutes. Uncover and stir in cheese, 2 tablespoons water, salt, and cilantro. Yield: 4 servings (serving size: about 1⅓ cups).

CALORIES 398 (29% from fat); FAT 12.8g (sat 7.7g, mono 1.8g, poly 0.3g); PROTEIN 24.7g; CARB 43.2g; FIBER 2.3g; CHOL 64mg; IRON 2.6mg; SODIUM 984mg; CALC 224mg
EXCHANGES: 3 Starch, 2 Lean Meat, 1 Fat

SIMPLEsubstitution

• • • • • • • • • • • • • • • • • • • •

Use any type of cooked chicken breast *in this risotto: deli-roasted chicken, rotisserie chicken (skin removed), refrigerated grilled chicken strips, or frozen diced cooked chicken. You'll need about ½ pound cooked chicken breast.*

Microwave Green Chile-Chicken Risotto

asian chicken and rice

with fresh fruit medley   serves 4 · total time 27 minutes

Pretend like you're dining at your favorite Asian-style bistro—serve the chicken and rice mixture wrapped in lettuce leaves.

SUPPER plan

1. Bring water to a boil.

2. Chop zucchini, cilantro, and cashews.

3. Prepare Asian Chicken and Rice.

4. While chicken mixture cooks, prepare fresh fruit medley using cubed pineapple, sliced strawberries, and sliced kiwifruit.

Asian Chicken and Rice

prep: 6 minutes   cook: 21 minutes

2	cups water
1¾	cups frozen chopped cooked chicken breast
1	cup converted rice, uncooked
1	cup frozen chopped onion
¼	cup hoisin sauce
2	tablespoons low-sodium soy sauce
2	tablespoons chopped fresh cilantro
2	teaspoons bottled minced garlic
¼	teaspoon crushed red pepper
2	small zucchini, coarsely chopped
3	tablespoons coarsely chopped unsalted cashews, divided
	Iceberg lettuce leaves (optional)

Bring water to a boil in a covered large deep skillet.

Add chicken and next 8 ingredients to pan, stirring well. Bring to a boil; cover, reduce heat, and simmer 21 minutes or until rice is just tender and liquid is nearly absorbed.

Sprinkle each serving with chopped cashews. Serve on lettuce leaves or wrap chicken mixture in lettuce leaves, if desired. Yield: 4 servings (serving size: 1 cup chicken-rice mixture and 2¼ teaspoons cashews).

CALORIES 360 (12% from fat); FAT 4.8g (sat 0.8g, mono 2.1g, poly 0.9g); PROTEIN 21.4g; CARB 57.1g; FIBER 3.5g; CHOL 33mg; IRON 3mg; SODIUM 724mg; CALC 66mg
EXCHANGES: 3 Starch, 2 Vegetable, 1 Lean Meat

NUTRITIONnote

• • • • • • • • • • • • • • • • • • •

Heart-healthy and full of nutrients, *nuts are back on the A-list. Research is showing that people who eat nuts are less likely to die from heart disease than those who don't eat nuts.*

Generally, one-fourth cup of any nut contains about 20 grams of fat. The fat in nuts, however, is highly monounsaturated—the same form found in abundance in heart-healthy olive oil and canola oil. Nuts are also rich in polyunsaturated fat, the other form known to lower cholesterol levels. Nuts contain relatively modest amounts of artery-clogging saturated fat.

Like mackerel, salmon, and other cold-water fish, nuts tend to be high in omega-3 fatty acids. This type of fat may help reduce the risk of strokes and heart attacks.

Nuts are full of disease-fighting nutrients such as vitamin E, folic acid, niacin, copper, magnesium, potassium, flavonoids, and isoflavones.

chicken portobello with romaine salad
and italian bread serves 4 • total time 27 minutes

The earthiness of the mushrooms and the rich flavor of the dark meat from chicken thighs combine for a very satisfying supper.

SUPPER plan

1. Thaw onions in microwave.

2. Chop mushrooms and thyme; cut chicken into pieces.

3. Prepare Chicken Portobello.

4. While chicken simmers:
 • Prepare salad using a package of salad greens (with romaine and radicchio) and low-fat olive oil vinaigrette.
 • Toast bread, if desired.

Chicken Portobello

prep: 6 minutes   cook: 21 minutes

 1 tablespoon olive oil, divided
 1 (6-ounce) package portobello mushroom caps, coarsely chopped
 1 (16-ounce) package frozen pearl onions, thawed
 ¾ teaspoon salt, divided
 ½ teaspoon black pepper, divided
 1 (16-ounce) package skinless, boneless chicken thighs, each cut into thirds
 1 tablespoon all-purpose flour
 Cooking spray
 ¼ cup port or other sweet red wine
 ½ cup fat-free, less-sodium chicken broth
 1 tablespoon chopped fresh thyme

Heat 1 teaspoon oil in a large nonstick skillet over medium-high heat. Add mushrooms and onions; cook 8 minutes or until lightly browned and liquid is absorbed, stirring frequently. Sprinkle with ¼ teaspoon each of salt and pepper. Transfer mushroom mixture to a plate.

Sprinkle chicken pieces with flour, ½ teaspoon salt, and ¼ teaspoon pepper. Toss lightly, and coat with cooking spray. Add remaining 2 teaspoons oil to pan; add chicken, and cook 3 minutes on each side or until browned on each side. Push chicken to one side of pan, and add wine; cook 2 minutes or until liquid evaporates, scraping pan to loosen browned bits. Return mushroom mixture to pan; add broth. Cover, reduce heat, and simmer 5 minutes or until chicken is done. Stir in thyme. Yield: 4 servings (serving size: 1½ cups).

CALORIES 287 (35% from fat); FAT 11.2g (sat 2.5g, mono 5.2g, poly 2.1g); PROTEIN 25g, CARB 20.7g; FIBER 1.4g; CHOL 74mg; IRON 2mg; SODIUM 600mg; CALC 52mg
EXCHANGES: 1 Starch, 1 Vegetable, 3 Lean Meat

SERVEwith

• • • • • • • • • • • • • • • • •

If you want to go beyond one dish *for this meal, the chicken would be wonderful served over white or brown rice, quick-cooking polenta, or frozen mashed potatoes.*

If you drink wine, we recommend a dry red wine to complement the rich flavors of the chicken thighs and the mushrooms.

pizza pasta salad with mixed green salad and focaccia wedges   serves 6 • total time 21 minutes

It tastes like pizza, but it's a pasta salad. Stir in other favorite pizza toppings such as green pepper strips, onions, or mushrooms.

SUPPER plan

1. Cook pasta.

2. While pasta cooks:
  • Drain artichokes and peppers.
  • Slice basil; halve tomatoes; cube cheese.
  • Process peppers.

3. Combine ingredients for pasta salad.

4. Prepare tossed green salad using prepackaged salad greens and low-fat vinaigrette.

5. Slice focaccia into wedges. Or you can use a Boboli (Italian bread shell) if focaccia isn't available.

Pizza Pasta Salad

prep: 10 minutes   cook: 9 minutes

You can make this salad the day before; cover and store in the refrigerator until serving time.

  8   ounces uncooked rotini pasta
  1   (14-ounce) can quartered artichoke hearts, drained
  4   ounces sliced turkey pepperoni
  6   ounces cubed part-skim mozzarella cheese
  2   cups grape tomatoes, halved
  ¼   cup sliced ripe olives
  1   (12-ounce) jar roasted red peppers, drained
  ⅓   cup reduced-fat Italian salad dressing
  ½   cup sliced fresh basil
  ¼   teaspoon freshly ground black pepper

Cook pasta according to package directions, omitting salt or fat; drain and rinse under cold water immediately. Place drained pasta in a large serving bowl.

Combine artichoke hearts and next 4 ingredients; set aside.

Place roasted peppers in blender, and process until almost smooth. Stir in salad dressing, basil, and black pepper.

Add pepper mixture to pasta. Add artichoke mixture to pasta, and toss well. Yield: 6 servings (serving size: 1⅔ cups).

CALORIES 323 (30% from fat); FAT 10.9g (sat 3.8g, mono 2.2g, poly 1.2g); PROTEIN 19.7g; CARB 36.5g; FIBER 3.8g; CHOL 40mg; IRON 2.6mg; SODIUM 1,074mg; CALC 218mg
EXCHANGES: 2 Starch, 1 Vegetable, 2 Medium-Fat Meat

NUTRITIONnote

• • • • • • • • • • • • • • • • • • • •

What's a pizza without cheese? *Compare the fat and calories in the following cheeses.*

CHEESE (1 OUNCE)	FAT (g)	CALORIES
Cheddar	9.4	114
Cheddar, 2% reduced-fat	6.1	91
Mozzarella, part-skim	4.9	79
Monterey Jack	8.6	106
Parmesan	7.3	111
Swiss	7.8	106
Swiss, reduced-fat	6.1	91

Pizza Pasta Salad

"The best time for me to exercise is right after work. But by the time I get home from the gym, change clothes, and cook supper, it's close to 9 p.m. before we eat."

slow cooker
SUPPERS

Speed up supper preparation with a slow cooker. This timesaving appliance turns a few minutes of morning prep time into a meal that's ready to serve when you get home.

Curried Lamb and Carrots, page 154

time is on your side

After a hectic day, there's nothing better than coming home in the evening to a hot meal, ready and waiting for you just to sit down and pick up your fork.

but how can you enjoy this luxury when you're the one who has to get that hot meal on the table? Put a slow cooker to work in your kitchen. No, not your spouse or your children—but an appliance that has been around for a while and is now making a comeback in busy households: a slow cooker.

here's how it works

In the morning you put in the recipe ingredients, ideally those that require very little preparation. Plug in the cooker, and let the ingredients simmer for hours on low heat. You're free to go about your day without ever checking on the cooker, and when you return to the kitchen in the evening, dinner is served!

flavor booster

Because the ingredients simmer together for a long time, you get the benefit of rich, intense flavor that you often can't get with quick cooking methods.

Slow cooking is an ideal method for lean cuts of meat because they simmer for a long time in liquid and become quite tender. Some less-tender cuts that are great for the slow cooker include:

- chuck or rump roast
- tip roast
- beef stew meat
- Boston butt roast
- lamb stew meat
- venison roast
- venison stew meat

slow moves

Here are some tips for making the most of your slow cooker.

Keep a lid on it

In most recipes, stirring isn't necessary. You lose heat (up to 20 minutes) each time you lift the lid, and that slows down the cooking process.

Location, location

Some vegetables, especially root vegetables, take a long time to cook in the slow cooker. Place these vegetables near the bottom and sides where they will be covered in liquid. Layer the ingredients in the order specified.

No attendance required

It's safe to leave the slow cooker unattended, even if you're not at home, because it operates on such a low wattage.

The chill factor

For some recipes you can assemble the ingredients in the insert (if you have a removable insert) the night before, and place it in the refrigerator overnight. The chilled insert can go directly into the heating base, but the cooking time might be a little longer if you start with a cold insert and cold ingredients.

Brown out

It's usually best to brown ground meat before putting it in the cooker with the rest of the ingredients. Browning usually enhances both the flavor and the appearance of the meat.

Cut the fat

Here are some ways to minimize the amount of fat in slow cooker dishes:

- Use lean cuts of meat.
- Trim excess fat from meat and poultry before placing in the cooker.
- Remove skin from poultry either before or after cooking.
- Skim visible fat from the cooking liquid before serving. One quick trick is to place a few ice cubes in the liquid. When the fat begins to cling to the cubes, remove and discard the cubes. There's enough heat in the cooker at this point, so the ice won't cool the mixture significantly.

safety first

There are a few safety issues to keep in mind when you're using a slow cooker.

1. The U.S. Department of Agriculture (USDA) recommends that, if possible, when you cook meat in a slow cooker that you cook on the HIGH heat setting for 1 hour and then reduce to the LOW heat setting.

2. Thaw frozen meats completely before cooking; don't cook meats from a frozen or partially frozen state. Thaw meats in the microwave before placing in the slow cooker, if necessary.

3. Don't cook whole poultry (such as a roasting hen) in the slow cooker because it can't heat up fast enough and some parts will be in the temperature range that is ideal for bacterial growth.

4. Use a quick-read thermometer to check the internal temperature of large pieces of meat. Here are the safe temperatures to reach:

Meat	Temperature
Beef	at least 155°
Pork	at least 160°
Lamb	at least 155°
Poultry	at least 170°

5. Don't reheat leftovers in the slow cooker. They can't heat up fast enough, so there's a chance of bacteria contamination.

Barley-Black Bean Burritos

barley-black bean burritos
and chocolate-banana smoothies

serves 6 • total time 6½ hours, 6 minutes

No need to stop by the local cantina when a warm Mexican meal waits for you at home.

SUPPER plan

1. Rinse and drain beans.

2. Place all ingredients for burritos in slow cooker.

3. While the barley mixture cooks, peel and slice 2 bananas, place on a baking sheet or plate, and freeze until firm.

4. After bean-barley mixture has cooked 6½ hours (or 3 hours and 15 minutes on high-heat setting):
   - Shred cheese.
   - Heat tortillas.
   - Assemble burritos.
   - Prepare Chocolate-Banana Smoothies.

Chocolate-Banana Smoothies

prep: 5 minutes

    2   cups frozen sliced banana (about 2 large)
    4   cups 1% low-fat chocolate milk
    1⅓   cups low-fat chocolate fudge ice cream

Combine all ingredients in a blender. Process until smooth, stopping once to scrape down sides. Serve immediately. Yield: 6 servings (serving size: about 1 cup).

CALORIES 225 (12% from fat); FAT 3g (sat 1.8g, mono 0.5g, poly 0.1g); PROTEIN 8.1g; CARB 43g; FIBER 2g; CHOL 16mg; IRON 0.6mg; SODIUM 143mg; CALC 259mg
EXCHANGES: 2 Starch, 1 Fruit

Barley-Black Bean Burritos

prep: 6 minutes   cook: 6½ hours OR
                               3 hours, 15 minutes

    1   cup uncooked fine barley
    1   cup frozen whole-kernel corn
    ⅓   cup water
    1   tablespoon fresh lime juice (½ lime)
    2   teaspoons Mexican seasoning
    2   teaspoons bottled minced garlic
    1   (15-ounce) can no-salt-added black beans, rinsed and drained
    1   (14-ounce) can vegetable broth (such as Swanson's)
    1   (10-ounce) can diced tomatoes with green chiles, undrained
    ¼   cup chopped fresh cilantro
    12   (6 to 7-inch) flour tortillas
    ¾   cup (3 ounces) shredded Monterey Jack cheese with jalapeño peppers
Shredded iceberg lettuce (optional)
Salsa (optional)

Place first 9 ingredients in a 3- to 4-quart electric slow cooker; stir well. Cover with lid; cook on low-heat setting 6½ hours or on high-heat setting 3 hours 15 minutes or until barley is tender and liquid is absorbed. Stir in cilantro.

Heat tortillas according to package directions. Spoon ½ cup barley mixture down center of each tortilla; sprinkle each with 1 tablespoon cheese. Serve on shredded lettuce and top with salsa, if desired. Yield: 6 servings (serving size: 2 burritos).

CALORIES 442 (20% from fat); FAT 9.6g (sat 3.9g, mono 0.1g, poly 0.2g); PROTEIN 16.3g; CARB 74.4g; FIBER 8.6g; CHOL 15mg; IRON 2.3mg; SODIUM 1,054mg; CALC 166mg
EXCHANGES: 4 Starch, 2 Vegetable, ½ High-Fat Meat, ½ Fat

vegetable-beef soup with grilled cheese sandwiches
and caramel apple slices   serves 8 • total time 7 hours, 11 minutes

Come home to a steaming bowl of vegetable beef soup and warm both body and soul on a wintry night.

SUPPER plan

1. Cut steak into cubes; coat in flour.

2. Brown beef cubes in skillet.

3. Place all ingredients in slow cooker.

4. While soup cooks, slice apples, and sprinkle with lemon juice to keep from browning. Serve apple slices with fat-free caramel dip.

5. Prepare grilled cheese sandwiches just before serving:
   • For each sandwich use 2 slices whole wheat bread and 2 ounces reduced-fat cheese.
   • Coat each side of sandwich with cooking spray.
   • Cook sandwiches in a nonstick skillet or griddle 2 to 3 minutes on each side or until golden and cheese melts.

FINDit

• • • • • • • • • • • • • • • • • •

Look for fat-free caramel dip *(such as T. Marzetti's) in the produce section along with other cartons of dip and refrigerated salad dressings. One tablespoon of this sweet, golden dip has 60 calories and 0 grams of fat. Serving fruit with caramel dip is a great way to encourage your kids to eat more fruit.*

Vegetable-Beef Soup

prep: 11 minutes   cook: 7 hours

¼   cup all-purpose flour
1½   pounds lean top round steak, cut into 1-inch cubes
Cooking spray
2   teaspoons spicy herb blend (such as Mrs. Dash)
2   (16-ounce) packages frozen gumbo vegetables mix
1   (10-ounce) package frozen chopped onion
2   (14.5-ounce) cans diced tomatoes with garlic, undrained
2   (14.5-ounce) cans fat-free beef broth
1   tablespoon bottled minced garlic
1   tablespoon low-sodium Worcestershire sauce
½   teaspoon salt
½   teaspoon pepper

Place flour in a large zip-top plastic bag; add steak cubes. Seal and shake to coat. Remove steak from bag; set aside.

Place a large nonstick skillet coated with cooking spray over medium-high heat until hot. Add steak, and cook until browned on all sides.

Place steak and remaining ingredients in a 4-quart electric slow cooker; stir well. Cover with lid; cook on high-heat setting 1 hour.

Reduce heat to low; cook 6 hours or until meat is done and vegetables are tender. Yield: 8 servings (serving size: about 1¾ cups).

CALORIES 256 (20% from fat); FAT 5.6g (sat 2g, mono 2.2g, poly 0.4g); PROTEIN 26g; CARB 26g; FIBER 6.2g; CHOL 49mg; IRON 3.4mg; SODIUM 542mg; CALC 66mg
EXCHANGES: 1 Starch, 2 Vegetable, 2 Lean Meat

Vegetable-Beef Soup

slow-cooker lasagna with tossed green salad
and french bread   serves 8 • total time 6 hours, 12 minutes

Cooking lasagna in a slow cooker is our favorite way to make this family favorite. Because the noodles and meat sauce simmer together for hours, you get a lasagna with deep, rich flavor. And it takes only 12 minutes to assemble.

SUPPER plan

1. Brown meat.

2. Layer lasagna ingredients in slow cooker.

3. After lasagna has cooked for 6 hours:
- Prepare salad with a bag of salad greens and low-fat olive oil vinaigrette.
- Slice bread.

Slow-Cooker Lasagna

prep: 12 minutes   cook: 6 hours

  1   pound ground round
  2   teaspoons bottled minced garlic
  1   teaspoon dried Italian seasoning
  1   (26-ounce) jar chunky garden-style pasta sauce
 ⅓   cup water
  8   uncooked lasagna noodles
Cooking spray
  1   (4½-ounce) jar sliced mushrooms, undrained
  1   (15-ounce) carton part-skim ricotta cheese
1½   cups (6 ounces) shredded part-skim mozzarella cheese, divided

Cook beef, garlic, and Italian seasoning in a large nonstick skillet over medium-high heat until beef is browned, stirring to crumble. Drain; set aside.

Combine pasta sauce and water in a small bowl; set aside.

Place 4 uncooked noodles in a 4-quart electric slow cooker coated with cooking spray, breaking noodles to fit. Layer with half each of beef mixture, pasta sauce mixture, and mushrooms. Spread ricotta cheese over mushrooms. Sprinkle with 1 cup mozzarella cheese. Layer with remaining noodles, meat, pasta sauce mixture, and mushrooms. Sprinkle with remaining ½ cup mozzarella cheese. Cover with lid; cook on high-heat setting 1 hour.

Reduce heat setting to low; cook 5 hours. Yield: 8 servings (serving size: 1 cup).

CALORIES 361 (30% from fat); FAT 12.2g (sat 6.5g, mono 3.7g, poly 0.6g); PROTEIN 28.6g; CARB 31.1g; FIBER 3.2g; CHOL 61mg; IRON 2.9mg; SODIUM 595mg; CALC 307mg
EXCHANGES: 2 Starch, 3 Medium-Fat Meat

SIMPLEsubstitutions

• • • • • • • • • • • • • • • • • •

Any flavor or brand of pasta sauce *will work in this lasagna—just make sure that you use a comparable jar size. A 26-ounce jar has about 3 cups of sauce.*

If you're trying to increase your fiber and complex carbohydrates intake, use whole wheat lasagna noodles.

slow-cooker fajitas
and mexi-corn   serves 6   •   total time 7 to 8 hours

Try this no-stress, no-mess way to make full-flavored fajitas. Instead of the usual two-step process of marinating the meat then grilling or pan-frying, the slow cooker cooks the meat and intensifies its flavor in one easy step.

SUPPER plan

1. Slice peppers; cut meat into pieces.

2. Place all ingredients in slow cooker.

3. After meat mixture has cooked 7 to 8 hours on low, (or 4 to 5 hours on high) heat canned or frozen mexi-corn in the microwave.

Slow-Cooker Fajitas

prep: 7 minutes   cook: 7 to 8 hours OR 4 to 5 hours

1½	pounds flank steak, cut into 6 pieces
1	cup frozen chopped onion
1	green bell pepper, sliced
1	jalapeño pepper, seeded and sliced
1	tablespoon bottled minced garlic
2	teaspoons salt-free Mexican seasoning
1	(10-ounce) can diced tomatoes and green chiles, drained
6	(8-inch) flour tortillas
6	tablespoons low-fat sour cream

Salsa (optional)

Place flank steak in bottom of a 5-quart electric slow cooker; top with chopped onion and next 5 ingredients.

Cover with lid; cook on high-heat setting 1 hour. Reduce heat setting to low; cook 6 to 7 hours or until meat is tender. Or cook on high-heat setting 4 to 5 hours. Remove meat, and shred with a fork. Return meat to slow cooker, and stir.

Serve shredded meat mixture with flour tortillas, low-fat sour cream, and, if desired, salsa. Yield: 6 servings (serving size: 1 tortilla, ⅔ cup meat mixture, and 1 tablespoon sour cream.)

CALORIES 379 (33% from fat); FAT 13.9g (sat 5.7g, mono 5g, poly 0.9g); PROTEIN 29.7g; CARB 32.6g; FIBER 1.2g; CHOL 66mg; IRON 3.7mg; SODIUM 534mg; CALC 145mg
EXCHANGES: 3 Starch, 3 Medium-Fat Meat

HOWto

• • • • • • • • • • • • • • • • • •

The heat in jalapeño peppers *is in the seeds and the membranes. If you like your foods hot, don't seed the peppers.*

While you're seeding the pepper, wear rubber gloves so your hands don't get burned.

❝My slow cooker is my new best friend.
I just love being able to dump the ingredients in before I leave for work, and when I get home, dinner is ready. All I have to do is spoon it out.❞

Susan Payne,
Executive Editor

curried lamb and carrots with pappadam
and seedless grapes   serves 6 · total time 8 hours, 11 minutes

Come home to the aroma of curry, cinnamon, and chutney; then let your taste buds travel to exotic, mysterious India where hot and sweet is always a desirable flavor combination.

SUPPER plan

1. Cut carrots.

2. Cut lamb into cubes; coat in flour. Brown lamb in skillet.

3. Place all ingredients in slow cooker.

4. After lamb mixture has cooked about 8 hours, prepare couscous according to package directions.

5. Heat pappadam in microwave at HIGH for 30 seconds per pappadam or just until crisp.

Curried Lamb and Carrots

prep: 6 minutes   cook: 8 hours, 5 minutes

Serve the lamb with additional chutney, if desired.

  6   carrots, cut into 1-inch pieces (about 7 cups)
  1   (10-ounce) package frozen chopped onion
  2   tablespoons all-purpose flour
1½   pounds lean boneless lamb, cut into 1-inch cubes
Cooking spray
 ½   cup apple cider
 ¼   cup mango chutney
  1   tablespoon bottled minced garlic
  1   tablespoon Thai seasoning (such as McCormick)
  2   teaspoons curry powder
 ¾   teaspoon salt
 ¼   teaspoon freshly ground black pepper
  1   (10-ounce) package couscous

Place carrot and onion in a 4-quart electric slow cooker.

Place flour in a zip-top plastic bag; add lamb. Seal and shake to coat. Heat a large nonstick skillet over medium-high heat until hot. Coat with cooking spray; add lamb, and cook, stirring often, 5 minutes or until lightly browned. Place lamb, cider, and next 6 ingredients in slow cooker. Cover with lid; cook on high-heat setting 1 hour.

Reduce heat setting to low; cook 7 hours. Remove lid, and stir mixture.

Prepare couscous according to package directions, omitting salt and fat. Yield: 6 servings (serving size: ¾ cup lamb mixture and ¾ cup couscous).

CALORIES 447 (18% from fat); FAT 8.8g (sat 3.2g, mono 3.4g, poly 1g); PROTEIN 30g; CARB 60.2g; FIBER 5.7g; CHOL 73mg; IRON 3.6mg; SODIUM 773mg; CALC 60mg
EXCHANGES: 3 Starch, 2 Vegetable, 2 Medium-Fat Meat

FOODfacts

• • • • • • • • • • • • • • • • • • •

Thai seasoning is a blend *of a variety of spices including coriander, nutmeg, cinnamon, red pepper, and black pepper. Although these spices are used a lot in Thai cooking, these same flavors are predominant in the cuisines of India, Turkey, and Morocco.*

Pappadam *is an Indian wafer-thin bread that resembles a tortilla but is made with lentil flour. It's often fried, but can be grilled or heated in the microwave. Pappadam is available in the ethnic foods section of some supermarkets and in Indian markets. Pita bread is a good substitute.*

Curried Lamb and Carrots

BBQ Pork Sandwiches with
Tangy Apple Coleslaw

bbq pork sandwiches with tangy apple coleslaw
and watermelon wedges   serves 8 • total time 8 hours, 7 minutes

When the heat index soars, here's a no-sweat way to barbecue. The pork simmers in the slow cooker all day, so you get full-flavored meat without having to stand over the grill.

SUPPER plan

1. Chop onion.

2. Place pork in slow cooker.

3. While pork mixture cooks, prepare Tangy Apple Coleslaw; cover and chill.

4. Cut watermelon into wedges just before serving.

BBQ Pork Sandwiches

prep: 7 minutes   cook: 8 hours

¼	cup packed brown sugar, divided
1	cup chopped onion (about 1 large)
1½	tablespoons Mexican seasoning
3	tablespoons Worcestershire sauce
3	tablespoons cider vinegar
3	tablespoons molasses
1	teaspoon dry mustard
1	(6-ounce) can tomato paste
¾	teaspoon pepper
¼	teaspoon salt
1	(2-pound) boneless pork loin roast
8	(2¼-ounce) whole wheat hamburger buns

Combine 3 tablespoons brown sugar, onion, and next 6 ingredients in a 3½-quart electric slow cooker; stir well. Combine remaining tablespoon brown sugar, pepper, and salt; rub pork roast with sugar mixture. Cut pork roast into 4 large pieces; add to slow cooker, turning to coat with sauce. Cover with lid; cook on high-heat setting 1 hour.

Reduce heat setting to low; cook 7 hours or until pork roast is tender. Remove pork roast from slow cooker, reserving sauce in cooker.

Shred pork roast with 2 forks. Return shredded pork to slow cooker, and stir well to coat with sauce. Spoon ⅔ cup pork mixture on bottom half of each bun, using a slotted spoon. Cover with tops of buns. Yield: 8 servings (serving size: 1 bun and about ⅔ cup pork mixture).

CALORIES 398 (19% from fat); FAT 8.4g (sat 2.2g, mono 2.9g, poly 0.8g); PROTEIN 33.3g; CARB 49.7g; FIBER 4.7g; CHOL 67mg; IRON 4.4mg; SODIUM 726mg; CALC 109mg
EXCHANGES: 3 Starch, 3 Lean Meat

Tangy Apple Coleslaw

prep: 7 minutes   chill: 4 hours

1	(12-ounce) package broccoli coleslaw
1⅔	cups chopped apple (about 1 large)
¼	cup light mayonnaise
3	tablespoons brown sugar
2	teaspoons chopped fresh rosemary
1	teaspoon cider vinegar
¾	teaspoon salt

Combine all ingredients in a large bowl, and toss well. Cover and chill. Yield: 8 servings (serving size: ⅓ cup).

CALORIES 79 (28% from fat); FAT 2.5g (sat 0.4g, mono 0g, poly 0g); PROTEIN 1.3g; CARB 13.1g; FIBER 2.4g; CHOL 3mg; IRON 0.6mg; SODIUM 297mg; CALC 10mg
EXCHANGES: ½ Fruit, 1 Vegetable, ½ Fat

chicken-white bean soup with low-fat tortilla chips
and salsa serves 6 · total time 8 hours, 12 minutes

When you need a change from chili, try this satisfying chicken and bean soup. You're still getting hot and spicy flavor, but with chicken instead of beef and white beans instead of red.

SUPPER plan

1. Rinse and drain beans; drain chiles.

2. Chop onion, and sauté.

3. Mash beans.

4. Place all ingredients, except cheese, in slow cooker.

5. While soup cooks, shred cheese.

Chicken-White Bean Soup

prep: 12 minutes   cook: 8 hours

Olive oil-flavored cooking spray
- 1 large onion, chopped (about 2 cups)
- 2 (19-ounce) cans cannellini beans, rinsed, drained, and divided
- 4 cups fat-free, less-sodium chicken broth
- 1 cup frozen shoepeg corn
- 1 tablespoon bottled minced garlic
- 1½ teaspoons ground cumin
- ½ teaspoon ground oregano
- ¼ teaspoon black pepper
- ¼ teaspoon salt
- 1 (20-ounce) bag frozen chopped cooked chicken
- 2 (4.5-ounce) cans chopped green chiles, drained
- ¾ cup (3 ounces) shredded reduced-fat Monterey Jack cheese

Coat a large nonstick skillet with cooking spray; place over medium-high heat until hot. Add onion, and sauté 4 minutes or until onion is tender.

Place 1 can of beans in a small bowl; mash with a fork. Place mashed beans, remaining can of beans, onion, broth, and next 8 ingredients in a 3-quart electric slow cooker; stir well. Cover with lid; cook on high-heat setting 1 hour.

Reduce to low-heat setting; cook 7 hours.

Ladle soup into bowls; sprinkle each serving with 2 tablespoons cheese. Yield: 6 servings (serving size: 2 cups).

CALORIES 310 (13% from fat); FAT 4.6g (sat 1.6g, mono 0.1g, poly 0.6g); PROTEIN 35.9g; CARB 31.8g; FIBER 7.6g; CHOL 58mg; IRON 2.6mg; SODIUM 1,067mg; CALC 198mg
EXCHANGES: 2 Starch, 4 Very Lean Meat

ADDons

• • • • • • • • • • • • • • • • • •

Top this spicy soup with *your ingredient of choice. Here are some of our suggestions:*
- *tomatillo salsa*
- *tomato salsa*
- *low-fat sour cream*
- *plain fat-free yogurt*
- *chopped green onions*
- *sliced jalapeño peppers*
- *crumbled low-fat tortilla chips*
- *shredded reduced-fat Monterey Jack cheese with jalapeño peppers*
- *shredded reduced-fat Cheddar cheese*

saucy italian-style chicken thighs
with balsamic mixed greens and crusty peasant-style bread   serves 6 · total time 5 to 6 hours, 3 minutes

Because the simple tomato sauce simmers for hours along with the chicken thighs, it develops an intensely rich flavor. You'll want to serve the dish with bread, pasta, or potatoes so you can sop up the sauce.

SUPPER plan

1. Chop onion.

2. Place all ingredients in slow cooker.

3. After chicken has cooked 5 to 6 hours, prepare salad with 1 package of mixed greens (including radicchio) and ¼ cup reduced-fat balsamic vinaigrette.

Saucy Italian-Style Chicken Thighs

prep: 3 minutes   cook: 5 hours

Look for skinned chicken thighs at the super-market. Or buy thighs with skins, and remove them yourself. When you remove the skins, you remove most of the fat.

12   chicken thighs (about 3 pounds), skinned
 1   (14.5-ounce) can Italian-style diced tomatoes
 1   (6-ounce) can tomato paste
 ½   cup chopped onion
 1   tablespoon bottled minced garlic
 1   teaspoon dried Italian seasoning
 ¼   teaspoon salt
 ¼   teaspoon pepper

Place chicken in a 4-quart electric slow cooker. Combine tomatoes and remaining ingredients; stir well. Pour sauce over chicken. Cover with lid, and cook on high-heat setting 1 hour.

Reduce heat setting to low; cook 4 to 5 hours or until chicken is tender. Yield: 6 servings (serving size: 2 thighs and about ¾ cup sauce).

CALORIES 202 (24% from fat); FAT 5.4g (sat 1.4g, mono 1.6g, poly 1.4g); PROTEIN 27.8g; CARB 9.6g; FIBER 2.1g; CHOL 109mg; IRON 2.3mg; SODIUM 526mg; CALC 35mg
EXCHANGES: 2 Vegetable, 3 Lean Meat

SERVEwith

● ● ● ● ● ● ● ● ● ● ● ● ● ● ● ● ● ●

These saucy chicken thighs *are also wonderful served over hot cooked spinach fettuccine or mashed potatoes.*

For quick mashed potatoes, start with a package of refrigerated mashed potatoes (such as Simply Potatoes), and cook them in the microwave according to package directions. All you need to add is a bit of light butter, and you'll have creamy, low-fat mashed potatoes in about 4 minutes.

" *Since it's just the two of us—cooking and cleaning up is almost more trouble than it's worth.* **"**

table
for **TWO**

Two's company, so there's no need to cut out special meals when you're serving two.

Whether it's a romantic dinner with your sweetie, a simple supper with a college buddy,

a weeknight meal with your child, or an

indulgent meal for yourself, these no-fuss

menus are just the right size.

Peppered Beef Tenderloin, page 176

amaretto french toast and
strawberry-banana smoothies serves 2 · total time 14 minutes

For nights when breakfast for supper sounds good, this sweet French toast meal is just what you need.

SUPPER plan

1. Prepare Amaretto French Toast.

2. Place toast in oven to keep warm.

3. Make Strawberry-Banana Smoothie.

Amaretto French Toast

prep: 3 minutes   cook: 9 minutes

Place French toast in a preheated 200° oven to keep warm while the second batch cooks or until ready to serve.

     2   large egg whites
     1   large egg
    ½   cup fat-free amaretto-flavored coffee creamer
          (such as International Delight)
    ½   teaspoon ground cinnamon
     4   slices sweet buttermilk bread (such as
          Pepperidge Farm Farmhouse)
Cooking spray
    ¼   cup reduced-calorie maple syrup

   Combine first 4 ingredients with a wire whisk in a shallow dish.
   Dredge 2 slices of bread in egg mixture, letting slices soak 15 to 20 seconds on each side.
   Heat a large nonstick skillet coated with cooking spray over medium heat. Place dredged bread slices in pan; cook 2 to 3 minutes on each side until lightly browned. Repeat with remaining bread slices. Serve with maple syrup. Yield: 2 servings (serving size: 2 slices French toast and 2 tablespoons syrup).

CALORIES 446 (9% from fat); FAT 4.5g (sat 0.8g, mono 1g, poly 0.3g); PROTEIN 14.7g; CARB 86g; FIBER 2.3g; CHOL 106mg; IRON 2.6mg; SODIUM 616mg; CALC 99mg
EXCHANGES: 5½ Starch, ½ Fat

Strawberry-Banana Smoothies

prep: 2 minutes

When you need breakfast in a hurry, this smoothie can be a meal in itself.

     1   large ripe banana, cut in half
     1   cup frozen unsweetened whole strawberries
    ¾   cup orange juice or pineapple juice
     1   (8-ounce) carton vanilla low-fat yogurt

   Place all ingredients in a blender; process 1 minute or until smooth. Serve immediately. Yield: 2 servings (serving size: 1½ cups).

CALORIES 227 (8% from fat); FAT 2.1g (sat 1.1g, mono 0.5g, poly 0.2g); PROTEIN 7.4g; CARB 47.8g; FIBER 3.4g; CHOL 6mg; IRON 1mg; SODIUM 78mg; CALC 220mg
EXCHANGES: 3 Fruit, ½ Skim Milk

puffy ham and swiss omelet with toasted english muffins
and fresh fruit cup serves 2 • total time 22 minutes

Share a hearty omelet for a late-night dinner after the show. You can make this one with ingredients you probably have on hand.

SUPPER plan

1. Prepare fruit cup with fresh strawberries, green grapes, and fresh or canned pineapple chunks.

2. Chop onion and ham for omelet.

3. Prepare omelet.

4. While omelet cooks, toast muffins.

Puffy Ham and Swiss Omelet

prep: 4 minutes   cook: 14 minutes

You can cut the prep time if you buy a package of diced ham.

Cooking spray
- ¼ cup chopped onion
- ½ cup chopped lean ham
- 2 large egg whites
- ¾ cup egg substitute
- 2 tablespoons water
- ¼ teaspoon salt
- ¼ teaspoon pepper
- ⅓ cup (1.3 ounces) shredded reduced-fat Swiss cheese

Place a large nonstick skillet coated with cooking spray over medium-high heat until hot. Add onion; sauté 5 minutes or until tender. Stir in ham, and sauté 1 minute. Remove from pan; keep warm.

Beat egg whites with a mixer at high speed until stiff peaks form (do not overbeat). Combine egg substitute and next 3 ingredients in a large bowl. Fold beaten egg white into egg substitute mixture.

Wipe pan with paper towels. Coat pan with cooking spray; place over medium heat until hot. Spread egg mixture in pan. Cover; reduce heat to low. Cook 5 minutes or until puffy. Increase heat to medium; cook 3 minutes or until golden on bottom. Transfer omelet to a serving plate. Spoon ham mixture over half of omelet; sprinkle with cheese. Fold omelet in half. Serve immediately. Yield: 2 servings (serving size: ½ of omelet).

CALORIES 173 (30% from fat); FAT 5.7g (sat 3.2g, mono 0.8g, poly 0.2g); PROTEIN 24.6g; CARB 4.7g; FIBER 0.4g; CHOL 29mg; IRON 2.3mg; SODIUM 1042mg; CALC 205mg
EXCHANGES: 3 Lean Meat

SIMPLEsubstitutions

• • • • • • • • • • • • • • • • • •

If you don't have ham *on hand, use chopped turkey. Or make it a meat-free omelet, and stir in ½ cup chopped mushrooms or bell pepper. Instead of Swiss cheese, you can use reduced-fat Cheddar, American, or Monterey Jack.*

black bean soup with pepper cheese toasts

and frozen lime pops   serves 2 · total time 14 minutes

This south-of-the-border soup is proof that soups don't have to simmer for a long time to have sensational flavor.

SUPPER plan

1. Chop ham, onion, bell pepper, and cilantro; rinse and drain beans.

2. Cook soup.

3. While soup simmers, prepare Pepper Cheese Toasts.

Ladle soup into individual bowls; dollop each serving evenly with sour cream, and sprinkle with cilantro. Yield: 2 servings (serving size: 1¼ cups).

CALORIES 258 (12% from fat); FAT 3.3g (sat 1.4g, mono 0.7g, poly 0.5g); PROTEIN 21.1g; CARB 38.2g; FIBER 12.1g; CHOL 21mg; IRON 3.8mg; SODIUM 987mg; CALC 74mg
EXCHANGES: 2 Starch, 1 Vegetable, 2 Very Lean Meat

Black Bean Soup

prep: 4 minutes   cook: 10 minutes

For a shortcut, you can use frozen chopped onion and chopped pepper instead of fresh.

 ¼ cup chopped onion
 ¼ cup chopped green bell pepper
 ½ cup chopped lower-sodium ham
 1 (15-ounce) can no-salt-added black beans, rinsed and drained
 1 (14-ounce) can fat-free, less-sodium chicken broth
1½ tablespoons basil, garlic, and oregano-flavored tomato paste (such as Hunt's)
 1 teaspoon ground cumin
 2 tablespoons reduced-fat sour cream
 1 tablespoon chopped fresh cilantro

Place a large nonstick saucepan over medium-high heat until hot. Add onion and pepper; sauté 3 minutes or until vegetables are crisp-tender.

Add chopped ham, beans, and chicken broth to onion mixture. Stir in tomato paste and cumin; bring soup to a boil, reduce heat, and simmer 5 to 6 minutes or until soup is slightly thickened.

Pepper Cheese Toasts

prep: 1 minute   cook: 5 minutes

A toaster oven is ideal for toasting a small amount of bread.

 4 (½-inch-thick) slices French bread baguette
 ¼ cup shredded Monterey Jack cheese with jalapeño peppers

Preheat oven to 350°.

Sprinkle 1 tablespoon cheese on each bread slice. Place bread on a baking sheet. Bake at 350° for 5 minutes or until cheese melts. Yield: 2 servings (serving size: 2 slices).

CALORIES 111 (40% from fat); FAT 4.9g (sat 2.8g, mono 1.5g, poly 0.3g); PROTEIN 5.3g; CARB 11.1g; FIBER 0.6g; CHOL 13mg; IRON 0.6mg; SODIUM 205mg; CALC 121mg
EXCHANGES: 1 Starch, ½ High-Fat Meat

VEGETARIANoption

• • • • • • • • • • • • • • • • • •

To make this a meat-free soup, *leave out the ham, and add an additional ½ cup chopped bell pepper; use a 14-ounce can of vegetable broth instead of the chicken broth.*

Black Bean Soup with
Pepper Cheese Toasts (right)

quick vegetable fried rice
and cucumber salad   serves 2 · total time 18 minutes

This fried rice is a simple, meat-free supper, but you can vary it by stirring in leftover diced chicken, pork, or cooked shrimp.

SUPPER plan

1. Prepare Cucumber Salad; chill.

2. Slice celery, halve snow peas, and drain water chestnuts.

3. Prepare Quick Vegetable Fried Rice.

Quick Vegetable Fried Rice

prep: 6 minutes   cook: 7 minutes

Fried rice is best when you make it with chilled or leftover rice because chilled rice maintains its texture during stir-frying. If you don't have any rice on hand, cook 1 bag of boil-in-bag brown rice while you prepare the salad and chop the vegetables. Spread the rice on a jelly roll pan, and chill.

　2　teaspoons dark sesame oil, divided
⅓　cup diagonally sliced celery
½　cup diagonally halved trimmed snow peas
¾　cup frozen green peas
¼　cup drained canned sliced water chestnuts
　1　large egg, beaten
　2　cups cooked instant brown rice, chilled
　3　tablespoons low-sodium soy sauce
¼　teaspoon freshly ground black pepper

Heat 1 teaspoon oil in a large nonstick skillet over medium-high heat. Add celery and snow peas to pan; sauté 3 minutes. Add green peas and water chestnuts; sauté 1 minute.

Push vegetables to one side of pan. Pour egg into other side of pan. Cook, stirring often, until done.

Add cooked rice, tossing well. Stir in remaining sesame oil, soy sauce, and pepper. Cook 1 minute or until rice mixture is thoroughly heated, tossing occasionally. Serve immediately. Yield: 2 servings (serving size: about 1¾ cups).

CALORIES 369 (23% from fat); FAT 9.3g (sat 1.9g, mono 3.5g, poly 3g); PROTEIN 13g; CARB 58.7g; FIBER 7.5g; CHOL 106mg; IRON 3.1mg; SODIUM 919mg; CALC 64mg
EXCHANGES: 3 Starch, 2 Vegetable, 1½ Fat

Cucumber Salad

prep: 5 minutes

　3　tablespoons rice wine vinegar
　2　teaspoons sugar
¼　teaspoon salt
⅛　teaspoon ground red pepper
　2　pickling cucumbers, peeled and thinly sliced
　2　tablespoons chopped green onions

Combine first 4 ingredients in a small bowl. Add cucumber and onions; toss to coat. Cover and chill. Yield: 2 servings (serving size: ¾ cup).

CALORIES 30 (5% from fat); FAT 0.2g (sat 0g, mono 0g, poly 0.1g); PROTEIN 0.5g; CARB 7g; FIBER 0.9g; CHOL 0mg; IRON 0.2mg; SODIUM 297mg; CALC 13mg
EXCHANGE: 1 Vegetable

FINDit

● ● ● ● ● ● ● ● ● ● ● ● ● ● ● ● ● ●

Pickling cucumbers, *also called salad cucumbers, are small, unwaxed cucumbers with bumpy skins. For more information and a photograph, turn to page 27.*

mustard-dill salmon
and creamy lima beans   serves 2 • total time 20 minutes

For an out-of-the-ordinary vegetable pairing for salmon, try the savory lima bean purée. It got a "WOW!" response in our test kitchens.

SUPPER plan

1. Thaw limas in microwave; mince onion and garlic; chop dill.

2. Broil salmon.

3. While salmon broils:
 • Cook beans in microwave.
 • Prepare sauce for salmon.

4. Prepare Creamy Lima Beans.

Mustard-Dill Salmon

prep: 4 minutes   cook: 11 minutes

Cooking spray
 2 (6-ounce) skinless salmon fillets
 ¼ teaspoon salt
 ¼ teaspoon freshly ground black pepper
 1 tablespoon sweet hot mustard
 1 tablespoon finely minced onion
 1 garlic clove, minced
 2 tablespoons plain fat-free yogurt
 1 teaspoon sweet hot mustard
 1½ teaspoons chopped fresh dill

Preheat broiler.

Place salmon on a broiler pan coated with cooking spray; sprinkle with salt and pepper. Broil 7 minutes. Remove from oven, and spread 1½ teaspoons mustard over each fillet. Broil 3 minutes or until salmon flakes easily when tested with a fork.

Place a small nonstick skillet coated with cooking spray over medium-high heat. Add onion and garlic, and sauté 1 to 2 minutes or until tender. Transfer onion mixture to a small bowl; stir in yogurt, mustard, and dill. Spoon yogurt mixture over salmon. Yield: 2 servings (serving size: 1 salmon fillet and about 2 table-spoons sauce).

CALORIES 225 (30% from fat); FAT 7.4g (sat 1.1g, mono 2.1g, poly 3.1g); PROTEIN 34.8g; CARB 3.1g; FIBER 0.3g; CHOL 89mg; IRON 1.5mg; SODIUM 437mg; CALC 48mg
EXCHANGES: 4 Lean Meat

Creamy Lima Beans

prep: 5 minutes   cook: 6 minutes

Fordhook lima beans give you a slightly creamier result, but regular limas will work fine, too.

 1 (10-ounce) package frozen fordhook lima beans, thawed
 ¼ cup 2% reduced-fat milk
 1½ tablespoons prepared horseradish
 2 tablespoons light butter
 ¼ teaspoon salt
 ¼ teaspoon freshly ground black pepper

Cook lima beans with 2 tablespoons water in a 2-quart microwave-safe dish at HIGH 6 minutes or until just tender. (Do not cook according to package directions.) Drain well.

Combine beans and remaining ingredients in food processor; process 1 to 2 minutes, stopping 3 times to scrape down sides of bowl, or until mixture is smooth. Serve immediately. Yield: 2 servings (serving size: ¾ cup).

CALORIES 221 (29% from fat); FAT 7.2g (sat 4.5g, mono 0.2g, poly 0.3g); PROTEIN 11.3g; CARB 31g; FIBER 8.2g; CHOL 22mg; IRON 2.3mg; SODIUM 496mg; CALC 79mg
EXCHANGES: 1 Starch, 1 Low-Fat Milk, ½ Fat

Maple-Glazed Salmon with Nutmeg Zucchini

maple-glazed salmon with nutmeg zucchini
and french rolls   serves 2 • total time 14 minutes

Show that special someone how much you care with this menu featuring a heart-healthy fish and a cancer-fighting vegetable.

SUPPER plan

1. Grate zucchini.

2. Prepare Maple-Glazed Salmon.

3. While salmon broils, sauté zucchini.

Maple-Glazed Salmon

prep: 1 minute   cook: 10 minutes

You can also cook salmon on the grill in the same amount of time.

1	tablespoon maple syrup
1	tablespoon hoisin sauce
1	teaspoon Dijon mustard
¼	teaspoon coarsely ground black pepper
2	(6-ounce) salmon fillets (about 1 inch thick)

Cooking spray

Preheat broiler.

Combine first 4 ingredients in a small bowl; stir with a whisk.

Place salmon, skin side down, on a broiler pan coated with cooking spray. Brush with maple mixture. Broil 10 to 12 minutes or until fish flakes easily when tested with a fork, brushing with maple mixture after 5 minutes and again after 10 minutes. Yield: 2 servings (serving size: 1 fillet).

CALORIES 320 (38% from fat); FAT 13.6g (sat 3.2g, mono 5.8g, poly 3.4g); PROTEIN 36.6g; CARB 10.7g; FIBER 0.3g; CHOL 87mg; IRON 0.9mg; SODIUM 273mg; CALC 34mg
EXCHANGES: ½ Starch, 5 Lean Meat

Nutmeg Zucchini

prep: 3 minutes   cook: 4 minutes

We used a food processor to shred the zucchini. A box grater or other hand-held grater works fine, too.

1	tablespoon light butter
3	cups shredded zucchini (about 3)
¼	teaspoon salt
¼	teaspoon coarsely ground black pepper
⅛	teaspoon ground nutmeg

Melt butter in a large nonstick skillet over medium-high heat. Add zucchini, and sauté 4 to 5 minutes or until crisp-tender. Stir in salt, pepper, and nutmeg. Yield: 2 servings (serving size: ¾ cup).

CALORIES 61 (52% from fat); FAT 3.5g (sat 2.2g, mono 0g, poly 0.2g); PROTEIN 2.6g; CARB 7.7g; FIBER 3.4g; CHOL 10mg; IRON 0.8mg; SODIUM 332mg; CALC 36mg
EXCHANGES: 1 Vegetable, 1 Fat

QUICKtip

• •

Instead of running by the fish market
on your way home, you can keep a package of individually wrapped 6-ounce salmon fillets in your freezer to pull out whenever you need them. Thaw the fillets in the refrigerator overnight or in the microwave according to the package directions. Look for the packages of salmon fillets in the freezer section of the supermarket or warehouse grocery.

thai orange-basil mussels with sesame bread
and fresh pineapple slices   serves 2 · total time 20 minutes

Stop by the seafood market on your way home to buy fresh mussels. Then you'll need only 20 minutes to get dinner on the table.

SUPPER plan

1. Prepare butter for Sesame Bread.
2. Grate ginger; slice onions and basil; scrub and debeard mussels.
3. Prepare Thai Orange-Basil Mussels.
4. While mussels cook, broil bread.

Thai Orange-Basil Mussels

prep: 6 minutes   cook: 11 minutes

  1 (14-ounce) can light coconut milk
  1 (8-ounce) bottle clam juice
 ¼ cup orange juice
  1 tablespoon grated peeled fresh ginger
  1 teaspoon curry powder
  2 teaspoons sugar
 ½ teaspoon salt
  2 dozen mussels, scrubbed and debearded
 ¾ cup thinly sliced green onions
  3 tablespoons thinly sliced fresh basil leaves

Combine first 7 ingredients in a 4-quart Dutch oven. Bring to a boil; reduce heat, and simmer, uncovered, 5 minutes.

Add mussels to coconut broth mixture. Bring to a boil; cover and cook 2 minutes or until shells open. Discard unopened shells. Place mussels in 2 large serving bowls. Stir green onions and basil into broth; pour broth over mussels. Yield: 2 servings (serving size: 12 mussels and 1¼ cups broth).

CALORIES 235 (47% from fat); FAT 12.3g (sat 7.3g, mono 0.4g, poly 0.5g); PROTEIN 9.1g; CARB 21.2g; FIBER 2.1g; CHOL 23mg; IRON 4.8mg; SODIUM 1,097mg; CALC 48mg
EXCHANGES: 1 Starch, ½ Fruit, 1 Very Lean Meat, 2 Fat

Sesame Bread

prep: 3 minutes   cook: 4 minutes

The bread is great for soaking up the rich, flavorful broth.

  1 tablespoon light butter, softened
  1 teaspoon sesame seeds
 ⅛ teaspoon pepper
  4 (1-ounce) slices French bread

Preheat broiler.

Combine butter, sesame seeds, and pepper in a small bowl. Spread mixture evenly onto each of 4 bread slices. Place bread on a baking sheet, and broil 4 to 5 minutes or until bread is lightly browned and butter mixture is bubbly. Yield: 2 servings (serving size: 2 slices).

CALORIES 191 (22% from fat); FAT 4.7g (sat 2.4g, mono 0.7g, poly 0.4g); PROTEIN 5.5g; CARB 29.5g; FIBER 1.7g; CHOL 10mg; IRON 3.6mg; SODIUM 380mg; CALC 43mg
EXCHANGES: 2 Starch, 1 Fat

HOWto

· ·

When purchasing mussels, *look for those with tightly closed shells or those that close when tapped; discard any that haven't opened after cooking.*
To clean, *scrub mussels with a stiff brush, and rinse them well with running water. Some mussels will need to be debearded, although some don't have beards when they're harvested. The "beard" is the strands of tissue attached to the shell.*
To debeard, *simply pull off the strands. Mussels spoil quickly after debearding, so prepare them immediately.*

Thai Orange-Basil Mussels
with Sesame Bread

Shrimp and Snow Pea Stir-Fry

shrimp and snow pea stir-fry with basmati rice
and frozen lemon yogurt   serves 2 • total time 20 minutes

Here's a no-stress, no-mess menu featuring a simple shrimp stir-fry.

SUPPER plan

1. Cook basmati rice according to package directions. Use 1 cup uncooked rice to get 3 cups cooked.

2. Mince garlic; slice onions; chop parsley; squeeze lemon juice.

3. Sauté shrimp and peas.

Shrimp and Snow Pea Stir-Fry

prep: 5 minutes   cook: 6 minutes

Have everything chopped, sliced, and minced, but don't begin cooking the stir-fry until the rice is just about ready.

  1   teaspoon olive oil
  ¾   pound peeled and deveined large shrimp
  1   small garlic clove, minced
  1   cup trimmed snow peas
  ¼   cup chopped fresh flat-leaf parsley
  2   green onions, thinly sliced
  2   teaspoons fresh lemon juice (½ small lemon)
  ⅛   teaspoon salt
  ⅛   teaspoon coarsely ground black pepper

    Heat oil in a large nonstick skillet over medium-high heat. Add shrimp and garlic, and sauté 5 minutes or until done. Add snow peas and remaining ingredients; sauté 30 seconds. Yield: 2 servings (serving size: 1½ cups).

CALORIES 173 (19% from fat); FAT 3.7g (sat 0.7g, mono 1.9g, poly 0.8g); PROTEIN 27.2g; CARB 5.9g; FIBER 2.2g; CHOL 242mg; IRON 5mg; SODIUM 430mg; CALC 76mg
EXCHANGES: 1 Vegetable, 4 Very Lean Meat

HOWto

• • • • • • • • • • • • • • • • • • • •

Ask for peeled *and deveined shrimp at the seafood counter. You'll need to buy about 1 pound of unpeeled shrimp if you plan to peel and devein it yourself.*

1. *To peel your own shrimp, grasp the tail in one hand and the legs in the other.*

2. *In one motion, pull off the legs.*

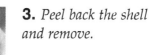

3. *Peel back the shell and remove.*

vermouth scallops over vermicelli
and steamed zucchini   serves 2 • total time 15 minutes

Fresh seafood and capers combine to create a fine dining experience in your home in just 15 minutes.

SUPPER plan

1. Bring water to a boil for pasta.

2. Chop basil; cut zucchini into strips.

3. While pasta cooks:
   • Steam zucchini, and toss with seasonings.
   • Cook scallop mixture.

4. Spoon scallop mixture over cooked pasta.

Vermouth Scallops over Vermicelli

prep: 1 minute   cook: 13 minutes

If you don't have vermouth or dry white wine, you can use ½ cup chicken broth.

   1   teaspoon olive oil
   1   teaspoon butter
Cooking spray
   ¾ pound sea scallops
   2 teaspoons capers
   ¼ teaspoon salt
   ¼ teaspoon coarsely ground black pepper
   ½ cup dry vermouth or dry white wine
   2 cups hot cooked vermicelli (about 4 ounces uncooked pasta)
   2 tablespoons chopped fresh basil

   Heat oil and butter over medium-high heat in a large nonstick skillet coated with cooking spray. Add scallops; cook about 3 minutes on each side until browned and cooked through. Add capers, salt, pepper, and vermouth. Cook 30 seconds or until vermouth evaporates.

Spoon mixture over pasta. Sprinkle evenly with basil. Yield: 2 servings (serving size: 1 cup scallop mixture, ¼ cup sauce, and 1 cup pasta).

CALORIES 389 (15% from fat); FAT 6.5g (sat 1.8g, mono 2.4g, poly 1.1g); PROTEIN 35.5g; CARB 45g; FIBER 2.7g; CHOL 61mg; IRON 2.9mg; SODIUM 678mg; CALC 62mg
EXCHANGES: 3 Starch, 4 Very Lean Meat

Steamed Zucchini

prep: 3 minutes   cook: 5 minutes

   1 large zucchini, halved crosswise and cut into strips
   2 teaspoons olive oil
   2 teaspoons lemon pepper

   Place zucchini in a microwave-safe casserole dish; cover with lid or heavy-duty plastic wrap. Microwave at HIGH 5 minutes or until tender. Drizzle with olive oil, sprinkle with lemon pepper, and toss gently to combine. Yield: 2 servings (serving size: about 1 cup).

CALORIES 60 (71% from fat); FAT 4.7g (sat 0.6g, mono 3.3g, poly 0.4g); PROTEIN 1.4g; CARB 4.3g; FIBER 1.3g; CHOL 0mg; IRON 0.4mg; SODIUM 393mg; CALC 15mg
EXCHANGES: 1 Vegetable, 1 Fat

SIMPLEsubstitutions

• •

Serve this flavorful *scallop mixture over any type of long thin pasta: angel hair, spaghettini, linguine, or fettuccine. Generally, 4 ounces of uncooked pasta will yield 2 cups cooked.*

Vermouth Scallops over Vermicelli
and Steamed Zucchini

peppered beef tenderloin
with orange-herbed asparagus
and crusty french rolls   **serves 2 • total time 25 minutes**

For meat lovers, there's nothing more satisfying than a simply seasoned tenderloin steak served with a crisp green vegetable.

SUPPER plan

1. Peel and slice shallots; trim asparagus; grate orange rind; mince garlic; chop thyme.

2. Prepare orange butter.

3. Broil steaks.

4. While steaks broil:
- Make shallot sauce.
- Broil asparagus.
- Toss asparagus with orange butter.

Peppered Beef Tenderloin

prep: 4 minutes   cook: 17 minutes

You can use 1 small, thinly sliced onion instead of shallots, but you'll get a bolder onion flavor.

  2 (4-ounce) beef tenderloin steaks, trimmed (about 1 inch thick)
  1 teaspoon freshly ground black pepper
  ⅛ teaspoon salt
Cooking spray
  4 shallots, peeled and sliced
  1 cup fat-free, low-sodium beef broth
  2 teaspoons Dijon mustard
Fresh thyme (optional)

Preheat broiler.
Sprinkle steaks with pepper and salt. Place steaks on a broiler pan coated with cooking spray; broil 5 minutes on each side or to desired degree of doneness.
Heat a nonstick skillet over medium-high heat. Coat shallots with cooking spray, and add to pan; sauté 2 minutes. Add broth; bring to a boil. Cook, stirring frequently, 5 minutes. Stir in mustard. Spoon sauce over steaks. Garnish with thyme, if desired. Yield: 2 servings (serving size: 1 steak and ¼ cup sauce).

CALORIES 232 (35% from fat); FAT 8.9g (sat 3.2g, mono 3.3g, poly 0.5g); PROTEIN 26.6g; CARB 10.8g; FIBER 1.5g; CHOL 70mg; IRON 4.1mg; SODIUM 553mg; CALC 39mg
EXCHANGES: 2 Starch, 3 Lean Meat

Orange-Herbed Asparagus

prep: 4 minutes   cook: 7 minutes

Place the asparagus on the broiler pan next to the steaks, and broil them at the same time.

  1 tablespoon light butter, softened
  1 teaspoon freshly grated orange rind
  1 garlic clove, minced
  1 teaspoon chopped fresh thyme
  ⅛ teaspoon salt
  ⅛ teaspoon freshly ground black pepper
  ¾ pound asparagus spears
Cooking spray

Preheat broiler.
Combine first 6 ingredients. Set aside.
Snap off tough ends of asparagus. Place spears on a broiler pan. Coat with cooking spray.
Broil 7 minutes or until lightly browned. Toss asparagus with butter mixture. Yield: 2 servings.

CALORIES 75 (36% from fat); FAT 3.0g (sat 2g, mono 0g, poly 0g); PROTEIN 4.3g; CARB 8.3g; FIBER 3.9g; CHOL 10mg; IRON 0.8mg; SODIUM 182mg; CALC 43mg
EXCHANGES: 1 Vegetable, 1 Fat

Peppered Beef Tenderloin with
Orange-Herbed Asparagus

beef tenderloins in wine sauce
with onion-garlic mashed potatoes
and steamed broccoli   **serves 2 • total time 22 minutes**

When you need a menu for a special evening, this elegant meat and potatoes dinner will not disappoint. Be sure to spoon a little of the rich wine sauce over your potatoes.

SUPPER plan

1. Chop onions and mince garlic for potatoes.

2. Prepare steaks.

3. While steaks cook:
- Prepare potatoes.
- Steam broccoli in microwave.

Beef Tenderloins in Wine Sauce

prep: 1 minute   cook: 14 minutes

You can use an additional ¼ cup beef broth in place of the wine.

¼	cup low-sodium beef broth
¼	cup ruby port or other sweet red wine
¾	teaspoon all-purpose flour
½	teaspoon Worcestershire sauce
½	teaspoon Dijon mustard
¼	teaspoon salt
¼	teaspoon coarsely ground black pepper

Cooking spray
½	teaspoon butter
2	(4-ounce) beef tenderloin steaks, trimmed (1 to 1¼ inch thick)

Combine first 7 ingredients, whisking to dissolve flour.

Coat a medium nonstick skillet with cooking spray; add butter. Place over medium-high heat until hot. Add steaks, and cook 4 minutes on each side or to desired degree of doneness. Transfer steaks to a plate; keep warm.

Whisk broth mixture; add to pan. Bring to a boil; cook 1 minute or until reduced to ¼ cup, scraping pan to loosen browned bits. Serve sauce over steaks. Yield: 2 servings (serving size: 1 steak and 2 tablespoons sauce).

CALORIES 195 (44% from fat); FAT 9.5g (sat 3.8g, mono 3.5g, poly 0.4g); PROTEIN 24.2g; CARB 1.7g; FIBER 0.1g; CHOL 73mg; IRON 3.4mg; SODIUM 459mg; CALC 13mg
EXCHANGES: 3½ Lean Meat

Onion-Garlic Mashed Potatoes

prep: 6 minutes   cook: 8 minutes

Cooking spray
¼	cup finely chopped red onion
¼	cup thinly sliced green onions
2	garlic cloves, minced
⅔	cup 1% low-fat milk
1⅓	cups frozen mashed potatoes
1	teaspoon light butter
¼	teaspoon salt
¼	teaspoon freshly ground black pepper

Coat a small saucepan with cooking spray; place over medium heat until hot. Add onions and garlic; sauté 3 minutes. Add milk to pan; cook until thoroughly heated. Stir in potatoes, and cook, stirring constantly, 3 minutes or until creamy. Stir in butter, salt, and pepper. Yield: 2 servings (serving size: ¾ cup).

CALORIES 151 (23% from fat); FAT 3.9g (sat 2.2g, mono 0.2g, poly 0g); PROTEIN 4.8g; CARB 24.1g; FIBER 1.8g; CHOL 8mg; IRON 0.4mg; SODIUM 498mg; CALC 109mg
EXCHANGES: 1½ Starch, 1 Fat

broiled lamb chops with mango-mint salsa

with brown and wild rice   serves 2 • total time 18 minutes

Pair a sweet fruit salsa with savory grilled lamb chops for a meal with flavor you won't forget.

SUPPER plan

1. Toast pine nuts in skillet over medium heat for 1 minute.

2. Peel and dice mango; peel and mince shallot; chop mint; halve garlic cloves. Prepare mango mixture; cover and chill.

3. Broil lamb chops.

4. While lamb broils, cook boil-in-bag brown and wild rice mix according to package directions.

Broiled Lamb Chops with Mango-Mint Salsa

prep: 9 minutes   cook: 8 minutes

1   cup diced peeled ripe mango (about 2)
1   large shallot, peeled and minced
2   tablespoons pine nuts, toasted
2   tablespoons chopped fresh mint
1   tablespoon honey
1   tablespoon rice wine vinegar
4   (3-ounce) lamb rib chops, trimmed (about 1 inch thick)
2   garlic cloves, halved
¼   teaspoon salt
¼   teaspoon freshly ground black pepper
Cooking spray

Preheat broiler.
Combine first 6 ingredients in a medium bowl. Cover and chill.
Rub chops with garlic, salt, and pepper. Place chops on a broiler pan coated with cooking spray. Broil 4 to 5 minutes on each side or until desired degree of doneness. Serve with salsa. Yield: 2 servings (serving size: 2 lamb chops and ½ cup plus 2 tablespoons salsa).

CALORIES 464 (36% from fat); FAT 18.7g (sat 6.8g, mono 7.3g, poly 2.5g); PROTEIN 37.9g; CARB 38.4g; FIBER 3.6g; CHOL 112mg; IRON 4.8mg; SODIUM 440mg; CALC 59mg
EXCHANGES: ½ Starch, 2 Fruit, 5 Lean Meat

HOWto

• • • • • • • • • • • • • • • • • • • •

Broiling is a low-fat cooking method *that is particularly good for relatively small, tender cuts of meat, such as rib chops.*

When you broil, the food is placed on a broiler pan, and the heat source is above the food. Generally, you need to turn the meat about halfway through the cooking time to get both sides of the meat evenly browned. Like grilling, broiling is a low-fat cooking method because some of the fat cooks out of the meat into the pan.

garam masala lamb chops
with **indian spiced couscous**   serves 2 • total time 16 minutes

Bring the taste of exotic India to your table with this spiced lamb and couscous dinner.

SUPPER plan

1. Combine spice mixture, and dredge lamb.

2. While lamb broils and stands:
• Cook couscous.
• Chop green onions.
• Let couscous stand.

Garam Masala Lamb Chops

prep: 5 minutes   cook: 6 minutes

Garam masala is an Indian spice blend which can be found in the spice section of the grocery store.

1½   tablespoons prune baby food
1   teaspoon garam masala
½   teaspoon minced garlic
½   teaspoon salt
4   (4-ounce) lamb rib chops, trimmed (about 1 inch thick)
⅓   cup dry breadcrumbs
Cooking spray

   Preheat broiler.
   Combine first 4 ingredients in a shallow dish. Rub lamb chops with prune mixture; dredge in breadcrumbs. Coat lamb with cooking spray. Place lamb on broiler pan coated with cooking spray. Broil 3 to 4 minutes on each side or to desired degree of doneness. Let stand 5 minutes before serving. Yield: 2 servings (serving size: 2 lamb chops).

CALORIES 263 (38% from fat); FAT 11g (sat 3.8g, mono 4.4g, poly 1.1g); PROTEIN 23.8g; CARB 16g; FIBER 1g; CHOL 67mg; IRON 3.1mg; SODIUM 808mg; CALC 64mg
EXCHANGES: 1 Starch, 3 Lean Meat

Indian Spiced Couscous

prep: 3 minutes   cook: 7 minutes

Black pepper, cardamom, and cinnamon are three spices commonly found in garam masala.

1   cup water
½   cup dried fruit bits (such as Sunmaid)
2   teaspoons light butter
¼   teaspoon salt
¼   teaspoon freshly ground black pepper
¼   teaspoon ground turmeric
Dash of ground cardamom
¼   teaspoon ground cinnamon
½   cup whole wheat or plain couscous, uncooked
3   tablespoons thinly sliced green onions

   Combine first 8 ingredients in a medium saucepan; bring to a boil over medium-high heat. Stir in couscous; return to a boil. Cover and reduce heat to low; simmer 2 minutes or until water is absorbed.
   Remove from heat; add green onions. Cover and let stand 5 minutes. Fluff before serving. Yield: 2 servings (serving size: ¾ cup).

CALORIES 241 (10% from fat); FAT 2.7g (sat 1.3g, mono 0g, poly 0g); PROTEIN 6.5g; CARB 50.3g; FIBER 6.4g; CHOL 7mg; IRON 2.2mg; SODIUM 186mg; CALC 38mg
EXCHANGES: 2 Starch, 1 Fruit

FOODfact

• • • • • • • • • • • • • • • • • • • •

"Garam" is the Indian word for warm.
"Masala" means a blend of spices. Garam masala is a combination of 10 or more spices that are dry roasted and ground to create a spice blend. Garam masala adds flavor and "heat" to Indian dishes.

Garam Masala Lamb Chops
with Indian Spiced Couscous

cuban pork chops
and fruited curry rice
serves 2 • total time 23 minutes

Let the passion of the island be yours with this Cuban-inspired menu featuring hot and spicy pork and banana slices splashed with fresh, tart lime juice.

SUPPER plan

1. Bring water to a boil for rice.

2. Chop cilantro; mince garlic, grate lime rind, squeeze lime juice, and slice banana.

3. While rice cooks and stands:
  • Cook pork.
  • Cook banana mixture for pork.

Cuban Pork Chops

prep: 5 minutes   cook: 8 minutes

Choose a banana that is firm, yet ripe, so that it will hold its shape when cooked.

  2   teaspoons ground cumin
  ¼   teaspoon ground red pepper
  ¼   teaspoon ground cloves
  ¼   teaspoon salt
  2   (4-ounce) boneless center-cut pork loin chops (about ½ inch thick)
Cooking spray
  1   banana, diagonally cut into ¼-inch-thick slices
  1   large garlic clove, minced
  2   teaspoons grated lime rind
  1   tablespoon fresh lime juice (about ½ lime)

Combine first 4 ingredients; rub spice mixture evenly over both sides of pork.

Heat a large nonstick skillet coated with cooking spray over medium-high heat. Add pork, and cook 3 minutes on each side or until done. Transfer pork to a plate, and keep warm.

Coat pan with cooking spray; add banana and garlic, and sauté 1 minute. Stir in lime rind and juice; cook 30 seconds.

Place pork chops on plates; spoon banana mixture over pork. Yield: 2 servings (serving size: 1 pork chop and about ¼ cup banana mixture).

CALORIES 244 (30% from fat); FAT 8g (sat 2.8g, mono 3.2g, poly 0.7g); PROTEIN 26.9g; CARB 16.4g; FIBER 2.6g; CHOL 73mg; IRON 1.9mg; SODIUM 352mg; CALC 48mg
EXCHANGES: 1 Fruit, 3 Lean Meat

Fruited Curry Rice

prep: 2 minutes   cook: 3 minutes   stand: 5 minutes

  ½   cup water
  ½   teaspoon butter
  ⅛   teaspoon salt
  ¼   teaspoon curry powder
  ½   cup instant long-grain rice
  ¼   cup chopped tropical dried fruit
  2   tablespoons chopped fresh cilantro

Bring water to a boil in a medium saucepan. Add butter and next 4 ingredients; stir gently. Cover and remove from heat. Let stand 5 minutes or until water is absorbed. Add cilantro, and fluff with a fork. Yield: 2 servings (serving size: ½ cup).

CALORIES 141 (8% from fat); FAT 1.2g (sat 0.6g, mono 0.4g, poly 0.1g); PROTEIN 2.3g; CARB 30.9g; FIBER 1.8g; CHOL 3mg; IRON 1.6mg; SODIUM 155mg; CALC 13mg
EXCHANGES: 1 Starch, 1 Fruit

pork medaillons in cherry sauce with curried pecan rice
and steamed spinach · serves 2 · total time 22 minutes

Treat yourself to this elegant meal that's worthy of the holiday season. For a festive finish, serve the Pear Custard Tarts on page 347.

SUPPER plan

1. Pound pork, and dredge in breadcrumbs.

2. Cook pork and sauce.

3. While pork cooks:
- Cook rice.
- Toast pecans in skillet.
- Chop parsley.
- Cook spinach in microwave.

Pork Medaillons in Cherry Sauce

prep: 8 minutes   cook: 14 minutes

If you don't care to use wine, add 2 more tablespoons of chicken broth.

½	pound pork tenderloin, trimmed and cut crosswise into 4 slices
¼	cup fat-free, less-sodium chicken broth
2	tablespoons ruby port
2	tablespoons cherry preserves
½	teaspoon cornstarch
¼	teaspoon salt
¼	teaspoon coarsely ground black pepper
⅛	teaspoon ground cloves
2	teaspoons seasoned breadcrumbs
1	teaspoon olive oil

Cooking spray
1   teaspoon chopped fresh parsley

Pound pork medaillons to ½-inch thickness, using the palm of your hand.

Combine chicken broth and next 6 ingredients in a medium bowl; whisk until smooth.

Dredge pork in breadcrumbs. Heat oil in a nonstick skillet coated with cooking spray over medium-high heat. Add pork; cook 1½ minutes on each side or until golden brown. Add broth mixture; cover, reduce heat, and simmer 8 minutes or until pork is done. Transfer pork to serving plates. Spoon cherry sauce over pork, and sprinkle evenly with parsley. Yield: 2 servings (serving size: 2 slices pork and about 2½ tablespoons sauce).

CALORIES 220 (25% from fat); FAT 6.2g (sat 1.7g, mono 3.5g, poly 0.6g); PROTEIN 24.8g; CARB 15.9g; FIBER 0.5g; CHOL 74mg; IRON 1.8mg; SODIUM 504mg; CALC 16mg
EXCHANGES: 1 Starch, 3 Lean Meat

Curried Pecan Rice

prep: 1 minute   cook: 10 minutes

1	(4-ounce) package boil-in-bag long-grain and wild rice mix
2	teaspoons light butter
2	tablespoons pecan pieces
½	teaspoon curry powder
¼	teaspoon salt
¼	teaspoon freshly ground black pepper
1	tablespoon chopped fresh parsley

Prepare rice according to package directions, omitting butter, fat, salt, and seasoning packet. Drain well.

Melt 2 teaspoons butter in a nonstick skillet over medium heat. Add pecans; sauté 3 minutes. Add curry powder, and sauté 1 minute.

Combine rice, pecans, salt, pepper, and parsley. Yield: 2 servings (serving size: 1 cup).

CALORIES 295 (29% from fat); FAT 9.4g (sat 1.8g, mono 3.1g, poly 1.6g); PROTEIN 6.4g; CARB 46.5g; FIBER 3.7g; CHOL 7mg; IRON 1mg; SODIUM 329mg; CALC 12mg
EXCHANGES: 3 Starch, 1½ Fat

grilled chicken salad with sesame seed vinaigrette and won ton crisps serves 2 · total time 16 minutes

When you don't want to heat up the kitchen, try this fruited grilled chicken salad.

SUPPER plan

1. Grill chicken.

2. While chicken cooks:
- Halve grapes and toast sesame seeds.
- Prepare vinaigrette.
- Prepare Won Ton Crisps.

3. Assemble salad.

Grilled Chicken Salad with Sesame Seed Vinaigrette

prep: 6 minutes   cook: 10 minutes

      2   (4-ounce) skinless, boneless chicken breast
          halves
    ¼   teaspoon salt, divided
    ¼   teaspoon pepper, divided
Cooking spray
      3   cups packed prepackaged fresh baby
          spinach leaves
    ½   cup seedless red grapes, halved
      2   teaspoons sesame seeds, toasted
      1   tablespoon red wine vinegar
      3   tablespoons unsweetened white grape juice
      2   teaspoons sesame oil

   Prepare grill.
   Sprinkle chicken evenly with ⅛ teaspoon each salt and pepper. Place chicken on grill rack coated with cooking spray; grill 5 to 7 minutes on each side or until done.
   Combine spinach, grapes, and sesame seeds in a large bowl. Combine vinegar, grape juice, sesame oil, and remaining salt and pepper.

   Slice chicken diagonally into thin slices. Toss chicken with spinach mixture. Drizzle vinaigrette over salad. Yield: 2 servings (serving size: 3 ounces chicken and 1½ cups salad).

CALORIES 231 (30% from fat); FAT 7.7g (sat 1.1g, mono 2.2g, poly 2.4g); PROTEIN 28.6g; CARB 13.7g; FIBER 2.7g; CHOL 66mg; IRON 2.5mg; SODIUM 406mg; CALC 68mg
EXCHANGES: ½ Fruit, 1 Vegetable, 4 Very Lean Meat, 1 Fat

Won Ton Crisps

prep: 1 minute   cook: 4 minutes

Make extra won ton crisps, and store them in an airtight container to keep on hand for snacks.

      6   won ton wrappers
Cooking spray
    ½   teaspoon sesame oil
    ¼   teaspoon salt

   Preheat oven to 375°.
   Place won ton wrappers on a baking sheet coated with cooking spray. Brush lightly with sesame oil, and sprinkle with salt.
   Bake at 375° for 4 minutes or until golden brown. Serve warm or at room temperature. Yield: 2 servings (serving size: 3 won ton crisps).

CALORIES 80 (17% from fat); FAT 1.5g (sat 0.2g, mono 0.5g, poly 0.6g); PROTEIN 2.4g; CARB 13.9g; FIBER 0.4g; CHOL 2mg; IRON 0.8mg; SODIUM 431mg; CALC 12mg
EXCHANGE: 1 Starch

orange-sauced chicken
with roasted cauliflower

serves 2 • total time 20 minutes

Jazz up your usual baked chicken breast and steamed vegetable menu with this saucy skillet chicken and hearty roasted vegetable.

SUPPER plan

1. Prepare orange sauce for chicken.

2. Dredge chicken.

3. Cook chicken.

4. While chicken cooks:
- Toss cauliflower with olive oil.
- Roast cauliflower.

Orange-Sauced Chicken

prep: 8 minutes   cook: 10 minutes

¼   cup fresh orange juice
¼   cup fat-free, less-sodium chicken broth
1   tablespoon orange marmalade
1   teaspoon fresh lemon juice
¾   teaspoon cornstarch
⅛   teaspoon dried crushed rosemary
⅛   teaspoon salt
¼   teaspoon freshly ground black pepper
2   (4-ounce) skinless, boneless, chicken breast halves
1   tablespoon Italian-seasoned breadcrumbs
1   teaspoon olive oil
Cooking spray
1   teaspoon chopped fresh flat-leaf parsley

Combine first 8 ingredients in a medium bowl, stirring with a whisk.

Dredge chicken in breadcrumbs.

Heat oil in a large nonstick skillet coated with cooking spray over medium-high heat. Add chicken, and cook 3 to 4 minutes on each side or just until lightly browned on both sides. Add broth mixture; cover, reduce heat, and simmer, stirring occasionally, 4 to 5 minutes or until chicken is done. Sprinkle with parsley. Yield: 2 servings (serving size: 1 chicken breast half and about ¼ cup sauce).

CALORIES 204 (17% from fat); FAT 3.8g (sat 0.7g, mono 2.1g, poly 0.6g); PROTEIN 27.4g; CARB 14g; FIBER 0.4g; CHOL 66mg; IRON 1.2mg; SODIUM 398mg; CALC 27mg
EXCHANGES: 1 Starch, 4 Very Lean Meat

Roasted Cauliflower

prep: 2 minutes   cook: 8 minutes

Buy a package of cauliflower florets instead of a head of cauliflower.

1   tablespoon olive oil
3   cups cauliflower florets
¼   teaspoon salt
¼   teaspoon freshly ground black pepper

Preheat oven to 425°.

Combine oil and cauliflower in a large bowl, tossing well.

Arrange cauliflower in 1 layer on a jelly roll pan. Bake at 425° for 8 minutes or until crisp-tender, stirring once. Sprinkle with salt and pepper. Yield: 2 servings (serving size: 1 cup).

CALORIES 98 (65% from fat); FAT 7.1g (sat 1g, mono 5g, poly 0.7g); PROTEIN 3g; CARB 8g; FIBER 3.8g; CHOL 0mg; IRON 0.8mg; SODIUM 336mg; CALC 34mg
EXCHANGES: 1 Vegetable, 1½ Fat

Pan-Seared Chicken in Prosciutto-Fig
Sauce with Roasted Green Beans

pan-seared chicken in prosciutto-fig sauce
with **roasted green beans,** caesar-style green salad, and whole grain rolls **serves 2 • total time 20 minutes**

Because this menu features simple ingredients with big flavors, it takes only 20 minutes to get this full-course meal to the table.

SUPPER PLAN

1. Trim green beans; chop prosciutto.

2. Sear chicken.

3. Roast beans.

4. While beans roast:
- Cook chicken and sauce mixture.
- Prepare salad with packaged mixed greens and reduced-fat Caesar dressing.

Pan-Seared Chicken in Prosciutto-Fig Sauce

prep: 3 minutes   cook: 12 minutes

Prosciutto is Italian-style ham that has been seasoned, salt-cured (not smoked), and air-dried. After it's dried, the meat is pressed, so it has a firm, dense texture. Prosciutto is a little pricey, but the flavor it adds is worth it. If you can't find it, you can substitute lean ham.

2   (4-ounce) skinless, boneless chicken breast halves
¼   teaspoon salt
1   teaspoon olive oil
⅓   cup fig preserves
2   tablespoons chopped prosciutto
1   tablespoon balsamic vinegar
2   tablespoons water

Sprinkle chicken evenly with salt. Heat oil in a 10-inch nonstick skillet over medium-high heat. Add chicken to pan, and cook 2 to 3 minutes on each side until seared.

Combine fig preserves and remaining ingredients. Add to chicken. Cover, reduce heat to medium, and cook 6 minutes or until chicken is done. Uncover and cook 1 minute over medium-high heat until sauce is slightly thickened. Yield: 2 servings (serving size: 1 chicken breast half and ¼ cup sauce).

CALORIES 299 (16% from fat); FAT 5.2g (sat 1.2g, mono 2g, poly 0.5g); PROTEIN 30.3g; CARB 30.7g; FIBER 0g; CHOL 73mg; IRON 1.1mg; SODIUM 622mg; CALC 15mg
EXCHANGES: 1 Starch, 1 Fruit, 3 Lean Meat

Roasted Green Beans

prep: 5 minutes   cook: 10 minutes

If you line the jelly roll pan with foil, you won't have to clean the pan after roasting.

½   pound green beans, trimmed
Butter-flavored cooking spray
¼   teaspoon salt
¼   teaspoon pepper

Preheat oven to 450°.
Coat beans with cooking spray; sprinkle with salt and pepper. Arrange beans in a single layer in a jelly roll pan lined with aluminum foil. Bake at 450° for 10 minutes or until lightly browned. Yield: 2 servings.

CALORIES 42 (17% from fat); FAT 0.8g (sat 0.1g, mono 0g, poly 0.1g); PROTEIN 2.1g; CARB 8.4g; FIBER 3.9g; CHOL 0mg; IRON 1.3mg; SODIUM 300mg; CALC 43mg
EXCHANGES: 2 Vegetable

chicken piccata with garlic-basil pasta
and steamed green beans   serves 2 • total time 20 minutes

Instead of dashing out to a restaurant, stay home and enjoy an intimate Italian-style dinner.

SUPPER plan

1. Bring water to a boil for pasta.

2. Pound chicken; cook chicken.

3. While chicken cooks:
- Cook pasta.
- Chop parsley; squeeze lemon juice.
- Chop basil for pasta.
- Steam beans in microwave.

Chicken Piccata

prep: 7 minutes   cook: 8 minutes

You can use this basic piccata recipe with either pork or veal cutlets, too. Just make sure you pound the meat to ¼-inch thickness.

2   (4-ounce) skinless, boneless chicken breast halves
¼   teaspoon salt
2   teaspoons olive oil
¼   cup fat-free, less-sodium chicken broth
2   tablespoons fresh lemon juice (about 1 lemon)
1   tablespoon capers in white balsamic vinegar (such as Alessi) or regular capers
¼   teaspoon freshly ground black pepper
2   tablespoons chopped fresh parsley

Place chicken between 2 sheets of heavy duty plastic wrap; pound to ¼-inch thickness. Sprinkle chicken with salt.

Heat oil in a large nonstick skillet over medium-high heat. Add chicken. Cook over medium-high heat 3 to 4 minutes on each side until golden brown.

Remove chicken from pan; keep warm. Add broth and lemon juice to pan, scraping pan with a wooden spoon to loosen browned bits. Cook, uncovered, over high heat 30 seconds or until slightly reduced. Stir in capers. Pour sauce over chicken. Sprinkle with pepper and parsley. Yield: 2 servings (serving size: 1 chicken breast half and about 3 tablespoons sauce).

CALORIES 173 (31% from fat); FAT 6g (sat 1g, mono 3.7g, poly 0.7g); PROTEIN 26.9g; CARB 2.1g; FIBER 0.4g; CHOL 66mg; IRON 1.2mg; SODIUM 574mg; CALC 22mg
EXCHANGES: 4 Very Lean Meat, ½ Fat

Garlic-Basil Pasta

prep: 7 minutes   cook: 4 minutes

Use refrigerated fresh pasta—it cooks in less than half the time it takes dry pasta to cook.

2   ounces uncooked refrigerated angel hair pasta
1½   teaspoons olive oil
1   teaspoon fresh lemon juice (about ½ small lemon)
½   teaspoon bottled minced garlic
¼   teaspoon salt
¼   teaspoon freshly ground black pepper
2   tablespoons chopped fresh basil

Cook pasta according to package directions, omitting salt and fat; drain, reserving 1 tablespoon pasta water.

Combine pasta water, olive oil, and next 4 ingredients; toss with pasta and basil. Yield: 2 servings (serving size: about ¾ cup).

CALORIES 115 (32% from fat); FAT 4.1g (sat 0.6g, mono 2.6g, poly 0.6g); PROTEIN 3.4g; CARB 16.3g; FIBER 1.3g; CHOL 21mg; IRON 1.1mg; SODIUM 301mg; CALC 11mg
EXCHANGES: 1 Starch, 1 Fat

mushroom-marsala chicken with steamed broccoli and long-grain rice

serves 2 • total time 22 minutes

Like all classics, a chicken marsala dish is perfect for any occasion—a simple weeknight supper or a special occasion.

SUPPER plan

1. Pound chicken; mince shallots.

2. Prepare chicken and sauce.

3. While chicken cooks:
   - Steam broccoli in microwave.
   - Prepare rice from boil-in-bag package.

Mushroom-Marsala Chicken

prep: 7 minutes   cook: 15 minutes

Instead of Marsala, you can use the same amount of white wine or additional chicken broth in the mushroom sauce.

½   cup fat-free, less-sodium chicken broth
1   teaspoon cornstarch
2   (4-ounce) skinless, boneless chicken breast halves
Cooking spray
¼   teaspoon salt
¼   teaspoon pepper
¼   cup Italian-seasoned breadcrumbs
1   (8-ounce) package sliced mushrooms
2   tablespoons minced shallots
¼   cup dry Marsala
1   tablespoon light butter

   Combine chicken broth and cornstarch, stirring well; set aside.
   Place chicken between 2 pieces of heavy-duty plastic wrap; pound to ½-inch thickness, using a meat mallet or rolling pin. Coat with cooking spray; sprinkle with salt and pepper. Sprinkle 2 tablespoons breadcrumbs evenly over each chicken breast half; coat with cooking spray.

   Place a large nonstick skillet over medium heat until hot; add chicken. Cook 3 minutes on each side or until done. Remove chicken from pan; cover and keep warm.
   Heat same skillet, coated with cooking spray, over medium-high heat. Add mushrooms and shallots; cook 4 to 5 minutes or until tender, stirring occasionally. Add wine; cook 1 minute. Add chicken broth mixture; cook 2 to 3 minutes or until sauce is thickened. Remove from heat; add butter, stirring until butter melts. Yield: 2 servings (serving size: 1 chicken breast half and ½ cup sauce).

CALORIES 247 (20% from fat); FAT 5.6g (sat 2.4g, mono 0.4g, poly 0.5g); PROTEIN 32.6g; CARB 17.9g; FIBER 2g; CHOL 76mg; IRON 2.9mg; SODIUM 925mg; CALC 56mg
EXCHANGES: 1 Starch, 1 Vegetable, 4 Very Lean Meat

HOWto

• • • • • • • • • • • • • • • • • •

Pounding the chicken *(or pork or veal), tenderizes the meat and decreases the cooking time because the pieces are thin. Thinner pieces of meat also help with portion control—they look like a large piece of meat.*

"We're not meat eaters, so it's hard to find a variety of dishes to make for dinner that everyone in our family will like."

MEATLESS
main dishes

With a focus on grain products, legumes, soy protein, vegetables, and fruits, these vegetarian-style main dishes offer a variety of flavors and textures, plus a number of health benefits. Whether you're a vegetarian or simply cutting back on meat, these easy menus are sure to satisfy.

Pad Thai, page 234

vegging out

Can a vegetarian diet supply you with all the nutrients you need? Yes, if you make good choices.

nutrient needs

If you eat dairy products and eggs, the nutrient issues are no different than those for nonvegetarians, as long as you don't eat too much saturated fat and cholesterol. For those who don't eat dairy products or eggs, the nutrients below are the ones that need special attention.

Protein: Animal sources of protein are usually more concentrated sources, but legumes, nuts, seeds, grain products, and vegetables can supply enough protein.

BEST SOURCES OF B12

- fortified breakfast cereals
- soy milk products
- vegetarian burger patties
- Vitamin B12 supplement (you don't need any more than 100 percent of the Recommended Dietary Allowance or RDA)

Note: Seaweed, algae, spirulina, and fermented plant foods such as tempeh and miso aren't good sources of vitamin B12, because it's not in a form that the body can use. Vitamin B12 in beer and other fermented foods isn't a reliable source, either.

Vitamin B12: Over time, a deficiency of this vitamin can cause anemia and severe, irreversible nerve damage. If you're a vegan, you need a reliable source of vitamin B12. (See the list on the left.)

Vitamin D: If you're regularly exposed to sunlight, you should be getting enough vitamin D. If not, some breakfast cereals and soy milks are fortified with this vitamin. Check the Nutrition Facts on food labels for vitamin D content.

Calcium: You can get enough calcium from plant sources, but it takes a little more planning in order to include those high-calcium foods. (See the list on the right.)

Iron: Because the iron in plant foods isn't as well absorbed as iron in animal products, adequate intake can be a challenge when you're not eating meat. Here's what you need to do:

- Eat plant foods that are good sources of iron such as legumes, iron-fortified cereals and breads, whole grain products, tofu, dark leafy greens, seeds, prune juice, dried fruit, and black-strap molasses.
- Include a vitamin C-rich food at every meal because the vitamin C helps you absorb iron from plant sources.
- Cook foods in iron skillets. Some of the iron from the pan passes into the food.

Zinc: The best sources of this mineral are meats, poultry, and seafood. However, some plant sources of zinc are whole wheat bread, whole grains, legumes, tofu, seeds, and nuts.

PLANT-BASED CALCIUM SOURCES

- Broccoli
- Calcium-fortified orange juice and breakfast cereals
- Calcium-fortified soy beverages
- Dried figs
- Greens such as collards, kale, mustard greens
- Legumes
- Nuts
- Okra
- Rutabaga
- Sunflower seeds
- Tofu processed with calcium
- Tortillas (made from lime-processed corn)

breakfast burritos
and fresh fruit salad   serves 4 • total time 20 minutes

If you don't have time for a cooked breakfast in the morning, have one for dinner.

SUPPER plan

1. Prepare Fresh Fruit Salad.

2. Slice onion; drain and slice bell peppers.

3. Prepare Breakfast Burritos.

Breakfast Burritos

prep: 6 minutes   cook: 11 minutes

This recipe uses a combination of whole eggs and egg substitute. Using both gives you a product with great flavor and texture but less fat than if you use all whole eggs.

½   teaspoon cumin seeds
½   teaspoon salt
¼   teaspoon ground red pepper
4   large eggs
1   (8-ounce) carton egg substitute
1   teaspoon butter or margarine
½   cup thinly sliced red onion
1   (7-ounce) jar roasted red bell peppers, drained and cut into ¼-inch strips
4   (8-inch) flour tortillas
¾   cup (3 ounces) shredded reduced-fat Cheddar cheese

Heat a large nonstick skillet over medium-low heat. Add cumin seeds, and cook, stirring constantly, 1 to 2 minutes or until fragrant. Combine cumin seeds, salt, pepper, eggs, and egg substitute in a bowl, stirring with a whisk.

Melt butter in same skillet over medium-high heat. Add onion; cook 2 minutes or until tender. Stir in roasted red pepper. Pour egg mixture into pan. Reduce heat to medium; cook without stirring until mixture begins to set on bottom. Draw a spatula across bottom of pan to form large curds. Continue cooking until eggs are thickened and firm throughout, but still moist. (Do not stir constantly.)

Heat tortillas according to package directions. Spoon egg mixture evenly down centers of tortillas; sprinkle each with 3 tablespoons cheese; roll up tortilla. Yield: 4 servings (serving size: 1 burrito).

CALORIES 340 (35% from fat); FAT 13.2g (sat 5.2g, mono 3.7g, poly 1.4g); PROTEIN 24g; CARB 31.2g; FIBER 0.6g; CHOL 230mg; IRON 3.2mg; SODIUM 1,073mg; CALC 341mg
EXCHANGES: 2 Starch, 2 High-Fat Meat, 1 Fat

Fresh Fruit Salad

prep: 3 minutes

2   cups sliced banana (about 2)
1   cup sliced strawberries
1   cup sliced peeled kiwifruit (about 3)
3   tablespoons pineapple juice

Combine all ingredients. Yield: 4 servings (serving size: 1 cup).

CALORIES 115 (5% from fat); FAT 0.7g (sat 0.2g, mono 0.1g, poly 0.3g); PROTEIN 1.5g; CARB 28.7g; FIBER 4.3g; CHOL 0mg; IRON 0.6mg; SODIUM 4mg; CALC 24mg
EXCHANGES: 2 Fruit

huevos rancheros with salsa-topped salad
and warm flour tortillas   serves 4 · total time 17 minutes

Even if you haven't been working on a ranch all day these hearty "rancher's eggs," served with potatoes, will fill you up at suppertime.

SUPPER plan

1. Prepare Huevos Rancheros.

2. While egg dish cooks, chop cilantro, and assemble salads.

3. Heat tortillas just before serving.

Huevos Rancheros

prep: 1 minute   cook: 16 minutes

If you cook eggs in simmering liquid until the whites are completely set and the yolks begin to thicken but are not hard (about 3 to 5 minutes), the eggs will reach the safe egg temperature of 160°.

1	(14.5-ounce) can diced tomatoes with green pepper, celery, and onions
2	cups diced potatoes with onion (such as Simply Potatoes)
½	cup vegetable broth
1	tablespoon tomato paste
1	teaspoon chili powder
½	teaspoon ground cumin
¼	teaspoon salt
⅛	teaspoon coarsely ground black pepper
4	large eggs
½	cup (2 ounces) shredded reduced-fat Cheddar cheese
4	teaspoons finely chopped fresh cilantro

Combine first 8 ingredients in a large non-stick skillet; stir gently. Bring to a boil; cover, reduce heat, and simmer 5 minutes.

Break 1 egg into a custard cup; slip egg from cup into potato mixture. Repeat with

remaining eggs, spacing evenly apart in pan. Cover and simmer 4 to 5 minutes or until eggs are done. Sprinkle with cheese; cover and cook 15 to 20 seconds or until cheese melts. Spoon onto individual serving plates, and sprinkle with cilantro. Yield: 4 servings (serving size: 1 egg and about 1 cup potato mixture).

CALORIES 221 (34% from fat); FAT 8.3g (sat 3.6g, mono 1.9g, poly 0.7g); PROTEIN 12.6g; CARB 23.1g; FIBER 3.6g; CHOL 223mg; IRON 1.6mg; SODIUM 1,013mg; CALC 147mg
EXCHANGES: 1 Starch, 1 Vegetable, 1 High-Fat Meat

Salsa-Topped Salad

prep: 2 minutes

1	(10-ounce) package shredded iceberg lettuce
½	cup reduced-fat sour cream
¼	cup salsa

Place 1½ cups lettuce on serving plates. Top each serving with 2 tablespoons sour cream and 1 tablespoon salsa. Yield: 4 servings (serving size: 1½ cups).

CALORIES 60 (59% from fat); FAT 3.9g (sat 2.4g, mono 0g, poly 0.1g); PROTEIN 2.3g; CARB 4.5g; FIBER 1.3g; CHOL 16mg; IRON 0.5mg; SODIUM 95mg; CALC 68mg
EXCHANGES: 1 Vegetable, 1 Fat

Huevos Rancheros

spinach-potato frittata
with tomato caesar salad   serves 4 • total time 20 minutes

When you've had a long, hard day, sometimes the best supper is the simplest supper: eggs, cheese, potatoes, and a green salad.

SUPPER plan

1. Thaw frozen spinach in the microwave; drain and squeeze dry.

2. Prepare frittata.

3. While frittata broils, prepare salad.

Spinach-Potato Frittata

prep: 5 minutes   cook: 15 minutes

If the handle of your skillet isn't ovenproof, wrap it in aluminum foil to protect it from heat damage.

  4   large eggs
  2   large egg whites
⅓   cup 1% low-fat milk
½   teaspoon dried basil
¼   teaspoon salt
⅛   teaspoon coarsely ground black pepper
  2   cups diced potatoes with onion (such as Simply Potatoes)
  1   (10-ounce) package frozen chopped spinach, thawed, drained, and squeezed dry
  1   teaspoon butter
Cooking spray
⅓   cup (1.3 ounces) shredded Asiago cheese
  1   cup marinara sauce

    Preheat broiler.
    Combine first 6 ingredients in a large bowl; stir with a whisk. Stir in potatoes and spinach.
    Melt butter in a large ovenproof skillet coated with cooking spray over medium heat. Add egg mixture to pan, spreading evenly. Cook over medium-low heat 5 minutes or until center is almost set; sprinkle with cheese.
    Broil 7 minutes or until top is golden brown. Cut into wedges, and top with marinara sauce. Yield: 4 servings (serving size: 1 wedge and ¼ cup sauce).

CALORIES 246 (37% from fat); FAT 10.2g (sat 4.1g, mono 3.5g, poly 1.4g); PROTEIN 15.7g; CARB 23.3g; FIBER 4.5g; CHOL 224mg; IRON 3.5mg; SODIUM 722mg; CALC 228mg
EXCHANGES: 1 Starch, 1 Vegetable, 2 Medium-Fat Meat

Tomato Caesar Salad

prep: 2 minutes

  1   (10-ounce) package torn romaine lettuce
  1   cup grape tomatoes
½   cup reduced-fat Caesar dressing
½   cup fat-free croutons

    Combine all ingredients; toss. Yield: 4 servings (serving size: 2 cups).

CALORIES 66 (22% from fat); FAT 1.6g (sat 0.3g, mono 0.4g, poly 0.8g); PROTEIN 2.1g; CARB 11.5g; FIBER 1.6g; CHOL 1mg; IRON 1mg; SODIUM 375mg; CALC 35mg
EXCHANGES: ½ Starch, 1 Vegetable

HOWto

• • • • • • • • • • • • • • • • • •

Drain the spinach well *so that your frittata won't be watery from excess spinach liquid. Place thawed spinach in a strainer, and press to remove liquid. Place drained spinach on several layers of paper towels. Wrap towels around spinach, and squeeze to remove excess liquid.*

spicy beans and greens with warm corn tortillas and sliced mango

serves 4 • total time 18 minutes

Instead of the usual Tex-Mex fare, try this unique Mexican meal. It's a version of a dish called quelites, *which features beans, wild greens, and pine nuts.*

SUPPER plan

1. Cook turnip greens in the microwave.

2. While greens cook:
- Chop onion.
- Mince garlic.
- Rinse and drain beans.
- Toast pine nuts.
- Drain refrigerated mango slices.

3. Prepare Spicy Beans and Greens.

4. Wrap tortillas in a paper towel, and heat in the microwave at HIGH 30 seconds.

Spicy Beans and Greens

prep: 6 minutes   cook: 17 minutes

1	(16-ounce) package fresh turnip greens
2	cups fat-free, less-sodium chicken broth, divided
2	teaspoons ground cumin
1	teaspoon ground coriander
¾	teaspoon hot chili powder
¾	teaspoon dried oregano
1	cup finely chopped onion
2	garlic cloves, minced
2	(16-ounce) cans pinto beans, rinsed and drained
¼	cup pine nuts, toasted

Combine greens and ½ cup broth in a large microwave-safe bowl; cover with plastic wrap, and vent. Microwave at HIGH 8 to 10 minutes or until tender; drain well.

Combine cumin, coriander, and chili powder in a large nonstick skillet; place over medium-low heat. Cook, stirring constantly, 2 minutes or until fragrant. Add remaining broth, oregano, onion, and garlic; bring to a simmer and cook 5 minutes. Stir in beans; cook 2 minutes. Stir in greens. Spoon onto plates; top each serving with 1 tablespoon pine nuts. Serve immediately. Yield: 4 servings (serving size: 1½ cups).

CALORIES 228 (25% from fat); FAT 6.3g (sat 1g, mono 1.9g, poly 2.4g); PROTEIN 12.7g; CARB 33.8g; FIBER 11.9g; CHOL 0mg; IRON 4.7mg; SODIUM 760mg; CALC 304mg
EXCHANGES: 2 Starch, 1 Very Lean Meat, 1 Fat

HOWto

• •

Bring out the flavor of dried spices *by toasting them. Place the spices in a dry skillet, and cook over medium-low heat for 1 to 2 minutes until the spices are fragrant. Stir the spices constantly so they won't burn.*

"Since I started cutting back on salt *I've become a spice fiend. I just love the intense flavor that you can get from just a little sprinkle of the right spice. It's the easiest way to enjoy a different cuisine every night of the week.* **"**

Julie Christopher,
Assistant Director,
Test Kitchens

Barley and Black
Bean Salad

barley and black bean salad with baked tortilla chips
and fresh pineapple slices serves 4 · total time 21 minutes

When you need a simple, hearty supper, a bowl of barley and beans won't leave you hungry. Plus, you can kick up the flavor a notch with extra peppers.

SUPPER plan

1. Bring water to a boil, and cook barley.

2. While barley cooks:
- Rinse and drain beans.
- Halve tomatoes; chop bell pepper; cube cheese.

3. Combine salad ingredients.

Barley and Black Bean Salad

prep: 11 minutes   cook: 10 minutes

For an extra kick, substitute 1 finely chopped poblano chile pepper for the green bell pepper, and add the ground red pepper.

1	cup uncooked quick-cooking pearl barley
1	(15-ounce) can black beans, rinsed and drained
1	pint grape or cherry tomatoes, halved
½	cup finely chopped green bell pepper
½	cup (2 ounces) Monterey Jack cheese with jalapeño peppers, cut into ¼-inch cubes
⅓	cup lemon juice
2	tablespoons olive oil
1	teaspoon salt
¾	cup fresh cilantro leaves (optional)
⅛	teaspoon ground red pepper (optional)

Cook barley according to package directions, omitting salt. Drain barley in a colander, and rinse with cold water until completely cooled.

Combine black beans, next 6 ingredients, and, if desired, cilantro and red pepper in a medium bowl. Add barley to black bean mixture; toss gently. Yield: 4 servings (serving size: about 1½ cups).

CALORIES 349 (31% from fat); FAT 12g (sat 3.8g, mono 6.4g, poly 1.1g); PROTEIN 11.9g; CARB 53.5g; FIBER 12.2g; CHOL 13mg; IRON 2.9mg; SODIUM 874mg; CALC 156mg
EXCHANGES: 2 Starch, 1 Vegetable, 2 Fat

NUTRITIONnote

• • • • • • • • • • • • • • • • • • •

Barley is a hearty grain *that dates back to the Stone Age, but it provides some very modern health benefits. Hulled or whole grain barley has only the outer husk removed and is the most nutritious form of the grain. Pearl barley has the outer husk removed and has been steamed and polished. Pearl barley is the form you'll see most often in the grocery store.*

Pearl barley is an excellent source of soluble fiber—that's the kind of fiber that helps lower cholesterol. With 6 grams of fiber per ½-cup serving, it's one of the top five cereal sources of fiber. Plus, it's practically fat and sodium free. The new quick-cooking barley provides the same nutritional benefits as regular barley, but cooks in 10 minutes.

rice and black bean pilaf with field greens salad
and watermelon wedges serves 4 • total time 22 minutes

When you've got instant rice and canned beans on hand, you can always come up with a meal. Add cumin and lime juice, and you get a Southwestern-flavored meal.

SUPPER plan

1. Chop celery and onion; rinse and drain beans; squeeze lime juice.

2. Prepare Rice and Black Bean Pilaf.

3. While pilaf simmers, make Field Greens Salad.

4. Slice watermelon.

Rice and Black Bean Pilaf

prep: 8 minutes   cook: 14 minutes

  2 teaspoons olive oil
Cooking spray
  ¾ cup chopped celery (about 2½ ribs)
  ½ cup chopped onion (about ½)
1½ cups uncooked instant brown rice
  1 (14-ounce) can vegetable broth
  1 (15.5-ounce) can black beans, rinsed and drained
  ½ teaspoon dried oregano
  ¼ teaspoon ground cumin
  ¼ teaspoon salt
  ¼ teaspoon coarsely ground black pepper
  1 tablespoon fresh lime juice (about ½ lime)
  ½ cup (2 ounces) shredded reduced-fat Cheddar cheese

Heat oil in a large nonstick skillet coated with cooking spray over medium-high heat. Add celery and onion; cook 4 minutes, stirring occasionally. Add rice and next 6 ingredients; stir gently. Bring to a boil; reduce heat, and simmer 10 minutes or until liquid is absorbed. Add lime juice, and mix gently. Sprinkle with cheese before serving. Yield: 4 servings (serving size: 1¼ cups rice mixture and 2 tablespoons cheese).

CALORIES 297 (21% from fat); FAT 6.9g (sat 2.3g, mono 1.7g, poly 0.2g); PROTEIN 11.1g; CARB 50.3g; FIBER 6.6g; CHOL 10mg; IRON 2.2mg; SODIUM 930mg; CALC 164mg
EXCHANGES: 3 Starch, 1 Fat

Field Greens Salad

prep: 3 minutes

  1 (5-ounce) package mixed greens
1½ cups chopped tomato (about 1 large)
  ½ cup low-fat tomato vinaigrette

Combine all ingredients in a bowl; toss gently. Yield: 4 servings (serving size: 1½ cups).

CALORIES 80 (71% from fat); FAT 6.3g (sat 0.5g, mono 0g, poly 0.1g); PROTEIN 1.1g; CARB 7.2g; FIBER 1.5g; CHOL 0mg; IRON 0.8mg; SODIUM 255mg; CALC 23mg
EXCHANGES: 1 Vegetable, 1 Fat

QUICKtip

• • • • • • • • • • • • • • • • • • • •

Keep a food chopper *on the countertop to make short work out of chopping vegetables.*

Mini food choppers are especially good for chopping small amounts of vegetables such as celery, onions, bell peppers, carrots, and other firm vegetables. You can get an electric chopper or a nonelectric version that has a hand-held plunger with sharp blades. Look for food choppers at kitchen specialty stores.

yucatan black beans and rice with low-fat tortilla chips and fruit salsa serves 3 · total time 15 minutes

If you think rice and beans sound boring, think again. This hearty bean mixture boasts the vibrant flavors of authentic Mexican cuisine: jalapeño pepper, cilantro, and lime.

SUPPER plan

1. Cook rice.

2. While rice cooks:
- Chop onion; halve tomatoes; seed and mince pepper; mince garlic; mince cilantro.
- Rinse and drain beans.
- Cut lime into wedges.

3. Prepare Yucatan Black Beans and Rice.

4. Serve with tortilla chips and bottled peach salsa. (Look for fruit salsas on the grocery shelves with the tomato salsas.)

Yucatan Black Beans and Rice

prep: 5 minutes   cook: 10 minutes

For extra heat, add another jalapeño pepper.

1 cup uncooked instant rice
1 cup water
1 tablespoon olive oil, divided
1 cup finely chopped onion (about 1)
1 jalapeño pepper, seeded and minced
2 garlic cloves, minced
1 (15-ounce) can black beans, rinsed and drained
1½ cups grape tomatoes, halved
½ teaspoon salt
2 tablespoons minced fresh cilantro
1 lime, cut into wedges

Cook rice in 1 cup water according to package directions, omitting salt and fat.

Heat 1 teaspoon olive oil in a large nonstick skillet over medium-high heat. Add onion; sauté 3 minutes. Add jalapeño pepper and garlic; sauté 1 minute. Add beans, tomatoes, and salt. Cover, reduce heat, and simmer 5 minutes. Remove from heat. Stir in remaining oil. Serve over rice, and top with cilantro and lime wedges. Yield: 3 servings (serving size: 1 cup bean mixture and ⅔ cup rice).

CALORIES 244 (19% from fat); FAT 5.1g (sat 0.7g, mono 3.4g, poly 0.6g); PROTEIN 7.2g; CARB 46.7g; FIBER 7.4g; CHOL 0mg; IRON 2.5mg; SODIUM 765mg; CALC 58mg
EXCHANGES: 3 Starch

NUTRITIONnote

● ● ● ● ● ● ● ● ● ● ● ● ● ● ● ● ● ●

Add a touch of global cuisine *to your plate with black beans. They're popular in the foods of Mexico, Central and South America, and the Caribbean.*

Black beans are an excellent source of protein, low in fat, and high in fiber. They also provide iron and folic acid, two nutrients that are especially important for women.

If you're concerned about the sodium in canned black beans, it's helpful to know that you reduce the sodium content by 40 percent when you rinse and drain the beans.

saucy cannellini beans with tossed green salad and sourdough rolls

serves 4 • total time 17 minutes

Serve this saucy bean dish in shallow bowls so you won't miss one drop of the flavorful tomato sauce.

SUPPER plan

1. Slice zucchini; chop parsley; rinse and drain beans.

2. Prepare Saucy Cannellini Beans, and let it simmer.

3. While bean mixture simmers:
   • Prepare tossed green salad.
   • Heat rolls, if desired.

Saucy Cannellini Beans

prep: 2 minutes   cook: 15 minutes

The bean mixture is also delicious served over pasta.

   2   teaspoons olive oil
   2   medium zucchini, halved lengthwise and sliced (about 2 cups)
   2   (14.5-ounce) cans diced tomatoes with balsamic vinegar and basil
   1   (15.5-ounce) can cannellini beans, rinsed and drained
   ¼   teaspoon dried or ½ teaspoon fresh oregano
   ¼   teaspoon coarsely ground black pepper
   4   teaspoons chopped flat-leaf parsley
   ¼   cup (1 ounce) preshredded fresh Parmesan cheese

   Heat olive oil in a large saucepan over medium-high heat. Add zucchini, and sauté 3 minutes or until tender.

   Add tomatoes and next 3 ingredients. Simmer, uncovered, 10 to 12 minutes or to desired consistency. Ladle into bowls; sprinkle evenly with parsley and Parmesan cheese just before serving. Yield: 4 servings (serving size: 1¼ cups).

CALORIES 186 (19% from fat); FAT 4g (sat 1.2g, mono 2.1g, poly 0.5g); PROTEIN 8.8g; CARB 30g; FIBER 5.3g; CHOL 4mg; IRON 4.4mg; SODIUM 1285mg; CALC 230mg
EXCHANGES: 2 Starch, ½ Fat

QUICKtip

● ● ● ● ● ● ● ● ● ● ● ● ● ● ● ● ● ● ● ●

Serving a salad *with your meal has never been easier. Most grocery stores now offer a wide variety of prepackaged salad greens and an even more extensive array of reduced-fat salad dressings.*

We like to rinse the prepackaged salad greens in cold water, and drain them well. A salad spinner works great! The cold water crisps and freshens the greens.

Another option is to pick up fresh salad ingredients from the supermarket salad bar. And some grocery stores sell premade salads in the produce department. For side salads, select the ones containing greens and veggies only (not the ones with lots of meats and cheese).

tortellini and broccoli alfredo with citrus salad
and italian bread   serves 4 • total time 13 minutes

If your weakness is fettuccine Alfredo, this low-fat tortellini Alfredo with fresh veggies might become your favorite new indulgence.

SUPPER plan

1. Boil water for pasta.

2. Prepare Citrus Salad.

3. Cook pasta and broccoli.

4. While pasta cooks, prepare sauce.

Tortellini and Broccoli Alfredo

prep: 1 minute   cook: 9 minutes

1	(9-ounce) package fresh three-cheese tortellini (such as Contadina)
1	(12-ounce) package fresh broccoli florets
1	(1.6-ounce) envelope Alfredo sauce mix (such as Knorr)
1½	cups fat-free milk
2	teaspoons light butter
⅛	teaspoon ground nutmeg
¼	cup preshredded fresh Parmesan cheese
¼	teaspoon freshly ground black pepper

Cook tortellini according to package directions, omitting salt and fat; add broccoli during the last 3 minutes of cooking time. Drain well.

Prepare sauce mix according to package directions, using fat-free milk, butter, and ⅛ teaspoon nutmeg.

Combine sauce, pasta, and broccoli; toss well to coat. Top each serving evenly with cheese and pepper. Yield: 4 servings (serving size: 1¼ cups).

CALORIES 337 (26% from fat); FAT 9.6g (sat 5.7g, mono 1.3g, poly 0.3g); PROTEIN 18.9g; CARB 43.7g; FIBER 3.3g; CHOL 36mg; IRON 1.7mg; SODIUM 900mg; CALC 375mg
EXCHANGES: 3 Starch, 1 High-Fat Meat

Citrus Salad

prep: 3 minutes

Take a citrus shortcut and use refrigerated orange sections. If you have more time, fresh work fine, too.

1	cup refrigerated orange sections
2	teaspoons olive oil
2	teaspoons balsamic vinegar
6	cups mixed salad greens
¼	cup chopped red onion
¼	teaspoon freshly ground black pepper

Drain orange sections, reserving 2 tablespoons juice. Combine reserved orange juice, olive oil, and vinegar, stirring with a whisk.

Combine salad greens, orange sections, and onion; add vinaigrette, and toss gently. Sprinkle with freshly ground black pepper. Yield: 4 servings (serving size: 1½ cups).

CALORIES 64 (37% from fat); FAT 2.6g (sat 0.4g, mono 1.7g, poly 0.3g); PROTEIN 1.9g; CARB 9.9g; FIBER 3.1g; CHOL 0mg; IRON 1.2mg; SODIUM 22mg; CALC 67mg
EXCHANGES: ½ Fruit, 1 Vegetable

HOWto

• • • • • • • • • • • • • • • • • •

If you want to use fresh oranges, *you'll need 2 oranges. To section a fresh orange, peel it, then cut between the white membranes to expose the flesh. Hold the peeled orange over a bowl to catch the juice.*

Nutty Vegetable Pasta

nutty vegetable pasta with sesame breadsticks
and fresh plum slices serves 4 • total time 16 minutes

Grown-ups will love this menu because it reminds them of their favorite Thai restaurant; kids will love it because it contains peanut butter.

SUPPER plan

1. Cut asparagus; chop peanuts.

2. Cook pasta.

3. While pasta cooks:
- Prepare peanut sauce.
- Slice plums.

Nutty Vegetable Pasta

prep: 6 minutes   cook: 10 minutes

Look for packages of matchstick-cut carrots in the produce section near the bagged salads.

1	pound fresh asparagus
8	ounces uncooked angel hair pasta
¾	cup matchstick-cut carrots
⅓	cup reduced-fat creamy peanut butter
¼	cup vegetable broth
2	tablespoons brown sugar
3	tablespoons low-sodium soy sauce
3	tablespoons rice wine vinegar
½	teaspoon crushed red pepper
¼	cup unsalted peanuts, chopped

Snap off tough ends of asparagus. Cut asparagus into 1-inch pieces. Set aside.

Cook pasta according to package directions, omitting salt and fat. Add asparagus pieces to pasta during the last 2 minutes of cooking time. Add carrots during the last 30 seconds of cooking time.

Combine peanut butter and next 5 ingredients in a small saucepan. Cook over medium heat, stirring occasionally, until mixture comes to a boil. Remove from heat.

Drain pasta, and place in a large serving bowl. Stir in peanut sauce, tossing to coat. Top evenly with peanuts. Yield: 4 servings (serving size: 1¼ cups).

CALORIES 390 (30% from fat); FAT 12.9g (sat 1.9g, mono 6g, poly 3.7g); PROTEIN 18.6g; CARB 53.3g; FIBER 6.4g; CHOL 0mg; IRON 3mg; SODIUM 785mg; CALC 51mg
EXCHANGES: 3 Starch, 2 Vegetable, 1 Medium-Fat Meat, 1 Fat

NUTRITIONnote

• • • • • • • • • • • • • • • • • •

Peanut butter-lovers, *take heart. It turns out that even though peanuts and peanut butter are high in fat, it's a healthy kind of fat. Peanuts contain mostly monounsaturated fat, which has been shown to reduce total cholesterol levels without decreasing good cholesterol, thus reducing the risk of heart disease.*

portobello tetrazzini with lemon pepper broccoli
and crisp breadsticks serves 4 • total time 19 minutes

Portobello mushrooms add a rich, hearty flavor to this spinoff of chicken tetrazzini. Even meat-lovers won't miss the meat.

SUPPER plan

1. Thaw and drain vegetable seasoning blend; chop mushrooms.

2. Cook pasta.

3. While pasta cooks:
 • Prepare mushroom mixture.
 • Steam broccoli in the microwave.

Portobello Tetrazzini

prep: 5 minutes   cook: 14 minutes

To remove any excess water from the seasoning blend, drain well, and lightly press between two paper towels.

4	ounces uncooked spaghetti

Cooking spray
2	(6-ounce) packages sliced portobello mushrooms, coarsely chopped
1	cup frozen vegetable seasoning blend, thawed and drained (such as McKenzie's)
1	(10¾-ounce) can condensed reduced-fat, reduced-sodium cream of mushroom soup, undiluted
½	cup fat-free milk
3	tablespoons sherry
½	teaspoon salt
¼	teaspoon freshly ground black pepper
¼	cup preshredded Parmesan cheese

Cook spaghetti according to package directions, omitting salt and fat; drain and set aside.

Heat a large nonstick skillet coated with cooking spray over high heat. Add mushrooms, and sauté 4 minutes or until tender. Add seasoning blend, and cook 1 minute. Add soup and next 4 ingredients; reduce heat to medium, and simmer 5 minutes or until thickened. Add spaghetti; toss well.

Place pasta mixture on each of 4 plates; top each serving with Parmesan cheese. Serve immediately. Yield: 4 servings (serving size: 1¼ cups pasta mixture and 1 tablespoon Parmesan cheese).

CALORIES 233 (18% from fat); FAT 4.6g (sat 2.3g, mono 0.1g, poly 0.3g); PROTEIN 10.5g; CARB 35.9g; FIBER 2g; CHOL 11mg; IRON 1mg; SODIUM 650mg; CALC 179mg
EXCHANGES: 2 Starch, 1 Vegetable, 1 Fat

Lemon Pepper Broccoli

prep: 2 minutes   cook: 3 minutes

4	cups fresh broccoli florets
1	tablespoon water
1	tablespoon light butter
½	teaspoon lemon pepper

Place broccoli and water in a medium microwave-safe bowl. Cover with plastic wrap. Microwave at HIGH 3 minutes or until crisp-tender; drain. Toss broccoli with butter and lemon pepper. Yield: 4 servings (serving size: ¾ cup).

CALORIES 66 (39% from fat); FAT 3.5g (sat 2.1g, mono 0g, poly 0.2g); PROTEIN 4.8g; CARB 7.8g; FIBER 4.1g; CHOL 10mg; IRON 1.3mg; SODIUM 171mg; CALC 68mg
EXCHANGES: 1 Vegetable, 1 Fat

tomato-vegetable pasta with fruited green salad
and italian bread · serves 4 · total time 20 minutes

When you need a quick and hearty meal, just add fresh vegetables to a prepared pasta sauce, and serve it over any pasta you have on hand.

SUPPER plan

1. Boil water for pasta.
2. Quarter mushrooms, and slice zucchini.
3. Cook pasta.
4. While pasta cooks:
   • Prepare sauce.
   • Prepare Fruited Green Salad.

Tomato-Vegetable Pasta

prep: 5 minutes   cook: 15 minutes

6   ounces (about 2½ cups) whole wheat rotini (corkscrew pasta)
1   teaspoon olive oil
Cooking spray
1   (8-ounce) package mushrooms, quartered (about 3½ cups)
1   medium zucchini, quartered lengthwise and sliced into ½-inch cubes (about 2 cups)
1   (26-ounce) jar tomato-basil pasta sauce
¼   teaspoon salt
¼   teaspoon coarsely ground black pepper
¼   cup (1 ounce) preshredded fresh Parmesan cheese

Cook pasta according to package directions, omitting salt and fat.

Heat olive oil in large nonstick skillet coated with cooking spray over medium-high heat. Add mushrooms and zucchini; sauté 7 minutes or until lightly browned.

Add pasta sauce, salt, and pepper to zucchini mixture; stir gently. Cover, reduce heat, and simmer 5 minutes, stirring once.

Drain pasta, and transfer to a large bowl. Spoon pasta sauce over pasta; toss well. Sprinkle with cheese just before serving. Yield: 4 servings (serving size: about 1¾ cups).

CALORIES 287 (15% from fat); FAT 4.9g (sat 1.2g, mono 1.4g, poly 0.5g); PROTEIN 12.8g; CARB 49.7g; FIBER 5.6g; CHOL 4mg; IRON 3.7mg; SODIUM 818mg; CALC 203mg
EXCHANGES: 3 Starch, 1 Vegetable, ½ Fat

Fruited Green Salad

prep: 3 minutes

1   (5-ounce) bag gourmet salad greens (about 6 cups)
1   cup seedless red grapes, halved
½   cup fat-free red wine vinaigrette

Combine all ingredients in a large bowl; toss gently. Yield: 4 servings (serving size: about 1¾ cups).

CALORIES 74 (4% from fat); FAT 0.3g (sat 0.1g, mono 0g, poly 0.1g); PROTEIN 0.8g; CARB 18.2g; FIBER 1.2g; CHOL 0mg; IRON 0.6mg; SODIUM 310mg; CALC 24mg
EXCHANGES: 1 Vegetable, 1 Fruit

White Bean-Tomato Pasta

white bean-tomato pasta with strawberry-spinach salad
and french baguettes   serves 4 • total time 16 minutes

Be good to your heart, and eat the Mediterranean way: olive oil, beans, greens, and fruit. And enjoy a glass of wine for good measure.

SUPPER plan

1. Boil water for pasta.

2. Halve tomatoes; chop basil; slice strawberries for salad.

3. Cook pasta.

4. While pasta cooks:
   - Combine ingredients for tomato mixture.
   - Prepare Strawberry-Spinach Salad.

5. Combine pasta, tomato mixture, and beans.

White Bean-Tomato Pasta

prep: 6 minutes   cook: 10 minutes

Drain, rinse, and heat the beans all in one step by placing the beans in a colander and draining the hot pasta over the beans.

2¼	cups uncooked penne pasta (6 ounces)
1½	cups halved grape tomatoes
½	cup chopped pitted kalamata olives
¼	cup chopped fresh basil
1½	tablespoons balsamic vinegar
1	tablespoon olive oil
¼	teaspoon salt
¼	teaspoon freshly ground black pepper
1	(19-ounce) can cannellini beans, rinsed and drained

Basil sprig (optional)

Cook pasta according to package directions, omitting salt and fat.

Combine tomatoes and next 6 ingredients in a large serving bowl; set aside.

Place beans in a colander; drain pasta over beans, reserving 2 tablespoons water. Add beans, pasta, and reserved water to tomato mixture; toss well. Garnish with a basil sprig, if desired. Serve immediately. Yield: 4 servings (serving size: 1¾ cups).

CALORIES 337 (16% from fat); FAT 6g (sat 0.8g, mono 3.9g, poly 1g); PROTEIN 15.1g; CARB 55.2g; FIBER 6.7g; CHOL 0mg; IRON 3.1mg; SODIUM 459mg; CALC 65mg
EXCHANGES: 3 Starch, 1 Very Lean Meat, 1 Fat

Strawberry-Spinach Salad

prep: 5 minutes

1	(7-ounce) bag baby spinach (about 8 cups)
2	cups sliced strawberries
⅓	cup fat-free balsamic vinaigrette

Combine all ingredients in a large bowl; toss well. Yield: 4 servings (serving size: 2 cups).

CALORIES 52 (9% from fat); FAT 0.5g (sat 0g, mono 0.1g, poly 0.2g); PROTEIN 1.9g; CARB 11.6g; FIBER 3.3g; CHOL 0mg; IRON 1.7mg; SODIUM 307mg; CALC 61mg
EXCHANGES: ½ Fruit, 1 Vegetable

NUTRITIONnote

• • • • • • • • • • • • • • • • • • • •

Spinach and other greens, *such as beet greens and Swiss chard, contain calcium, but these foods also contain compounds called oxalates that bind calcium and block its absorption.*

tortellini in tomato broth with mixed green salad and french bread

serves 4 · total time 14 minutes

Whether you call it a soup or a pasta dish with a rich tomato broth, you'll certainly name it one of your favorite suppers for cold winter nights.

SUPPER plan

1. Cook tortellini.

2. While tortellini cooks:
- Prepare green salad.
- Slice French bread.

Tortellini in Tomato Broth

prep: 7 minutes   cook: 5 minutes
stand: 2 minutes

1	(14-ounce) can vegetable broth
1	cup water
1	(14.5-ounce) can diced tomatoes with balsamic vinegar, basil, and olive oil
¼	cup dry white wine
1	(9-ounce) package refrigerated cheese-filled tortellini
2	cups baby spinach leaves
½	cup fresh basil leaves
¼	teaspoon freshly ground black pepper
8	teaspoons preshredded fresh Parmesan cheese

Combine first 4 ingredients in a large saucepan; bring to a boil. Add tortellini; cook, uncovered, 5 minutes. Remove pan from heat. Place spinach and basil in pan over broth mixture; cover and let stand 2 minutes or until spinach and basil wilt. Stir spinach, basil, and pepper into broth.

Ladle pasta and broth into bowls; top each serving with 2 teaspoons Parmesan cheese. Yield: 4 servings (serving size: 1½ cups).

CALORIES 236 (24% from fat); FAT 6.2g (sat 3.3g, mono 0.3g, poly 0g); PROTEIN 12.5g; CARB 32g; FIBER 1.3g; CHOL 26mg; IRON 1.9mg; SODIUM 685mg; CALC 238mg
EXCHANGES: 2 Starch, 1 Medium-Fat Meat

SERVEwith

• • • • • • • • • • • • • • • • • • • •

Pump up the flavor *of plain French bread with these ideas:*

- *Rub a garlic clove on the cut side of the bread before toasting.*
- *Spread light butter on the bread, and sprinkle with chopped fresh basil, oregano, rosemary, or dill.*
- *Sprinkle with Parmesan cheese.*
- *Top with a yogurt-based spread (such as Brummel & Brown).*
- *Top with a thin layer of light cream cheese and chopped herbs.*
- *Try whole wheat French bread.*

❝It's all about organization. *I get out all my ingredients (the fewer the better!) before I start, and figure out what needs to be cooked first so that everything will be ready at the same time.❞*

Gayle Sadler,
Recipe Editor

roasted tomato-cannellini pasta
with sautéed spinach   **serves 4 • total time 23 minutes**

Treat yourself to a taste of Tuscany with a pasta meal featuring beans, pasta, and greens.

SUPPER plan

1. Bring water to a boil for pasta.
2. Slice garlic; rinse and drain beans.
3. Roast tomatoes.
4. While tomatoes roast:
   - Cook pasta.
   - Sauté sage; toast garlic; prepare bean mixture.
   - Sauté spinach (can use same skillet used for bean mixture).

Roasted Tomato-Cannellini Pasta

prep: 2 minutes   cook: 21 minutes

Toasting the sage leaves brings out their flavor.

2	pints grape tomatoes
1	teaspoon olive oil
3/4	teaspoon salt, divided
8	ounces uncooked fusilli (short, twisted spaghetti)
2	tablespoons olive oil
20	fresh sage leaves
8	garlic cloves, thinly sliced
1	(19-ounce) can cannellini beans, rinsed and drained
1/4	cup vegetable broth
1/4	teaspoon freshly ground black pepper
1/4	cup preshredded Romano or Asiago cheese

Preheat oven to 450°.

Place tomatoes on a 15 x 10-inch jelly roll pan covered with foil. Drizzle with 1 teaspoon oil; sprinkle with 1/4 teaspoon salt. Bake at 450° for 15 minutes.

Cook pasta according to package directions, omitting salt and fat.

Heat 2 tablespoons oil in a large nonstick skillet over medium heat. Add sage leaves; cook 1 minute or until crisp. Remove sage from pan with a slotted spoon; set aside. Place garlic in pan, and cook 1 minute or until lightly toasted. Add beans to pan; cook 2 minutes. Stir in broth, remaining salt, and pepper; simmer 2 minutes or until thoroughly heated. Drain pasta; stir in tomatoes and bean mixture.

Reserve 4 sage leaves. Crumble remaining sage leaves; stir into pasta mixture. Spoon pasta into shallow bowls; top each with 1 tablespoon cheese. Garnish with reserved sage leaves, if desired. Yield: 4 servings (serving size: 2 cups).

CALORIES 419 (25% from fat); FAT 11.5g (sat 2.3g, mono 6.5g, poly 1.6g); PROTEIN 14.0g; CARB 64.8g; FIBER 6.7g; CHOL 7mg; IRON 4.3mg; SODIUM 787mg; CALC 135mg
EXCHANGES: 4 Starch, 1 Vegetable, 2 Fat

Sautéed Spinach

prep: 1 minute   cook: 2 minutes

1	(5-ounce) package fresh baby spinach
1	teaspoon olive oil
1/4	teaspoon salt
1/4	teaspoon crushed red pepper
1	teaspoon red wine vinegar

Combine spinach and oil in a large nonstick skillet. Cook over medium heat 2 minutes or until wilted. Sprinkle with salt, pepper, and vinegar. Yield: 4 servings (serving size: 1/2 cup).

CALORIES 18 (65% from fat); FAT 1.3g (sat 0.2g, mono 0.8g, poly 0.2g); PROTEIN 1g; CARB 1.3g; FIBER 1g; CHOL 0mg; IRON 1mg; SODIUM 175mg; CALC 35mg
EXCHANGE: 1/2 Vegetable

roasted red pepper and arugula pizza
with romaine-mushroom salad
and chocolate sorbet   serves 4 • total time 21 minutes

If you're craving a pizza but you're not really a pepperoni person, here's a pizza with a slightly sophisticated slant.

SUPPER plan

1. Bake crust.

2. While crust bakes:
 • Slice onion and drain peppers for pizza.
 • Shred lettuce, slice mushrooms, and squeeze lemon juice for salad.

3. Arrange toppings on pizza, and bake.

4. While pizza bakes, prepare Romaine-Mushroom Salad.

Roasted Red Pepper and Arugula Pizza

prep: 7 minutes   cook: 14 minutes

  1 tablespoon yellow cornmeal
Cooking spray
  1 (10.5-ounce) package refrigerated pizza dough
  1 (7-ounce) jar roasted red bell pepper, drained
  1 (1.75-ounce) package arugula or 2 cups loosely packed baby spinach leaves
1½ tablespoons pine nuts
¼ cup thinly sliced red onion
¼ teaspoon crushed red pepper
  1 cup preshredded pizza cheese blend

Preheat oven to 425°.
Sprinkle 1 tablespoon cornmeal onto a large baking sheet coated with cooking spray. Unroll pizza dough onto prepared baking sheet, and stretch sides gently into an 11 x 15-inch rectangle. Bake at 425° for 7 minutes. Remove crust from oven.

Layer red pepper strips and arugula over crust. Sprinkle with pine nuts, red onion, and crushed red pepper. Bake at 425° for 5 minutes; sprinkle with cheese, and bake 2 minutes or until cheese melts. Cut into 8 pieces. Yield: 4 servings (serving size: 2 slices).

CALORIES 333 (31% from fat); FAT 11.6g (sat 4.8g, mono 0.6g, poly 0.9g); PROTEIN 14.6g; CARB 41.1g; FIBER 2.2g; CHOL 20mg; IRON 2.9mg; SODIUM 903mg; CALC 222mg
EXCHANGES: 2 Starch, 2 Vegetable, 1 Medium-Fat Meat, 1 Fat

Romaine-Mushroom Salad

prep: 3 minutes

Look for bags of hearts of romaine in the produce section. To shred, cut lettuce crosswise into ½-inch slices.

  1 tablespoon fresh lemon juice (about ½ lemon)
  2 teaspoons extravirgin olive oil
¼ teaspoon salt
¼ teaspoon pepper
  3 cups shredded romaine lettuce
½ cup sliced mushrooms

Combine first 4 ingredients in a medium bowl. Add lettuce and mushrooms. Toss well. Yield: 3½ cups (serving size: about 1 cup).

CALORIES 29 (74% from fat); FAT 2.4g (sat 0.3g, mono 1.7g, poly 0.3g); PROTEIN 1g; CARB 1.7g; FIBER 0.9g; CHOL 0mg; IRON 0.6mg; SODIUM 151mg; CALC 17mg
EXCHANGE: 1 Vegetable

Roasted Red Pepper and
Arugula Pizza

tomato-basil-artichoke pizza
with **easy three-bean salad**   serves 4 • total time 15 minutes

You can make this meal entirely from items you have on hand in the pantry or refrigerator.

SUPPER plan

1. Chop artichokes.

2. Assemble and bake pizza.

3. While pizza bakes, prepare Easy Three-Bean Salad.

Tomato-Basil-Artichoke Pizza

prep: 5 minutes   cook: 10 minutes

Use your kitchen shears to quickly chop artichoke hearts in the can.

1	(10-ounce) Italian cheese-flavored thin pizza crust (such as Boboli)
1	cup tomato-basil pasta sauce
1	(14-ounce) can quartered artichoke hearts, drained and coarsely chopped
1	cup (4 ounces) shredded part-skim mozzarella cheese

Preheat oven to 450°.

Place pizza crust on a baking sheet. Spoon pasta sauce over top, leaving a 1-inch border. Top with chopped artichoke, and sprinkle with cheese.

Bake at 450° for 10 minutes or until cheese melts. Cut into 4 pieces. Yield: 4 servings (serving size: 1 slice).

CALORIES 313 (26% from fat); FAT 9.1g (sat 4.3g, mono 1.4g, poly 0.1g);
PROTEIN 17.8g; CARB 39g; FIBER 1.6g; CHOL 15mg; IRON 3mg;
SODIUM 868mg; CALC 434mg
EXCHANGES: 2 Starch, 2 Vegetable, 1 High-Fat Meat

Easy Three-Bean Salad

prep: 4 minutes

Since this recipe calls for whole cans of beans, you'll have enough salad left over for another meal. Just store the extra in an airtight container in the refrigerator, and it will keep for up to one week.

1	(16-ounce) can kidney beans, rinsed and drained
1	(15-ounce) can black beans, rinsed and drained
1	(15-ounce) can chickpeas, rinsed and drained
½	cup chopped fresh parsley
¼	cup olive oil
¼	cup balsamic vinegar
	Romaine lettuce leaves (optional)

Combine all ingredients in a bowl; toss. Cover and chill. Serve on lettuce leaves, if desired. Yield: 8 servings (serving size: ¾ cup).

CALORIES 153 (46% from fat); FAT 7.8g (sat 0.9g, mono 5.3g, poly 1.3g);
PROTEIN 4.9g; CARB 16g; FIBER 5.3g; CHOL 0mg; IRON 1.9mg;
SODIUM 288mg; CALC 36mg
EXCHANGES: 1 Starch, ½ Fat

mushroom-spinach pizza with baby carrots and low-fat ice cream sandwiches

serves 4 • total time 17 minutes

What better way to add more veggies to your meal than on top of a cheesy pizza?

SUPPER plan

1. Chop spinach.

2. Prepare pizza.

Mushroom-Spinach Pizza

prep: 7 minutes   cook: 10 minutes

Crushed red pepper adds a nice spiciness to this simple pizza.

1	(10-ounce) Italian cheese-flavored thin pizza crust (such as Boboli)
1⅓	cups tomato-basil pasta sauce
1	(8-ounce) package presliced mushrooms
1	cup coarsely chopped baby spinach
1	cup (4 ounces) shredded part-skim mozzarella cheese
¼	teaspoon crushed red pepper

Preheat oven to 450°.

Place pizza crust on a pizza pan or baking sheet. Spoon pasta sauce over crust, leaving a 1-inch border. Top with mushrooms and spinach; sprinkle with cheese and red pepper.

Bake at 450° for 10 minutes or until cheese melts. Cut into 4 pieces. Yield: 4 servings (serving size: 1 slice).

CALORIES 308 (27% from fat); FAT 9.1g (sat 4.1g, mono 1.3g, poly 0.2g); PROTEIN 17.5g; CARB 39.3g; FIBER 2.9g; CHOL 16mg; IRON 3.1mg; SODIUM 773mg; CALC 433mg
EXCHANGES: 2 Starch, 2 Vegetable, 1 High-Fat Meat

FOODfacts

• • • • • • • • • • • • • • • • • • • •

The best way to store *fresh mushrooms is to put them in a paper bag, and refrigerate. Don't store them in an airtight plastic bag because moisture will accumulate and cause spoilage. Stored properly, mushrooms should keep for at least five days.*

Always clean mushrooms just before you use them. Wipe them off with a damp cloth or paper towel, or rinse quickly with cold water. Don't soak them in water.

Mushrooms are mostly water and can dehydrate in a short time. If you have wrinkled mushrooms in your refrigerator, they're fine to eat—just chop or slice them, and add to a soup, stew, or sauce.

Asparagus-Parmesan
Pita Rounds

asparagus-parmesan pita rounds
with **triple chocolate smoothies**
and fresh pear slices   **serves 4 • total time 20 minutes**

No more fussing about who gets the last slice of pizza—everybody gets a whole pita pizza all to themselves.

SUPPER plan

1. Freeze bananas for smoothies.

2. Prepare pitas, and bake.

3. While pitas bake:
- Slice pears.
- Prepare smoothies, and chill.

Asparagus-Parmesan Pita Rounds

prep: 5 minutes   cook: 9 minutes

Most any cheese will work in this recipe. Blue cheese and mozzarella are especially good options.

2	cups (2-inch) sliced asparagus (about 1 pound)
2	teaspoons extravirgin olive oil
2	garlic cloves, minced
4	(6-inch) pitas
3	plum tomatoes, thinly sliced (about ½ pound)
1	teaspoon dried basil
¼	teaspoon crushed red pepper (optional)
¼	teaspoon salt
6	tablespoons preshredded Parmesan cheese

Preheat oven 450°.

Steam asparagus, covered, 2 minutes or until crisp-tender. Rinse with cold water; drain.

Combine oil and garlic. Brush over pitas. Arrange tomato slices and asparagus on pitas. Sprinkle with basil, pepper, and salt. Top evenly with Parmesan cheese. Bake at 450° for 7 to 8 minutes or until edges are golden. Yield: 4 servings (serving size: 1 pita).

CALORIES 245 (20% from fat); FAT 5.4g (sat 1.8g, mono 2.4g, poly 0.7g); PROTEIN 10.5g; CARB 40g; FIBER 3.5g; CHOL 5mg; IRON 2.7mg; SODIUM 601mg; CALC 177mg
EXCHANGES: 2 Starch, 2 Vegetable, 1 Fat

Triple Chocolate Smoothies

prep: 4 minutes   freeze: 20 minutes

1	ripe banana, peeled and sliced
3½	cups chocolate fat-free frozen yogurt
1	cup chocolate soy milk
3	tablespoons fat-free chocolate sundae syrup

Place banana on a plate in a single layer, and freeze 20 minutes.

Combine banana and remaining ingredients in a blender. Process until smooth. Serve immediately. Yield: 4 servings (serving size: 1 cup).

CALORIES 288 (5% from fat); FAT 1.9g (sat 1g, mono 0.5g, poly 0.1g); PROTEIN 11.5g; CARB 63.3g; FIBER 3.6g; CHOL 2mg; IRON 2.1mg; SODIUM 118mg; CALC 316mg
EXCHANGES: 3 Starch, 1 Fruit

NUTRITIONnote

• • • • • • • • • • • • • • • • • • • •

Toast your health *with a Triple Chocolate Smoothie. Bananas are a fat-free source of potassium, which can offset sodium's tendency to raise blood pressure. Soy milk may help reduce cholesterol and decrease the risk of certain kinds of cancer. And chocolate contains flavenoids—substances that have been shown to help reduce heart disease.*

kalamata-artichoke pita pizzas
and roasted asparagus

serves 4 · total time 15 minutes

When pizza night has become routine at your house, get out of the rut and try Middle Eastern-flavored toppings on a pita. If you need something sweet to end your meal, try Grape and Mango Compote (page 334).

SUPPER plan

1. Chop onion; quarter tomatoes; drain and chop artichokes; chop and pit olives; trim asparagus.

2. Top pitas with hummus, vegetables, basil, and cheese.

3. Roast asparagus, and bake pizzas at the same time, removing pizzas after 5 minutes.

Kalamata-Artichoke Pita Pizzas

prep: 6 minutes   cook: 5 minutes

To add different flavors to this pizza, try using a flavored hummus such as roasted red pepper or garlic-flavored.

4	(6-inch) pitas
½	cup hummus
1	cup cherry tomatoes, quartered
¼	cup finely chopped red onion
½	(14-ounce) can quartered artichoke hearts, drained and coarsely chopped
½	teaspoon dried basil
12	kalamata olives, pitted and chopped
⅓	cup crumbled feta cheese with basil and sun-dried tomatoes

Preheat oven to 450°.

Place pitas on a baking sheet. Spread 2 tablespoons hummus over each pita. Top with tomato and remaining ingredients.

Bake at 450° for 5 minutes or until edges are lightly browned. Yield: 4 servings (serving size: 1 pita).

CALORIES 287 (25% from fat); FAT 7.9g (sat 2.2g, mono 1.7g, poly 0.6g); PROTEIN 11g; CARB 43.4g; FIBER 4.2g; CHOL 11mg; IRON 3.5mg; SODIUM 773mg; CALC 146mg
EXCHANGES: 3 Starch, 1 Fat

Roasted Asparagus

prep: 1 minute   cook: 8 minutes

1	pound asparagus spears
	Olive oil-flavored cooking spray
⅛	teaspoon salt
⅛	teaspoon black pepper

Preheat oven to 450°.

Snap off tough ends of asparagus. Place asparagus on a baking sheet. Coat with cooking spray; sprinkle with salt and pepper.

Bake at 450° for 8 to 10 minutes or until tender. Yield: 4 servings.

CALORIES 55 (5% from fat); FAT 0.3g (sat 0.1g, mono 0.1g, poly 0.1g); PROTEIN 3.5g; CARB 11.1g; FIBER 5g; CHOL 0mg; IRON 3.2mg; SODIUM 77mg; CALC 66mg
EXCHANGES: 2 Vegetable

italian eggplant with spinach fettuccine and mixed green salad   serves 4 • total time 18 minutes

Instead of eggplant Parmesan, try this sausage-topped variation, and round out the meal with fettuccine and an Italian-style salad.

SUPPER plan

1. Cook spinach fettuccine according to package directions, omitting salt and fat. Cook 8 ounces of dry fettuccine to get 4 cups of cooked pasta.

2. While fettuccine cooks:
- Thaw and crumble patties.
- Slice eggplant, and broil.
- Prepare mixed green salad with packaged salad greens and fat-free balsamic vinaigrette.

3. Complete eggplant dish.

Italian Eggplant

prep: 10 minutes   cook: 8 minutes

If frozen veggie sausage crumbles are available, use them; you'll need about 1¾ cups.

    4   (1.3-ounce) frozen vegetable protein sausage
        breakfast patties (such as Morningstar Farms)
    1   (1½-pound) eggplant
Cooking spray
    ¼   teaspoon salt
    ¾   cup tomato and basil pasta sauce (such as
        Classico)
    1   teaspoon dried basil leaves
    ⅛   teaspoon crushed red pepper
    1   cup (4 ounces) shredded part-skim
        mozzarella cheese

Preheat broiler.

Partially thaw breakfast patties in microwave at HIGH 10 to 15 seconds; crumble into small pieces.

Remove stem end of eggplant; slice eggplant lengthwise into 4 (½-inch) slices. Arrange slices on a baking sheet coated with cooking spray. Lightly coat slices with spray, and broil 4 minutes. Turn slices, coat with cooking spray, and broil 2 minutes.

Sprinkle salt over eggplant; top evenly with crumbled breakfast patties, and broil 1 minute.

Combine pasta sauce, basil, and red pepper.

Spoon sauce over eggplant, and top with cheese. Broil 1 minute or until cheese melts. Yield: 4 servings (serving size: 1 eggplant slice, about 1 ounce sausage, and 3 tablespoons sauce).

CALORIES 219 (33% from fat); FAT 8g (sat 3.4g, mono 2g, poly 1.6g); PROTEIN 19.3g; CARB 19.5g; FIBER 7.3g; CHOL 17mg; IRON 2.9mg; SODIUM 730mg; CALC 260mg
EXCHANGES: 1 Starch, 1 Vegetable, 2 Lean Meat

NUTRITIONnote

• • • • • • • • • • • • • • • • • • •

Veggie breakfast patties *are made with textured vegetable (soy) protein and have 75 percent less fat than pork sausage patties. Research shows that soy products offer major health benefits such as reducing the risk of certain cancers, decreasing "bad" cholesterol, and minimizing menopause symptoms.*

See page 226 for more information on soy products.

roasted asparagus on parmesan polenta
with **roasted pesto tomatoes**   serves 4 • total time 21 minutes

This bountiful vegetable meal features the best produce of the season. Serve fresh blackberries for dessert, and this meal provides 80 percent of the recommended daily vegetable and fruit servings.

SUPPER plan

1. Cut asparagus and onions; halve mushrooms; mince chives; squeeze lemon juice.

2. Roast asparagus.

3. While asparagus roasts:
- Prepare polenta.
- Prepare Roasted Pesto Tomatoes.

Roasted Asparagus on Parmesan Polenta

prep: 8 minutes   cook: 13 minutes

2	pounds asparagus spears
1	small red onion, cut into wedges
1	(8-ounce) package whole mushrooms, halved
1½	tablespoons olive oil
½	teaspoon salt, divided
4	cups water, divided
1	cup yellow cornmeal
¾	cup preshredded fresh Parmesan cheese
¼	cup minced fresh chives
2	tablespoons fresh lemon juice (about 1 lemon)

Preheat oven to 500°.

Snap off tough ends of asparagus; cut spears into thirds.

Combine asparagus, onion, and mushrooms on a foil-lined baking sheet. Drizzle with oil, and sprinkle with ¼ teaspoon salt; toss gently. Bake at 500° for 8 minutes or until roasted.

Combine 3 cups water and remaining ¼ teaspoon salt in a large saucepan; bring to a boil.

Stir cornmeal into remaining cup of water. Add cornmeal mixture to boiling water, stirring constantly. Cook 4 to 5 minutes or until thickened, stirring occasionally. Stir in cheese.

Sprinkle vegetable mixture with chives and lemon juice; toss gently. Serve over polenta. Yield: 4 servings (serving size: 1 cup vegetables and ⅔ cup polenta).

CALORIES 321 (27% from fat); FAT 9.8g (sat 3.4g, mono 5.2g, poly 0.8g); PROTEIN 16g; CARB 42.3g; FIBER 8.7g; CHOL 11mg; IRON 1.8mg; SODIUM 557mg; CALC 252mg
EXCHANGES: 2 Starch, 2 Vegetable, 1 High-Fat Meat

Roasted Pesto Tomatoes

prep: 1 minute   cook: 10 minutes

The tomatoes can roast in the oven at the same time the asparagus roasts.

2	large tomatoes, seeded and halved
2	tablespoons commercial pesto
4	teaspoons preshredded fresh Parmesan cheese

Preheat oven to 500°.

Place tomato halves, cut sides up, in a nonstick muffin pan. Top each with 1½ teaspoons pesto; top each with 1 teaspoon Parmesan cheese. Bake at 500° for 10 minutes or until roasted. Yield: 4 servings (serving size: ½ tomato).

CALORIES 65 (59% from fat); FAT 4.3g (sat 1.3g, mono 2.4g, poly 0.4g); PROTEIN 2.8g; CARB 4.8g; FIBER 1.2g; CHOL 4mg; IRON 0.7mg; SODIUM 96mg; CALC 81mg
EXCHANGES: 1 Vegetable, 1 Fat

Roasted Asparagus on Parmesan
Polenta with Roasted Pesto
Tomatoes

Garam Masala Vegetables

garam masala vegetables with minted mango slices and pappadum

serves 4 • total time 19 minutes

This spicy blend of vegetables is like a thick vegetable-beef stew without the beef.

SUPPER plan

1. Cook potatoes in the microwave.

2. While potatoes cook:
   • Prepare Minted Mango Slices.
   • Toast spices.

3. Cook vegetable mixture.

4. Heat pappadum in the microwave at HIGH for about 30 seconds per pappadum or just until crisp.

Garam Masala Vegetables

prep: 3 minutes   cook: 16 minutes

Garam masala is a spice blend typically used in Indian dishes. (See page 180 for more information on garam masala.)

1½	pounds red potatoes, cut into large chunks
3	tablespoons vegetable oil
2	teaspoons garam masala
¼	teaspoon ground turmeric
1	(14.5-ounce) can diced tomatoes with garlic and onion, undrained
1	cup matchstick-cut carrots
1	cup frozen green peas
1	cup vegetable broth
¼	teaspoon salt
¼	cup fresh cilantro leaves, tightly packed

Place potato in a microwave-safe bowl; cover with heavy-duty plastic wrap. Microwave at HIGH 3 minutes or until almost done.

Heat oil in a Dutch oven over medium heat. Add garam masala and turmeric; sauté 45 seconds or until spices are toasted. Add potato; cook 2 minutes or until potato begins to brown. Stir in tomatoes; cook 3 minutes or until mixture begins to thicken. Stir in carrots, peas, and broth. Bring to a boil; reduce heat, and simmer, uncovered, 4 minutes or until vegetables are tender. Stir in salt and cilantro. Yield: 4 servings (serving size: about 1½ cups).

CALORIES 291 (36% from fat); FAT 11.6g (sat 0.8g, mono 6g, poly 3.1g); PROTEIN 9.2g; CARB 46.7g; FIBER 7.8g; CHOL 0mg; IRON 3.8mg; SODIUM 941mg; CALC 65mg
EXCHANGES: 3 Starch, 2 Fat

Minted Mango Slices

prep: 2 minutes

Look for bottled mango slices in the produce section of your grocery store.

1	(1-pound, 8-ounce) jar mango slices (about 2 cups)
¼	cup fresh mint leaves, chopped

Combine mango slices and mint; toss. Yield: 4 servings (serving size: about ½ cup).

CALORIES 55 (3% from fat); FAT 0.2g (sat 0.1g, mono 0.1g, poly 0.1g); PROTEIN 0.5g; CARB 14.3g; FIBER 1.6g; CHOL 0mg; IRON 0.2mg; SODIUM 2mg; CALC 12mg
EXCHANGE: 1 Fruit

FINDit

• •

Pappadum are wafer-thin *tortilla-shaped crackers made with lentil flour. Look for them at an Indian market or in the ethnic foods section of your grocery store. Pita rounds are a good substitute.*

grilled vegetable sandwich with apple slices and low-fat frozen yogurt   serves 4 • total time 20 minutes

Dispel the myth that grilling is only for meats with this "mile-high" vegetable sandwich that's packed with great grill flavor. It's a nice option for a summertime patio party.

SUPPER plan

1. Slice bell pepper, eggplant, onion, and zucchini; mince basil.
2. Prepare mayonnaise mixture, and chill.
3. Grill vegetables; grill bread.
4. Assemble sandwich.
5. Slice apples.

Grilled Vegetable Sandwich

prep: 6 minutes   cook: 14 minutes

    2   tablespoons light mayonnaise
    1   tablespoon minced fresh basil
    2   tablespoons olive oil
    3   tablespoons balsamic vinegar
    ¼   teaspoon salt
    ¼   teaspoon freshly ground black pepper
    1   red bell pepper, cut into eighths
    1   (1-pound) eggplant, cut crosswise into
        ½-inch-thick slices
    1   sweet onion, cut crosswise into ¼-inch-
        thick slices
    1   zucchini, cut lengthwise into ¼-inch slices
Cooking spray
    1   (8-ounce) loaf French bread, cut in half
        lengthwise
    6   (1-ounce) slices part-skim mozzarella cheese,
        divided

Prepare grill.

Combine mayonnaise and minced basil; cover and chill.

Combine oil and next 3 ingredients in a large bowl. Add bell pepper, eggplant, onion, and zucchini to dressing mixture; toss vegetable mixture well to coat.

Place bell pepper and eggplant on grill rack coated with cooking spray; grill 6 minutes. Add onion and zucchini; grill 5 minutes. Turn vegetables often, baste with dressing, and cook just until tender. Remove from grill, and keep warm.

Place bread on grill, cut side down, and grill 2 minutes. Turn bread, cut side up, and place half of cheese slices on bottom half of bread. Grill 1 minute or until cheese begins to melt.

Spread mayonnaise mixture over top half of bread. Top bottom half with vegetables, remaining cheese slices, and top half of bread. Cut crosswise into fourths. Yield: 4 servings (serving size: one-fourth of sandwich).

CALORIES 423 (39% from fat); FAT 18.5g (sat 6.3g, mono 7.8g, poly 1.3g); PROTEIN 19.2g; CARB 46.3g; FIBER 6.2g; CHOL 26mg; IRON 2.4mg; SODIUM 784mg; CALC 386mg
EXCHANGES: 2 Starch, 3 Vegetable, 1 High-Fat Meat, 2 Fat

QUICKtip

• • • • • • • • • • • • • • • • • • • •

To keep vegetables from falling through the grill rack, *use a grill basket coated with cooking spray. Or if you don't want to go outside, grill the vegetables on the stovetop using a grill pan.*

Grilled Vegetable
Sandwich

soy story

Soy is a current culinary darling because of its potential health benefits and versatility.

health benefits

Soy products contain isoflavones—plant chemicals—that have impressive disease-fighting properties. Take a look at some of the health benefits:

- reduces risk of breast and prostate cancers, and possibly colon cancer
- reduces risk of heart disease by increasing "good cholesterol" and decreasing "bad cholesterol"
- strengthens bones and reduces risk of osteoporosis
- decreases hot flashes associated with menopause

soy store

If you want to increase the soy in your diet, you've got plenty of options. Here's a quick guide to soy products.

Edamame: fresh soybeans. These beans are available in Asian markets from late spring to early fall. Frozen soybeans are available year-round in the pods or shelled.

Tofu: or soybean curd, is a soft, cheeselike food that's made from curdled soy milk. Tofu is available in firm, extrafirm, soft, silken, and low-fat varieties.

- Soft or silken tofu can be used as a substitute for sour cream, yogurt, cream cheese, or cottage cheese in beverages, dips, puddings, soups, and salad dressings.

- Firm tofu can be cubed, crumbled, or sliced, and used in salads, stir-frys, and pasta dishes.
- Low-fat firm silken tofu has 1.0 gram of fat per 3-ounce serving; regular firm silken tofu has 2.3 grams.

Soy milk: the milk of the soybean. It's lactose-free and comes in regular and low-fat versions. Soy milk isn't naturally high in calcium, but many brands are fortified with calcium, as well as vitamins D and B12.

Tempeh: a fermented soybean cake with a texture similar to that of tofu and a yeasty flavor. Tempeh is often used in stir-fry recipes.

Miso: fermented soybean paste with the consistency of peanut butter. It comes in a variety of flavors and colors; the flavor can vary based on the length of time the paste is aged.

Veggie Sausage: made from textured soy protein with a variety of flavors added to mimic the flavor of sausages. Veggie sausages are available in patties, links, and crumbles.

Veggie Burgers and Burger Crumbles: made with textured soy protein with a flavor and texture similar to that of ground beef. Use the patties and the crumbles just as you would ground beef, but with slightly less cooking time.

saucy enchiladas with shredded lettuce salad
and mexican-style corn   serves 4 • total time 24 minutes

If you're trying to please fans of south-of-the-border fare, this easy menu will get you rave reviews. And, to keep everyone happy, you can make the enchiladas with or without meat.

SUPPER plan

1. Assemble enchiladas.

2. Bake enchiladas.

3. While enchiladas bake:
   • Heat canned or frozen corn according to package directions.
   • Prepare Shredded Lettuce Salad.

Saucy Enchiladas

prep: 8½ minutes   cook: 15 minutes

For the meat-lovers at your table, you can use ½ pound ground round, cooked and crumbled, instead of the burger crumbles.

¾	cup fat-free refried beans
1	tablespoon 40%-reduced-sodium taco seasoning
4	(8-inch) flour tortillas
1	cup frozen burger-style vegetable crumbles (such as Boca Burger)
¾	cup enchilada sauce
½	cup (2 ounces) shredded reduced-fat Cheddar cheese

Preheat oven to 400°.

Combine beans and taco seasoning in a small bowl. Spread each tortilla with 3 tablespoons bean mixture, leaving a ¾-inch border around edges. Sprinkle vegetable crumbles down center of each tortilla; roll up tortillas. Arrange, seam sides down, in an 8-inch-square baking dish. Pour enchilada sauce over tortillas; sprinkle with cheese.

Bake at 400° for 15 minutes or just until sides are bubbly. Yield: 4 servings (serving size: 1 enchilada).

CALORIES 296 (28% from fat); FAT 9.2g (sat 2.8g, mono 2.3g, poly 1.4g); PROTEIN 15.4g; CARB 38.1g; FIBER 3.2g; CHOL 10mg; IRON 2.9mg; SODIUM 897mg; CALC 254mg
EXCHANGES: 2½ Starch, 1 High-Fat Meat

Shredded Lettuce Salad

prep: 2 minutes

Iceberg lettuce is now available, preshredded, in the bagged salad section of the produce department.

4	cups shredded iceberg lettuce
4	tablespoons reduced-fat ranch dressing

Place 1 cup shredded lettuce on each plate. Top each with 1 tablespoon dressing. Yield: 4 servings.

CALORIES 57 (65% from fat); FAT 4.1g (sat 0.8g, mono 0g, poly 0.1g); PROTEIN 0.6g; CARB 3.7g; FIBER 0.8g; CHOL 3mg; IRON 0.3mg; SODIUM 125mg; CALC 10mg
EXCHANGES: 1 Vegetable, ½ Fat

NUTRITIONnote

• • • • • • • • • • • • • • • • • •

If you use ½ pound ground round *instead of the meatless burger crumbles, one serving of Saucy Enchiladas will have 339 calories, 10.3 grams of fat, 3.5 grams of saturated fat, 42 milligrams of cholesterol, and 836 milligrams of sodium.*

santa fe soup with cheese toast and iceberg lettuce salad   serves 5 • total time 21 minutes

A dump and stir soup is the star of this no-stress meal. The only real work you have to do is mince a pepper.

SUPPER plan

1. Drain peas and olives; seed and mince jalapeño.

2. While soup simmers, prepare Iceberg Lettuce Salad and Cheese Toast.

Santa Fe Soup

prep: 7 minutes   cook: 14 minutes

    2   cups burger-style vegetable crumbles
    1   (15-ounce) can black-eyed peas, rinsed and
        drained
    1   (10-ounce) package frozen whole kernel corn
    1   cup frozen chopped onion
    1   (14½-ounce) can no-salt-added diced
        tomatoes
    1   small jalapeño pepper, seeded and minced
    1   (1.25-ounce) package 40%-less-sodium taco
        seasoning
    ½   (1-ounce) package ranch-style dip mix (such
        as Hidden Valley)
    2   cups water
    1   (2¼-ounce) can sliced ripe olives, drained
    5   tablespoons reduced-fat sour cream

    Combine first 9 ingredients in a large
saucepan. Bring to a boil; reduce heat, and simmer, uncovered, 10 minutes. Stir in olives.
Ladle into individual bowls; top each serving
with sour cream. Yield: 5 servings (serving size:
1⅓ cups and 1 tablespoon sour cream).

CALORIES 250 (29% from fat); FAT 8.1g (sat 2.5g, mono 2.6g, poly 2g);
PROTEIN 12.8g; CARB 34.9g; FIBER 6.4g; CHOL 8mg; IRON 3.7mg;
SODIUM 1,109mg; CALC 104mg
EXCHANGES: 2 Starch, 1 Vegetable, 1 Very Lean Meat, 1 Fat

Cheese Toast

prep: 1 minute   cook: 2 minutes

    5   (1-ounce) slices French bread
    5   ounces reduced-fat sharp Cheddar cheese,
        sliced

    Preheat broiler.
    Place bread slices on a baking sheet. Top
each slice with 1 slice cheese. Broil 2 to 3 minutes or until cheese melts. Yield: 5 servings
(serving size: 1 slice).

CALORIES 159 (33% from fat); FAT 5.9g (sat 3.2g, mono 0.3g, poly 0.2g);
PROTEIN 11.6g; CARB 15.2g; FIBER 0.9g; CHOL 20mg; IRON 0.7mg;
SODIUM 395mg; CALC 274mg
EXCHANGES: 1 Starch, 1 Medium-Fat Meat

Iceberg Lettuce Salad

prep: 1 minute

    7½   cups shredded iceberg lettuce
     5   tablespoons reduced-fat Thousand Island
         dressing

    Place lettuce on individual plates. Top each
serving with 1 tablespoon dressing. Yield: 5
servings (serving size: 1½ cups).

CALORIES 34 (48% from fat); FAT 1.8g (sat 0.3g, mono 0.4g, poly 1g);
PROTEIN 1g; CARB 4.2g; FIBER 1.3g; CHOL 2mg; IRON 0.5mg;
SODIUM 161mg; CALC 17mg
EXCHANGE: 1 Vegetable

Santa Fe Soup with
Cheese Toast

veggie sausage-cheddar frittata with broiled tomatoes
and whole grain bread   serves 4 • total time 16 minutes

Bulk up a cheesy egg dish with savory veggie sausage, and serve this frittata for a late-night supper.

SUPPER plan

1. Thaw vegetable patties in microwave.

2. Chop bell pepper for frittata; slice tomatoes.

3. Prepare frittata; cook in skillet.

4. While frittata cooks, prepare tomatoes.

5. Broil frittata and tomatoes.

Veggie Sausage-Cheddar Frittata

prep: 5 minutes   cook: 11 minutes

Vegetable sausage is easier to crumble if you microwave it at HIGH for 15 seconds.

Cooking spray
- 1   green bell pepper, chopped
- 1   (8-ounce) package presliced mushrooms
- 4   (1.3-ounce) frozen vegetable protein sausage patties, thawed and crumbled
- ⅛   teaspoon salt
- ⅛   teaspoon freshly ground black pepper
- 1   cup egg substitute
- ¼   cup fat-free half-and-half
- ½   cup (2 ounces) shredded reduced-fat sharp Cheddar cheese

Preheat broiler.

Place a 12-inch ovenproof nonstick skillet over medium-high heat. Coat pan with cooking spray. Add chopped bell pepper and mushrooms; sauté 3 minutes. Add sausage, salt, and pepper; reduce heat to medium-low, and cook 1 minute.

Combine egg substitute and half-and-half; carefully pour over sausage mixture. Cover and cook 6 minutes. (Frittata will be slightly moist on top.) Sprinkle with cheese.

Broil 1 to 2 minutes or until cheese melts. Cut into 8 wedges. Yield: 4 servings (serving size: 2 wedges).

CALORIES 184 (29% from fat); FAT 5.9g (sat 2.5g, mono 0.7g, poly 1.4g); PROTEIN 21g; CARB 10.4g; FIBER 3.2g; CHOL 11mg; IRON 3.7mg; SODIUM 588mg; CALC 154mg
EXCHANGES: 2 Vegetable, 2 Lean Meat

Broiled Tomatoes

prep: 2 minutes   cook: 3 minutes

- 2   large tomatoes
- 2   tablespoons reduced-fat olive oil vinaigrette
- 2   teaspoons salt-free garlic and herb blend
- 2   tablespoons preshredded fresh Parmesan cheese
- 2   tablespoons Italian-seasoned breadcrumbs

Preheat broiler.

Cut each tomato into 4 slices; place tomato slices on a broiler pan. Drizzle with vinaigrette; sprinkle with salt-free garlic and herb blend.

Combine cheese and breadcrumbs; sprinkle over tomato slices.

Broil 3 to 5 minutes or until cheese melts. Yield: 4 servings (serving size: ½ tomato).

CALORIES 58 (40% from fat); FAT 2.6g (sat 0.6g, mono 0.3g, poly 0.2g); PROTEIN 2.3g; CARB 7.7g; FIBER 1.2g; CHOL 2mg; IRON 0.6mg; SODIUM 210mg; CALC 40mg
EXCHANGES: 1 Vegetable, ½ Fat

Veggie Sausage-Cheddar
Frittata

Wild Rice and Sausage-Stuffed Acorn Squash

wild rice and sausage-stuffed acorn squash
with sliced tomatoes and red grapes   serves 4 • total time 20 minutes

Celebrate the flavors of fall with this elegantly simple stuffed squash menu.

SUPPER plan

1. Cook squash in microwave.

2. While squash cooks:
 • Cube apple.
 • Shred cheese.
 • Chop parsley.
 • Prepare sausage-rice mixture.

3. Spoon sausage-rice mixture into squash.

4. Slice 2 Roma tomatoes, and drizzle evenly with ¼ cup reduced-fat olive oil vinaigrette.

Wild Rice and Sausage-Stuffed Acorn Squash

prep: 8 minutes   cook: 14 minutes

To make it easier to cut the squash in half, cook the whole squash in the microwave at HIGH for about 4 minutes.

2	acorn squash
¼	cup water
1	(14-ounce) can fat-free, less-sodium chicken broth
1	cup frozen chopped onion
¼	teaspoon black pepper
1	(6.2-ounce) package fast-cooking long-grain and wild rice mix (such as Uncle Ben's)
2	teaspoons vegetable oil
1	(14-ounce) package bulk sausage-style vegetable product
1	cup cubed golden delicious apple (about 1)
1	teaspoon bottled minced garlic
½	cup chopped fresh flat-leaf parsley
½	cup shredded Gruyère cheese

Cut squash in half lengthwise; scoop out seeds. Place squash halves, cut sides down, in a shallow baking dish. Pour ¼ cup water into dish. Cover with plastic wrap, and vent. Microwave at HIGH 10 to 12 minutes or until tender.

Combine broth, onion, and pepper in a small saucepan; bring to a boil. Stir in rice and 1½ tablespoons seasoning from packet. (Discard remaining seasoning in packet.) Bring to a boil; cover, reduce heat, and simmer 7 minutes or until liquid is absorbed.

Heat oil in a large nonstick skillet over medium-high heat. Add sausage, apple, and garlic; cook 4 to 5 minutes, stirring to crumble sausage. Stir in rice and parsley.

Spoon 1¼ cups rice mixture into each squash half. Sprinkle evenly with cheese. Yield: 4 servings (serving size: ½ acorn squash and 1¼ cups rice mixture).

CALORIES 480 (14% from fat); FAT 7.8g (sat 3.3g, mono 1.9g, poly 1.7g); PROTEIN 28.1g; CARB 77.7g; FIBER 7.5g; CHOL 15mg; IRON 6.8mg; SODIUM 1,128mg; CALC 331mg
EXCHANGES: 4 Starch, 2 Medium-Fat Meat

NUTRITIONnote

• • • • • • • • • • • • • • • • • •

Low-fat, meat-free products *that replace regular breakfast sausage are now available in supermarkets across the nation. These soy protein-based products come in links, patties, and crumbles and are lower in calories, fat, and cholesterol than pork sausage.*

pad thai
with bok choy salad
serves 4 • total time 22 minutes

Instead of going out for your favorite Thai food, you can have it at home in a matter of minutes.

SUPPER plan

1. Boil water for pasta.

2. Drain tofu.

3. Cook pasta.

4. While tofu drains and pasta cooks:
- Slice green onions.
- Combine ingredients for sauce.
- Prepare Bok Choy Salad.

5. Stir-fry tofu, and combine with pasta.

Pad Thai

prep: 10 minutes   cook: 12 minutes

Draining the tofu reduces the amount of water, so the tofu is more dense. A denser tofu is easier to cut and retains its cut shape as it cooks.

1	(15-ounce) package extrafirm tofu
6	ounces uncooked linguine
⅓	cup rice wine vinegar
¼	cup sugar
¼	teaspoon crushed red pepper
¼	cup reduced-fat peanut butter
3	tablespoons fish sauce
1	tablespoon ketchup
2	teaspoons vegetable oil
2	tablespoons bottled minced garlic
1	cup sliced green onions (about 4 large)

Cut each block of tofu in half lengthwise. Place tofu slices on several layers of paper towels; cover with additional paper towels. Let stand 10 minutes, pressing down occasionally.

Cook pasta according to package directions; drain.

Combine vinegar and next 5 ingredients; stir with a whisk.

Cut tofu into cubes. Heat a large nonstick skillet over high heat until very hot; add oil. Add tofu; stir-fry 2 minutes. Add garlic; stir-fry 1 minute. Stir in vinegar mixture; cook 1 minute. Add pasta and green onions; toss well. Yield: 4 servings (serving size: 1 cup).

CALORIES 443 (30% from fat); FAT 14.7g (sat 2.7g, mono 4.6g, poly 7g); PROTEIN 21.3g; CARB 58g; FIBER 2.8g; CHOL 0mg; IRON 3.9mg; SODIUM 1,185mg; CALC 122mg
EXCHANGES: 4 Starch, 1 Lean Meat, 2 Fat

Bok Choy Salad

prep: 5 minutes

4	cups sliced bok choy or napa cabbage (1 head)
1	cup red bell pepper strips (about 1 pepper)
2	tablespoons finely chopped unsalted dry-roasted peanuts
¼	cup low-fat ginger vinaigrette

Combine all ingredients, tossing well. Yield: 4 servings (serving size: 1½ cups).

CALORIES 62 (51% from fat); FAT 3.5g (sat 0.3g, mono 1.1g, poly 0.8g); PROTEIN 2.8g; CARB 6g; FIBER 1.5g; CHOL 0mg; IRON 0.8mg; SODIUM 181mg; CALC 78mg
EXCHANGES: 1 Vegetable, 1 Fat

Pad Thai

cashew broccoli and tofu with grapefruit-pineapple medley

serves 4 · total time 16 minutes

A stir-fry is always a good choice for a superfast meal—especially one like this that requires very little chopping. If you buy broccoli florets, the only vegetable you have to chop is the red bell pepper.

SUPPER plan

1. Drain and cut tofu into strips; slice pepper; mince ginger; chop nuts.

2. Cook rice.

3. While rice cooks:
  • Prepare Grapefruit-Pineapple Medley.
  • Prepare Cashew Broccoli and Tofu.

Cashew Broccoli and Tofu

prep: 4 minutes   cook: 12 minutes

To get 4 cups cooked rice, use 2 regular-sized boil-in-bag rice bags.

  1 (15-ounce) package extrafirm tofu, drained and cut into ½-inch-thick strips
  1 cup vegetable broth, divided
  ¼ cup low-sodium soy sauce, divided
  2 teaspoons cornstarch
  1½ tablespoons dark sesame oil, divided
  3 cups broccoli florets
  2 cups thinly sliced red bell pepper (about 2)
  2 tablespoons minced peeled fresh ginger
  ½ teaspoon crushed red pepper (optional)
  4 cups hot cooked rice
  ¼ cup dry-roasted unsalted cashews, chopped

   Place tofu strips on several layers of paper towels; cover with additional paper towels, and press to remove moisture.
   Combine ½ cup broth, 2 tablespoons soy sauce, and cornstarch; set aside.
   Drizzle remaining 2 tablespoons soy sauce over tofu strips. Heat 1 tablespoon oil in a large nonstick skillet over medium-high heat. Add tofu; cook 5 to 6 minutes or until browned, turning occasionally. Remove tofu from pan; keep warm. Heat remaining ½ tablespoon oil in same pan. Add broccoli, bell pepper, ginger, and, if desired, crushed red pepper. Cook 2 to 3 minutes, stirring constantly. Add remaining ½ cup broth; cover and simmer 2 to 3 minutes or until broccoli is crisp-tender. Add cornstarch mixture; cook 1 minute or until thickened. Gently stir tofu into vegetables. Serve over rice; sprinkle with cashews. Yield: 4 servings (serving size: 1¼ cups tofu mixture, 1 cup rice, and 1 tablespoon cashews).

CALORIES 424 (34% from fat); FAT 16.2g (sat 3g, mono 5.7g, poly 6.8g); PROTEIN 18.4g; CARB 53g; FIBER 4.5g; CHOL 0mg; IRON 4.1g; SODIUM 806mg; CALC 128mg
EXCHANGES: 3 Starch, 1 Vegetable, 1 Lean Meat, 2 Fat

Grapefruit-Pineapple Medley

prep: 2 minutes

Buy fresh pineapple chunks in the produce department of the supermarket.

  2 cups bottled grapefruit sections
  2 cups fresh pineapple chunks
  3 tablespoons chopped fresh cilantro

   Combine all ingredients. Yield: 4 servings (serving size: ½ cup).

CALORIES 84 (5% from fat); FAT 0.5g (sat 0g, mono 0.1g, poly 0.1g); PROTEIN 1.2g; CARB 21.1g; FIBER 1.4g; CHOL 0mg; IRON 0.6mg; SODIUM 10mg; CALC 25mg
EXCHANGES: 1½ Fruit

Cashew Broccoli and Tofu

Spicy Asparagus-Tempeh
Stir-Fry

spicy asparagus-tempeh stir-fry
and tropical fruit salad   serves 4 · total time 22 minutes

Not your "run-of-the-mill" stir-fry, this one features the nutty, earthy flavors of tempeh, mushrooms, and brown rice.

SUPPER plan

1. Trim asparagus and slice tempeh for stir-fry.

2. Stir-fry tempeh.

3. Cook rice.

4. While rice cooks:
- Prepare fruit salad by sprinkling 2 tablespoons of coconut over 2 cups of refrigerated tropical fruit (such as Del Monte Sun Fresh).
- Prepare stir-fry.

Spicy Asparagus-Tempeh Stir-Fry

prep: 12 minutes   cook: 10 minutes

Prepare 3 cups cooked brown rice by using 1 large bag of boil-in-bag brown rice.

¾   pound asparagus spears
¾   cup vegetable broth
¼   cup low-sodium soy sauce
2   teaspoons cornstarch
2   tablespoons sesame oil, divided
1   (8 ounce) package multigrain tempeh (such as White Wave Five-Grain), thinly sliced
4   garlic cloves, minced
½   teaspoon crushed red pepper
1   (6-ounce) package sliced shiitake mushrooms
3   cups hot cooked instant brown rice

Snap off tough ends of asparagus. Cut spears diagonally into 2-inch pieces. Set aside.

Combine vegetable broth, soy sauce, and cornstarch in a small bowl; stir with a whisk until smooth. Set aside.

Heat 1 tablespoon sesame oil in a large non-stick skillet over medium-high heat. Add tempeh, and stir-fry 4 to 5 minutes or until golden. Remove tempeh from pan; set aside.

Heat remaining 1 tablespoon sesame oil in same pan. Add garlic, red pepper, asparagus, and mushrooms to pan, and stir-fry 3 minutes or until asparagus is crisp-tender. Add broth mixture; bring to a boil, and cook 2 to 3 minutes or until thickened. Add tempeh, and cook 1 minute or until thoroughly heated. Serve over brown rice. Yield: 4 servings (serving size: 1 cup stir-fry and ¾ cup brown rice).

CALORIES 390 (33% from fat); FAT 14.7g (sat 2.5g, mono 4.9g, poly 5.6g); PROTEIN 18.6g; CARB 49.4g; FIBER 8.2g; CHOL 0mg; IRON 4mg; SODIUM 745mg; CALC 104mg
EXCHANGES: 3 Starch, 1 Vegetable, 1 High-Fat Meat, 1 Fat

FINDit

• • • • • • • • • • • • • • • • • • • •

Look for tempeh *(fermented soybean cake) in the produce section of the grocery store along with tofu and other soy products. Or you can usually find it at a health-food store.*

> **"** *I don't get home until 6 p.m. and then have to cook supper, so I have very little time to relax with my kids before their bedtime at 8 p.m. I need some recipes that will get me in and out of the kitchen fast.* **"**

easy
ENTRÉES

With over 40 meals that you can have on the table in about 20 minutes or less, these superfast suppers let you spend time doing the things you'd really rather be doing. To help you quickly locate the types of meals you're looking for, this chapter is divided into 3 sections: Fish and Shellfish (page 242), Meats (page 261), and Poultry (page 292).

Fish & Shellfish Entrées

Basil Scallops with Spinach Fettuccine, page 253

Beef Entrées

Seared Steaks with Creamy Horseradish Sauce, page 269

Poultry Entrées

Kalamata-Feta Chicken, page 299

go fish

At last, there is one nutrition recommendation that almost everyone agrees with: **Eat more fish.** You can prepare fish to perfection if you follow the simple guidelines below.

buying it

- Fresh fish is firm, bright, and has no discoloration. If the fish smells "fishy" or like ammonia, don't buy it.

- Be sure that the fish you buy is wrapped separately in a leak-proof package.

- Don't buy cooked fish that is displayed next to raw fish because there is a risk of cross-contamination.

- Store fresh fish in the refrigerator up to 2 days or wrap tightly in airtight wrap, and freeze up to 3 months.

- Frozen fish is a great option. Because of modern techniques, fish that is frozen at sea can be just as tasty as fresh. If you buy frozen fish, thaw it overnight on the lowest shelf of the refrigerator.

cooking it

- Cut down on odors by adding a little wine, vinegar, or lemon juice to the liquid used to cook or marinate fish.

- A general guideline for baking, broiling, pan-frying, or grilling fish is to cook it 10 minutes per inch of thickness. But some delicate fish may require less time, as do some firm-fleshed fish such as tuna.

- Fish is done when it flakes easily with a fork or when the flesh looks opaque. As soon as the fish stops looking raw in the middle, remove it from the heat. If you're using a thermometer, fish is thoroughly cooked at 145°.

simple shellfish

Don't pass up shellfish because you think that it's too complicated to cook. This chapter features shellfish recipes that require very little effort.

Shrimp: You can buy shrimp already peeled and deveined at the seafood counter. In most markets, you can buy it steamed, too. Frozen cooked shrimp is available in the frozen food section. If you prefer to buy unpeeled fresh shrimp, see pages 127 and 173 for information on how much to buy and how to peel and devein.

Scallops: These mollusks are removed from their shells at sea, so when you buy them, they're ready to cook. Fresh scallops should be either creamy white, tan, or slightly pink and not dry or dark around the edges.

Crabmeat: Instead of cooking fresh crabs in the shell, you can buy a container of fresh cooked lump or flaked crabmeat (you'll need to pick out the shells). Or you can buy imitation crabmeat (surimi) which is cooked and ready to use.

easy seafood salad with crisp breadsticks
and raspberry sorbet   serves 4 • total time 16 minutes

This shortcut salad is similar to a traditional Crab Louis (lump crabmeat on a bed of shredded lettuce topped with a dressing of mayonnaise and chili sauce) but without the expense of fresh crabmeat.

SUPPER plan

1. Cook egg.

2. While egg cooks:
   - Slice green onions.
   - Chop imitation crabmeat.
   - Slice tomatoes.

3. Assemble salads.

Easy Seafood Salad

prep: 6 minutes   cook: 10 minutes

If you have a hard-cooked egg on hand, this chilled salad takes only 6 minutes to make.

1	large egg
½	cup light mayonnaise
2	tablespoons chili sauce
1	teaspoon white wine Worcestershire sauce
2	teaspoons lemon juice
2	tablespoons sliced green onions (1 small)
1	pound imitation crabmeat, coarsely chopped
6	cups preshredded iceberg lettuce
4	plum tomatoes, thinly sliced lengthwise

Place egg in a saucepan; add enough water to measure at least 1 inch above egg. Cover and bring to a boil over high heat. Remove from heat, and let stand, covered, in hot water 10 minutes. Drain; run cold water over egg to cool. Remove shell, and coarsely chop egg.

Combine mayonnaise and next 5 ingredients in a medium bowl.

Place lettuce on each plate; top with crabmeat mixture. Sprinkle with egg; garnish with tomato slices. Yield: 4 servings (serving size: about ⅔ cup crabmeat mixture, 1½ cups lettuce, 1 tomato).

CALORIES 276 (42% from fat); FAT 12.9g (sat 2.2g, mono 0.8g, poly 1g); PROTEIN 16.9g; CARB 24.4g; FIBER 2.9g; CHOL 86mg; IRON 1mg; SODIUM 1,498mg; CALC 68mg
EXCHANGES: 1 Starch, 2 Vegetable, 1 Lean Meat, 2 Fat

FINDit

• • • • • • • • • • • • • • • • • • • •

Imitation crabmeat, or surimi, is fish pulp that is formed into various shapes. Most surimi found in this country is made from pollock and is usually in the shape of crab legs, lobster chunks, shrimp, and scallops.

Look for surimi in the refrigerator or freezer section of supermarkets. You can keep it unopened in the refrigerator up to 2 months and in the freezer up to 6 months. Once you open the package, you need to use it within 3 days. Surimi is best in salads, casseroles, and soups.

Although the calories and fat aren't much different in fresh seafood and their comparable surimi form, the sodium content of a surimi product is twice as high. If you're using the imitation product in a recipe that includes salt, leave out the salt until you taste-test the recipe.

Salmon with Mustard Cream and Pan-Roasted Potatoes

salmon with mustard cream
and **pan-roasted potatoes**   serves 4 • total time 12 minutes

Enjoy this succulent salmon with a glass of pinot noir and double the benefit to your heart. Both the omega-3 fats in the fish and the resveratrol in the wine appear to reduce the risk of heart disease.

SUPPER plan

1. Cook potatoes.

2. Broil salmon.

3. While potatoes and salmon cook, prepare sauce for salmon.

Salmon with Mustard Cream

prep: 1 minute   cook: 8 minutes

4   (6-ounce) skinless salmon fillets
Cooking spray
⅛   teaspoon coarsely ground black pepper
½   cup reduced-fat sour cream
1½   tablespoons Dijon mustard
2   teaspoons chopped fresh dill
¼   teaspoon coarsely ground black pepper
1½   teaspoons lemon juice
1   garlic clove, minced
¼   teaspoon salt

Preheat broiler.
Place fish on a broiler pan; coat fish with cooking spray, and sprinkle with ⅛ teaspoon pepper. Broil 8 minutes or until fish flakes easily when tested with a fork.
Combine sour cream and next 6 ingredients.
Place fillets on plates. Spoon sauce over fish. Yield: 4 servings (serving size: 1 fillet and about 2 tablespoons sauce).

CALORIES 254 (36% from fat); FAT 10.1g (sat 3.3g, mono 1.8g, poly 2.5g); PROTEIN 35.8g; CARB 3.2g; FIBER 0.2g; CHOL 104mg; IRON 1.6mg; SODIUM 421mg; CALC 82mg
EXCHANGES: 5 Lean Meat

Pan-Roasted Potatoes

prep: 1 minute   cook: 10 minutes

1   tablespoon olive oil
1   (20-ounce) package refrigerated new potato wedges (such as Simply Potatoes)
1   teaspoon Greek seasoning
¼   teaspoon freshly ground black pepper

Heat oil in a large skillet over medium-high heat. Add potato, and cook 10 to 12 minutes or until golden brown, stirring frequently. Remove from heat, and sprinkle with seasoning and pepper. Yield: 4 servings (serving size: ¾ cup).

CALORIES 118 (26% from fat); FAT 3.4g (sat 0.5g, mono 2.5g, poly 0.3g); PROTEIN 3.5g; CARB 17.6g; FIBER 3.5g; CHOL 0mg; IRON 0.7mg; SODIUM 169mg; CALC 0mg
EXCHANGES: 1 Starch, 1 Fat

NUTRITION**note**

• • • • • • • • • • • • • • • • • •

Eating salmon is good for your heart
because it's rich in omega-3 fatty acids—fats which appear to offer a number of health benefits. These fats have been shown to:
- *lower triglycerides*
- *help maintain normal heart rhythm*
- *decrease the risk of clot formation in the arteries*
- *provide partial relief for the inflammation associated with rheumatoid arthritis*

snapper with tomato-caper topping
with **sautéed zucchini** and crusty french bread

serves 4 • total time 22 minutes

The zesty flavor of the tomato-caper topping provides a delightful contrast to the mild, sweet snapper.

SUPPER plan

1. Halve tomatoes, drain capers, chop parsley, squeeze lemon, and cut lemon wedges for fish; slice zucchini.

2. Bake fish.

3. While fish bakes, sauté zucchini.

Snapper with Tomato-Caper Topping

prep: 4 minutes   cook: 15 minutes

Halibut, sea bass, redfish, or pompano will also work well in this recipe.

2	cups halved grape tomatoes
2	tablespoons capers, drained
2	tablespoons fresh lemon juice (about 1 lemon)
2	teaspoons olive oil
1½	teaspoons dried or 1 tablespoon chopped fresh basil
¼	teaspoon salt
⅛	teaspoon crushed red pepper (optional)
4	(6-ounce) snapper or grouper fillets (about ¾ inch thick)

Cooking spray
1	teaspoon paprika
2	tablespoons chopped fresh parsley
1	lemon, cut into 4 wedges

Preheat oven to 450°.

Combine first 6 ingredients and crushed red pepper, if desired; set aside.

Place snapper on a broiler pan lined with aluminum foil; coat foil with cooking spray. Sprinkle snapper with paprika; coat with cooking spray. Bake at 450° for 10 minutes.

Top snapper with tomato mixture; bake 5 minutes or until fish flakes easily when tested with a fork. Sprinkle with parsley, and serve with lemon wedges. Yield: 4 servings (serving size: 1 fillet and ¼ cup topping).

CALORIES 215 (21% from fat); FAT 4.9g (sat 0.9g, mono 2.1g, poly 1.1g); PROTEIN 36.1g; CARB 5.8g; FIBER 1.7g; CHOL 63mg; IRON 1.4mg; SODIUM 391mg; CALC 85mg
EXCHANGES: 1 Vegetable, 5 Very Lean Meat

Sautéed Zucchini

prep: 3 minutes   cook: 5 minutes

Cooking spray
3	zucchini, sliced
½	teaspoon olive oil
1	teaspoon Greek seasoning
1	tablespoon preshredded fresh Parmesan cheese

Heat a large nonstick skillet coated with cooking spray over medium-high heat. Add zucchini; sauté 5 minutes or until lightly browned. Drizzle with oil; sprinkle with seasoning and cheese. Yield: 4 servings (serving size: 1 cup).

CALORIES 40 (20% from fat); FAT 0.9g (sat 0.3g, mono 0.5g, poly 0.1g); PROTEIN 2g; CARB 6g; FIBER 3g; CHOL 1mg; IRON 0.6mg; SODIUM 41mg; CALC 46mg
EXCHANGES: 2 Vegetable

Snapper with Tomato-Caper Topping

grilled tuna-couscous salad
and feta pita rounds   serves 4 • total time 20 minutes

Add grilled tuna to this Mediterranean-style grain salad for a simple summer supper.

SUPPER plan

1. Chop parsley, mint, and onion; halve tomatoes.

2. Assemble pita rounds.

3. Prepare couscous.

4. While couscous stands:
   • Grill tuna.
   • Grill pita rounds.

5. Prepare vinaigrette; combine with couscous mixture and tuna.

Grilled Tuna-Couscous Salad

prep: 6 minutes   cook: 12 minutes

```
  2  cups water
  ½  cup lemon juice, divided
1¼  teaspoons salt, divided
  1  (10-ounce) package couscous
  1  cup chopped fresh parsley
  ¼  cup chopped fresh mint
  ¼  cup finely chopped red onion
  1  pint cherry tomatoes, halved
  2  (6-ounce) tuna steaks (about ½ inch thick)
  2  tablespoons plus 2 teaspoons olive oil
Olive oil-flavored cooking spray
  ½  teaspoon freshly ground black pepper
```

Prepare grill.

Combine water, 2 teaspoons lemon juice, and ¼ teaspoon salt in a saucepan. Bring to a boil over high heat. Stir in couscous. Remove from heat; cover and let stand 5 minutes. Place couscous in a bowl; stir in parsley and next 3 ingredients.

Brush tuna with 2 teaspoons oil and ¼ teaspoon salt. Place fish on grill rack coated with cooking spray. Cover and grill 2 minutes on each side or until desired degree of doneness. Remove from grill, and flake into large pieces.

Whisk together 2 tablespoons olive oil, remaining lemon juice, and ¾ teaspoon salt. Pour vinaigrette over couscous mixture. Add tuna, and toss. Sprinkle with pepper. Yield: 4 servings (serving size: 2 cups).

CALORIES 453 (23% from fat); FAT 11.4g (sat 1.7g, mono 7g, poly 1.8g); PROTEIN 30.8g; CARB 60.1g; FIBER 4.6g; CHOL 38mg; IRON 3.5mg; SODIUM 797mg; CALC 73mg
EXCHANGES: 4 Starch, 3 Lean Meat

Feta Pita Rounds

prep: 1 minute   cook: 2 minutes

Put the pita rounds on the grill right after you turn the tuna.

```
  1  (6-inch) pita
Olive oil-flavored cooking spray
  ¼  cup (1 ounce) finely crumbled reduced-fat
     feta cheese
  ¼  teaspoon dried oregano
```

Split pita in half lengthwise to get 2 thin rounds. Coat each half with cooking spray.

Combine feta cheese and oregano; sprinkle mixture evenly over each round. Place on grill rack coated with cooking spray, and grill 2 minutes or until crisp. Cut each half into 4 wedges. Yield: 4 servings (serving size: 2 wedges).

CALORIES 57 (19% from fat); FAT 1.2g (sat 0.7g, mono 0g, poly 0.1g); PROTEIN 2.6g; CARB 8.7g; FIBER 0.4g; CHOL 3mg; IRON 0.4mg; SODIUM 174mg; CALC 27mg
EXCHANGE: ½ Starch

sesame tuna with coconut-cilantro rice and asian coleslaw
serves 4 · total time 15 minutes

The clean, crisp flavors of this Asian-style meal will satisfy your desire for simplicity as well as your hearty appetite.

SUPPER plan

1. Cut onion into strips, grate lime rind, squeeze juice, and chop cilantro.

2. Cook rice.

3. While rice cooks:
   • Prepare Sesame Tuna.
   • Prepare Asian Coleslaw.

4. Stir lime juice, rind, and cilantro into rice.

Sesame Tuna

prep: 3 minutes   cook: 7 minutes

½   teaspoon salt
4   (6-ounce) tuna steaks (about ½ inch thick)
2   tablespoons sesame seeds
2   teaspoons sesame oil
12 green onion tops, cut into 2-inch strips
1   tablespoon low-sodium soy sauce

Sprinkle salt evenly on fish. Sprinkle sesame seeds on both sides of fish, pressing seeds gently into fish.

Heat oil in a large nonstick skillet over medium-high heat. Add fish; cook 2 minutes on each side or until fish flakes easily when tested with a fork. Remove from pan, and keep warm.

Add green onions and soy sauce to pan; sauté 3 minutes. Spoon over fish. Yield: 4 servings (serving size: 1 tuna steak).

CALORIES 249 (22% from fat); FAT 6.1g (sat 1g, mono 2g, poly 2.4g); PROTEIN 40.8g; CARB 4.8g; FIBER 2.2g; CHOL 77mg; IRON 2mg; SODIUM 499mg; CALC 72mg
EXCHANGES: 1 Vegetable, 5 Very Lean Meat, 1 Fat

Coconut-Cilantro Rice

prep: 5 minutes   cook: 7 minutes

1⅔ cups water
⅓   cup light coconut milk
½   teaspoon salt
2   cups uncooked instant rice
¼   teaspoon grated lime rind
1   tablespoon fresh lime juice (½ lime)
¼   cup chopped fresh cilantro

Combine first 3 ingredients in a saucepan; bring to a boil over medium-high heat. Add rice. Cover and let stand 5 minutes or until rice is tender. Stir in lime rind, juice, and cilantro. Yield: 4 servings (serving size: ¾ cup).

CALORIES 175 (7% from fat); FAT 1.3g (sat 0.7g, mono 0.1g, poly 0.1g); PROTEIN 3.5g; CARB 36.3g; FIBER 1.2g; CHOL 0mg; IRON 1.2mg; SODIUM 307mg; CALC 19mg
EXCHANGES: 2 Starch

Asian Coleslaw

prep: 2 minutes

2   tablespoons rice vinegar
1   tablespoon sesame oil
1   teaspoon sugar
¼   teaspoon crushed red pepper
2   cups angel hair shredded cabbage

Whisk together first 4 ingredients. Pour dressing over cabbage, stirring to coat. Yield: 4 servings (serving size: ½ cup).

CALORIES 43 (73% from fat); FAT 3.5g (sat 0.5g, mono 1.4g, poly 1.5g); PROTEIN 0.5g; CARB 3g; FIBER 0.8g; CHOL 0mg; IRON 0.2mg; SODIUM 7mg; CALC 17mg
EXCHANGES: 1 Vegetable, ½ Fat

tuna with jalapeño sour cream
and pepper slaw   serves 4 · total time 19 minutes

Chili-flavored tuna with jalapeño cream and tangy slaw give this menu big flavor.

SUPPER plan

1. Seed and chop jalapeño; squeeze lime juice; chop cilantro.
2. Prepare sour cream mixture.
3. Prepare Pepper Slaw.
4. Rub tuna with chili powder and salt; cook tuna.

Tuna with Jalapeño Sour Cream

prep: 8 minutes   cook: 6 minutes

½   cup reduced-fat sour cream
1   jalapeño pepper, seeded and finely chopped
1   tablespoon fresh lime juice (½ lime)
¼   cup chopped fresh cilantro
¼   teaspoon salt
1   tablespoon chili powder
¼   teaspoon salt
4   (6-ounce) tuna steaks (about 1 inch thick)
Cooking spray

Combine first 5 ingredients; set aside.
Combine chili powder and ¼ teaspoon salt. Rub tuna with chili powder mixture; coat with cooking spray. Place a large nonstick skillet over medium-high heat until hot; add tuna. Cook 3 minutes on each side or until desired degree of doneness. Serve with sour cream mixture. Yield: 4 servings (serving size: 1 tuna steak and about 2½ tablespoons jalapeño sour cream).

CALORIES 239 (21% from fat); FAT 5.7g (sat 2.8g, mono 0.3g, poly 0.6g); PROTEIN 41.5g; CARB 3.6g; FIBER 0.9g; CHOL 92mg; IRON 1.6mg; SODIUM 396mg; CALC 85mg
EXCHANGES: 5 Very Lean Meat, 1 Fat

Pepper Slaw

prep: 5 minutes

Look for a package of coleslaw mix that doesn't include a dressing packet.

3   cups coleslaw mix (about ½ of a 16-ounce package)
½   cup chopped green bell pepper
¼   cup sugar
¼   cup red wine vinegar
2   tablespoons water
⅛   teaspoon salt
⅛   teaspoon black pepper

Combine coleslaw mix and bell pepper. Combine sugar and remaining 4 ingredients; stir well. Pour over cabbage mixture; toss. Cover and chill. Yield: 4 servings (serving size: ¾ cup).

CALORIES 71 (2% from fat); FAT 0.1g (sat 0g, mono 0g, poly 0.1g); PROTEIN 0.8g; CARB 16.6g; FIBER 1.6g; CHOL 0mg; IRON 0.5mg; SODIUM 84mg; CALC 28mg
EXCHANGES: ½ Starch, 1 Vegetable

NUTRITIONnote

• • • • • • • • • • • • • • • • • •

Some fish contain high levels of a form of mercury *that can harm an unborn child's developing nervous system. If you're pregnant, considering pregnancy, or nursing, it's best not to eat the following fish:*

- *halibut*
- *king mackerel*
- *large mouth bass*
- *marlin*
- *oysters (Gulf of Mexico)*
- *sea bass*
- *shark*
- *swordfish*
- *tilefish*
- *tuna*
- *walleye*
- *white croaker*

Tuna with Jalapeño Sour
Cream and Pepper Slaw

Basil Scallops with Spinach
Fettuccine

basil scallops with spinach fettuccine
and french bread rolls   serves 4   •   total time 17 minutes

This no-fuss seafood dinner is one to keep in mind for last-minute entertaining. It's elegant enough to impress your guests, but simple enough to ease your stress.

SUPPER plan

1. Bring water to a boil for pasta.

2. Chop basil, onions, and parsley.

3. Cook pasta.

4. While pasta cooks, prepare scallops.

Basil Scallops with Spinach Fettuccine

prep: 2 minutes   cook: 15 minutes

8	ounces uncooked spinach fettuccine
1½	pounds sea scallops
¾	teaspoon freshly ground black pepper
	Cooking spray
2	tablespoons extravirgin olive oil
1	tablespoon Dijon mustard
1	tablespoon chopped fresh basil
¼	teaspoon salt
¾	cup dry white wine or low-sodium chicken broth
⅓	cup finely chopped green onion (about 2)
3	tablespoons chopped fresh parsley

Cook pasta according to package directions, omitting salt and fat. Drain.

Rinse scallops, and pat dry with a paper towel. Sprinkle scallops with pepper. Place a large nonstick skillet coated with cooking spray over medium-high heat until hot. Add half of scallops; cook 3 minutes on each side or until done. Remove scallops from pan; keep warm. Repeat procedure with remaining scallops.

Combine olive oil and next 3 ingredients; set aside.

Place same pan over high heat until hot. Add wine and green onions, and cook 1 minute. Add olive oil mixture; cook 15 seconds. Add scallops and any accumulated juices; cook 15 seconds, stirring constantly. Spoon scallops and juices over pasta. Sprinkle with parsley. Yield: 4 servings (serving size: about ¾ cup scallops and 1 cup pasta).

CALORIES 375 (23% from fat); FAT 9.7g (sat 1.1g, mono 5.2g, poly 1.1g); PROTEIN 34.8g; CARB 36.9g; FIBER 2.1g; CHOL 56mg; IRON 2.7mg; SODIUM 635mg; CALC 94mg
EXCHANGES: 2 Starch, 1 Vegetable, 4 Very Lean Meat, 1 Fat

SERVEwith

• • • • • • • • • • • • • • • • • •

If you're having guests, *we recommend offering a cool, crisp Chenin Blanc and serving Lemon-Raspberry Tarts (page 346) for dessert. You can make the tarts in 6 minutes, and let them chill while you're enjoying dinner.*

fresh ginger scallops with cilantro rice

and steamed snow peas   serves 4 • total time 22 minutes

There's nothing mellow about this meal. The vibrant flavors of the lime, ginger, and cilantro provide an exciting background for the sweet scallops.

SUPPER plan

1. Chop shallots and cilantro; peel and grate ginger; grate lime rind; cut limes into wedges.

2. Cook rice.

3. While rice cooks, prepare scallops.

4. Steam snow peas in microwave for 1 minute or just until crisp-tender.

Fresh Ginger Scallops with Cilantro Rice

prep: 9 minutes   cook: 13 minutes

One regular-sized bag of boil-in-bag rice will give you 2 cups of cooked rice.

1	regular-sized bag boil-in-bag long-grain rice
2	tablespoons chopped fresh cilantro
1	tablespoon light butter
¾	cup dry white wine or low-sodium chicken broth
3	tablespoons finely chopped shallots
1	tablespoon grated peeled fresh ginger
1	teaspoon grated lime rind
½	teaspoon salt
1½	pounds sea scallops
3	tablespoons light butter, melted
2	limes, cut into 8 wedges

Cook rice according to package directions, omitting salt and fat. Stir cilantro and 1 tablespoon butter into cooked rice.

Combine wine and next 4 ingredients in a small bowl; set aside.

Rinse scallops, and pat dry with paper towels. Pour melted butter over scallops, and toss well.

Place a nonstick skillet over medium-high heat until hot. Add half of scallop mixture; cook 3 minutes on each side. Remove scallops from heat, and keep warm. Wipe pan with a paper towel. Repeat procedure with remaining scallop mixture.

Pour wine sauce into pan; cook over medium heat 1 minute or until thoroughly heated. Spoon sauce over scallops. Serve with rice and lime wedges. Yield: 4 servings (serving size: 1 cup scallop mixture and ½ cup rice).

CALORIES 294 (23% from fat); FAT 7.5g (sat 4.2g, mono 0.1g, poly 0.5g); PROTEIN 31.7g; CARB 25.1g; FIBER 1g; CHOL 76mg; IRON 1.4mg; SODIUM 645mg; CALC 59mg
EXCHANGES: 1½ Starch, 4 Very Lean Meat, 1 Fat

HOWto

• • • • • • • • • • • • • • • • • •

To chop fresh cilantro *(and other herbs such as parsley, basil, and mint), wash the leaves in cold water, nip off the stems, and pat the leaves dry with paper towels. Hold the herbs tightly together on a cutting board with one hand; as you cut, move the fingertips of this hand to the blade. Use your other hand to hold the blade on the cutting board, rocking the knife up and down and scraping the cilantro into a pile as you cut.*

asian shrimp and vermicelli salad
with sesame breadsticks and orange wedges

serves 4 • total time 19 minutes

Toss tender pasta, shrimp, and veggies in a tangy, sweet sauce for a fresh, colorful one-dish meal.

SUPPER plan

1. Bring water to a boil for pasta.

2. Cut pepper into strips; peel and mince ginger.

3. Prepare sauce for salad.

4. Cook pasta and shrimp mixture.

5. While pasta and shrimp cook, slice oranges into wedges.

Asian Shrimp and Vermicelli Salad

prep: 10 minutes   cook: 9 minutes

1/3	cup cider vinegar
1/3	cup packed dark brown sugar
1/4	cup low-sodium soy sauce
1 1/2	teaspoons cornstarch
1	(7-ounce) package vermicelli, uncooked and broken in half
1	pound peeled and deveined large shrimp
1/2	(16-ounce) package frozen sugar snap peas (about 1 1/2 cups)
1	red bell pepper, seeded and cut into thin strips
1	tablespoon low-sodium soy sauce
2	teaspoons minced peeled fresh ginger

Combine first 4 ingredients in a small saucepan, stirring until smooth. Bring to a boil over high heat, and cook, stirring constantly, 30 seconds or until thickened. Cool completely.

Cook pasta in boiling water 5 minutes, omitting salt and fat. Stir in shrimp, and cook 2 minutes or until shrimp are done. Place shrimp mixture in a colander; add peas, and rinse with cold water. Drain well.

Place shrimp mixture in a large bowl. Stir soy sauce mixture, bell pepper, 1 tablespoon soy sauce, and ginger into shrimp mixture; toss gently to coat. Yield: 4 servings (serving size: 1 3/4 cups).

CALORIES 402 (4% from fat); FAT 1.9g (sat 0.4g, mono 0.3g, poly 0.8g); PROTEIN 26.9g; CARB 68.9g; FIBER 5.8g; CHOL 161mg; IRON 6.1mg; SODIUM 862mg; CALC 114mg
EXCHANGES: 4 Starch, 2 Vegetable, 1 Very Lean Meat

VEGETARIANoption

• • • • • • • • • • • • • • • • •

For a meatless alternative *to this pasta salad, leave out the shrimp, and toss in 1/2 cup toasted peanuts.*

buttery lemon shrimp with quick caesar salad
and french bread   serves 4 · total time 14 minutes

You'll need the French bread to sop up every bit of the buttery sauce from this simple shrimp dish.

SUPPER plan

1. Chop parsley; combine ingredients for sauce.

2. Prepare Quick Caesar Salad.

3. Cook shrimp.

Buttery Lemon Shrimp

prep: 5 minutes   cook: 5 minutes

Buy peeled and deveined shrimp from the seafood market or the seafood counter at the grocery store.

¼   cup yogurt-based spread (such as Brummel & Brown)
2   tablespoons lemon juice
1   teaspoon low-sodium Worcestershire sauce
½   teaspoon paprika
Cooking spray
1½   pounds peeled and deveined large shrimp
1   teaspoon Old Bay seasoning
2   tablespoons chopped fresh parsley

Combine first 4 ingredients in a small bowl; set aside.

Place a large nonstick skillet coated with cooking spray over medium heat until hot. Add shrimp and seasoning; sauté 2 minutes. Add yogurt spread mixture, and cook 3 minutes or until shrimp are done. Spoon shrimp and liquid into individual serving bowls, and sprinkle with parsley. Yield: 4 servings (serving size: 6 ounces shrimp and 3 tablespoons sauce).

CALORIES 171 (34% from fat); FAT 6.4g (sat 1.4g, mono 0.3g, poly 0.6g); PROTEIN 26.1g; CARB 0.9g; FIBER 0.2g; CHOL 242mg; IRON 4mg; SODIUM 959mg; CALC 53mg
EXCHANGES: 4 Very Lean Meat

Quick Caesar Salad

prep: 4 minutes

1   (10-ounce) package hearts of romaine
1   cup fat-free croutons (about 2 ounces)
1   tablespoon preshredded fresh Parmesan cheese
½   cup reduced-fat Caesar dressing
¼   teaspoon freshly ground black pepper

Combine first 3 ingredients in a large serving bowl. Pour dressing over lettuce mixture, tossing gently to coat. Sprinkle with pepper. Yield: 4 servings (serving size: 2 cups).

CALORIES 115 (20% from fat); FAT 2.5g (sat 0.7g, mono 0.1g, poly 0.1g); PROTEIN 3.6g; CARB 18.8g; FIBER 1.2g; CHOL 11mg; IRON 0.8mg; SODIUM 497mg; CALC 42mg
EXCHANGES: 1 Starch, ½ Fat

Buttery Lemon Shrimp with
Quick Caesar Salad

quick creole shrimp and grits
with crusty french bread   serves 5 · total time 18 minutes

This quick version of a traditional Louisiana favorite will leave you with plenty of time to listen to jazz or to kick up your heels to some Cajun tunes.

SUPPER plan

1. Chop pepper; crumble bacon.

2. Cook tomato mixture.

3. While tomato mixture cooks, cook grits.

4. Add shrimp to tomato mixture, and cook.

Quick Creole Shrimp and Grits

prep: 5 minutes   cook: 13 minutes

Cooking spray
- 2   cups chopped green bell pepper (about 2)
- 1   (14.5-ounce) can petite diced tomatoes with garlic and olive oil
- 4   slices precooked bacon, crumbled
- ½   teaspoon Creole seasoning
- 1½   pounds peeled and deveined large shrimp
- 1⅔   cups fat-free milk
- 2   cups fat-free, less-sodium chicken broth
- 1   cup uncooked quick-cooking grits
- 1   tablespoon light butter
- ¾   cup light cream cheese, softened

Heat a large skillet coated with cooking spray over medium-high heat. Add chopped pepper; sauté 5 minutes. Add tomatoes, bacon, and Creole seasoning; cook 5 minutes. Add shrimp, and cook 3 minutes or until shrimp are done.

Combine milk and broth in a saucepan; bring to a boil over medium-high heat. Stir in grits; return to a boil. Reduce heat; simmer, uncovered, 5 minutes or until thickened. Stir in butter and cream cheese until melted. Serve shrimp mixture over grits. Yield: 5 servings (serving size: about ¾ cup grits and 1 cup shrimp mixture).

CALORIES 411 (24% from fat); FAT 10.9g (sat 6g, mono 0.3g, poly 0.7g); PROTEIN 34.6g; CARB 42.5g; FIBER 2.1g; CHOL 221mg; IRON 5.9mg; SODIUM 1,225mg; CALC 206mg
EXCHANGES: 2 Starch, 2 Vegetable, 3 Lean Meat

FINDit

Look for precooked bacon *in the section of the grocery store where you find the other types of bacon, sausage, and cold cuts.*

Since the bacon is fully cooked, all you have to do is heat it in the microwave at HIGH for about 5 seconds per slice. Or you can heat it in a conventional oven at 425° for 2 to 4 minutes until the bacon is the desired crispness.

The bacon is packaged in a low-oxygen pouch and can be stored unrefrigerated, refrigerated, or in the freezer. After opening the pouch, store in the refrigerator up to 2 weeks.

Precooked bacon is available in premium cut, thick-slice, lower-sodium, and maple-flavored varieties.

You can also buy 2.5- or 3-ounce packages of cooked and crumbled real bacon pieces. They're usually near the shelves with the bottles of imitation bacon bits, croutons, and salad dressings.

curried coconut shrimp
and fresh citrus fruit   serves 4 · total time 20 minutes

Celebrate the flavors of the islands with this uncomplicated curry dinner.

SUPPER plan

1. Cook basmati rice according to package directions, omitting salt and fat.

2. While rice cooks:
- Cut pepper into strips; slice onion; peel and grate ginger.
- Cook shrimp and vegetable mixture.
- Drain jar of refrigerated citrus fruit.

Curried Coconut Shrimp

prep: 8 minutes   cook: 20 minutes

Cooking spray
1½   pounds peeled and deveined medium shrimp
1   large red bell pepper, cut into ¼-inch strips
1   cup thinly sliced onion (about 1)
1   cup light coconut milk
2   teaspoons cornstarch
½   cup water
1½   tablespoons grated peeled fresh ginger
    or bottled minced ginger
1   teaspoon curry powder
¾   teaspoon salt
½   cup frozen petite green peas
3   cups hot cooked basmati rice

Heat a large nonstick skillet coated with cooking spray over medium-high heat. Add shrimp; sauté 1 to 2 minutes or until almost done. Remove shrimp from pan; keep warm.

Add red bell pepper and onion to pan; cook over medium-high heat 5 minutes or until crisp-tender, stirring frequently. Combine coconut milk and cornstarch in a small bowl. Add cornstarch mixture, water, and next 3 ingredients to pan. Bring to a boil; simmer 1 to 2 minutes or until sauce is thickened. Add shrimp and peas; cook 1 minute or until thoroughly heated. Serve over basmati rice. Yield: 4 servings (serving size: 1 cup shrimp mixture and ¾ cup rice).

CALORIES 383 (12% from fat); FAT 4.9g (sat 2.5g, mono 0.4g, poly 0.7g); PROTEIN 31g; CARB 51.3g; FIBER 2.8g; CHOL 242mg; IRON 7mg; SODIUM 756mg; CALC 70mg
EXCHANGES: 3 Starch, 1 Vegetable, 3 Very Lean Meat

HOWto

• • • • • • • • • • • • • • • • • • •

The freshest gingerroot *has smooth skin; wrinkled skin means the root is old and the flesh will be dry.*

The best flavor in a piece of fresh gingerroot is just under the skin. So carefully peel away only the tough outer skin.

To store fresh ginger, wrap it tightly in plastic wrap, and keep it in the refrigerator up to 1 week or in the freezer up to 2 months.

creamy seafood-parmesan pasta
with **nutty fruited green salad**
and french bread rolls   serves 4 · total time 15 minutes

Sometimes there's nothing more soothing than creamy, rich pasta for dinner.

SUPPER plan

1. Bring water to a boil for noodles.

2. Mince garlic, and chop onions.

3. Cook noodles.

4. While noodles cook:
- Cook shrimp mixture.
- Prepare Nutty Fruited Green Salad.

Creamy Seafood-Parmesan Pasta

prep: 3 minutes   cook: 11 minutes

- 6   ounces uncooked medium egg noodles
- 8   ounces sea scallops
- Cooking spray
- ½   pound peeled and deveined medium shrimp
- 1   teaspoon seafood seasoning (such as Old Bay)
- 2   garlic cloves, minced or 2 teaspoons bottled minced garlic
- ½   cup fat-free half-and-half
- 2   tablespoons yogurt-based spread (such as Brummel & Brown)
- ½   cup finely chopped green onions (about 2)
- ¼   cup grated Parmesan cheese

Cook noodles according to package directions, omitting salt and fat.

Rinse scallops, and pat dry with paper towels.

Place a large nonstick skillet coated with cooking spray over medium heat until hot. Add scallops, shrimp, seasoning, and garlic; cook 5 minutes, stirring frequently, or until shrimp and scallops are done. Add half-and-half, yogurt spread, and green onions. Remove from heat. Add noodles and cheese, tossing to coat. Yield: 4 servings (serving size: 1¼ cups).

CALORIES 330 (19% from fat); FAT 7.1g (sat 2.2g, mono 1.2g, poly 0.9g); PROTEIN 27.1g; CARB 36.2g; FIBER 1.5g; CHOL 145mg; IRON 3.6mg; SODIUM 973mg; CALC 161mg
EXCHANGES: 2½ Starch, 3 Very Lean Meat, ½ Fat

Nutty Fruited Green Salad

prep: 4 minutes

- 4   cups mixed salad greens
- 1   Gala apple, cored and thinly sliced
- 3   tablespoons golden raisins
- ⅓   cup fat-free red wine vinaigrette
- 2   tablespoons chopped pecans

Combine first 4 ingredients in a large bowl; toss well. Sprinkle with pecans. Yield: 4 servings (serving size: 1½ cups).

CALORIES 105 (25% from fat); FAT 2.9g (sat 0.3g, mono 1.5g, poly 0.9g); PROTEIN 1.5g; CARB 20.4g; FIBER 3.1g; CHOL 0mg; IRON 1mg; SODIUM 213mg; CALC 37mg
EXCHANGES: 1 Fruit, 1 Vegetable, ½ Fat

meats in minutes

When you're living fast and cooking light, quick-cooking meats are what you need in your kitchen.

Consider this gift to the time challenged: Some of the leanest cuts of meat are the ones that require the least amount of cooking. For busy weeknights, here are the cuts that will have you in and out of the kitchen in no time, but also offer the benefit of being low in fat and calories, high in protein and iron.

Beef
- Ground round
- Flank steak
- Sirloin steak
- Tenderloin steak
- Top round steak

Veal
- Cutlet
- Loin chop

Lamb
- Loin chop
- Leg of lamb, cubed

Pork
- Boneless loin chop
- Center loin chop
- Cutlet
- Tenderloin

quick tips

Here are a few secrets to the art of cooking meats quickly.

- Cut meat into small pieces. The smaller the pieces, the quicker they cook. For example, when you cut beef or pork into cubes or thin strips for a stir-fry, the meat cooks in about 5 minutes or less.

- Pound meat. The thinner the meat, the quicker it cooks. Pounding with a meat mallet or rolling pin also helps tenderize the meat. When you make a pork or veal piccata, you pound the meat to a ¼-inch thickness.

- Cook a healthy portion. To control fat and calories, the recommended serving size of meat is 4 ounces of raw meat or 3 ounces of cooked meat per person. Chops and steaks that are about 4 ounces will cook more quickly than larger pieces of meat.

HEAT-AND-EAT MEATS If you'd rather just "heat something up" than cook, there are plenty of options. Check labels for fat and sodium content as precooked, packaged meats are sometimes made with higher-fat cuts and usually have more sodium than fresh meats.

PRODUCT	WHERE TO FIND IT	COMMENTS
Deli roast beef and ham	Deli	Ready to use
Cooked burger crumbles	Refrigerated meats section	Fully cooked; heat per package directions
Cooked pot roast	Refrigerated meats section	Fully cooked; heat per package directions
Cooked meat loaf	Refrigerated meats section	Fully cooked; heat per package directions
Cooked beef tips	Refrigerated meats section	Fully cooked; heat per package directions
Cooked beef stew	Refrigerated meats section	Fully cooked; heat per package directions
Premarinated pork tenderloin	Refrigerated meats section	Cook per package directions
Barbecue pork	Refrigerated meats section	Fully cooked; heat per package directions
Frozen meatballs*	Freezer section	Cook per package directions
Ground beef patties*	Freezer section	Cook per package directions

Fat content higher than ground round

gingered flank steak
and jícama-lime slaw serves 4 • total time 22 minutes

Peppery sweet ginger adds just the right amount of spice to this flavorful flank steak. Jícama and lime juice perk up ordinary coleslaw with crunch and zest.

SUPPER plan

1. Prepare and combine ingredients for wine mixture; brush on steak, and broil.

2. While steak broils:
• Peel and cube jícama; chop onion; squeeze lime juice.
• Prepare Jícama-Lime Slaw; cover and chill.

3. Cook sauce while steak stands; slice steak.

Gingered Flank Steak

prep: 5 minutes   cook: 17 minutes

¼   cup dry red wine
3   tablespoons low-sodium soy sauce
3   tablespoons Worcestershire sauce
2   tablespoons lemon juice
1   tablespoon grated peeled fresh ginger or bottled minced ginger
2   garlic cloves, minced or 2 teaspoons bottled minced garlic
2   teaspoons sugar
1   (1-pound) flank steak, trimmed (about ½ inch thick)
Cooking spray

Preheat broiler.
Combine first 7 ingredients in a small saucepan; stir well.
Place steak on a broiler pan coated with cooking spray. Brush steak with 1 tablespoon wine mixture, and broil 6 minutes. Turn steak; brush with 1 tablespoon wine mixture. Broil 6 minutes or until desired degree of doneness. Let stand 5 minutes before slicing.
Bring remaining wine mixture to a boil; cook 5 minutes or until reduced to ¼ cup.
Cut steak diagonally across grain into thin slices. Serve steak with wine sauce. Yield: 4 servings (serving size: 3 ounces steak and 1 tablespoon sauce).

CALORIES 210 (36% from fat); FAT 8.4g (sat 3.6g, mono 3.4g, poly 0.3g); PROTEIN 25.6g; CARB 6.7g; FIBER 0.2g; CHOL 46mg; IRON 3mg; SODIUM 599mg; CALC 26mg
EXCHANGES: ½ Starch, 3 Lean Meat

Jícama-Lime Slaw

prep: 10 minutes

1   medium jícama, peeled and cut into ¼-inch cubes
1   cup preshredded green cabbage
¼   cup finely chopped red onion
⅓   cup fresh lime juice (about 2 large limes)
2   teaspoons olive oil
1½ teaspoons sugar
¼   teaspoon salt
¼   teaspoon freshly ground black pepper

Combine all ingredients in a medium bowl, tossing well to coat. Serve at room temperature or chilled. Yield: 4 servings (serving size: 1 cup).

CALORIES 103 (22% from fat); FAT 2.5g (sat 0.4g, mono 1.7g, poly 0.3g); PROTEIN 1.7g; CARB 19.8g; FIBER 8.8g; CHOL 0mg; IRON 1.2mg; SODIUM 157mg; CALC 33mg
EXCHANGES: ½ Starch, 2 Vegetable

dijon sirloin
and **chipotle mashed potatoes**   serves 4 • total time 15 minutes

A meal this full of flavor is hard to come by in only 15 minutes. Mustard and lime juice pump up the flavor of the steak, while chipotle chiles, lime, and cilantro transform plain mashed potatoes into spuds that are simply smashing!

SUPPER plan

1. Chop parsley; mince garlic; drain and chop chile; chop cilantro; squeeze lime juice.

2. Cook potatoes.

3. While potatoes cook, spread mustard mixture over steak, and broil steak.

Dijon Sirloin

prep: 5 minutes   cook: 7 minutes

To vary the flavor slightly, use any type of flavored mustard. Honey mustard or Creole mustard are two good choices.

 3   tablespoons whole grain Dijon mustard
 1   tablespoon fresh lime juice (about ½ lime)
 ¼   teaspoon salt
 2   garlic cloves, minced or 2 teaspoons
     bottled minced garlic
 1   pound boneless sirloin steak (¾ inch thick)
Cooking spray
 2   tablespoons chopped fresh parsley
 ½   teaspoon coarsely ground black pepper

Preheat broiler.
Combine first 4 ingredients in a small bowl; stir well.
Place steak on a broiler pan coated with cooking spray. Spoon half of mustard mixture evenly over steak, and broil 4 minutes. Turn steak, and spread remaining mustard mixture over steak. Broil 3 minutes or until desired degree of doneness. Place steak on a serving platter; sprinkle with parsley and pepper. Yield: 4 servings (serving size: 3 ounces steak).

CALORIES 193 (37% from fat); FAT 8g (sat 2.7g, mono 3.3g, poly 0.6g); PROTEIN 27.1g; CARB 2.3g; FIBER 0.3g; CHOL 77mg; IRON 3.4mg; SODIUM 490mg; CALC 32mg
EXCHANGES: 4 Lean Meat

Chipotle Mashed Potatoes

prep: 2 minutes   cook: 8 minutes

If you want your potatoes to be extra-creamy, increase the milk to 1¼ cups.

 1   cup 1% low-fat milk
 2¾   cups frozen mashed potatoes (such as
      Ore-Ida)
 1   drained canned chipotle chile in adobo
      sauce, chopped
 ¼   cup chopped fresh cilantro
 1   tablespoon fresh lime juice (about ½ lime)
 ¼   teaspoon salt
 ¼   teaspoon freshly ground black pepper

Heat milk in a medium saucepan over medium heat. Add potato; cook, stirring occasionally, 5 minutes or until thoroughly heated. Remove from heat; add chipotle pepper and remaining ingredients, stirring well. Yield: 4 servings (serving size: ⅔ cup).

CALORIES 122 (21% from fat); FAT 2.8g (sat 1.4g, mono 0.2g, poly 0g); PROTEIN 3.1g; CARB 20.2g; FIBER 1.1g; CHOL 2mg; IRON 0.1mg; SODIUM 355mg; CALC 79mg
EXCHANGES: 1½ Starch

Sirloin with Chipotle-
Tomato Sauce

sirloin with chipotle-tomato sauce

with yellow rice and flour tortillas   serves 4 • total time 21 minutes

The combination of chili powder, cumin, and chipotle chile peppers adds an earthy sort of heat to the meat instead of a "makes your head sweat" heat.

SUPPER plan

1. Slice onion; drain and chop chile.

2. Prepare ½ package of yellow rice mix according to package microwave directions, omitting fat. Use ½ package of rice (about ¾ cup uncooked rice) and 1¾ cups of water to get about 2½ cups cooked rice.

3. While rice cooks, prepare Sirloin with Chipotle-Tomato Sauce.

4. Wrap 4 tortillas in damp paper towels, and heat in the microwave at HIGH for 30 seconds.

Sirloin with Chipotle-Tomato Sauce

prep: 5 minutes   cook: 16 minutes

- 1   tablespoon chili powder
- 1   teaspoon ground cumin
- ¼   teaspoon salt
- 1   pound boneless sirloin steak, trimmed (about ½ inch thick)
- Cooking spray
- 1½   cups thinly sliced onion
- 1   (14½-ounce) can diced tomatoes with green peppers and onions, undrained
- 1   drained canned chipotle chile in adobo sauce, finely chopped
- 1   teaspoon sugar
- 4   (8-inch) warm flour tortillas

Preheat broiler.

Combine first 3 ingredients. Sprinkle steak with chili powder mixture. Place on a broiler pan coated with cooking spray. Broil 4 minutes on each side or until desired degree of doneness. Let stand 5 minutes before slicing.

Heat a large nonstick skillet coated with cooking spray over medium-high heat. Add onion; sauté 4 minutes. Add tomatoes, chile, and sugar; bring to a boil. Reduce heat, and simmer, uncovered, 4 minutes. Thinly slice steak across grain. Serve steak with tomato mixture and warm tortillas. Yield: 4 servings (serving size: 3 ounces steak, ½ cup sauce, and 1 tortilla).

Note: Use your remaining chipotle chiles in adobo sauce in Chipotle Mashed Potatoes (page 263) or Chipotle Black Bean Chili (page 100).

CALORIES 368 (22% from fat); FAT 8.8g (sat 2.5g, mono 3.5g, poly 0.9g); PROTEIN 30.4g; CARB 41.2g; FIBER 3.6g; CHOL 69mg; IRON 5mg; SODIUM 934mg; CALC 148mg
EXCHANGES: 2 Starch, 2 Vegetable, 3 Lean Meat

SERVEwith

• • • • • • • • • • • • • • • • • •

Offer a refreshing dessert *with this hearty beef meal. Grape and Mango Compote (page 334) or Mixed Fruit Compote with Rum (page 335) are both good choices and each takes only 4 minutes to prepare.*

sirloin tips with vegetables and **toasted polenta rounds**

serves 4 • total time 23 minutes

This hearty dish is like a beef and vegetable kabob minus the skewers—it's all cooked in the skillet. The toasted polenta rounds are a nice switch from rice.

SUPPER plan

1. Cut onion and bell peppers into pieces.

2. Prepare Toasted Polenta Rounds.

3. While polenta rounds bake:
- Cook sirloin tips.
- Cook onion and peppers.

Sirloin Tips with Vegetables

prep: 5 minutes   cook: 10 minutes

If you can't find precut sirloin tips, have the butcher cut a trimmed sirloin steak into 1½-inch pieces.

2	teaspoons olive oil
1	pound sirloin tips
½	teaspoon salt, divided
¼	teaspoon freshly ground black pepper
1	large Vidalia or other sweet onion, cut into 1½-inch pieces
1	green bell pepper, seeded and cut into 1½-inch pieces
1	red bell pepper, seeded and cut into 1½-inch pieces
¼	cup plus 2 tablespoons water, divided
2	teaspoons tomato, basil, and garlic seasoning blend (such as Mrs. Dash)

Heat oil in a large nonstick skillet over high heat. Sprinkle sirloin tips with ¼ teaspoon salt and pepper. Add beef to pan, and cook 3 to 5 minutes, stirring frequently, or until desired degree of doneness. Remove beef from pan; set aside, and keep warm.

Reduce heat to medium-high. Add onion and peppers to pan; sauté 3 minutes. Add 2 tablespoons water; cook 1 minute.

Add beef to onion mixture; sprinkle with seasoning blend and remaining ¼ teaspoon salt. Add ¼ cup water to pan; bring to boil, scraping browned bits from bottom of pan. Cook, stirring constantly, 1 minute. Yield: 4 servings (serving size: 1½ cups).

CALORIES 240 (32% from fat); FAT 8.4g (sat 2.4g, mono 4.1g, poly 0.5g); PROTEIN 33.4g; CARB 6.3g; FIBER 1.7g; CHOL 92mg; IRON 3.7mg; SODIUM 370mg; CALC 18mg
EXCHANGES: 1 Vegetable, 4 Lean Meat

Toasted Polenta Rounds

prep: 3 minutes   cook: 15 minutes

Look for tubes of polenta in the refrigerated produce section of the supermarket.

1	(16-ounce) tube of polenta, cut into 8 slices
	Olive oil-flavored cooking spray
2	tablespoons preshredded fresh Parmesan cheese
1	teaspoon Italian seasoning

Preheat oven to 450°.

Coat both sides of polenta slices with cooking spray, and place on a baking sheet. Sprinkle evenly with cheese and seasoning.

Bake at 450° for 15 minutes or until golden. Yield: 4 servings (serving size: 2 slices).

CALORIES 91 (7% from fat); FAT 0.7g (sat 0.4g, mono 0.2g, poly 0g); PROTEIN 3g; CARB 16.1g; FIBER 2g; CHOL 2mg; IRON 0.7mg; SODIUM 241mg; CALC 31mg
EXCHANGE: 1 Starch

Sirloin Tips with Vegetables and
Toasted Polenta Rounds

Seared Steaks with Creamy
Horseradish Sauce with
Roasted Onions and Peppers

seared steaks with creamy horseradish sauce
with roasted onions and peppers
and sourdough rolls   serves 4 · total time 21 minutes

Searing steaks in a skillet is a great way to maximize their flavor without having to go to the grill.

SUPPER plan

1. Slice onion and peppers; halve 2 garlic cloves; mince 1 clove; cut steak into 4 pieces.

2. Roast onions and peppers.

3. While onions and peppers roast:
- Cook steaks in skillet.
- Prepare horseradish sauce.

Seared Steaks with Creamy Horseradish Sauce

prep: 4 minutes   cook: 9 minutes

- 1   pound boneless sirloin steak, trimmed (about 1 inch thick)
- 3   garlic cloves, divided
- Cooking spray
- ½   teaspoon salt, divided
- ⅛   teaspoon coarsely ground black pepper
- ⅓   cup fat-free sour cream
- 1½ tablespoons light mayonnaise
- 1   tablespoon prepared horseradish
- ¼   teaspoon coarsely ground black pepper

Cut steak into 4 equal pieces. Cut 2 garlic cloves in half, and rub both sides of each steak with garlic. Place a large nonstick skillet or grill pan coated with cooking spray over high heat until hot. Add steaks; cook 4 minutes. Turn steaks, and cook 3 minutes. Reduce heat to medium; sprinkle steaks with ¼ teaspoon salt and ⅛ teaspoon black pepper. Cook 2 minutes or to desired degree of doneness.

Mince remaining garlic clove. Combine garlic, sour cream, mayonnaise, horseradish, ¼ teaspoon pepper, and remaining ¼ teaspoon salt. Serve steaks with horseradish sauce. Yield: 4 servings (serving size: 3 ounces steak and 2 tablespoons sauce).

CALORIES 218 (38% from fat); FAT 9.1g (sat 3.1g, mono 3g, poly 0.3g); PROTEIN 27.4g; CARB 5g; FIBER 0.2g; CHOL 81mg; IRON 3mg; SODIUM 423mg; CALC 47mg
EXCHANGES: 4 Lean Meat

Roasted Onions and Peppers

prep: 4 minutes   cook: 15 minutes

- 1   Vidalia or other sweet onion, thinly sliced
- 1   green bell pepper, seeded and cut into thin strips
- 1   red bell pepper, seeded and cut into thin strips
- Cooking spray
- 2   teaspoons olive oil
- 2   teaspoons Creole seasoning

Preheat oven to 475°.

Place first 3 ingredients in a single layer in a large roasting pan. Coat vegetables with cooking spray; drizzle with olive oil. Sprinkle with Creole seasoning. Bake at 475° for 15 to 17 minutes or until lightly browned. Yield: 4 servings (serving size: about ½ cup).

CALORIES 46 (47% from fat); FAT 2.4g (sat 0.3g, mono 1.7g, poly 0.3g); PROTEIN 0.9g; CARB 6.2g; FIBER 1.6g; CHOL 0mg; IRON 0.3mg; SODIUM 302mg; CALC 11mg
EXCHANGES: 1 Vegetable, ½ Fat

pepper-beef stir-fry
and pineapple with brown sugar   serves 4 • total time 20 minutes

With this sweet red pepper and beef stir-fry, you can do Chinese takeout—all the way from the kitchen to the table.

SUPPER plan

1. Bring water to a boil for noodles.

2. Slice steak; mince garlic; seed and slice bell pepper; drain water chestnuts; trim snow peas.

3. Cook noodles while you stir-fry beef and peppers.

4. Prepare Pineapple with Brown Sugar.

Pepper-Beef Stir-Fry

prep: 8 minutes   cook: 8 minutes

1	(5-ounce) package Japanese curly noodles (chucka soba), uncooked
⅓	cup low-sodium soy sauce
¼	cup low-salt beef broth
3	tablespoons dark brown sugar
2	teaspoons cornstarch

Cooking spray

¾	pound top round steak, thinly sliced
1	teaspoon light sesame oil
2	garlic cloves, minced
1	red bell pepper, seeded and cut into thin strips
1	(8-ounce) can sliced water chestnuts, drained
3	ounces snow peas, trimmed

Cook noodles according to package directions, omitting salt and fat.

Combine soy sauce and next 3 ingredients in a small bowl; stir well with a whisk.

Place a nonstick skillet coated with cooking spray over medium-high heat until hot; add beef. Stir-fry 4 minutes or until browned.

Remove beef from pan; set aside, and keep warm. Coat pan with oil. Add garlic and bell pepper; stir-fry 2 minutes. Add water chestnuts and snow peas; stir-fry 1 minute. Return beef, juices, and soy sauce mixture to pan, and cook 30 seconds or until slightly thickened. Serve over noodles. Yield: 4 servings (serving size: 1 cup beef mixture and ¾ cup noodles).

CALORIES 349 (20% from fat); FAT 7.9g (sat 2.5g, mono 2.9g, poly 0.8g); PROTEIN 24.9g; CARB 44.6g; FIBER 3.8g; CHOL 51mg; IRON 12.9mg; SODIUM 980mg; CALC 28mg
EXCHANGES: 3 Starch, 2 Lean Meat

Pineapple with Brown Sugar

prep: 4 minutes

Buy fresh cubed pineapple in the produce section.

2	cups cubed fresh pineapple
½	cup reduced-fat sour cream
¼	cup firmly packed brown sugar

Spoon pineapple into individual bowls. Top each serving with sour cream. Sprinkle each with sugar. Yield: 4 servings (serving size: ½ cup pineapple, 2 tablespoons sour cream, and 1 tablespoon sugar).

CALORIES 137 (27% from fat); FAT 4.1g (sat 2.4g, mono 0g, poly 0.1g); PROTEIN 1.7g; CARB 25g; FIBER 1g; CHOL 16mg; IRON 0.6mg; SODIUM 24mg; CALC 67mg
EXCHANGES: ½ Starch, 1 Fruit, 1 Fat

Pepper-Beef Stir-Fry

balsamic pan-seared steaks
and jalapeño-corn salad   serves 4 • total time 21 minutes

You don't need to do much to beef tenderloin steaks to get great flavor. These are seared in the skillet and served with a simple sauce of olive oil, balsamic vinegar, and beef broth—ingredients you probably have on hand.

SUPPER plan

1. Mince garlic; seed and mince jalapeño; chop tomato; chop cilantro; squeeze lime juice.

2. Prepare Jalapeño-Corn Salad; cover and chill.

3. Prepare Balsamic Pan-Seared Steaks.

Balsamic Pan-Seared Steaks

prep: 2 minutes   cook: 11 minutes

    4   (4-ounce) lean boneless beef tenderloin
        steaks (1 inch thick)
    1   teaspoon garlic-pepper seasoning
    ¼   teaspoon salt
    1   teaspoon olive oil
    ½   cup balsamic vinegar
    ⅓   cup beef broth

Sprinkle both sides of steaks with garlic-pepper seasoning and salt. Heat oil in a large nonstick skillet over medium-high heat. Add steaks, and cook 3 minutes on each side or until done. Remove steaks from pan; keep warm.

Combine vinegar and broth in pan. Bring to a boil; reduce heat to medium-high, and cook 5 minutes or until sauce is reduced to a ¼ cup, stirring occasionally. Spoon sauce over steaks. Yield: 4 servings (serving size: 1 steak and 1 tablespoon sauce).

CALORIES 213 (41% from fat); FAT 9.8g (sat 3.3g, mono 4g, poly 0.4g); PROTEIN 24.5g; CARB 5.1g; FIBER 0g; CHOL 71mg; IRON 3.3mg; SODIUM 367mg; CALC 16mg
EXCHANGES: 4 Lean Meat

Jalapeño-Corn Salad

prep: 8 minutes

It makes a nice presentation to serve the corn salad spooned over the meat.

    ½   cup frozen whole-kernel corn
    2   garlic cloves, minced
    1   jalapeño pepper, seeded and minced
    ¼   cup chopped tomato
    ¼   cup chopped fresh cilantro
    ¼   cup fresh lime juice (about 2 limes)
    2   teaspoons olive oil
    ¼   teaspoon salt
    ¼   teaspoon ground cumin
    ¼   teaspoon black pepper

Place corn in a colander, and rinse with cold water until thawed; drain.

Combine all ingredients in a bowl; toss well. Yield: 4 servings (serving size: ¾ cup).

CALORIES 49 (46% from fat); FAT 2.5g (sat 0.3g, mono 1.7g, poly 0.3g); PROTEIN 1g; CARB 7g; FIBER 0.9g; CHOL 0mg; IRON 0.3mg; SODIUM 149mg; CALC 9mg
EXCHANGE: ½ Starch

SERVEwith

• • • • • • • • • • • • • • • • •

This high-flavor meal *warrants a mouthwatering dessert. We suggest Warm Nectarine-Caramel Sundaes (page 340).*

veal with sherry-mushroom sauce
with egg noodles and **steamed yellow squash**

serves 4 • total time 26 minutes

Tender veal is at its best when you serve it with a light, creamy sauce. The mellow flavor of sherry and mushrooms in this rich-tasting sauce is hard to resist.

SUPPER plan

1. Bring water to a boil for noodles.

2. Slice squash; chop onion and parsley.

3. Brown veal.

4. While veal cooks, cook noodles according to package directions using 8 ounces dry noodles and omitting salt and fat.

5. While noodles cook:
- Cook sherry-mushroom sauce.
- Steam squash.

Veal with Sherry-Mushroom Sauce

prep: 4 minutes   cook: 20 minutes

  1   teaspoon olive oil, divided
  1   pound veal cutlets (¼ inch thick)
Cooking spray
  1   (8-ounce) package presliced mushrooms
  ½   cup chopped onion
  2   tablespoons light butter
  1   tablespoon all-purpose flour
  ½   teaspoon sugar
  ¼   teaspoon salt
  ¼   teaspoon freshly ground black pepper
  1   cup low-salt beef broth
  ¼   cup dry sherry
  2   tablespoons chopped fresh parsley

Heat ½ teaspoon oil in a large skillet over high heat. Add half of veal, and cook 4 minutes; turn and cook 1 minute. Transfer cooked veal to a plate, and keep warm. Repeat with remaining ½ teaspoon oil and veal.

Coat pan with cooking spray; add mushrooms and onion; sauté 5 minutes or until mushrooms are tender. Stir in butter and next 6 ingredients. Bring to a boil; cook 5 minutes or until thickened, stirring occasionally. Spoon sauce over veal. Sprinkle with parsley. Yield: 4 servings (serving size: 3 ounces veal and ½ cup sauce).

CALORIES 194 (28% from fat); FAT 6.1g (sat 2.8g, mono 1.4g, poly 0.6g); PROTEIN 28.5g; CARB 6.5g; FIBER 1.2g; CHOL 117mg; IRON 2.8mg; SODIUM 344mg; CALC 18mg
EXCHANGES: 1 Vegetable, 3 Lean Meat

Steamed Yellow Squash

prep: 2 minutes   cook: 2 minutes

  4   cups sliced yellow squash (about 4 squash)
  1   tablespoon water
  ¼   teaspoon salt
  ¼   teaspoon freshly ground black pepper
  1   tablespoon light butter

Place squash and water in a microwave-safe dish. Cover and cook at HIGH 2 to 2½ minutes or just until squash is tender; drain. Toss with salt, pepper, and butter. Yield: 4 servings (serving size: about 1 cup).

CALORIES 36 (45% from fat); FAT 1.8g (sat 1.1g, mono 0g, poly 0.1g); PROTEIN 1.8g; CARB 5.1g; FIBER 2.3g; CHOL 5mg; IRON 0.6mg; SODIUM 166mg; CALC 26mg
EXCHANGE: 1 Vegetable

Blue Cheese Veal Chops

blue cheese veal chops with sourdough rolls
and fresh pear slices serves 4 • total time 23 minutes

This veal menu goes beyond the average supper fare—with artichokes, turmeric rice, and blue cheese, plus a bottle of red wine, it's definitely entertainment-worthy.

SUPPER plan

1. Bring water to a boil for rice.

2. Drain and chop artichokes; chop green onions.

3. Broil veal chops.

4. While veal cooks:
  • Prepare blue cheese mixture.
  • Cook rice.
  • Slice pears.

5. Top veal with cheese, and broil.

Blue Cheese Veal Chops

prep: 10 minutes   cook: 14 minutes
stand: 5 minutes

  1 cup water
  ½ teaspoon salt
  ¼ teaspoon coarsely ground black pepper
  ¼ teaspoon paprika
  4 (6-ounce) veal loin chops, trimmed (1 inch thick)
Cooking spray
  1 cup uncooked instant rice
  ½ teaspoon ground turmeric
  ¼ teaspoon salt
  1 (14-ounce) can quartered artichoke hearts, drained and coarsely chopped
  ½ cup chopped green onions
  ¼ cup (1 ounce) crumbled blue cheese
  1 tablespoon yogurt-based spread (such as Brummel & Brown)

Preheat broiler.

Bring water to a boil in a medium saucepan.

Combine ½ teaspoon salt, pepper, and paprika in a small bowl. Sprinkle both sides of chops with seasoning mixture. Place chops on a broiler pan coated with cooking spray, and broil 6 to 7 minutes on each side or until desired degree of doneness.

Add rice to boiling water; remove from heat, cover, and let stand 5 minutes. Stir in turmeric, ¼ teaspoon salt, artichokes, and green onions.

Combine blue cheese and yogurt spread in a small bowl; spoon over veal chops. Broil chops and blue cheese 20 seconds or until cheese melts. Serve chops over rice mixture. Yield: 4 servings (serving size: 1 veal chop and ¾ cup rice mixture).

CALORIES 262 (23% from fat); FAT 6.8g (sat 2.6g, mono 1.7g, poly 0.5g); PROTEIN 24.7g; CARB 23g; FIBER 1.1g; CHOL 84mg; IRON 2.3mg; SODIUM 809mg; CALC 64mg
EXCHANGES: 1½ Starch, 3 Lean Meat

SERVEwith

• • • • • • • • • • • • • • • • • •

If you're serving this meal to guests, *replace the sliced pears with a simple salad and a sensational dessert. We recommend Cherry Tomato and Greens Salad (page 312) and Caramel Apple-Cranberry Crisp (page 348).*

veal chops with apple with steamed brussels sprouts
and whole wheat rolls serves 4 • total time 21 minutes

Take advantage of the bounty of autumn orchards with apple-enhanced veal. Tender Brussels sprouts complement the sweetness of the fruit.

SUPPER plan

1. Cook veal chops.

2. While veal cooks:
- Steam frozen Brussels sprouts in the microwave.
- Chop onion and slice apple.

3. Cook onion and apple mixture; spoon over veal.

Veal Chops with Apple

prep: 8 minutes   cook: 19 minutes

Applejack, a strong brandy made from apple cider, adds a distinctive apple flavor to this recipe. You can substitute 2 tablespoons apple cider or juice for the applejack.

3	tablespoons all-purpose flour
½	teaspoon salt
½	teaspoon dried thyme
¼	teaspoon pepper
4	(6-ounce) veal loin chops, trimmed
1	tablespoon olive oil
½	cup chopped Vidalia or other sweet onion
½	cup apple juice concentrate, thawed
2	tablespoons applejack
1½	tablespoons brown sugar
1	teaspoon all-purpose flour
2	cups thinly sliced Braeburn apples (about 1½ apples)

Combine first 4 ingredients; sprinkle over veal chops.

Heat oil in a large nonstick skillet over medium-high heat. Add veal chops, and cook 6 minutes on each side or until desired degree of doneness. Remove from pan, and keep warm.

Add onion, and sauté 2 minutes or until tender. Combine apple juice and next 3 ingredients; stir with a whisk. Pour apple juice mixture into pan, and add sliced apple. Cook apple mixture 5 minutes or until mixture is slightly thickened. Spoon apple mixture over veal chops. Yield: 4 servings (serving size: 1 veal chop and ½ cup apple mixture).

CALORIES 295 (22% from fat); FAT 7.1g (sat 1.5g, mono 3.6g, poly 0.8g); PROTEIN 21.1g; CARB 34.7g; FIBER 2.3g; CHOL 79mg; IRON 1.8mg; SODIUM 395mg; CALC 40mg
EXCHANGES: 1 Starch, 1 Fruit, 3 Lean Meat

SIMPLEsubstitutions

• •

If you can't find Braeburn apples *use another variety of cooking apple that will keep its texture and flavor during the cooking process. Some good choices include Baldwin, Rome Beauty, Winesap, Granny Smith, and York Imperial.*

lamb with tomato-lentil couscous
and spinach with pine nuts   serves 4 · total time 20 minutes

Lamb lovers will delight in this quick-cooking robust dish, which features small pieces of lamb instead of the whole leg.

SUPPER plan

1. Bring water to a boil for couscous.

2. Trim lamb and cube; chop onion; mince garlic.

3. Sear lamb; cook lamb mixture.

4. While lamb mixture cooks:
   - Cook couscous.
   - Prepare Spinach with Pine Nuts.

Lamb with Tomato-Lentil Couscous

prep: 5 minutes   cook: 12 minutes

- ½   cup fat-free, less-sodium chicken broth
- 1   teaspoon cornstarch
- 1   teaspoon olive oil
- 1   pound boneless leg of lamb, trimmed and cut into 1-inch pieces
- 1   (6.1-ounce) package tomato and lentil couscous mix (such as Near East)
- ½   cup chopped onion
- ¾   teaspoon minced garlic
- 2   tablespoons balsamic vinegar
- 2   teaspoons Dijon mustard
- ¼   teaspoon black pepper

Combine chicken broth and cornstarch, stirring well. Set aside.

Heat olive oil in a large nonstick skillet over high heat. Add lamb; sauté 4 minutes or until browned.

Prepare couscous according to package directions, omitting salt and fat.

Remove lamb from pan. Add onion and garlic; sauté 2 minutes or until onion is tender.

Return lamb to pan. Stir in balsamic vinegar and mustard; cook 3 minutes or until liquid is reduced by half. Stir in chicken broth mixture; cook 2 minutes or until thickened. Stir in pepper.

Spoon couscous onto a platter; spoon lamb mixture over couscous. Yield: 4 servings (serving size: ½ cup lamb and ⅔ cup couscous).

CALORIES 334 (22% from fat); FAT 8.1g (sat 2.5g, mono 3.8g, poly 0.7g); PROTEIN 29.8g; CARB 36.3g; FIBER 2.7g; CHOL 73mg; IRON 2.8mg; SODIUM 701mg; CALC 38mg
EXCHANGES: 2½ Starch, 3 Lean Meat

Spinach with Pine Nuts

prep: 1 minute   cook: 8 minutes

- 4   teaspoons pine nuts
- 1   teaspoon olive oil
- 2   (7-ounce) packages fresh baby spinach
- 1   teaspoon minced garlic
- ½   teaspoon salt
- ¼   teaspoon freshly ground black pepper
- ¼   cup raisins

Place pine nuts in a large nonstick skillet over medium-high heat. Cook, stirring frequently, 3 minutes or until lightly toasted. Remove from pan, and set aside.

Heat oil in same pan over medium-high heat. Add spinach and garlic; cook, stirring occasionally, 3 to 4 minutes or just until spinach wilts. Sprinkle with salt and pepper; add pine nuts and raisins. Toss well. Yield: 4 servings (serving size: ¾ cup).

CALORIES 76 (36% from fat); FAT 3g (sat 0.4g, mono 1.4g, poly 0.9g); PROTEIN 3.9g; CARB 11.4g; FIBER 3.2g; CHOL 0mg; IRON 3.2mg; SODIUM 373mg; CALC 106mg
EXCHANGES: 1 Vegetable, ½ Fruit, ½ Fat

lamb quesadillas
and cucumber salad   serves 4 • total time 21 minutes

Try quesadillas with a Mediterranean mix—lamb and spinach—and top them with a cool, creamy cucumber salad.

SUPPER plan

1. Chop dill, cucumber, and onion for salad; drain and chop roasted peppers; slice onion.

2. Cook lamb and spinach.

3. While lamb and spinach cook, bake 4 tortillas.

4. Fill and bake quesadillas.

5. While quesadillas bake, combine ingredients for salad.

Lamb Quesadillas

prep: 10 minutes   cook: 12 minutes

- 1   pound lean ground lamb
- 1   teaspoon dried Italian seasoning
- ¼   teaspoon pepper
- 2   cups fresh baby spinach
- 8   (8-inch) fat-free flour tortillas
- Cooking spray
- ½   cup roasted garlic and onion pasta sauce
- 1   (7-ounce) bottle roasted red bell peppers, drained and chopped
- ½   cup thinly sliced red onion
- 1   cup (4 ounces) preshredded part-skim mozzarella cheese

Preheat oven to 500°.

Place a large nonstick skillet over medium-high heat until hot. Add first 3 ingredients. Cook 3 minutes, stirring until meat crumbles; drain. Return lamb to pan, and add spinach; cook, stirring frequently, 2 minutes or until spinach wilts.

Place 4 tortillas on a baking sheet coated with cooking spray; bake at 500° for 2 minutes or until lightly browned. Spread 2 tablespoons pasta sauce over each tortilla. Top evenly with lamb mixture, pepper, onion, and cheese. Top with remaining 4 tortillas.

Coat each quesadilla with cooking spray; bake at 500° for 5 minutes or until cheese melts and tortillas are crisp. Cut each into 4 wedges. Yield: 4 servings (serving size: 4 wedges).

CALORIES 491 (30% from fat); FAT 16.2g (sat 7.6g, mono 6.1g, poly 1.2g); PROTEIN 29g; CARB 55.6g; FIBER 3.6g; CHOL 72mg; IRON 4.4mg; SODIUM 1,143mg; CALC 234mg
EXCHANGES: 3 Starch, 2 Vegetable, 2 High-Fat Meat

Cucumber Salad

prep: 6 minutes

- ½   cup reduced-fat sour cream
- 1   tablespoon red wine vinegar
- ½   teaspoon chopped fresh dill
- ¼   teaspoon salt
- ¼   teaspoon freshly ground black pepper
- 2   cups chopped English cucumber (about 1)
- ¼   cup chopped red onion (about ½ small)

Combine first 5 ingredients.

Place cucumber and onion in a medium bowl. Spoon sour cream mixture over vegetables; toss gently to coat. Serve immediately, or cover and chill. Yield: 4 servings (serving size: ¾ cup).

CALORIES 59 (58% from fat); FAT 3.8g (sat 2.4g, mono 0g, poly 0g); PROTEIN 1.9g; CARB 4.5g; FIBER 0.7g; CHOL 16mg; IRON 0.2mg; SODIUM 167mg; CALC 61mg
EXCHANGES: 1 Vegetable, 1 Fat

Lamb Quesadillas
and Cucumber Salad

mediterranean lamb wraps and
greek-style steak fries   serves 4 · total time 17 minutes

If you're tired of the usual burger on a bun, try lamb in a wrap. The Greek-seasoned lamb is topped with a refreshing cucumber mixture that includes crumbled feta and mint.

SUPPER plan

1. Cube cucumber; prepare cucumber sauce, and chill.

2. Prepare Greek-Style Steak Fries, and broil.

3. While fries broil:
- Brown lamb.
- Slice tomato; quarter and slice onion.
- Assemble wraps.

Mediterranean Lamb Wraps

prep: 7 minutes   cook: 6 minutes

Instead of flour tortillas, you can also use a Mediterranean-style flat bread (such as Toufayan).

1	cup unpeeled cubed cucumber (about ½)
½	cup reduced-fat sour cream
2	teaspoons red wine vinegar
⅓	cup (1.3-ounces) crumbled feta cheese
¼	teaspoon freshly ground black pepper
⅛	teaspoon dried mint flakes

Cooking spray
1	pound lean boneless leg of lamb, cut into ¼-inch slices
1	onion, cut into quarters and thinly sliced
1	teaspoon Greek seasoning
4	(8-inch) flour tortillas
1	large tomato, thinly sliced
1	cup packed baby spinach leaves

Combine first 6 ingredients in a small bowl; stir well. Cover and chill.

Coat a large nonstick skillet with cooking spray; add lamb and onion, and cook over medium-high heat, stirring occasionally, 6 to 7 minutes or until lamb is done. Remove from heat; stir in Greek seasoning.

Divide lamb mixture evenly among 4 tortillas; top each evenly with cucumber sauce, tomato, and spinach. Roll up tortillas, and cut each wrap in half; secure with wooden picks, if necessary. Yield: 4 servings.

CALORIES 397 (33% from fat); FAT 14.8g (sat 6.8g, mono 4.1g, poly 1.1g); PROTEIN 32g; CARB 33.4g; FIBER 1.5g; CHOL 99mg; IRON 3.9mg; SODIUM 507mg; CALC 235mg
EXCHANGES: 2 Starch, 4 Lean Meat

Greek-Style Steak Fries

prep: 2 minutes   cook: 12 minutes

12	ounces frozen steak fries (such as Ore-Ida)
	Olive oil-flavored cooking spray
2	teaspoons Greek seasoning

Preheat broiler.

Place fries in a single layer on a baking sheet. Coat fries with cooking spray, and sprinkle evenly with Greek seasoning.

Broil 12 minutes or until fries are done, turning occasionally. Yield: 4 servings (serving size: about 7 fries).

CALORIES 133 (34% from fat); FAT 5g (sat 0.8g, mono 3.2g, poly 0.5g); PROTEIN 2.1g; CARB 20.7g; FIBER 2.6g; CHOL 0mg; IRON 0.8mg; SODIUM 60mg; CALC 5mg
EXCHANGES: 1 Starch, 1 Fat

tarragon mustard lamb with fruited quinoa
and roasted asparagus   serves 3 • total time 24 minutes

If you've never tried "the Mother Grain"—quinoa—you'll wonder what took you so long once you taste this fruited version.

SUPPER plan

1. Trim asparagus; halve garlic cloves; squeeze lemon juice.

2. Prepare Fruited Quinoa.

3. While quinoa cooks and stands:
   • Prepare mustard mixture.
   • Broil lamb.

4. Coat asparagus with cooking spray, and place in the oven with lamb when you turn chops. Roast asparagus for 9 minutes. Sprinkle with salt and pepper, if desired.

Tarragon Mustard Lamb

prep: 2 minutes   cook: 18 minutes

At testing, we broiled the lamb chops on the middle rack of the oven.

  6   (4-ounce) lamb loin chops, trimmed
  3   garlic cloves, halved
Cooking spray
  3   tablespoons Dijon mustard
 ¾ teaspoon dried tarragon
 ½ teaspoon salt
 ¼ teaspoon coarsely ground black pepper
 ¼ teaspoon paprika

Preheat broiler.
Rub both sides of each lamb chop with garlic. Place chops on a broiler pan coated with cooking spray.
Combine mustard, tarragon, salt, and pepper in a small bowl; spoon half of mustard mixture evenly over lamb. Broil 9 minutes.

Turn; spoon remaining mustard over lamb. Sprinkle with paprika; broil 9 minutes. Yield: 3 servings (serving size: 2 lamb chops).

CALORIES 201 (39% from fat); FAT 8.7g (sat 2.7g, mono 3.4g, poly 1.1g); PROTEIN 26.9g; CARB 3.1g; FIBER 0.4g; CHOL 81mg; IRON 3mg; SODIUM 854mg; CALC 47mg
EXCHANGES: 4 Lean Meat

Fruited Quinoa

prep: 1 minute   cook: 15 minutes
stand: 5 minutes

Quinoa is a high-protein grain that has been around since ancient times and is common in South American cuisines. Look for it in the organic section of the grocery store or in the grains section.

  1   cup water
 ¾ cup uncooked quinoa, rinsed and drained
 ¼ cup golden raisins
  1   teaspoon olive oil
  1   teaspoon fresh lemon juice (about ¼ lemon)
 ¼ teaspoon salt
 ¼ teaspoon freshly ground black pepper

Bring water to a boil in a medium saucepan; add quinoa and raisins. Cover, reduce heat, and simmer 15 minutes or until liquid is absorbed. Remove from heat; cover and let stand 5 minutes. Add oil, lemon juice, salt, and pepper; fluff with a fork. Yield: 3 servings (serving size: ½ cup).

CALORIES 215 (16% from fat); FAT 4g (sat 0.5g, mono 1.8g, poly 1.2g); PROTEIN 6.1g; CARB 40.4g; FIBER 3.5g; CHOL 0mg; IRON 4.2mg; SODIUM 209mg; CALC 36mg
EXCHANGES: 1½ Starch, 1 Fruit, 1 Fat

Greek-Style Lamb

greek-style lamb with orzo
and sourdough bread   serves 4 • total time 24 minutes

If cruising the Mediterranean Sea through the Greek isles isn't an option, maybe a Greek-style supper will suffice. Perhaps the flavors of the lamb, olive oil, oregano, lemon juice, and orzo will transport you—at least during dinner.

SUPPER plan

1. Bring water to a boil for orzo.

2. Cut lamb and bell pepper into pieces; slice zucchini; cut onion into wedges; mince garlic; squeeze fresh lemon juice.

3. Cook orzo.

4. While orzo cooks, grill lamb and vegetables.

Greek-Style Lamb

prep: 10 minutes   cook: 14 minutes

Cut the pieces of pepper, zucchini, and onion large enough so that they don't fall through the grill rack. Or use a grill basket, which is great for grilling small pieces of food.

  1   pound boneless leg of lamb, cut into 1-inch pieces
  1   yellow bell pepper, seeded and cut into large pieces
  1   small zucchini, cut into ½-inch-thick slices
  ½   red onion, cut into wedges
  3   garlic cloves, minced
  2   tablespoons fresh lemon juice (about 1 lemon)
  2   tablespoons olive oil
  1   tablespoon dried oregano
  ½   teaspoon salt
  ½   teaspoon pepper
Cooking spray

Prepare grill.

Combine first 4 ingredients in a large bowl. Add garlic and next 5 ingredients; toss gently to coat.

Arrange lamb mixture in grilling basket coated with cooking spray on grill rack. Grill covered, 14 minutes, turning once, until lamb is done and vegetables are tender. Yield: 4 servings (serving size: 1¾ cups).

CALORIES 232 (47% from fat); FAT 12g (sat 2.8g, mono 7g, poly 1.1g); PROTEIN 24.5g; CARB 6.1g; FIBER 2g; CHOL 73mg; IRON 3.1mg; SODIUM 368mg; CALC 44mg
EXCHANGES: 1 Vegetable, 3 Lean Meat, 1 Fat

SERVEwith

• • • • • • • • • • • • • • • • • •

For dessert, we recommend *Sliced Banana and Grape Ambrosia (page 334). Ambrosia is known as "the food of the gods." Or focus on other typical Greek flavors, and serve Pineapple Sundaes (page 340), featuring lemon sorbet and chopped fresh mint.*

bacon-tomato linguine
and basil green beans   serves 4 · total time 20 minutes

Instead of a BLT—it's a BTL: Bacon, Tomatoes, and Linguine. For bacon flavor without the fuss, this pasta features packaged real bacon pieces.

SUPPER plan

1. Bring water to a boil for pasta.

2. Halve tomatoes; mince garlic; trim green beans; chop basil.

3. Cook pasta.

4. While pasta cooks:
   - Sauté onion, bacon, and tomatoes.
   - Cook green beans in the microwave.

5. Combine pasta ingredients, and let stand.

Bacon-Tomato Linguine

prep: 2 minutes   cook: 15 minutes
stand: 3 minutes

If you can't find a package of cooked bacon pieces, buy a package of precooked bacon, and chop 8 slices.

8	ounces uncooked linguine
2	teaspoons olive oil
½	cup chopped onion
1	(2.5-ounce) package cooked bacon pieces (such as Hormel)
1⅓	cups grape tomatoes, halved
4	garlic cloves, minced
1	teaspoon dried oregano
1	teaspoon salt
¼	teaspoon pepper
¼	cup (1 ounce) preshredded fresh Parmesan cheese

Cook pasta according to package directions, omitting salt and fat. Drain, reserving ½ cup pasta water.

Heat oil in a large nonstick skillet over medium-high heat. Add onion; sauté 2 minutes. Add bacon bits; sauté 2 minutes. Add tomato, garlic, and oregano; sauté 30 seconds. Remove from heat.

Add pasta, reserved pasta water, salt, and pepper. Stir well, and cook 1 minute or until thoroughly heated and liquid is absorbed. Remove from heat; cover and let stand 3 minutes. Sprinkle with cheese. Yield: 4 servings (serving size: 1¼ cups).

CALORIES 301 (32% from fat); FAT 11g (sat 3.6g, mono 2.1g, poly 0.3g); PROTEIN 14.4g; CARB 37.1g; FIBER 2.8g; CHOL 21mg; IRON 2.1mg; SODIUM 745mg; CALC 81mg
EXCHANGES: 2 Starch, 1 Vegetable, 1 High-Fat Meat

Basil Green Beans

prep: 3 minutes   cook: 5 minutes

1	pound fresh green beans, trimmed
2	tablespoons chopped fresh basil
1½	teaspoons light butter
¼	teaspoon salt

Combine all ingredients in a microwave-safe dish. Cover and microwave at HIGH 5 minutes or until beans are crisp-tender, stirring after 2½ minutes. Yield: 4 servings.

CALORIES 42 (19% from fat); FAT 1g (sat 0.5g, mono 0g, poly 0.1g); PROTEIN 2.2g; CARB 8.2g; FIBER 3.9g; CHOL 3mg; IRON 1.2mg; SODIUM 162mg; CALC 44mg
EXCHANGE: 1 Vegetable

Bacon-Tomato Linguine and
Basil Green Beans

Country Rice and Sausage

country rice and sausage with whole wheat rolls
and fresh nectarine slices   serves 3 · total time 18 minutes

A skillet sausage dinner satisfies your need for comfort food with no stress and no mess.

SUPPER plan

1. Chop onion; slice celery; chop parsley.

2. Cook rice in the microwave.

3. While rice cooks and stands:
   • Brown sausage.
   • Cook vegetable mixture.
   • Slice nectarines.

4. Combine ingredients for rice and sausage mixture.

Country Rice and Sausage

prep: 5 minutes   cook: 13 minutes

1	cup uncooked instant rice
8	ounces 50%-less-fat pork sausage
1	cup chopped onion
½	cup water
½	cup thinly sliced celery
½	cup matchstick-cut carrots
¼	teaspoon salt
¼	teaspoon dried rubbed sage
⅛	teaspoon crushed red pepper
¼	cup chopped fresh parsley
⅛	teaspoon salt

Cook rice according to package microwave directions, omitting salt and fat.

Place a large nonstick skillet over medium-high heat until hot. Add sausage; cook 4 minutes or until browned, stirring to crumble. Remove sausage from pan; set aside, and keep warm.

Add onion and next 6 ingredients to pan; bring to a boil. Cover, reduce heat, and simmer, 4 minutes or until crisp-tender. Return cooked sausage to pan; stir in cooked rice, parsley, and ⅛ teaspoon salt. Yield: 3 servings (serving size: 1⅓ cups).

CALORIES 327 (39% from fat); FAT 14.1g (sat 4.9g, mono 0.1g, poly 0.1g); PROTEIN 16.1g; CARB 33.3g; FIBER 2g; CHOL 53mg; IRON 3mg; SODIUM 801mg; CALC 33mg
EXCHANGES: 2 Starch, 2 Medium-Fat Meat

VEGETARIANoption

● ● ● ● ● ● ● ● ● ● ● ● ● ● ● ● ● ●

To make this skillet dinner a meatless dish, *use veggie sausage or burger crumbles instead of the pork sausage.*

If you make it with veggie sausage, one serving will contain 301 calories, 18.8 grams of protein, 36.9 grams of carbohydrate, 5.8 grams of fiber, 8.5 grams of fat (2.1 grams saturated), and 777 milligrams of sodium. In a nutshell, you get slightly fewer calories, less total fat, saturated fat, and sodium, and more protein and fiber.

spicy pork au jus with yellow rice and orange-spinach salad

serves 4 · total time 16 minutes

Because of the juiciness of the meat and the zesty flavor of the seasonings, this 16-minute pork menu will soon become one of your standbys.

SUPPER plan

1. Rinse spinach; drain oranges; slice onion.

2. Cook one boil-in-bag yellow rice mix according to package directions, omitting fat.

3. Prepare Spicy Pork au Jus.

4. While pork cooks, combine salad ingredients.

Spicy Pork au Jus

prep: 3 minutes   cook: 9 minutes

   4   (4-ounce) boneless pork loin chops
   1   teaspoon blackened seasoning
   1   teaspoon vegetable oil
   ¼   cup water
1½   tablespoons low-sodium Worcestershire sauce
1½   tablespoons balsamic vinegar
1½   tablespoons low-sodium soy sauce
1½   teaspoons sugar

Sprinkle both sides of pork chops with seasoning. Place a large nonstick skillet over high heat until hot; add oil. Add pork chops, and cook 4 minutes on each side or just until done. Remove pork from pan; set aside, and keep warm.

Combine water and remaining ingredients. Add soy sauce mixture to hot pan, and cook over medium-high heat 45 seconds until mixture reduces to ¼ cup, scraping sides and bottom of pan to remove browned bits. Serve over pork. Yield: 4 servings (serving size: 1 pork chop and 1 tablespoon sauce).

CALORIES 185 (35% from fat); FAT 7.2g (sat 2.2g, mono 3g, poly 1.3g); PROTEIN 25g; CARB 3.3g; FIBER 0.1g; CHOL 62mg; IRON 1.1mg; SODIUM 355mg; CALC 28mg
EXCHANGES: 3 Lean Meat

Orange-Spinach Salad

prep: 4 minutes

   1   (10-ounce) package torn fresh spinach (about 6 cups)
   1   (11-ounce) can mandarin oranges, drained
   ½   cup thinly sliced red onion (about ½ small)
   ½   cup reduced-fat olive oil vinaigrette

Combine all ingredients in a large bowl, and toss well. Yield: 4 servings (serving size: 1½ cups).

CALORIES 110 (52% from fat); FAT 6.3g (sat 0.5g, mono 0g, poly 0g); PROTEIN 2.6g; CARB 13.4g; FIBER 1g; CHOL 0mg; IRON 2.5mg; SODIUM 310mg; CALC 86mg
EXCHANGES: 1 Vegetable, ½ Fruit, 1 Fat

SERVEwith

● ● ● ● ● ● ● ● ● ● ● ● ● ● ● ● ● ● ●

Complement the spicy pork dish *with a cool and creamy dessert such as Ice Cream Sandwich Dessert (page 348).*

Spicy Pork au Jus and
Orange-Spinach Salad

curried apricot pork with steamed snow peas and couscous   serves 4 • total time 20 minutes

The spicy sweetness of curry and apricots is a hard combination to beat—especially when it showcases tender pork.

SUPPER plan

1. Prepare apricot mixture for pork; bring water to a boil for couscous.

2. Season and cook pork chops.

3. While pork chops cook:
   • Prepare 1 (10-ounce) package of couscous according to package directions, omitting salt and fat.
   • Steam snow peas 1 to 2 minutes in the microwave until just crisp-tender.

4. Cook apricot mixture, and spoon over pork chops.

Curried Apricot Pork

prep: 4 minutes   cook: 16 minutes

- ¼ cup apricot fruit spread (such as Polaner)
- 2 teaspoons balsamic vinegar
- ½ cup water
- ⅛ teaspoon salt
- 1 teaspoon curry powder
- ¼ teaspoon salt
- ⅛ teaspoon ground red pepper
- 4 (4-ounce) boneless center-cut loin pork chops (about ½ inch thick)

Cooking spray

Combine first 4 ingredients; set aside.
Combine curry powder, ¼ teaspoon salt, and red pepper; rub curry mixture on both sides of pork. Coat pork with cooking spray. Place a large nonstick skillet over medium heat until hot; add pork, and cook 7 minutes on each side or until done. Remove pork from pan; keep warm.

Increase heat to high; add apricot mixture. Bring to a boil. Cook, stirring constantly, 2 minutes or until reduced to ¼ cup. Spoon apricot mixture over pork. Yield: 4 servings (serving size: 1 pork chop and 2 tablespoons sauce).

CALORIES 207 (28% from fat); FAT 6.5g (sat 2.2g, mono 2.9g, poly 0.7g); PROTEIN 24.5g; CARB 11g; FIBER 0.2g; CHOL 67mg; IRON 1.1mg; SODIUM 287mg; CALC 23mg
EXCHANGES: ½ Fruit, 3 Lean Meat

NUTRITIONnote

• • • • • • • • • • • • • • • • • • •

Pork has a place in a healthy diet *because certain cuts are low in fat and cholesterol. Some pork is comparable to lean cuts of beef and skinless chicken; compare their calorie, fat, and cholesterol contents.*

COOKED MEAT (3 ounces)	CALORIES	FAT (g)	CHOL (mg)
Pork tenderloin	139	4.1	67
Pork, boneless loin chop	171	6.9	70
Chicken, skinless breast	140	3.1	73
Chicken, skinless thigh	178	9.3	81
Beef, top round	169	4.3	76
Beef tenderloin	175	8.1	71
Beef, top sirloin	162	8.0	76

italian-style pork with quick focaccia
and steamed broccoli serves 4 • total time 23 minutes

When there's no time to simmer an all-day Italian sauce, try these speedy Italian-flavored pork chops with a shortcut version of focaccia.

SUPPER plan

1. Chop rosemary; halve garlic and tomatoes; chop parsley.

2. Prepare Quick Focaccia.

3. While focaccia bakes:
- Season pork, and cook.
- Steam broccoli in the microwave.
- Cook tomato mixture.

Italian-Style Pork

prep: 8 minutes   cook: 13 minutes

- 4 (6-ounce) bone-in center cut pork chops (about ½ inch thick)
- 2 garlic cloves, halved
- 1 teaspoon dried Italian seasoning
- ¼ teaspoon salt
- Cooking spray
- ½ cup grape tomatoes, halved
- ½ cup chopped bottled roasted red bell peppers
- ¼ cup chopped fresh parsley
- 2 tablespoons capers, drained
- 2 tablespoons cider vinegar
- ⅛ teaspoon crushed red pepper

Rub both sides of pork chops with garlic halves; sprinkle with Italian seasoning and salt. Coat pork chops with cooking spray. Place a large nonstick skillet over medium heat until hot. Add pork chops, and cook 6 minutes on each side or until done. Transfer pork to a serving platter; keep warm.

Add tomatoes and remaining 5 ingredients to pan; cook 1 minute or until thoroughly heated.

Spoon over pork. Yield: 4 servings (serving size: 1 pork chop and about ⅓ cup tomato mixture).

CALORIES 164 (32% from fat); FAT 5.9g (sat 2.1g, mono 2.6g, poly 0.5g); PROTEIN 21.9g; CARB 5.5g; FIBER 0.6g; CHOL 58mg; IRON 1.2mg; SODIUM 376mg; CALC 39mg
EXCHANGES: 1 Vegetable, 3 Lean Meat

Quick Focaccia

prep: 3 minutes   cook: 17 minutes

- 1 (10-ounce) can refrigerated pizza crust dough
- Olive oil-flavored cooking spray
- 2 teaspoons olive oil
- 1 tablespoon bottled minced garlic
- 1½ tablespoons chopped fresh rosemary
- ½ teaspoon kosher salt

Preheat oven to 400°.

Unroll dough into a rectangle on a baking sheet coated with cooking spray. Brush dough with 2 teaspoons olive oil, and sprinkle with garlic and rosemary. Bake at 400° for 17 minutes or until edges are lightly browned. Sprinkle with kosher salt. Yield: 4 servings (serving size: 1 piece).

CALORIES 194 (21% from fat); FAT 4.6g (sat 0.3g, mono 1.7g, poly 0.2g); PROTEIN 5.8g; CARB 31.4g; FIBER 1g; CHOL 0mg; IRON 1.7mg; SODIUM 666mg; CALC 6mg
EXCHANGES: 2 Starch, 1 Fat

quick chick

When you don't have a lot of time to pull together a meal, chicken is one of your best bets. With the variety of poultry products now available, "a chicken in every pot" is entirely possible.

i n addition to fresh you can buy chicken frozen, precooked, roasted, ground, seasoned, and sliced. You can even buy chicken sausage. As with most convenience products, many of the precooked chicken products are higher in sodium than their fresh counterparts. But when the skin is removed, the fat is about the same.

In *Superfast Suppers*, when chopped cooked chicken is called for in a recipe, you can choose the type you wish to use. (Always remove the skin.) Here are some of the products—fresh and cooked—that we've used in this book.

fresh (uncooked)

Refrigerated: In addition to boneless, skinless chicken breast halves and thighs, you can buy ground chicken, premarinated breast halves, and chicken tenders. Many stores offer fresh chicken in single-serving packages.

Frozen: Individual pieces of fresh chicken are marinated to enhance juiciness and tenderness, and then frozen and packaged loosely in resealable bags. Skinless breasts, tenderloins, breast halves, drumsticks, and wings are available in this form. The advantage of this form of chicken is that you can pull out the number of pieces that you need and leave the rest frozen.

cooked or precooked

Frozen: Look for bags of fully cooked chicken, cut into strips or chopped. The chicken isn't seasoned with any particular flavor, but because of the processing, it's higher in sodium than fresh cooked chicken.

Deli-roasted: Freshly roasted whole chickens can be found in the deli section of the grocery store. They're usually seasoned with salt and pepper and/or other seasonings. To decrease the fat, remove the skin.

Refrigerated: The refrigerated poultry section of the grocery store may have whole roasted chickens, chicken breasts, or single-serve portions of breasts or drumsticks. To reduced the fat, remove the skin.

Grilled: These chicken strips are available without skin, seasoned or unseasoned, in resealable 6-ounce packages. Look for them in the refrigerated poultry section.

Leftover: Use baked, broiled, or grilled chicken from other meals prepared at home.

Below are some helpful amounts to keep in mind when you're buying uncooked or cooked chicken to use in recipes.

AMOUNT/TYPE OF CHICKEN	AMOUNT OF CHOPPED, COOKED CHICKEN
1 pound uncooked boneless, skinless chicken	3 cups
5.5-ounce cooked boneless chicken breast half	1 cup
1 (2-pound) chicken	2¼ cups
1 (6-ounce) package grilled chicken strips	1⅓ cups
1 (9-ounce) package frozen chopped cooked chicken	1⅔ cups

pasta with grilled chicken and asparagus
with **berry-spinach salad**
and french rolls   **serves 5 · total time 17 minutes**

Celebrate spring with a menu that features the season's best offerings: asparagus and strawberries.

SUPPER plan

1. Bring water to a boil for pasta.

2. Slice green onions, and cut asparagus into pieces; slice strawberries for salad.

3. Roast vegetables and cook pasta at the same time.

4. While pasta and vegetables cook, assemble salad.

5. Toss vegetables and pasta.

Pasta with Grilled Chicken and Asparagus

prep: 4 minutes   cook: 8 minutes

    1   pound asparagus
    1   (8-ounce) package presliced mushrooms
    2   green onions, cut into 1-inch pieces
Cooking spray
    1   (9-ounce) package refrigerated angel hair pasta
    2   (6-ounce) packages grilled chicken strips (such as Louis Rich)
    2   tablespoons olive oil
    2   tablespoons hot water
    3   tablespoons balsamic vinegar
    ½   teaspoon pepper
    ½   cup preshredded fresh Parmesan cheese

Preheat oven to 450°.

Snap off tough ends of asparagus, and cut asparagus into 2-inch pieces. Arrange asparagus, mushrooms, and green onions in a single layer on a broiler pan coated with cooking spray. Bake at 450° for 8 to 10 minutes or until golden brown, stirring once.

Cook pasta according to package directions, omitting salt and fat. Drain, reserving 3 tablespoons pasta water.

Add roasted vegetables, reserved pasta water, and chicken to pasta; toss gently.

Combine olive oil, 2 tablespoons hot water, balsamic vinegar, and pepper; stir well with a whisk. Add to pasta mixture, and toss well. Sprinkle with cheese. Serve immediately. Yield: 5 servings (serving size: 2 cups).

CALORIES 401 (25% from fat); FAT 11.2g (sat 3.1g, mono 4.8g, poly 1g); PROTEIN 28.4g; CARB 47.5g; FIBER 4.1g; CHOL 50mg; IRON 4mg; SODIUM 771mg; CALC 135mg
EXCHANGES: 2 Starch, 3 Vegetable, 2 Lean Meat, 1 Fat

Berry-Spinach Salad

prep: 5 minutes

Instead of strawberries, you can use 2 cups of fresh raspberries.

    1   (10-ounce) package torn spinach
    2   cups sliced strawberries
    2   tablespoons fat-free poppy seed dressing

Combine all ingredients in a large bowl; toss well. Serve immediately. Yield: 5 servings (serving size: about 1⅔ cups).

CALORIES 91 (6% from fat); FAT 0.6g (sat 0.1g, mono 0.1g, poly 0.3g); PROTEIN 3.5g; CARB 19.3g; FIBER 3.8g; CHOL 0mg; IRON 2.2mg; SODIUM 137mg; CALC 122mg
EXCHANGES: 1 Fruit, 1 Vegetable

red curry chicken

with fresh pineapple slices serves 6 · total time 12 minutes

This chicken dish gets its Thai-style flavor from red curry paste, coconut milk, and peanuts. Serve it with cool, sweet pineapple to tame the spiciness.

SUPPER plan

1. Prepare rice according to package directions, omitting salt and fat. To get 4½ cups of cooked rice, use 1½ cups of uncooked rice and 2⅔ cups of water.

2. While rice cooks:
- Slice basil; chop peanuts.
- Cook vegetables in the microwave.
- Cook chicken mixture.

Red Curry Chicken

prep: 2 minutes   cook: 10 minutes

Instead of chicken, you can stir in ½ pound peeled and deveined shrimp.

    1   (16-ounce) package frozen broccoli, red
        peppers, onions, and mushrooms
Cooking spray
    1   (6-ounce) package grilled chicken breast
        strips (such as Louis Rich)
    1   (13.5-ounce) can light coconut milk
    2   teaspoons red curry paste (such as Thai
        Kitchen)
    ¼   teaspoon salt
    2   tablespoons thinly sliced fresh basil
  4½   cups hot cooked basmati rice
    6   tablespoons chopped unsalted dry-roasted
        peanuts

Place vegetables in a microwave-safe bowl; cover with plastic wrap, and vent. Microwave at HIGH 4 minutes; drain and set aside.

Place a large nonstick skillet coated with cooking spray over medium-high heat. Add chicken; sauté 1 minute. Add coconut milk; bring to a boil. Stir in red curry paste and salt. Cook 5 minutes over medium heat or just until sauce begins to thicken, stirring frequently.

Add vegetable mixture to chicken mixture, stirring well. Bring to a boil; cook 4 minutes or until sauce is slightly thickened. Stir in basil. Serve over rice, and sprinkle with peanuts. Yield: 6 servings (serving size: ¾ cup rice, ½ cup chicken mixture, and 1 tablespoon peanuts).

CALORIES 389 (35% from fat); FAT 15.2g (sat 4.2g, mono 4.4g, poly 4.7g); PROTEIN 13.1g; CARB 51.3g; FIBER 4.4g; CHOL 15mg; IRON 3.2mg; SODIUM 389mg; CALC 43mg
EXCHANGES: 3 Starch, 2 Vegetable, 2 Fat

NUTRITIONnote

● ● ● ● ● ● ● ● ● ● ● ● ● ● ● ● ● ●

Coconut milk is a common ingredient *in many Thai-style recipes and adds a distinct sweet creaminess to the food. The milk is made by simmering a combination of water and shredded fresh coconut until the mixture is foamy. Then the mixture is strained to extract as much liquid as possible from the coconut meat. The oil in coconuts is one of the few nonanimal sources of saturated fat, so coconut milk, too, is a source of saturated fat. You can significantly reduce the fat in recipes that call for coconut milk by using light coconut milk.*

COCONUT MILK (½ cup)	CALORIES	FAT (g)	SAT FAT (g)
Regular	223	24	21
Light	70	6	4

chicken with creamy dijon sauce
with **balsamic cucumber and tomato salad**
and french bread   serves 4 • total time 17 minutes

An effortlessly elegant dinner may be just what you need to perk up a hum-drum week.

SUPPER plan

1. Seed and cube cucumber; seed and chop tomato; mince garlic.

2. Broil chicken.

3. While chicken broils:
   • Prepare sauce.
   • Combine ingredients for salad.

Chicken with Creamy Dijon Sauce

prep: 2 minutes   cook: 10 minutes

4 (4-ounce) skinless, boneless chicken breast halves
Cooking spray
¼ teaspoon salt
¼ teaspoon pepper
½ teaspoon paprika
¼ cup light mayonnaise
1 tablespoon lemon juice (½ lemon)
½ teaspoon Dijon mustard
1 garlic clove, minced or 1 teaspoon bottled minced garlic
¼ teaspoon dried rosemary

Preheat broiler.

Coat chicken with cooking spray; sprinkle with salt, pepper, and paprika. Place chicken on broiler pan coated with cooking spray. Broil 5 to 6 minutes on each side or until done.

Combine mayonnaise and remaining 4 ingredients in a small bowl.

Serve chicken with sauce. Yield: 4 servings (serving size: 1 chicken breast half and 1 tablespoon sauce).

CALORIES 179 (33% from fat); FAT 6.5g (sat 1.1g, mono 0.4g, poly 0.4g); PROTEIN 26.4g; CARB 2.1g; FIBER 0.2g; CHOL 71mg; IRON 1mg; SODIUM 357mg; CALC 18mg
EXCHANGES: 3 Lean Meat

Balsamic Cucumber and Tomato Salad

prep: 7 minutes

1 cucumber, seeded and cubed (about 1½ cups)
1 tomato, seeded and chopped (about 1 cup)
2 tablespoons fat-free balsamic dressing
2 tablespoons preshredded fresh Parmesan cheese
¼ teaspoon salt
¼ teaspoon freshly ground black pepper

Combine all ingredients, tossing gently. Yield: 4 servings (serving size: about ⅔ cup).

CALORIES 31 (26% from fat); FAT 0.9g (sat 0.5g, mono 0.2g, poly 0.1g); PROTEIN 1.6g; CARB 4.8g; FIBER 0.8g; CHOL 2mg; IRON 0.4mg; SODIUM 294mg; CALC 40mg
EXCHANGE: 1 Vegetable

SERVE**with**

• • • • • • • • • • • • • • • • •

Indulge in a decadent dessert *that takes only 4 minutes to make: Chocolate-Banana Cream Tarts (page 346).*

jalapeño chicken with spanish rice and beans

serves 4 • total time 19 minutes

If you love Tex-Mex, but are tired of tacos, try this taco-flavored chicken, and serve it over a bed of rice and beans.

SUPPER plan

1. Bring water to a boil for rice.

2. Shred cheese; rinse and drain beans.

3. Cook rice.

4. While rice cooks, cook chicken.

5. Remove chicken from heat, and add cheese; let stand.

6. Combine rice, beans, and salsa.

Jalapeño Chicken

prep: 1 minute   cook: 14 minutes
stand: 3 minutes

To crank up the heat in this dish, top each piece of chicken with sliced jalapeños.

1   tablespoon 40%-less-sodium taco seasoning
4   (4-ounce) skinless, boneless chicken breast halves
Cooking spray
½   cup (2 ounces) shredded Monterey Jack cheese with jalapeño peppers
2   tablespoons sliced jalapeño peppers (optional)

Sprinkle taco seasoning over both sides of chicken.

Place a large nonstick skillet over medium heat until hot. Coat chicken with cooking spray.

Add chicken to pan, and cook 7 minutes on each side or until chicken is done.

Remove chicken from heat; sprinkle with cheese. Cover and let stand 3 to 4 minutes or until cheese melts. Garnish with jalapeño slices, if desired. Yield: 4 servings (serving size: 1 chicken breast half).

CALORIES 186 (29% from fat); FAT 6g (sat 3.4g, mono 0.3g, poly 0.3g); PROTEIN 29.7g; CARB 1.8g; FIBER 0g; CHOL 81mg; IRON 0.8mg; SODIUM 294mg; CALC 114mg
EXCHANGES: 4 Lean Meat

Spanish Rice and Beans

prep: 1 minute   cook: 15 minutes

1   (4.3-ounce) package boil-in-bag Spanish rice mix
1   (15-ounce) can black beans, rinsed and drained
¼   cup mild salsa

Prepare rice according to package directions, omitting fat.

Combine cooked rice, beans, and salsa. Cook over medium heat 1 minute or until thoroughly heated. Yield: 4 servings (serving size: about ¾ cup).

CALORIES 133 (2% from fat); FAT 0.3g (sat 0g, mono 0g, poly 0g); PROTEIN 5.1g; CARB 30.7g; FIBER 3.6g; CHOL 0mg; IRON 1.9mg; SODIUM 648mg; CALC 64mg
EXCHANGES: 2 Starch

SERVEwith

• • • • • • • • • • • • • • • • • • • •

For a cool and creamy dessert *to pair with this spicy meal, try Cookies and Cream Parfaits (page 339).*

Jalapeño Chicken with
Spanish Rice and Beans

Kalamata-Feta Chicken

kalamata-feta chicken with orzo and garlic butter spinach

serves 4 • total time 24 minutes

While it probably won't help you achieve goddess status, this Greek-style meal will still make you very popular with your family.

SUPPER plan

1. Bring water to a boil for orzo.

2. Prepare olive mixture.

3. Cook orzo.

4. While orzo cooks:
- Cook chicken.
- Prepare Garlic Butter Spinach.
- Deglaze skillet, and top chicken with olive mixture.

Kalamata-Feta Chicken

prep: 9 minutes   cook: 12 minutes

1	cup uncooked orzo (rice-shaped pasta)
½	teaspoon salt, divided
¼	teaspoon pepper, divided
10	pitted kalamata olives, chopped
8	grape tomatoes, finely chopped
¼	cup chopped fresh parsley
¼	cup (1 ounce) crumbled feta cheese with basil and sun-dried tomatoes
4	teaspoons chopped fresh or 1 teaspoon dried oregano, divided
4	(4-ounce) skinless, boneless chicken breast halves
	Cooking spray
½	cup water

Cook orzo according to package directions. Drain; stir in ¼ teaspoon salt and ⅛ teaspoon pepper.

Combine olives, tomato, parsley, cheese, 2 teaspoons fresh oregano, and ⅛ teaspoon salt.

Coat chicken with cooking spray; sprinkle with remaining ⅛ teaspoon salt, ⅛ teaspoon pepper, and 2 teaspoons fresh oregano.

Place a large nonstick skillet over medium-high heat. Add chicken; cook 6 minutes on each side. Transfer to a serving plate; keep warm.

Add water to pan; bring to a boil, scraping pan to loosen browned bits. Pour mixture over chicken. Top chicken with olive mixture, and serve with orzo. Yield: 4 servings (serving size: 1 chicken breast half, ¾ cup orzo, and 2 tablespoons olive mixture).

CALORIES 354 (17% from fat); FAT 6.8g (sat 2.2g, mono 2.8g, poly 1g); PROTEIN 33.9g; CARB 37.2g; FIBER 1.7g; CHOL 74mg; IRON 3.1mg; SODIUM 634mg; CALC 85mg
EXCHANGES: 2 Starch, 1 Vegetable, 3 Lean Meat

Garlic Butter Spinach

prep: 1 minute   cook: 2½ minutes

2	tablespoons light butter
2	teaspoons bottled minced garlic
¼	teaspoon salt
⅛	teaspoon freshly ground black pepper
1	(7-ounce) package fresh spinach (about 6 cups)

Combine first 4 ingredients in a 2-quart microwave-safe dish. Cover and microwave at HIGH 25 seconds or until butter melts. Add spinach; cover and microwave at HIGH 2 minutes or until spinach wilts. Serve immediately. Yield: 4 servings (serving size: ½ cup).

CALORIES 38 (76% from fat); FAT 3.2g (sat 2g, mono 0g, poly 0.1g); PROTEIN 2g; CARB 2.2g; FIBER 1.4g; CHOL 10mg; IRON 1.4mg; SODIUM 221mg; CALC 52mg
EXCHANGES: 1 Vegetable, ½ Fat

seared chicken with avocado with black beans and tortilla chips con queso

serves 4 • total time 22 minutes

This menu received our highest rating. It's easy and colorful, and the flavor combination of blackened chicken with buttery-tasting avocado pleased even our pickiest tasters.

SUPPER plan

1. Peel and dice avocado; seed and chop jalapeño; squeeze lime juice.

2. Cut tortillas into wedges, and sprinkle with chili powder and cheese.

3. Rinse and drain canned black beans; heat in a saucepan; season as desired.

4. Sear chicken.

5. While chicken cooks:
  • Prepare avocado mixture.
  • Bake tortilla chips.

Seared Chicken with Avocado

prep: 9 minutes   cook: 7 minutes

1½	teaspoons blackened seasoning
4	(4-ounce) skinless, boneless chicken breast halves
1	teaspoon olive oil
1	diced peeled avocado
2	tablespoons chopped fresh cilantro
1	jalapeño pepper, seeded and finely chopped
2	tablespoons fresh lime juice (about 1 lime)
¼	teaspoon salt
1	lime, cut into fourths

Sprinkle seasoning on both sides of chicken. Heat oil in a large nonstick skillet over high heat. Add chicken to pan, smooth side down; cook 1 minute or until seared. Reduce heat to medium; cook 3 minutes on each side or until lightly browned.

Combine avocado, cilantro, pepper, lime juice, and salt. Squeeze one-fourth lime over each piece of chicken before serving. Serve with avocado mixture. Yield: 4 servings (serving size: 1 chicken breast half and ¼ cup avocado mixture).

CALORIES 221 (42% from fat); FAT 10.3g (sat 1.8g, mono 6g, poly 1.4g); PROTEIN 27.4g; CARB 5.2g; FIBER 2.9g; CHOL 66mg; IRON 1.4mg; SODIUM 370mg; CALC 22mg
EXCHANGES: 1 Vegetable, 4 Very Lean Meat, 1 Fat

Tortilla Chips con Queso

prep: 4 minutes   cook: 5 minutes

Use kitchen scissors to cut the tortillas into wedges.

2	(8-inch) flour tortillas
	Cooking spray
¼	teaspoon chili powder
¼	cup (1 ounce) preshredded light Mexican cheese blend (such as Sargento)
⅔	cup salsa

Preheat oven to 400°.

Cut each tortilla into 8 wedges; arrange on a baking sheet in a single layer. Coat wedges with cooking spray; sprinkle evenly with chili powder and cheese. Bake at 400° for 5 minutes or until lightly browned. Serve with salsa. Yield: 4 servings (serving size: 4 tortilla wedges and about 2 tablespoons salsa).

CALORIES 105 (23% from fat); FAT 2.7g (sat 1.1g, mono 0.7g, poly 0.3g); PROTEIN 4.3g; CARB 15.4g; FIBER 0.1g; CHOL 3mg; IRON 0.5mg; SODIUM 303mg; CALC 100mg
EXCHANGES: 1 Starch, ½ Medium-Fat Meat

Seared Chicken with Avocado

Chicken Thighs with
Tomatoes and Capers

chicken thighs with tomatoes and capers
with linguine and **sautéed zucchini strips**

serves 4   •   total time 25 minutes

Just a short time of simmering gives you a rich, full-flavored chicken-tomato mixture to serve over pasta.

SUPPER plan

1. Bring water to a boil for pasta.

2. Cook chicken and pasta at the same time. (Cook 8 ounces of dry pasta to get 4 cups of cooked.)

3. While chicken and pasta cook, prepare Sautéed Zucchini Strips.

Chicken Thighs with Tomatoes and Capers

prep: 4 minutes   cook: 21 minutes

    4   (4-ounce) skinless, boneless chicken thighs,
        trimmed
Cooking spray
    1   tablespoon dried or 2 tablespoons chopped
        fresh basil
    2   (14.5-ounce) cans diced tomatoes with
        peppers, undrained
    1   tablespoon capers
    2   tablespoons sliced fresh basil (optional)

Coat chicken with cooking spray; sprinkle with basil. Place a large nonstick skillet over medium-high heat; add chicken, and cook 2 to 3 minutes on each side or until browned. Add tomatoes to pan. Bring to a boil; cover, reduce heat, and simmer 15 minutes, turning chicken occasionally. Increase heat to high; bring to a boil. Cook, uncovered, 2 minutes or until chicken is done and tomato mixture is slightly thick,

stirring frequently. Add capers. Sprinkle with fresh basil, if desired. Yield: 4 servings (serving size: 1 thigh and ½ cup sauce).

CALORIES 205 (20% from fat); FAT 4.5g (sat 1.1g, mono 1.4g, poly 1.1g);
PROTEIN 24.4g; CARB 15.5g; FIBER 3.9g; CHOL 94mg; IRON 2.6mg;
SODIUM 945mg; CALC 82mg
EXCHANGES: 1 Starch, 3 Very Lean Meat

Sautéed Zucchini Strips

prep: 4 minutes   cook: 7 minutes

    2   teaspoons olive oil
    2   teaspoons bottled minced garlic
    2   zucchini, cut lengthwise into 2-inch-thick
        strips
    2   teaspoons lemon juice
    1   teaspoon Greek seasoning

Heat olive oil in a large nonstick skillet over medium-high heat. Add garlic, zucchini, lemon juice, and Greek seasoning. Sauté 7 minutes or until zucchini is tender. Yield: 4 servings (serving size: ½ cup).

CALORIES 36 (60% from fat); FAT 2.4g (sat 0.3g, mono 1.7g, poly 0.3g);
PROTEIN 1.2g; CARB 3.5g; FIBER 1.2g; CHOL 0mg; IRON 0.5mg;
SODIUM 24mg; CALC 18mg
EXCHANGE: 1 Vegetable

curried turkey with pecans and carrots with lemon butter

serves 4 • total time 25 minutes

Plums and chutney add sweetness, and pecans add crunch to this not-so-ordinary curry meal.

SUPPER plan

1. Slice onion and chop plums; grate lemon rind and squeeze juice.

2. Prepare Curried Turkey with Pecans, and boil water for couscous.

3. While turkey and couscous stand, steam carrots.

Curried Turkey with Pecans

prep: 5 minutes   cook: 11 minutes
stand: 5 minutes

To get 3 cups of cooked couscous, use 1 cup of dry couscous and 1¼ cups water, and cook according to package directions.

1	tablespoon dark brown sugar
¾	teaspoon curry powder
½	teaspoon salt, divided
⅛	teaspoon ground red pepper
1	pound turkey cutlets
⅓	cup pecan pieces
	Cooking spray
½	small onion, thinly sliced (about 4 ounces)
¾	cup fat-free, less-sodium chicken broth, divided
8	orange essence dried plums, chopped
3	cups hot cooked couscous
4	tablespoons mango chutney (optional)

Combine brown sugar, curry powder, ¼ teaspoon salt, and red pepper; rub over turkey.

Place a large nonstick skillet over medium-high heat until hot. Add pecans, and cook 3 minutes or until lightly browned, stirring constantly. Transfer pecans to a small bowl.

Coat pan with cooking spray. Add turkey; cook 2 minutes on each side or until done. Transfer turkey to a platter, and keep warm.

Add onion and 6 tablespoons chicken broth to pan. Cook, uncovered, 2 minutes, stirring constantly. Stir in plums, remaining chicken broth, ¼ teaspoon salt, and pecans. Cook 2 minutes or until liquid is nearly absorbed. Spoon mixture over turkey; cover and let stand 5 minutes.

Serve turkey mixture over couscous. Top each serving with chutney, if desired. Yield: 4 servings (serving size: ¾ cup couscous, 4 ounces turkey, and ¼ cup onion mixture).

CALORIES 438 (17% from fat); FAT 8.3g (sat 0.9g, mono 4.3g, poly 2.5g); PROTEIN 37.6g; CARB 53.3g; FIBER 5.3g; CHOL 82mg; IRON 3mg; SODIUM 468mg; CALC 50mg
EXCHANGES: 3 Starch, ½ Fruit, 4 Very Lean Meat, 1 Fat

Carrots with Lemon Butter

prep: 3 minutes   cook: 7 minutes

1	(16-ounce) package baby carrots
½	teaspoon grated lemon rind
2	teaspoons fresh lemon juice (about ½ lemon)
1½	tablespoons light butter
¼	teaspoon salt

Steam carrots, covered, 6 to 7 minutes or until crisp-tender; drain well. Return carrots to pan. Add lemon rind and remaining ingredients; stir until butter melts. Yield: 4 servings (serving size: about ½ cup).

CALORIES 63 (41% from fat); FAT 2.9g (sat 1.6g, mono 0g, poly 0.3g); PROTEIN 1.3g; CARB 9.5g; FIBER 2.1g; CHOL 8mg; IRON 0.9mg; SODIUM 213mg; CALC 27mg
EXCHANGES: 2 Vegetable, ½ Fat

cranberry-orange turkey cutlets
with mashed potatoes and steamed brussels sprouts

serves 4 • total time 24 minutes

Enjoy the taste of Thanksgiving without spending all day in the kitchen.

SUPPER plan

1. Cook frozen Brussels sprouts in a saucepan according to package directions.

2. Dredge turkey, and cook.

3. Prepare and cook onion mixture.

4. While onion mixture cooks, cook frozen mashed potatoes according to package microwave directions using fat-free milk.

5. Add fruit to onion mixture, cook, and spoon over turkey.

Cranberry-Orange Turkey Cutlets

prep: 5 minutes   cook: 20 minutes

If you can't find turkey cutlets, you can use turkey tenderloin. Cut the tenderloin into slices, and pound to a ¼-inch thickness.

¼ cup all-purpose flour
¾ teaspoon salt
½ teaspoon dried thyme
½ teaspoon freshly ground black pepper
1 pound turkey cutlets
1 tablespoon olive oil, divided
¼ cup finely chopped onion
⅔ cup orange juice
½ cup fat-free, less-sodium chicken broth
½ cup cranberry-orange crushed fruit (such as Ocean Spray)

Combine first 4 ingredients in a shallow dish. Dredge turkey cutlets in flour mixture.

Heat 1½ teaspoons oil in a large nonstick skillet over medium-high heat. Add half of turkey cutlets, and cook 3 minutes on each side or until done. Remove cutlets to a serving platter; keep warm. Repeat process with remaining 1½ teaspoons oil and turkey cutlets.

Add onion to pan, and cook over medium heat 1 minute. Add juice and broth; stir, scraping bottom of pan with a wooden spoon to loosen browned bits. Bring to a boil, and cook 6 to 7 minutes or until slightly thickened. Add cranberry-orange crushed fruit, and cook 1 minute or until thoroughly heated. Spoon sauce over cutlets. Yield: 4 servings (serving size: 3 ounces turkey cutlets and ¼ cup sauce).

CALORIES 270 (14% from fat); FAT 4.3g (sat 0.7g, mono 2.6g, poly 0.5g); PROTEIN 29.5g; CARB 27.4g; FIBER 0.6g; CHOL 70mg; IRON 2mg; SODIUM 581mg; CALC 25mg
EXCHANGES: 2 Fruit, 4 Very Lean Meat

HOWto

• • • • • • • • • • • • • • • • • •

Enjoy creamy low-fat mashed potatoes
using these convenience products.
Frozen: *Add fat-free milk, and cook in the microwave for 6 to 8 minutes for 4 servings.*
Refrigerated: *Keep these potatoes in the container, and heat in the microwave at HIGH 3 minutes. Stir and microwave 1 minute. A 1-pound, 4-ounce container makes 4 (⅔-cup) servings.*
Dehydrated (instant): *Bring water and margarine (or butter) to a boil in a saucepan or microwave-safe dish. Remove from heat, and add fat-free milk. Stir in potato flakes, and let stand 1 to 2 minutes until flakes are moist. Whip with a fork.*

garlic turkey-broccoli stir-fry

with steamed rice   serves 4 · total time 14 minutes

Get out your chopsticks for a simple stir-fry supper featuring tender turkey and vegetables.

SUPPER plan

1. Bring water to a boil for rice.

2. Mince garlic; drain water chestnuts; cut turkey into strips; slice bell pepper.

3. Cook rice using 2 regular bags of boil-in-bag rice.

4. While rice cooks:
- Prepare broth mixture.
- Stir-fry turkey and vegetables.

Garlic Turkey-Broccoli Stir-Fry

prep: 6 minutes   cook: 8 minutes

If you can't find turkey tenderloin, use turkey cutlets or Butterball's fresh turkey breast for stir-fry, which is already cut into strips.

2	teaspoons sesame oil, divided
1	(1-pound) turkey tenderloin, cut into thin strips
1	cup fat-free, less-sodium chicken broth
4	garlic cloves, minced
1½	tablespoons cornstarch
¼	teaspoon crushed red pepper
¼	teaspoon salt
1	red bell pepper, cut into thin strips
2	cups fresh broccoli florets
1	(8-ounce) can sliced water chestnuts, drained
2	tablespoons low-sodium soy sauce

Place a large nonstick skillet over medium-high heat until hot. Add 1 teaspoon sesame oil to pan, and tilt to coat evenly. Add turkey, and stir-fry 5 minutes or until turkey is no longer pink in center. Remove turkey, and set aside.

Combine broth and next 4 ingredients in a small bowl; stir until cornstarch dissolves. Set aside.

Add remaining 1 teaspoon oil to pan; add pepper strips and broccoli; stir-fry 1 minute. Add water chestnuts, and stir-fry 30 seconds. Increase heat to high. Stir broth mixture, and add to pan with soy sauce, turkey, and any accumulated juices. Bring to a boil; cook 1 to 2 minutes or until slightly thickened. Yield: 4 servings (serving size: 1½ cups).

CALORIES 262 (38% from fat); FAT 11g (sat 2.6g, mono 4.1g, poly 3g); PROTEIN 27.6g; CARB 13.1g; FIBER 3.7g; CHOL 74mg; IRON 12.3mg; SODIUM 651mg; CALC 43mg
EXCHANGES: ½ Starch, 2 Vegetable, 3 Lean Meat

HOWto

● ● ● ● ● ● ● ● ● ● ● ● ● ● ● ● ● ●

Here are some tips for stir-fry success:

- *Make sure the skillet is very hot before adding the vegetables so that they'll cook quickly. If a drop of water sizzles when dropped in the skillet, it's hot enough.*

- *Use a big enough skillet so all the vegetables are in contact with the pan; that way they'll be stir-fried, not steamed.*

- *Don't overload the pan or the pieces will not cook evenly.*

Garlic Turkey-Broccoli
Stir-Fry

66 *What else can I serve with a main dish? I'm in a rut, cooking the same old frozen vegetables.* **99**

speedy
SIDES

Round out your meals with no-stress side dishes: salads, veggies, grains, and simple pastas. Pair these delicious sides with the entrées in this book or serve them with your favorite grilled meats, poultry, or fish. Sure, they're speedy— most take less than 15 minutes to prepare— but these sides are front and center when it comes to flavor.

Zucchini with Corn and Cilantro, page 325

Apple-Yogurt Salad

prep: 5 minutes

Serve this sweet, creamy apple salad for dinner with lamb or pork, as a breakfast treat, or as a quick dessert.

1   (8-ounce) carton vanilla fat-free yogurt
2   cups chopped Granny Smith apple (about 1 large)
1   teaspoon chopped fresh mint
2   teaspoons honey
2   tablespoons nutlike cereal nuggets (such as Grape-Nuts)

Combine first 4 ingredients.

Spoon mixture into bowls. Sprinkle each with cereal nuggets just before serving. Yield: 4 servings (serving size: ½ cup apple mixture and 1½ teaspoons cereal nuggets).

CALORIES 95 (1% from fat); FAT 0g (sat 0g, mono 0g, poly 0g); PROTEIN 3.1g; CARB 20.5g; FIBER 1g; CHOL 2mg; IRON 1mg; SODIUM 54mg; CALC 87mg
EXCHANGES: ½ Starch, 1 Fruit

SIMPLEsubstitutions

• • • • • • • • • • • • • • • • • •

Use cereal instead of nuts. *One of our food editors claims that she puts Grape-Nuts cereal on "everything" to add crunch and nutty flavor. Plus, you get fiber, iron, B-vitamins, and folic acid along with the crunch.*

Try sprinkling a tablespoon of nuggets on yogurt, frozen yogurt, low-fat ice cream, oatmeal, fruit salads, green salads, and vegetables. Oh, and it's also good in a bowl with milk and a spoon.

Since you're only using a few tablespoons at a time, store the cereal in the freezer in a zip-top plastic bag to keep it fresh.

Honey Grapefruit with Banana

prep: 5 minutes

When you're hungry for breakfast at supper time, enjoy a bowl of this sweet minted fruit with an omelet .

1   (24-ounce) jar refrigerated red grapefruit sections (about 2 cups)
1   cup sliced banana (about 1)
1   tablespoon fresh chopped mint
1   tablespoon honey

Drain grapefruit sections, reserving ¼ cup juice.

Combine grapefruit sections, juice, and remaining ingredients in a medium bowl. Toss gently to coat. Serve immediately, or cover and chill. Yield: 3 servings (serving size: 1 cup).

CALORIES 122 (3% from fat); FAT 0.4g (sat 0.1g, mono 0g, poly 0g); PROTEIN 1.5g; CARB 31.3g; FIBER 3.4g; CHOL 0mg; IRON 0.6mg; SODIUM 2mg; CALC 26mg
EXCHANGES: 2 Fruit

FINDit

• • • • • • • • • • • • • • • • • •

Look for jars of fresh fruit sections, *such as grapefruit, peaches, pears, and mangoes, in the refrigerated produce section of the grocery store. The fruit is usually located near the fresh squeezed juices.*

Because these fruits are packed fresh in their natural juices, you're not getting any extra syrup or sugar.

Honey Grapefruit with Banana

Pear Waldorf Salad

prep: 6 minutes

This variation on traditional Waldorf salad features pears instead of apples and red grapes in place of raisins for extra sweetness.

  1 tablespoon light mayonnaise
  2 tablespoons reduced-fat sour cream
  1 teaspoon fresh lemon juice
  ⅛ teaspoon salt
  2 cups (¾-inch) coarsely chopped Bartlett pear
     (about 2 pears)
  1 cup small seedless red grapes
  2 tablespoons chopped walnuts
     Arugula leaves or mixed greens (optional)

Combine first 4 ingredients in a small bowl; stir until smooth.

Combine pear, grapes, walnuts, and mayonnaise mixture in a large bowl; toss gently. Serve salad over arugula or mixed greens, if desired. Yield: 4 servings (serving size: ¾ cup).

CALORIES 116 (29% from fat); FAT 3.8g (sat 0.9g, mono 0.4g, poly 1.6g); PROTEIN 1.4g; CARB 21.6g; FIBER 2.6g; CHOL 4mg; IRON 0.4mg; SODIUM 114mg; CALC 29mg
EXCHANGES: 1 Fruit, 1 Fat

HOW**to**

● ● ● ● ● ● ● ● ● ● ● ● ● ● ● ●

Toasting nuts enhances their flavor. *To toast walnuts, cook them in a dry skillet over medium heat for 1 to 2 minutes, stirring constantly. Use your sense of smell to judge when they're toasted. Remove from the heat as soon as you begin to smell that wonderful nutty aroma; if left on much longer the nuts will begin to burn. Be especially careful when you're toasting a small amount of nuts—they can burn even more quickly.*

Cherry Tomato and Greens Salad

prep: 5 minutes

Toss together this very simple salad for a no-fuss supper.

  1 tablespoon red wine vinegar
  1 tablespoon tomato juice
  2 teaspoons olive oil
  ¼ teaspoon salt
  ⅛ teaspoon coarsely ground black pepper
  1 small garlic clove, pressed
  1 (5-ounce) package gourmet salad greens
     (about 6 cups)
  1 cup halved cherry tomatoes
  2 tablespoons (½ ounce) shredded Asiago or
     fresh Parmesan cheese

Combine first 6 ingredients in a small bowl, stirring with a whisk. Combine greens and tomatoes in a large bowl; add dressing, and toss well. Sprinkle with cheese. Yield: 4 servings (serving size: 1½ cups).

CALORIES 50 (61% from fat); FAT 3.4g (sat 1g, mono 2g, poly 0.3g); PROTEIN 2.3g; CARB 3.3g; FIBER 1.2g; CHOL 2.6mg; IRON 0.7mg; SODIUM 233mg; CALC 68mg
EXCHANGES: 1 Vegetable, ½ Fat

HOW**to**

● ● ● ● ● ● ● ● ● ● ● ● ● ● ● ●

Wash your greens *even though the package of salad greens says that the greens are prewashed. Rinse them lightly, and drain them on a paper towel or use a salad spinner. When you rinse them again, you can be confident that the greens are clean. It's a good idea to wash all fresh greens, vegetables, and fruits as soon as you get home from the grocery store so you'll have them ready to use in recipes.*

Iceberg Lettuce and Snow Peas with Creamy Dill Dressing

prep: 12 minutes

Buttermilk gives the creamy dressing a rich, full-bodied flavor.

¼ cup light mayonnaise
¼ cup low-fat buttermilk (1%)
2 tablespoons chopped fresh dill
1 teaspoon fresh lemon juice
¼ teaspoon salt
⅛ teaspoon coarsely ground black pepper
4 cups preshredded iceberg lettuce
1 cup thinly sliced trimmed snow peas
½ cup chopped celery

Combine first 6 ingredients in a small bowl, stirring with a whisk. Combine lettuce, snow peas, and celery in a large bowl; add dressing, and toss. Yield: 4 servings (serving size: 1 cup).

CALORIES 77 (62% from fat); FAT 5.3g (sat 1.1g, mono 0.1g, poly 0.1g); PROTEIN 1.9g; CARB 5.5g; FIBER 1.7g; CHOL 6mg; IRON 0.9mg; SODIUM 302mg; CALC 45mg
EXCHANGES: 1 Vegetable, 1 Fat

QUICKtip

● ● ● ● ● ● ● ● ● ● ● ● ● ● ● ● ●

Save a few minutes *of prep time by picking up chopped celery from the supermarket salad bar and bags of shredded lettuce from the produce section. In larger markets you may find small bags of chopped celery, onions, and carrots in the fresh produce section, especially during the holidays.*

Leafy Greens with Mandarin Oranges and Watercress

prep: 8 minutes

Since Mandarin oranges are fairly delicate, toss them gently so you don't tear up the sections.

2 (8-ounce) cans Mandarin oranges in light syrup
1½ tablespoons white wine vinegar
2 teaspoons olive oil
½ teaspoon sugar
¼ teaspoon salt
⅛ teaspoon coarsely ground black pepper
5 cups coarsely chopped red or green leaf lettuce
1 cup trimmed watercress

Drain oranges, reserving 2 tablespoons syrup. Combine syrup, vinegar, and next 4 ingredients in a small bowl, stirring with a whisk. Combine lettuce, watercress, and oranges in a large bowl. Add dressing, and toss well. Yield: 4 servings (serving size: 1½ cups).

CALORIES 92 (23% from fat); FAT 2.4g (sat 0.3g, mono 1.7g, poly 0.2g); PROTEIN 1.5g; CARB 19g; FIBER 2.5g; CHOL 0mg; IRON 0.4mg; SODIUM 181mg; CALC 51mg
EXCHANGES: 1 Fruit, 1 Vegetable

SIMPLEsubstitutions

● ● ● ● ● ● ● ● ● ● ● ● ● ● ● ● ●

Watercress adds a peppery bite, *which is a nice flavor contrast to the sweet oranges. If you can't find watercress, just use another cup of chopped lettuce.*

Field Salad with Pears and
Blue Cheese

Field Salad with Pears and Blue Cheese

prep: 5 minutes

Offer this colorful salad during the fall and winter when pears are in season and fresh walnuts are abundant.

  1   (5-ounce) package gourmet salad greens (about 6 cups)
  1   red pear, thinly sliced
  ¼   cup (1 ounce) crumbled blue cheese
  3   tablespoons fat-free raspberry vinaigrette (such as Maple Grove Farms)
  2   tablespoons finely chopped walnuts

  Combine first 3 ingredients in a large bowl. Add dressing, and toss gently. Spoon onto plates, and sprinkle evenly with walnuts. Yield: 4 servings (serving size: 1½ cups).

CALORIES 98 (47% from fat); FAT 5.1g (sat 1.8g, mono 1g, poly 1.9g); PROTEIN 3.1g; CARB 11g; FIBER 2g; CHOL 6mg; IRON 0.7mg; SODIUM 140mg; CALC 72mg
EXCHANGES: ½ Fruit, 1 Vegetable, 1 Fat

SIMPLEsubstitutions

● ● ● ● ● ● ● ● ● ● ● ● ● ● ● ● ● ● ●

Instead of using a fresh pear, *you can make this salad with coarsely chopped refrigerated or canned pears.*

Hearts of Palm Salad

prep: 5 minutes

Dress up a simple green salad with delicately flavored hearts of palm.

  1   (¾-ounce) package fresh basil leaves (about 12 large)
  1   (7.75-ounce) can hearts of palm, drained and sliced
  ½   cup sliced bottled roasted red bell peppers, drained
  ¼   cup fat-free balsamic vinaigrette

  Arrange basil leaves evenly on serving plates. Top evenly with hearts of palm and red peppers. Drizzle 1 tablespoon vinaigrette over each salad. Yield: 4 servings (serving size: 1 salad).

CALORIES 26 (10% from fat); FAT 0.3g (sat 0.1g, mono 0g, poly 0.1g); PROTEIN 1.1g; CARB 5.4g; FIBER 1.2g; CHOL 0mg; IRON 1.3mg; SODIUM 580mg; CALC 34mg
EXCHANGE: 1 Vegetable

FINDit

● ● ● ● ● ● ● ● ● ● ● ● ● ● ● ● ● ● ●

Hearts of palm are the edible *inner portions of the stem of the cabbage palm tree. They look like white asparagus without the tips, and the flavor is similar to that of an artichoke.*

Hearts of palm are available fresh only in Florida and in the tropical countries where they're grown. You can find canned hearts of palm, packed in water, in the canned vegetable section of the grocery store. They're considered somewhat of a delicacy and are more expensive than other canned vegetables. Once you've opened the can, transfer the hearts of palm (with liquid) to an airtight nonmetal container and store in the refrigerator for up to one week.

Coleslaw with Pineapple

prep: 9 minutes

Buy a coleslaw mix without the dressing packet, or discard the packet if there's one in the package.

  ¼   cup light mayonnaise
  ¼   cup reduced-fat sour cream
  1   tablespoon sugar
  ⅛   teaspoon salt
  1   (8-ounce) can crushed pineapple in juice,
      drained
  4   cups cabbage-and-carrot coleslaw mix
      (about 8 ounces)
  ⅓   cup (2-inch) pieces red bell pepper

Combine first 5 ingredients in a medium bowl, stirring with a whisk until blended.

Combine coleslaw and red pepper in a large bowl; add mayonnaise mixture, tossing gently to coat. Cover and chill. Yield: 6 servings (serving size: about ⅔ cup).

CALORIES 86 (50% from fat); FAT 4.7g (sat 1.3g, mono 0g, poly 0.1g); PROTEIN 1.4g; CARB 10.6g; FIBER 1.5g; CHOL 8.7mg; IRON 0.4mg; SODIUM 144mg; CALC 43mg
EXCHANGES: ½ Fruit, 1 Vegetable, 1 Fat

SIMPLE**substitutions**

● ● ● ● ● ● ● ● ● ● ● ● ● ● ● ● ● ● ●

Vary the flavor of this creamy coleslaw *by using either ½ cup chopped apple or an 8-ounce can of Mandarin oranges, drained, to replace the pineapple.*

Lemony Asparagus with Parsley

prep: 4 minutes   cook: 7 minutes

Welcome springtime (when asparagus is at its peak) with this tangy, fresh dish.

  1   teaspoon olive oil
  3   cups (2-inch) diagonally sliced asparagus
      (about ½ pound)
  2   tablespoons finely chopped fresh flat-leaf
      parsley
  1   tablespoon fresh lemon juice (about
      ½ lemon)
  ¼   teaspoon salt
  ¼   teaspoon coarsely ground black pepper

Heat oil in a large nonstick skillet over medium-high heat. Add asparagus; cook, stirring occasionally, 7 minutes or until crisp-tender. Remove from heat; stir in parsley and remaining ingredients. Yield: 4 servings (serving size: ½ cup).

CALORIES 35 (36% from fat); FAT 1.4g (sat 0.2g, mono 0.8g, poly 0.2g); PROTEIN 2.4g; CARB 5g; FIBER 2.2g; CHOL 0mg; IRON 1mg; SODIUM 151mg; CALC 25mg
EXCHANGE: 1 Vegetable

HOW**to**

● ● ● ● ● ● ● ● ● ● ● ● ● ● ● ● ● ● ●

To trim fresh asparagus, *snap off the tough ends and remove the scales, if desired, with a vegetable peeler or a knife. Cut spears diagonally into 2-inch pieces. You'll need to buy about ½ pound of fresh asparagus to get 3 cups of sliced.*

Lemony Asparagus with
Parsley

Balsamic Pan-Roasted Broccoli

prep: 1 minute   cook: 8 minutes

Instead of steaming broccoli, roast it quickly in a skillet to brown the florets and add flavor.

   1   teaspoon olive oil
Cooking spray
   1   (12-ounce) package fresh broccoli florets
   ¼   teaspoon salt
   ¼   teaspoon freshly ground black pepper
   1   tablespoon balsamic vinegar

   Heat oil in a large nonstick skillet coated with cooking spray over medium heat. Add broccoli; cook, turning occasionally, 8 minutes or until lightly browned and crisp-tender. Remove from heat; add salt, pepper, and vinegar. Yield: 4 servings (serving size: ¾ cup).

CALORIES 37 (35% from fat); FAT 1.4g (sat 0.2g, mono 0.9g, poly 0.2g); PROTEIN 2.6g; CARB 5.1g; FIBER 2.5g; CHOL 0mg; IRON 0.8mg; SODIUM 171mg; CALC 43mg
EXCHANGE: 1 Vegetable

FIND**it**

• • • • • • • • • • • • • • • • •

Balsamic vinegar *is made from Trebblano grape juice (a sweet white Italian grape) and gets its characteristic dark color and tangy sweetness from being aged in oak barrels for long periods of time. Some imported balsamic vinegars have been aged as long as 25 years and are quite expensive, but you can find reasonably priced bottles on the shelves with other vinegars at the supermarket.*

Sautéed Cabbage with Dill

prep: 7 minutes   cook: 4 minutes

This cabbage is good either warm or at room temperature. If you have any left over, try it as a lower-sodium substitution for sauerkraut on a Reuben sandwich.

   2   teaspoons butter
   4   cups cabbage-and-carrot coleslaw mix
       (about 8 ounces)
   1   cup thinly sliced leek (about 1 large)
   2   tablespoons chopped fresh dill
   2   teaspoons fresh lemon juice (about ½ lemon)
   ¼   teaspoon salt
   ⅛   teaspoon freshly ground black pepper

   Melt butter in a large nonstick skillet over medium heat. Stir in coleslaw and leek. Cover and cook 4 minutes or until cabbage wilts, stirring twice.
   Remove from heat. Add dill and remaining ingredients. Serve warm or at room temperature. Yield: 4 servings (serving size: ½ cup).

CALORIES 49 (40% from fat); FAT 2.2g (sat 1.2g, mono 0.6g, poly 0.2g); PROTEIN 1.4g; CARB 7.2g; FIBER 2g; CHOL 5mg; IRON 0.9mg; SODIUM 184mg; CALC 48mg
EXCHANGES: 1 Vegetable, ½ Fat

FIND**it**

• • • • • • • • • • • • • • • • •

Look for cabbage-and-carrot coleslaw mix *in the produce section with prepackaged lettuce and salads. Buy a coleslaw mix without a seasoning packet.*

Cauliflower with Chives and Lemon

prep: 5 minutes   cook: 5 minutes

The simple addition of butter and fresh lemon juice brings out the cauliflower's best flavor.

  3 cups fresh cauliflower florets (about ¾ pound)
  2 tablespoons finely chopped fresh chives
1½ tablespoons light butter, melted
  1 tablespoon fresh lemon juice (about ½ lemon)
  ¼ teaspoon salt
  ¼ teaspoon freshly ground black pepper

Place cauliflower in a medium saucepan, and add water to cover. Bring to a boil, and cook 5 minutes or until crisp-tender.

Transfer florets to a bowl; add chives and remaining ingredients. Yield: 4 servings (serving size: about ¾ cup).

CALORIES 39 (55% from fat); FAT 2.4g (sat 1.5g, mono 0g, poly 0.1g); PROTEIN 1.9g; CARB 4.3g; FIBER 2g; CHOL 8mg; IRON 0.4mg; SODIUM 196mg; CALC 19mg
EXCHANGES: ½ Fruit,1 Vegetable

FIND**it**

● ● ● ● ● ● ● ● ● ● ● ● ● ● ● ● ● ●

You'll find prepackaged cauliflower florets *in the produce section of the supermarket. If the bagged florets aren't available, use one head of cauliflower (about 1 pound) to get 3 cups of florets.*

Green Beans with Cilantro

prep: 11 minutes   cook: 10 minutes

Spice up bland beans by adding hot pepper and cilantro.

1½ teaspoons olive oil
     Cooking spray
  3 cups (2-inch) diagonally cut green beans (about ¾ pound)
  1 tablespoon minced fresh cilantro
  1 small jalapeño pepper, seeded and minced
  ¼ teaspoon salt

Heat oil in a large nonstick skillet coated with cooking spray over medium-high heat. Add green beans; sauté 10 minutes or until tender and browned in spots.

Stir in cilantro, minced pepper, and salt. Yield: 4 servings (serving size: ½ cup).

CALORIES 43 (40% from fat); FAT 1.9g (sat 0.3g, mono 1.3g, poly 0.2g); PROTEIN 1.6g; CARB 6.5g; FIBER 2.8g; CHOL 0mg; IRON 0.9mg; SODIUM 151mg; CALC 31mg
EXCHANGE: 1 Vegetable

QUICK**tip**

● ● ● ● ● ● ● ● ● ● ● ● ● ● ● ● ● ●

Use rubber gloves *when working with the jalapeño pepper so your hands won't get burned. If you want extra fire in the dish, don't remove the seeds.*

Lemony Green Beans

prep: 2 minutes   cook: 5 minutes

The light lemon flavor of these fresh beans is a nice complement to roasted turkey, chicken, or pork tenderloin.

  2   tablespoons light butter
  1   teaspoon grated lemon rind
  2   teaspoons fresh lemon juice (about ½ lemon)
  ¼   teaspoon salt
  ¼   teaspoon freshly ground black pepper
  4   cups green beans, trimmed (about 1 pound)
  2   tablespoons water

  Place butter in a microwave-safe bowl; microwave at HIGH 20 seconds or until melted. Stir in lemon rind and next 3 ingredients. Set aside.
  Place beans in a large microwave-safe bowl; add water. Cover and microwave at HIGH 3 to 4 minutes or until crisp-tender. Drain well. Toss beans with butter mixture. Yield: 4 servings (serving size: 1 cup).

CALORIES 53 (53% from fat); FAT 3.1g (sat 2g, mono 0g, poly 0g); PROTEIN 2.1g; CARB 6.5g; FIBER 1g; CHOL 10mg; IRON 0.9mg; SODIUM 187mg; CALC 33mg
EXCHANGES: 1 Vegetable, ½ Fat

HOW**to**

● ● ● ● ● ● ● ● ● ● ● ● ● ● ● ● ●

Buy about 1 pound of green beans *to get 4 cups trimmed beans. A good rule of thumb for green beans is to count on about ¼ pound of fresh beans per serving.*

Skillet Mushrooms and Water Chestnuts

prep: 5 minutes   cook: 9 minutes

Grilled steak, chicken, or fish, and roasted green beans or asparagus pair nicely with this Asian-style side dish.

  1   teaspoon sesame oil
  ¼   teaspoon toasted sesame oil
  2   garlic cloves, minced
  2   (8-ounce) packages presliced mushrooms
  1   (8-ounce) can sliced water chestnuts, drained
  ¼   teaspoon freshly ground black pepper
  ¼   teaspoon salt
  1   tablespoon low-sodium soy sauce
  2   tablespoons thinly sliced green onions

  Heat oils in a large nonstick skillet over medium-high heat. Add garlic and mushrooms; cook, stirring occasionally, 7 to 8 minutes or just until tender.
  Add water chestnuts and remaining ingredients, and cook 1 minute or until thoroughly heated. Yield: 4 servings (serving size: ¾ cup).

CALORIES 63 (27% from fat); FAT 1.9g (sat 0.3g, mono 0.6g, poly 0.8g); PROTEIN 3.9g; CARB 9.7g; FIBER 3.2g; CHOL 0mg; IRON 9.9mg; SODIUM 289mg; CALC 11mg
EXCHANGES: 2 Vegetable

HOW**to**

● ● ● ● ● ● ● ● ● ● ● ● ● ● ● ● ●

Keep mushrooms cool and dry *by leaving them in their plastic or paper containers until you're ready to use them.*

Garlicky Sautéed Spinach

prep: 2 minutes   cook: 3 minutes

Here's a five-minute side that goes with just about anything.

    1   tablespoon butter
    1   small garlic clove, minced
    ½   (10-ounce) package fresh spinach
    ⅛   teaspoon crushed red pepper
    1   tablespoon lemon juice

   Melt butter in a large nonstick skillet over medium heat. Add garlic, and sauté 30 seconds. Add spinach, red pepper, and lemon juice. Sauté 2 to 3 minutes or until spinach wilts. Yield: 2 servings (serving size: 1 cup).

CALORIES 71 (77% from fat); FAT 6g (sat 3.6g, mono 1.7g, poly 0.3g); PROTEIN 2.2g; CARB 3.5g; FIBER 2g; CHOL 16mg; IRON 2mg; SODIUM 116mg; CALC 76mg
EXCHANGES: 1 Vegetable, 1 Fat

HOWto

• • • • • • • • • • • • • • • •

To remove the garlic smell *from your fingers after mincing garlic, rub your fingers along the flat sides of a stainless steel knife (be careful not to touch the sharp edge) or a stainless steel sink.*

❝I rely on the microwave for cooking vegetables. *It's kind of a no-brainer, but I can be cooking something else in the oven or on the stovetop and just put the vegetable in at the last minute.*❞

Jane Gentry,
Assistant Foods Editor

Acorn Squash with Maple Syrup

prep: 4 minutes   cook: 16 minutes

A taste of the holidays, this steamed winter squash is bathed in butter and maple syrup.

    1   acorn squash (about 2¼ pounds)
    1½   tablespoons light butter
    3   tablespoons maple syrup
    ¼   teaspoon salt
    ⅛   teaspoon ground cinnamon

   Cut squash in half lengthwise; scoop out seeds and discard. Cut each piece in half.
   Place squash in a medium saucepan; cover with water. Bring to a boil; cover and cook 15 to 18 minutes or until tender. Drain well, and transfer to serving plates.
   Place butter, syrup, and salt in a small microwave-safe bowl. Microwave at HIGH 30 seconds; stir with a whisk. Spoon butter mixture over squash; sprinkle with cinnamon. Yield: 4 servings.

CALORIES 101 (21% from fat); FAT 2.4g (sat 1.5g, mono 0g, poly 0.1g); PROTEIN 1.2g, CARB 21.4g; FIBER 1.7g; CHOL 8mg; IRON 0.0mg; SODIUM 177mg; CALC 46mg
EXCHANGES: 1½ Starch

QUICKtip

• • • • • • • • • • • • • • • •

To make the squash easier to cut in half, *microwave the whole acorn squash for 1 to 2 minutes at HIGH.*

Summer Squash with
Tomatoes and Basil

Summer Squash with Tomatoes and Basil

prep: 5 minutes   cook: 7 minutes

When your summer garden bounty is coming in, this simple skillet dish is an ideal way to cook all the squash, tomatoes, and basil.

1   teaspoon olive oil
Cooking spray
5   cups cubed yellow squash (about 1¼ pounds)
1   cup grape tomatoes, halved
2   tablespoons chopped fresh basil
¼   teaspoon salt
¼   teaspoon freshly ground black pepper

Heat oil in a large nonstick skillet coated with cooking spray over medium heat. Add squash; cook, stirring occasionally, 6 minutes or until tender.

Add tomato and remaining ingredients; cook 1 minute or until thoroughly heated. Yield: 4 servings (serving size: 1 cup).

CALORIES 49 (31% from fat); FAT 1.7g (sat 0.3g, mono 0.9g, poly 0.3g); PROTEIN 1.9g; CARB 8.4g; FIBER 3.6g; CHOL 0mg; IRON 1mg; SODIUM 153mg; CALC 39mg
EXCHANGES: 2 Vegetable

SIMPLEsubstitutions

• • • • • • • • • • • • • • • • • •

For a flavor variation, use zucchini *instead of yellow squash, and fresh oregano or rosemary instead of basil.*

Zucchini with Garlic

prep: 5 minutes   cook: 7 minutes

There's nothing better than garden-fresh zucchini, simply seasoned with butter and garlic.

1   tablespoon light butter
3   garlic cloves, minced
2   cups cubed zucchini (about ¾ pound)
¼   teaspoon salt
¼   teaspoon freshly ground black pepper

Melt butter in a large nonstick skillet over medium-high heat. Add garlic, and sauté 1 minute. Add zucchini, and cook, stirring occasionally, 6 to 7 minutes or until crisp-tender. Stir in salt and pepper. Yield: 2 servings (serving size: ¾ cup).

CALORIES 55 (54% from fat); FAT 3.3g (sat 2.1g, mono 0g, poly 0.1g); PROTEIN 2.2g; CARB 6.6g; FIBER 2.3g; CHOL 10mg; IRON 0.7mg; SODIUM 331mg; CALC 32mg
EXCHANGES: 1 Vegetable, ½ Fat

FINDit

• • • • • • • • • • • • • • • • • •

Fresh zucchini is available year-round *in most supermarkets, but it's at its peak in late spring and early summer. Select small zucchini about 1½ inches in diameter and 6 inches in length. They're younger, have thinner skins, and are more tender than the larger ones.*

Zucchini with Corn and
Cilantro

Zucchini with Corn and Cilantro

prep: 6 minutes   cook: 7 minutes

Use this vegetable medley as a fresh substitute for salsa or guacamole salad on a Tex-Mex fiesta plate.

1	teaspoon olive oil
3½	cups cubed zucchini (about 1 pound)
1	cup frozen whole-kernel corn
1	tablespoon chopped fresh cilantro
1	teaspoon fresh lime juice
¼	teaspoon salt
⅛	teaspoon freshly ground black pepper

Heat oil in a large nonstick skillet over medium-high heat. Add zucchini and corn; cook, stirring occasionally, 7 to 8 minutes or until zucchini is crisp-tender.

Remove from heat, and stir in cilantro and remaining ingredients. Yield: 4 servings (serving size: ¾ cup).

CALORIES 62 (23% from fat); FAT 1.6g (sat 0.2g, mono 0.9g, poly 0.3g); PROTEIN 2.6g; CARB 12g; FIBER 2.4g; CHOL 0mg; IRON 0.7mg; SODIUM 152mg; CALC 19mg
EXCHANGES: ½ Starch, 1 Vegetable

SIMPLEsubstitutions

. . . .

Use canned corn *instead of frozen if you have it on hand. Canned corn has more sodium than the frozen (350 milligrams per cup versus 8 milligrams), so if you use canned, just omit the salt from the recipe.*

Cheddar Mashed Potatoes with Sage

prep: 3 minutes   cook: 6 minutes

You may be pleasantly surprised at the rich creaminess you can get from a package of frozen mashed potatoes.

1¼	cups 1% low-fat milk
3	cups frozen mashed potatoes (about 11 ounces)
½	cup (2 ounces) shredded reduced-fat sharp Cheddar cheese
1	teaspoon butter
¼	teaspoon dried rubbed sage
¼	teaspoon salt
⅛	teaspoon garlic powder
⅛	teaspoon freshly ground black pepper

Cook milk in a medium saucepan over medium-high heat until hot. Add potatoes, and cook, stirring constantly, 3 to 4 minutes or until thoroughly heated.

Reduce heat to low; add cheese and remaining ingredients. Cook 1 to 2 minutes or until cheese melts. Serve immediately. Yield: 5 servings (serving size: ½ cup).

CALORIES 147 (32% from fat); FAT 5.3g (sat 3g, mono 0.4g, poly 0.1g); PROTEIN 6.3g; CARB 17.6g; FIBER 0.9g; CHOL 13mg; IRON 0.1mg; SODIUM 375mg; CALC 181mg
EXCHANGES: 1 Starch, 1 Fat

SIMPLEsubstitutions

. . . .

You can substitute another dried herb *for the sage. Try dried basil, oregano, cilantro, or dill, and use the same amount—¼ teaspoon.*

Garlic Mashed Potatoes with Basil and Feta

prep: 9 minutes   cook: 14 minutes

Yukon Gold potatoes have a naturally yellow color and a rich, buttery-tasting flavor.

1½   pounds Yukon Gold potatoes, peeled and cut into eighths (about 3 medium)
  2   garlic cloves, halved
  2   teaspoons butter, softened
  ⅓   cup 1% low-fat milk
  ½   cup (2 ounces) crumbled feta cheese
  2   tablespoons finely chopped fresh basil
  ¼   teaspoon salt
  ¼   teaspoon pepper

Place potato and garlic in a 3-quart saucepan; add water to cover. Bring to a boil over high heat; partially cover, reduce heat, and simmer 14 minutes or until tender.

Drain potato; return to pan. Add butter and remaining ingredients to pan. Mash with a potato masher. Cook, stirring constantly, over low heat just until thoroughly heated. Yield: 4 servings (serving size: ¾ cup).

CALORIES 153 (31% from fat); FAT 5.3g (sat 3.4g, mono 1.3g, poly 0.2g); PROTEIN 6g; CARB 19.5g; FIBER 2.4g; CHOL 19mg; IRON 1mg; SODIUM 340mg; CALC 105mg
EXCHANGES: 1½ Starch, 1 Fat

SIMPLEsubstitutions

● ● ● ● ● ● ● ● ● ● ● ● ● ● ● ● ● ●

Use 2 ounces of another cheese *such as goat cheese, light cream cheese, or shredded Cheddar instead of feta to create a deliciously different version of these potatoes.*

Pan-Fried Potatoes with Dill

prep: 3 minutes   cook: 10 minutes

Instead of fresh, you can use about ½ teaspoon of dried dill.

  1   tablespoon olive oil
  1   (20-ounce) package cooked new potato wedges (such as Simply Potatoes)
  1   tablespoon grated Parmesan cheese
  1   tablespoon finely chopped fresh dill
  ¼   teaspoon salt
  ¼   teaspoon freshly ground black pepper

Heat oil in a large nonstick skillet over medium-high heat. Add potato wedges; cook, stirring occasionally, 10 to 15 minutes or until golden brown.

Remove from heat, and sprinkle with cheese and remaining ingredients; toss gently. Yield: 4 servings (serving size: ¾ cup).

CALORIES 168 (21% from fat); FAT 3.9g (sat 0.8g, mono 2.6g, poly 0.3g); PROTEIN 3.9g; CARB 29.5g; FIBER 3.3g; CHOL 1mg; IRON 0.7mg; SODIUM 453mg; CALC 23mg
EXCHANGES: 2 Starch

FINDit

● ● ● ● ● ● ● ● ● ● ● ● ● ● ● ● ● ●

Look for packages of cooked potatoes *in the refrigerated section of the supermarket. These potatoes are packaged fresh and refrigerated, not frozen. For best quality, you need to use the potatoes within five days of opening the package. If you use only part of a package, be sure to store the remaining potatoes in an airtight container.*

Refrigerated cooked potatoes are also available in the following varieties: Shredded Hash Browns, Southwest-Style Hash Browns, Diced Potatoes with Onions, Sliced Home Fries, and Country Mashed Potatoes.

Pan-Fried Potatoes with Dill

Couscous with Pistachios and Oranges

prep: 2½ minutes   cook: 5 minutes

Couscous is a perfect last-minute side dish; it "cooks" in about 5 minutes while it stands .

 1   cup vegetable broth
 ⅔   cup uncooked couscous
 1   (11-ounce) can Mandarin oranges in light syrup, undrained
 2   teaspoons fresh lemon juice
 ¼   teaspoon salt
 ⅛   teaspoon coarsely ground black pepper
 2   tablespoons chopped pistachios

Bring broth to a boil in a medium saucepan; stir in couscous. Remove from heat; cover and let stand 5 minutes or until broth is absorbed.

Drain oranges in a colander over a bowl, reserving 2 tablespoons syrup.

Transfer couscous to a large bowl; fluff with a fork. Stir in 2 tablespoons orange syrup, lemon juice, and next 3 ingredients. Add reserved orange sections, and toss gently. Yield: 4 servings (serving size: about ¾ cup).

CALORIES 165 (11% from fat); FAT 2g (sat 0.3g, mono 0.9g, poly 0.6g); PROTEIN 5.5g; CARB 31.9g; FIBER 2.2g; CHOL 0mg; IRON 0.7mg; SODIUM 308mg; CALC 16mg
EXCHANGES: 2 Starch

QUICKtip

• • • • • • • • • • • • • • • • • • •

Buy a bag of shelled pistachios (pistachio kernels) *so you don't have to spend time shelling. But if you do buy unshelled nuts, make sure the shells are partially open so it will be easier to get the nutmeat out. Also, closed shells mean that the nutmeat is immature and won't have the delicate flavor that the mature nuts offer.*

Tabbouleh-Style Couscous

prep: 12 minutes   cook: 5 minutes

This quick variation of the traditional grain salad uses couscous instead of bulgur, but keeps the distinctive flavor blend of mint, parsley, and lemon juice.

 1¼   cups fat-free, less-sodium chicken broth, divided
 ½   teaspoon dried mint
 ⅔   cup uncooked couscous
 1   tablespoon olive oil
 1   tablespoon fresh lemon juice (about ½ lemon)
 ¼   teaspoon salt
 ¼   teaspoon freshly ground black pepper
 1   cup grape tomatoes, halved
 ⅓   cup finely chopped fresh flat-leaf parsley
 2   tablespoons minced red onion

Bring 1 cup broth to a boil in a medium saucepan; remove from heat. Add mint and couscous to broth; cover and let stand 5 minutes.

Transfer to a bowl; fluff with a fork. Add remaining ¼ cup broth, oil, and remaining ingredients to couscous. Stir gently. Yield: 4 servings (serving size: about ¾ cup).

CALORIES 157 (22% from fat); FAT 3.8g (sat 0.5g, mono 2.6g, poly 0.4g); PROTEIN 5.2g; CARB 25.5g; FIBER 2.2g; CHOL 0mg; IRON 1.2mg; SODIUM 351mg; CALC 21mg
EXCHANGES: 1½ Starch, 1 Vegetable, ½ Fat

SIMPLEsubstitutions

• • • • • • • • • • • • • • • •

To vary this side dish, *use a flavored couscous instead of plain. The tomato-lentil or roasted garlic and olive oil versions are good options.*

Tabbouleh-Style
Couscous

Brown Rice with Peas

prep: 5 minutes   cook: 10 minutes

Make nutty-tasting brown rice a staple in your kitchen—it has twice the fiber of white rice.

1⅓	cups water
1	cup instant brown rice (such as Uncle Ben's)
1	cup frozen green peas
2	tablespoons thinly sliced green onions
1½	tablespoons preshredded fresh Parmesan cheese
1	teaspoon butter
⅛	teaspoon salt
⅛	teaspoon freshly ground black pepper

Combine water and rice in a medium saucepan. Bring to a boil; cover, reduce heat, and simmer 10 minutes or until water is absorbed and rice is tender.

Stir in green peas and remaining ingredients. Yield: 4 servings (serving size: ¾ cup).

CALORIES 130 (17% from fat); FAT 2.4g (sat 1g, mono 0.5g, poly 0.1g); PROTEIN 4.6g; CARB 22.3g; FIBER 2.8g; CHOL 4mg; IRON 0.8mg; SODIUM 161mg; CALC 32mg
EXCHANGES: 1 Starch, 1 Vegetable, ½ Fat

EASY**additions**

• • • • • • • • • • • • • • • • • • •

To transform this side dish *into the main attraction, double the recipe, and stir in about 2 cups of cooked shrimp, roasted chicken, or turkey.*

Sesame-Garlic Brown Rice

prep: 3 minutes   cook: 12 minutes

Instead of serving plain brown rice, pump up the flavor of your meal with this Asian-inspired brown rice.

1⅓	cups water
1	cup instant brown rice (such as Uncle Ben's)
2	teaspoons dark sesame oil
1	cup shredded carrot
1	tablespoon bottled minced garlic
¼	cup thinly sliced green onions
1	tablespoon low-sodium soy sauce
¼	teaspoon salt
¼	teaspoon coarsely ground black pepper

Combine water and rice in a medium saucepan; bring to a boil over medium heat. Cover, reduce heat, and simmer 10 minutes or until water is absorbed.

Heat sesame oil in a small skillet; add carrot, and sauté 2 to 3 minutes or until crisp-tender.

Remove rice from heat; stir in sautéed carrot, garlic, and remaining ingredients. Yield: 4 servings (serving size: ¾ cup).

CALORIES 155 (18% from fat); FAT 3.1g (sat 0.3g, mono 0.9g, poly 1g); PROTEIN 2.9g; CARB 29g; FIBER 2.8g; CHOL 0mg; IRON 0.9mg; SODIUM 295mg; CALC 30mg
EXCHANGES: 2 Starch

SIMPLE**substitutions**

• • • • • • • • • • • • • • • • • • •

If you have leftover brown rice, *this side dish is a great way to use it. Just reheat the rice in the skillet, and stir in the other ingredients. You'll need about 2 cups of cooked rice.*

Lemon Rice with Carrots

prep: 10 minutes   cook: 5 minutes

Golden raisins add a hint of sweetness to this savory, lemony rice.

  1 cup fat-free, less-sodium chicken broth
  1 cup uncooked long-grain instant rice
 ½ cup shredded carrot
  3 tablespoons golden raisins
  1 teaspoon grated lemon rind
  2 teaspoons light butter
 ¼ teaspoon salt
 ¼ teaspoon freshly ground black pepper

    Bring broth to a boil in a small saucepan over medium-high heat. Stir in rice, carrot, and raisins; remove from heat. Cover and let stand 5 minutes or until rice is tender. Add lemon rind and remaining ingredients. Yield: 4 servings (serving size: about ½ cup).

CALORIES 132 (8% from fat); FAT 1.1g (sat 0.7g, mono 0g, poly 0g);
PROTEIN 3.1g; CARB 27.8g; FIBER 1.2g; CHOL 3.3mg; IRON 1.2mg;
SODIUM 321mg; CALC 13mg
EXCHANGES: 1½ Starch, 1 Vegetable

SIMPLE**substitution**

● ● ● ● ● ● ● ● ● ● ● ● ● ● ● ●

Use either dark or golden raisins *in the rice. Golden raisins are slightly more moist and plump than the dark, but either will work fine.*

Orzo with Tomatoes and Pesto

prep: 5 minutes   cook: 12 minutes

Chop the tomato and the green onions while the orzo is cooking.

 ⅔ cup uncooked orzo (rice-shaped pasta)
2½ tablespoons pesto (such as Classico)
  1 cup chopped seeded tomato
  3 tablespoons thinly sliced green onions
 ¼ teaspoon salt
 ¼ teaspoon freshly ground black pepper

    Cook orzo according to package directions, omitting salt and fat. Drain and transfer to a serving bowl. Add pesto and remaining ingredients; toss well. Yield: 5 servings (serving size: ½ cup).

CALORIES 143 (26% from fat); FAT 4.1g (sat 1g, mono 2.2g, poly 0.5g);
PROTEIN 5g; CARB 21.6g; FIBER 1.4g; CHOL 2.5mg; IRON 1.5mg;
SODIUM 183mg; CALC 62mg
EXCHANGES: 1 Starch, 1 Vegetable, 1 Fat

HOW**to**

● ● ● ● ● ● ● ● ● ● ● ● ● ● ● ●

We recommend seeding the tomato *in this recipe so you won't unintentionally bite down on a seed "hiding" in the light-colored orzo.*

To remove the seeds from a tomato, cut the tomato in half crosswise and scoop out the seeds with a small spoon.

"Do you have any ideas for quick-fix desserts? I'm tired of having just a scoop of low-fat ice cream after supper."

deadline
DESSERTS

Life is too short to pass up dessert. And there's no need to when you can satisfy your sweet tooth with a low-fat treat in a matter of minutes. Whether you're entertaining at the last minute, or just need a "sweet fix," here are 26 decadent desserts to help you out. And over half can be made in 10 minutes or less.

White Bottom Chocolate Pies, page 345

Sliced Banana and Grape Ambrosia

prep: 9 minutes

This simple fruit dessert becomes quite elegant when served in stemmed dessert glasses or wine glasses.

- ½ cup orange juice
- 2 teaspoons sugar
- 2 teaspoons Triple Sec (orange-flavored liqueur)
- 1½ cups sliced bananas (2 medium)
- 2½ cups halved seedless red grapes
- 2 tablespoons flaked sweetened coconut, toasted

Combine first 3 ingredients in a medium bowl; stir with a whisk until sugar dissolves.

Add bananas and grapes; stir gently. Spoon into stemmed glasses, and sprinkle with coconut. Yield: 4 servings (serving size: 1 cup fruit and ½ tablespoon coconut).

CALORIES 164 (9% from fat); FAT 1.7g (sat 1g, mono 0.1g, poly 0.2g); PROTEIN 1.5g; CARB 38.4g; FIBER 2.5g; CHOL 0mg; IRON 0.5mg; SODIUM 9mg; CALC 18mg
EXCHANGES: 1 Starch, 1½ Fruit

SIMPLE**substitutions**

● ● ● ● ● ● ● ● ● ● ● ● ● ● ● ● ● ●

If you don't want to use the liqueur, *stir in 2 teaspoons of orange juice. The flavor of the extra orange juice will be a little less intense than that of the liqueur, but you'll still get a nice touch of orange.*

Almost any time a recipe calls for a fruit liqueur, you can substitute the same amount of fruit juice. Generally, fruit juice has about 88 percent fewer calories than a liqueur.

Grape and Mango Compote

prep: 4 minutes

The tartness of the lime juice complements the sweetness of the honey and fruit in this dessert.

- 1 (1 pound, 8-ounce) jar mango in extra light syrup, drained
- 1⅓ cups seedless red grapes, halved
- 1 tablespoon fresh lime juice
- 1 tablespoon honey

Combine all ingredients in a large bowl; stir gently. Yield: 3 cups (serving size: ¾ cup).

CALORIES 123 (2% from fat); FAT 0.3g (sat 0.1g, mono 0g, poly 0.1g); PROTEIN 0.7g; CARB 32.9g; FIBER 1.4g; CHOL 0mg; IRON 0.5mg; SODIUM 4mg; CALC 15mg
EXCHANGES: 2 Fruit

SIMPLE**substitutions**

● ● ● ● ● ● ● ● ● ● ● ● ● ● ● ● ● ●

To use fresh whole mangoes *instead of the refrigerated slices in a jar, you'll need 1½ cups sliced mango, or about 2 mangoes. One mango will usually yield about 1 to 1⅓ cups cubed fruit.*

1. *With a sharp knife, slice the fruit lengthwise on each side of the flat pit.*

2. *Holding the mango half in your hand, score the pulp. Be sure that you slice to, but not through, the skin.*

3. *Turn the mango inside out, and cut the chunks from the skin.*

Mixed Fruit Compote with Rum

prep: 4 minutes

If you don't want to use the rum, just leave it out. The mango nectar and lime juice add plenty of extra flavor to the fruit.

½   cup mango nectar
1   tablespoon sugar
1   tablespoon white rum
1   teaspoon fresh lime juice
3   cups mixed fresh cut fruit (about 1½ pounds)

Combine first 4 ingredients in a small bowl; stir with a whisk until sugar dissolves.

Add nectar mixture to fruit; toss gently.
Yield: 4 servings (serving size: about ¾ cup).

CALORIES 136 (4% from fat); FAT 0.6g (sat 0.1g, mono 0.1g, poly 0.2g); PROTEIN 1g; CARB 32.5g; FIBER 3.4g; CHOL 0mg; IRON 0.3mg; SODIUM 2mg; CALC 17mg
EXCHANGES: 2 Fruit

FIND**it**

● ● ● ● ● ● ● ● ● ● ● ● ● ● ● ● ●

Any combination of mixed fresh cut fruit, *such as cantaloupe, strawberries, grapes, and honeydew melon, will work in this compote. Most supermarkets have fresh fruit combos in plastic containers in the produce section.*

Strawberries with Orange Custard Sauce

prep: 10 minutes

It's hard to believe that this delicious sauce starts with snack pudding. Plus, it's easy to halve or double the number of servings.

2   (3.5-ounce) containers vanilla fat-free pudding (such as Handi Snacks)
2   tablespoons orange juice
2   tablespoons orange marmalade
2   cups quartered strawberries

Combine first 3 ingredients in a medium bowl; stir with a whisk.

Place strawberries in individual stemmed serving glasses; spoon sauce over strawberries.
Yield: 4 servings (serving size: ½ cup strawberries and ¼ cup sauce).

CALORIES 96 (4% from fat); FAT 0.4g (sat 0.1g, mono 0g, poly 0.2g); PROTEIN 1.6g; CARB 22.9g; FIBER 1.8g; CHOL 1mg; IRON 0.3mg; SODIUM 112mg; CALC 53mg
EXCHANGES: 1 Starch, 1 Fruit

SIMPLE**substitutions**

● ● ● ● ● ● ● ● ● ● ● ● ● ● ● ● ●

Fat-free instant pudding *is a good stand-in for the snack packs. Prepare it according to the package directions. You'll need about 1 cup of prepared pudding for this recipe, so use a 3.4-ounce package of pudding mix.*

The creamy sauce is good for other fresh berries such as blueberries, blackberries, and raspberries. You might even combine two or three kinds of fruit.

Fresh Berries with Maple
Cream

Fresh Berries with Maple Cream

prep: 4 minutes

Just by stirring a bit of maple syrup into sour cream, you get a sweet, creamy sauce that's wonderful over any kind of fresh fruit.

¾	cup fat-free sour cream
¼	cup maple syrup
1	cup fresh blueberries
1½	cups fresh raspberries

Combine sour cream and maple syrup in a small bowl; stir with a whisk.

Combine berries, and spoon into dessert dishes; pour maple cream over berries. Yield: 4 servings (serving size: about ⅔ cup berries and ¼ cup maple cream).

CALORIES 140 (3% from fat); FAT 0.4g (sat 0g, mono 0.1g, poly 0.2g); PROTEIN 2.2g; CARB 31.4g; FIBER 4.1g; CHOL 8mg; IRON 0.6mg; SODIUM 64mg; CALC 86mg
EXCHANGES: 1 Starch, 1 Fruit

NUTRITIONnote

● ● ● ● ● ● ● ● ● ● ● ● ● ● ● ● ● ●

The power of blueberries *is in the color. The same substances that cause the berries to be blue are also strong antioxidant and anti-inflammatory agents. These agents may help reduce the risk of Alzheimer's, heart disease, cancer, stroke, and diabetes. There is some new research showing that blueberries may reverse short-term memory loss and slow down other effects of aging.*

California-Style Peach Melbas

prep: 11 minutes

For another dessert option, serve the strawberry syrup and fruit over slices of fat-free pound cake.

1	(10-ounce) package frozen strawberries in light syrup, thawed
1½	tablespoons red currant jelly
1⅓	cups vanilla low-fat frozen yogurt
2	large ripe peaches, peeled and sliced
1	cup fresh raspberries
½	cup frozen fat-free whipped topping, thawed

Place strawberries and syrup in a blender; process 20 seconds.

Place jelly in a custard cup; microwave at HIGH 25 seconds. Stir into strawberry puree.

Spoon ⅓ cup frozen yogurt into each serving dish. Drizzle each serving with 5 tablespoons sauce, and top evenly with peaches and raspberries. Dollop each with 2 tablespoons whipped topping. Serve immediately. Yield: 4 servings.

CALORIES 218 (5% from fat); FAT 1.2g (sat 0.6g, mono 0.3g, poly 0.2g); PROTEIN 4.1g; CARB 50.8g; FIBER 5g; CHOL 3mg; IRON 0.7mg; SODIUM 50mg; CALC 121mg
EXCHANGES: 1 Starch, 2 Fruit

SIMPLEsubstitutions

● ● ● ● ● ● ● ● ● ● ● ● ● ● ● ● ● ●

To speed up preparation, *use 1½ cups frozen peaches, thawed, instead of 2 fresh peaches.*

Cookies and Cream Parfaits

Cookies and Cream Parfaits

prep: 7 minutes

If you don't want to use the liqueur, just leave it out. You'll still get a rich chocolate-coffee flavor from the syrup and the ice cream.

¼ cup lite chocolate syrup (such as Hershey's)
1 tablespoon coffee-flavored liqueur (such as Kahlúa)
1 cup chocolate or vanilla low-fat ice cream
4 reduced-fat cream-filled chocolate sandwich cookies (such as reduced-fat Oreos), crumbled
1 cup coffee low-fat ice cream

Combine chocolate syrup and liqueur in a small bowl, stirring well with a whisk. Place ¼ cup chocolate or vanilla ice cream into each of 4 glasses. Drizzle with 1½ teaspoons chocolate syrup mixture and about 2 tablespoons crumbled cookies. Spoon ¼ cup coffee ice cream over crumbs in each dish, and top with remaining syrup and cookies. Yield: 4 servings.

CALORIES 221 (14% from fat), FAT 3.5g (sat 1.3g, mono 0g, poly 1.2g); PROTEIN 4.6g; CARB 40.8g; FIBER 0.9g; CHOL 15mg; IRON 0.2mg; SODIUM 131mg; CALC 134mg
EXCHANGES: 2½ Starch, ½ Fat

SIMPLEsubstitutions

● ● ● ● ● ● ● ● ● ● ● ● ● ● ● ● ● ●

Vary the flavors of parfaits *by using any combination of low-fat ice creams and reduced-fat cream-filled sandwich cookies. The calories and fat content will be about the same.*

Chocolate-Peanut Butter Sundaes

prep: 5 minutes

The balance between smooth and crunchy, sweet and salty is just right in this 5-minute dessert.

2 tablespoons reduced-fat peanut butter
2 tablespoons lite chocolate syrup (such as Hershey's)
2 tablespoons finely chopped peanuts
1 tablespoon 1% low-fat milk
2 cups vanilla low-fat ice cream

Combine first 4 ingredients in a small bowl; stir with a whisk until blended.
Place ½ cup ice cream into each of 4 serving dishes; top each with 2 tablespoons peanut butter mixture. Yield: 4 servings.

CALORIES 191 (33% from fat); FAT 7g (sat 1.8g, mono 2.5g, poly 1.5g); PROTEIN 6.7g; CARB 25.5g; FIBER 2.1g; CHOL 5mg; IRON 0.2mg; SODIUM 123mg; CALC 113mg
EXCHANGES: 2 Starch, 1 Fat

NUTRITIONnote

● ● ● ● ● ● ● ● ● ● ● ● ● ● ● ● ● ●

Peanuts and peanut butter are high in monounsaturated fat—*a kind of fat that protects against heart disease. Monounsaturated fats appear to help reduce total cholesterol level without affecting HDL (good cholesterol). When you have more HDL than LDL (bad cholesterol), you have a lower risk of heart disease.*

Pineapple Sundaes

prep: 6 minutes

This citrus sundae gets an unexpected twist from mint and toasted almonds.

1⅓ cups lemon sorbet
1 (8-ounce) can pineapple chunks in juice, drained
2 teaspoons chopped fresh mint
4 teaspoons flaked sweetened coconut
4 teaspoons sliced almonds, toasted

Place ⅓ cup sorbet in each of 4 serving bowls. Top each with ¼ cup pineapple, ½ teaspoon mint, 1 teaspoon coconut, and 1 teaspoon almonds. Yield: 4 servings.

CALORIES 120 (11% from fat); FAT 1.5g (sat 0.5g, mono 0.7g, poly 0.3g); PROTEIN 0.7g; CARB 27.2g; FIBER 1g; CHOL 0mg; IRON 0.2mg; SODIUM 8mg; CALC 13mg
EXCHANGES: 2 Fruit

HOWto

• • • • • • • • • • • • • • • • • •

Toasting almonds is a cinch—*place them in a small dry skillet, and cook over medium heat for a minute or less, stirring constantly. Instead of toasting such a small amount of almonds, go ahead and toast about ½ cup and keep them on hand for other uses. Place extra nuts in an airtight container, and refrigerate 3 to 6 months or freeze up to a year.*

Warm Nectarine-Caramel Sundaes

prep: 5 minutes   cook: 5 minutes

The flesh of ripe nectarines is firmer than that of ripe peaches but should feel soft when gently squeezed.

1 tablespoon butter
1½ cups chopped nectarines (about 2)
½ teaspoon fresh lemon juice
½ cup fat-free caramel sundae syrup (such as Smucker's)
1⅓ cups vanilla low-fat ice cream
4 teaspoons low-fat granola without raisins

Melt butter in a large nonstick skillet over medium-high heat. Add nectarines; cook, turning occasionally, 5 minutes or until tender.
Remove from heat; add lemon juice and caramel syrup. Stir gently.
Place ice cream into 4 serving bowls; spoon nectarine mixture over ice cream. Sprinkle with granola. Yield: 4 servings (serving size: ⅓ cup ice cream, ¼ cup nectarine mixture, and 1 teaspoon granola).

CALORIES 243 (17% from fat); FAT 4.6g (sat 2.5g, mono 0.9g, poly 0.2g); PROTEIN 3.7g; CARB 45.6g; FIBER 1.6g; CHOL 11mg; IRON 0.4mg; SODIUM 172mg; CALC 91mg
EXCHANGES: 1 Starch, 2 Fruit, 1 Fat

SIMPLEsubstitutions

• • • • • • • • • • • • • • • • • •

Use fresh peaches *in this fruity sundae if you don't have nectarines. Peaches and nectarines are in the same fruit family and have a similar sweet flavor, but the skin on peaches is fuzzy, so you'll need to peel them before eating or using in recipes.*

Warm Nectarine-Caramel
Sundaes

Triple Raspberry Sundaes

prep: 5 minutes

For big citrus flavor, spoon the raspberry sauce and berries over lemon sorbet instead of the raspberry.

  ⅓ cup raspberry spread (such as Polaner All Fruit)
  2 teaspoons Triple Sec (orange-flavored liqueur)
  2 teaspoons water
  1½ cups fresh raspberries
  1⅓ cups raspberry sorbet
  4 fresh mint sprigs (optional)

Combine first 3 ingredients in a small bowl; stir with a whisk.

Combine raspberries and raspberry spread mixture in a medium bowl, stirring gently.

Spoon sorbet into 4 stemmed glasses; top with raspberry mixture. Garnish each with a mint sprig, if desired. Yield: 4 servings (serving size: ⅓ cup sorbet and about ⅓ cup raspberry mixture).

CALORIES 141 (2% from fat); FAT 0.3g (sat 0g, mono 0g, poly 0.2g); PROTEIN 1.4g; CARB 33.5g; FIBER 3.1g; CHOL 0mg; IRON 0.4mg; SODIUM 7.7mg; CALC 13.7mg
EXCHANGES: 1 Starch, 1 Fruit

NUTRITION**note**

● ● ● ● ● ● ● ● ● ● ● ● ● ● ● ● ● ●

Raspberries act as anti-inflammatories *(along with sweet cherries, blackberries, and strawberries). New research shows that because these foods can reduce inflammation, they may help arthritis-sufferers reduce pain and improve range of motion.*

Strawberry-Tapioca Parfaits

prep: 8 minutes

Use whatever berries you have on hand for these superquick pudding parfaits.

  2 cups hulled strawberries, divided
  2 tablespoons sugar
  2 cups refrigerated tapioca pudding (such as Kozy Shack)

Combine 1 cup strawberries and sugar in a blender; process until smooth. Thinly slice remaining 1 cup strawberries. Combine strawberry puree and sliced berries in a bowl.

Spoon about 1 tablespoon strawberry mixture into each of 4 stemmed glasses. Top each with ¼ cup tapioca pudding and 1½ tablespoons strawberry mixture. Repeat layers, ending with strawberry mixture. Yield: 4 servings.

CALORIES 163 (17% from fat); FAT 3.3g (sat 2g, mono 0g, poly 0.2g); PROTEIN 4.5g; CARB 34.1g; FIBER 1.9g; CHOL 20mg; IRON 0.3mg; SODIUM 136mg; CALC 92mg
EXCHANGES: 1 Starch, 1 Fruit, ½ Fat

FIND**it**

● ● ● ● ● ● ● ● ● ● ● ● ● ● ● ● ● ●

Look for cartons of tapioca pudding *in the dairy section of the supermarket. It comes in snack-pack cups as well as 22-ounce containers that contain about 3 cups of pudding.*

Strawberry-Tapioca
Parfaits

White Bottom
Chocolate Pies

White Bottom Chocolate Pies

prep: 16 minutes   chill: 4 minutes

Enjoy your own little chocolate pie—there's no need to share.

- 1   (3.9-ounce) package chocolate fudge-flavored instant pudding mix
- 1¾ cups 1% low-fat milk
- ½   teaspoon vanilla extract
- 4   ounces light cream cheese, softened
- 2   tablespoons sugar
- 1   (4-ounce) package mini graham cracker pie crusts (such as Keebler)
- 6   tablespoons frozen reduced-calorie whipped topping, thawed
- 2   tablespoons chocolate curls (optional)

Prepare pudding mix according to package directions, using 1¾ cups milk; stir in vanilla extract. Cover and chill.

Combine cream cheese and sugar, stirring until smooth. Spoon cream cheese mixture into pie crusts, carefully spreading to cover bottoms of crusts.

Spoon pudding over cream cheese mixture; top each pie with 1 tablespoon whipped topping. Sprinkle with chocolate curls, if desired. Yield: 6 servings.

CALORIES 257 (33% from fat); FAT 9.3g (sat 4.1g, mono 2.5g, poly 1.4g); PROTEIN 5.3g; CARB 38.3g; FIBER 0.7g; CHOL 12mg; IRON 0.8mg; SODIUM 496mg; CALC 118mg
EXCHANGES: 2 Starch, 2 Fat

HOWto

● ● ● ● ● ● ● ● ● ● ● ● ● ● ● ● ● ●

For easy chocolate curls, *start with a small piece of chocolate-flavored almond bark, and shave off pieces using a vegetable peeler. The almond bark works better because it's softer, and you get a smoother curl. You'll need about 1 ounce almond bark to make enough curls for six pies.*

Pineapple Mousse Pie with Raspberries

prep: 15 minutes   freeze: 2 hours

A frozen pie like this is ideal for entertaining because you can make it a few days ahead and keep it in the freezer.

- 1   tablespoon granulated sugar
- 2   teaspoons cornstarch
- 2   teaspoons fresh lemon juice
- 1   (8-ounce) can crushed pineapple in its own juice, undrained
- 1½ cups fresh raspberries
- 3   tablespoons low-sugar raspberry spread
- 1   (6-ounce) reduced-fat graham cracker pie crust
- ¾   cup tub-style light cream cheese
- 3   tablespoons powdered sugar
- 1   teaspoon vanilla extract
- 1   cup frozen fat-free whipped topping, thawed

Combine first 4 ingredients in a small saucepan; cook over medium heat, stirring often, until mixture comes to a boil and thickens. Cool to room temperature.

Gently combine raspberries and raspberry spread. Spoon into bottom of pie crust.

Combine cream cheese, sugar, and vanilla in a mixing bowl; beat with a mixer at medium speed until smooth and creamy. Fold pineapple mixture into cream cheese mixture. Fold whipping topping into cream cheese mixture. Spoon over berries. Cover and freeze at least 2 hours. Yield: 8 servings (serving size: 1 wedge).

CALORIES 217 (31% from fat); FAT 7.4g (sat 3.1g, mono 0g, poly 0.1g); PROTEIN 3.5g; CARB 32.7g; FIBER 2g; CHOL 11mg; IRON 0.9mg; SODIUM 207mg; CALC 47mg
EXCHANGES: 1 Starch, 1 Fruit, 1½ Fat

Chocolate-Banana Cream Tarts

prep: 4 minutes

Spoon into creamy chocolate pudding with a candy bar crunch—it's guaranteed to make you smile.

- 1 medium banana, thinly sliced
- 4 mini graham cracker pie crusts
- 2 (3.5-ounce) fat-free chocolate pudding cups
- 1 (1.4-ounce) English toffee candy bar, crushed

Arrange banana slices evenly in pie crusts. Spoon pudding over bananas. Sprinkle each with 2 teaspoons crushed candy. Yield: 4 servings.

CALORIES 246 (34% from fat); FAT 9.4g (sat 3.5g, mono 3.7g, poly 1.8g); PROTEIN 3.1g; CARB 38.9g; FIBER 1.7g; CHOL 6mg; IRON 0.9mg; SODIUM 255mg; CALC 64mg
EXCHANGES: 1½ Starch, 1 Fruit, 1½ Fat

HOWto

● ● ● ● ● ● ● ● ● ● ● ● ● ● ● ● ●

To crush the candy bar with no mess, *remove the wrapper, and place the bar in a zip-top plastic bag. Crush with a rolling pin or the flat side of a meat mallet.*

Lemon-Raspberry Tarts

prep: 8 minutes   chill: 1 hour

The tangy, sweet filling in these tarts may remind you of a key lime pie.

- 1 cup frozen fat-free whipped topping, thawed and divided
- ½ cup fat-free sweetened condensed milk (about ½ can)
- 1 teaspoon grated lemon rind
- ¼ cup fresh lemon juice (about 1 large lemon)
- 1 cup fresh raspberries, divided
- 1 (4-ounce) package mini graham cracker pie crusts

Combine ¾ cup whipped topping, milk, lemon rind, and lemon juice; stir until smooth.
Place 3 raspberries in each pie crust. Spoon filling evenly into crusts on top of berries. Cover and chill.
Dollop remaining ¼ cup whipped topping evenly on tarts, and top evenly with remaining fresh raspberries. Yield: 6 servings.

CALORIES 199 (22% from fat); FAT 4.9g (sat 1g, mono 2.2g, poly 1.4g); PROTEIN 3.3g; CARB 35.3g; FIBER 1.8g; CHOL 2mg; IRON 0.6mg; SODIUM 142mg; CALC 83mg
EXCHANGES: 1 Starch, 1½ Fruit, 1 Fat

EASYadditions

● ● ● ● ● ● ● ● ● ● ● ● ● ● ● ● ●

Make your tarts extra-tart *by topping them with very thin lemon slices instead of fresh raspberries.*

Pear Custard Tarts

prep: 4 minutes

Snack-pack puddings work great when you need a creamy filling in a hurry.

  2   (3.5-ounce) fat-free vanilla pudding cups
       (such as Hunt's)
  4   mini graham cracker pie crusts
 12   sliced refrigerated pear wedges, coarsely
       chopped (such as Del Monte)
 ¼   cup frozen fat-free whipped topping, thawed
Grated whole nutmeg

Spoon pudding into pie crusts; sprinkle evenly with chopped pear. Top each serving with 1 tablespoon whipped topping; sprinkle lightly with nutmeg. Yield: 4 servings.

CALORIES 206 (27% from fat); FAT 6.1g (sat 1.4g, mono 2.7g, poly 1.6g);
PROTEIN 2.4g; CARB 36g; FIBER 1.8g; CHOL 1mg; IRON 0.7mg;
SODIUM 254mg; CALC 54mg
EXCHANGES: 1½ Starch, 1 Fruit, 1 Fat

Shortcut Tiramisu

prep: 17 minutes   cook: 1 minute

No need to wait until your next meal at an Italian restaurant to indulge in tiramisu—you can make this low-fat version in minutes.

  2   cups cubed fat-free pound cake (about 5
       ounces), divided
  1   (0.82-ounce) envelope mocha-flavored
       cappuccino mix
  2   cups 1% low-fat milk, divided
  1   (8-ounce) package fat-free cream cheese,
       softened
  1   (3.3-ounce) package vanilla fat-free instant
       pudding mix
  1   (0.78-ounce) envelope vanilla-flavored
       cappuccino mix
  2   cups frozen fat-free whipped topping, thawed
 ½   ounce grated chocolate (optional)

Place half of cake cubes in bottom of an 8-inch square baking dish. Set aside. Combine mocha-flavored cappuccino mix and ½ cup milk in a small microwave-safe dish. Microwave at HIGH 35 seconds, stirring until mix dissolves. Set aside.

Beat cream cheese with a mixer at medium speed until smooth. Add 1 cup milk; beat until smooth. Add pudding mix; beat until blended. Combine vanilla-flavored cappuccino mix and remaining ½ cup milk in a small microwave-safe dish. Microwave at HIGH 35 seconds, stirring until mix dissolves. Add vanilla cappuccino mixture to cream cheese mixture. Fold in whipped topping.

Pour half of mocha cappuccino mixture over cake; top with half of cream cheese mixture. Place remaining cake cubes on top of cream cheese mixture, and drizzle with remaining mocha cappuccino mixture. Top with remaining cream cheese mixture. Sprinkle with grated chocolate, if desired. Cover and chill, or serve immediately. Yield: 6 servings (serving size: about 1⅓ cups).

CALORIES 258 (8% from fat); FAT 2.4g (sat 1.5g, mono 0.4g, poly 0.2g);
PROTEIN 9.9g; CARB 47g; FIBER 0.3g; CHOL 8mg; IRON 0.6mg;
SODIUM 603mg; CALC 175mg
EXCHANGES: 3 Starch

SIMPLEsubstitutions

• • • • • • • • • • • • • • • • •

To decrease the sugar in the tiramisu, *use a 1-ounce package of fat-free, sugar-free instant pudding mix and omit the grated chocolate topping. Using the sugar-free pudding mix will reduce the total carbohydrate to 37 grams per serving.*

Caramel Apple-Cranberry Crisp

prep: 15 minutes   cook: 45 minutes

Although this crisp takes 45 minutes to bake, the flavor is worth waiting for—it received our test kitchen's highest rating.

- ⅓ cup all-purpose flour
- ⅓ cup uncooked regular oats
- ½ cup firmly packed light brown sugar
- ¼ cup butter, cut into small pieces
- 7 cups sliced Granny Smith apple (about 5 apples)
- ¼ cup sweetened dried cranberries
- ¼ cup orange juice
- 1 tablespoon all-purpose flour
- ⅓ cup fat-free caramel sundae syrup

Preheat oven to 375°.

Lightly spoon ⅓ cup flour into a dry measuring cup; level with a knife. Combine flour, oats, and sugar in a medium bowl. Cut in butter with a pastry blender or 2 knives until mixture is crumbly.

Combine apple and next 4 ingredients in a large bowl. Spoon into an 8-inch square baking dish. Sprinkle flour mixture over apple mixture. Bake at 375° for 45 minutes or until golden brown. Yield: 8 servings (serving size: about ¾ cup).

CALORIES 208 (27% from fat); FAT 6.3g (sat 3.7g, mono 1.8g, poly 0.4g); PROTEIN 1.7g; CARB 37.1g; FIBER 2g; CHOL 16mg; IRON 0.7mg; SODIUM 99mg; CALC 22mg
EXCHANGES: 1 Starch, 1½ Fruit, 1 Fat

QUICKtip

● ● ● ● ● ● ● ● ● ● ● ● ● ● ● ● ● ●

Save a few minutes of prep time *by using packaged fresh apple slices. Look for them in the produce section.*

Ice Cream Sandwich Dessert

prep: 8 minutes   freeze: 2 hours

This frozen dessert is quick and has three kinds of chocolate plus whipped topping.

- 1 (8-ounce) container frozen fat-free whipped topping, thawed
- 2 tablespoons coffee-flavored liqueur (such as Kahlúa)
- 2 tablespoons chocolate syrup
- 6 (0.7-ounce) reduced-fat triple chocolate wafer bars (such as Hershey's Sweet Escapes), finely chopped and divided
- 6 (2.3-ounce) low-fat ice cream sandwiches

Spoon whipped topping into a large bowl.

Combine coffee liqueur and chocolate syrup, and fold into whipped topping. Stir in half of chopped wafer bars.

Arrange ice cream sandwiches in an 11 x 7-inch baking dish. Spread whipped topping mixture evenly over ice cream sandwiches. Sprinkle with remaining chopped wafer bars. Cover and freeze at least 2 hours or until firm. Cut into squares. Yield: 12 servings.

CALORIES 243 (17% from fat); FAT 4.5g (sat 2g, mono 0.3g, poly 0.1g); PROTEIN 4.2g; CARB 43.7g; FIBER 0.4g; CHOL 5mg; IRON 0.7mg; SODIUM 186mg; CALC 158mg
EXCHANGES: 2½ Starch, 1 Fat

SIMPLEsubstitutions

● ● ● ● ● ● ● ● ● ● ● ● ● ● ● ● ● ●

You can flavor the whipped topping *with 2 tablespoons of strongly brewed coffee or espresso plus 1 teaspoon of sugar instead of the liqueur.*

Ice Cream Sandwich Dessert

Cherry Snickerdoodles

Cherry Snickerdoodles

prep: 15 minutes   cook: 10 minutes per batch
cool: 3 minutes

With just a few simple additions, you can turn refrigerated cookie dough into extra-special treats.

2	tablespoons sugar
¼	teaspoon ground nutmeg
1	(18-ounce) package refrigerated sugar cookie dough

Cooking spray
25	candied red cherries

Preheat oven to 350°.

Combine sugar and nutmeg in a small dish. Slice and shape dough into 25 (1-inch) balls; roll in sugar mixture. Place cookies 2-inches apart on a baking sheet coated with cooking spray.

Bake at 350° for 10 to 12 minutes or until edges are lightly browned. Place cookie sheet on a wire rack, and press a cherry into the center of each cookie. Let cool 3 minutes; remove cookies to wire rack, and cool completely. Yield: 25 cookies (serving size: 1 cookie).

CALORIES 108 (35% from fat); FAT 4.2g (sat 1.1g, mono 2.4g, poly 0.5g); PROTEIN 0.9g; CARB 16.9g; FIBER 0g; CHOL 6mg; IRON 0.4mg; SODIUM 86mg; CALC 18mg
EXCHANGES: 1 Starch, 1 Fat

HOWto

• • • • • • • • • • • • • • • • • •

It's a good idea *to have several sturdy, shiny aluminum cookie or baking sheets on hand if you like to make cookies. Select fairly heavy cookie sheets that are at least 2 inches narrower and shorter than your oven so that heat can circulate evenly around the pans. Don't use pans with high sides for baking cookies because the sides deflect heat and cause the cookies to bake unevenly. If you have dark-surfaced nonstick cookie sheets, watch the cookies carefully as they bake. Dark-surfaced cookie sheets absorb more heat than the shiny sheets so the cookies tend to brown more quickly.*

Orange Crumb Cake

prep: 14 minutes   cook: 25 minutes
cool: 5 minutes

Whip up this orange-kissed cake in no time from ingredients you have on hand. Enjoy it warm with a cup of coffee or hot tea.

1¼	cups all-purpose flour
¾	cup sugar
4½	tablespoons butter, cut into small pieces
1	teaspoon water
½	teaspoon baking powder
¼	teaspoon baking soda
1	large egg
½	cup low-fat buttermilk (1%)
1	tablespoon grated orange rind (½ orange)

Cooking spray
¾	teaspoon powdered sugar

Preheat oven to 350°.

Lightly spoon flour into dry measuring cups, and level with a knife. Combine flour and sugar in a large bowl. Cut in butter with a pastry blender or 2 knives until mixture resembles coarse meal. Remove ⅓ cup crumb mixture; add water, stirring gently. Set aside.

Add baking powder and soda to remaining flour mixture; stir with a whisk. Add egg, buttermilk, and orange rind. Beat with a mixer at medium speed just until combined.

Pour batter into an 8-inch round cake pan coated with cooking spray. Sprinkle reserved crumb mixture over batter. Bake at 350° for 25 minutes or until a wooden pick inserted in center comes out clean. Let cool in pan 5 minutes. Remove cake from pan; cool on a wire rack. Sift powdered sugar over cake. Cut into wedges. Serve warm, if desired. Yield: 8 servings (serving size: 1 wedge).

CALORIES 219 (31% from fat); FAT 7.5g (sat 4.4g, mono 2.2g, poly 0.4g); PROTEIN 3.4g; CARB 35.1g; FIBER 0.6g; CHOL 45mg; IRON 1mg; SODIUM 164mg; CALC 32mg
EXCHANGES: 2 Starch, 1½ Fat

Almond Bundt Cake

prep: 10 minutes   cook: 40 minutes
cool: 20 minutes

Take 10 minutes to put together this simple cake, and let it bake while you eat dinner.

- 1 (18.25-ounce) package white cake mix with pudding (such as Pillsbury)
- 2 large eggs
- 2 large egg whites
- 1¾ cups low-fat buttermilk (1%)
- ½ teaspoon almond extract
- Cooking spray
- 1½ cups sifted powdered sugar
- ½ teaspoon almond extract
- 4¼ teaspoons warm water
- 2 tablespoons sliced almonds

Preheat oven to 350°.

Combine first 5 ingredients in a large bowl. Beat with a mixer at low speed 30 seconds or until moistened. Scrape sides of bowl; beat at medium speed 2 minutes or until well blended. Pour batter into a 12-cup Bundt pan coated with cooking spray.

Bake at 350° for 40 minutes or until a wooden pick inserted in center comes out clean. Cool in pan 20 minutes on a wire rack; remove from pan. Cool on wire rack.

Combine powdered sugar, almond extract, and water in a medium bowl; stir with a whisk until smooth. Pour glaze over top of cake; sprinkle with almonds. Yield: 16 servings (serving size: 1 slice).

CALORIES 202 (20% from fat); FAT 4.4g (sat 1.3g, mono 0.5g, poly 0.2g); PROTEIN 3.6g; CARB 36.5g; FIBER 0.6g; CHOL 28mg; IRON 0.6mg; SODIUM 249mg; CALC 35mg
EXCHANGES: 2 Starch, 1 Fat

NUTRITION**note**

Almonds contain more vitamin E *than any other food, and vitamin E can boost your immunity, reduce the risk of cancer, and slow the progression of Alzheimer's disease.*

This vitamin also slows down the buildup of "bad cholesterol" in the arteries, which helps prevent heart disease and stroke. In one study, researchers found that eating about a handful (a little over an ounce) of almonds each day was associated with a 4.4 percent decline of bad cholesterol.

Despite these benefits, almonds are still considered a high-fat food, so eat them in moderation.

Apricot Upside-Down Cake

prep: 12 minutes   cook: 35 minutes

We offer two versions of this cake so you can have a choice depending on the ingredients you have on hand. The "from scratch" cake and the cake mix version differ by about 15 calories.

 1   tablespoon light butter, melted
¼   cup firmly packed light brown sugar
 2   (8¼-ounce) cans apricot halves in light syrup, undrained
 1   cup all-purpose flour
¾   teaspoon baking powder
¼   teaspoon baking soda
⅛   teaspoon salt
¼   cup light butter, softened
⅔   cup sugar
 1   large egg
 1   teaspoon grated lemon rind
 1   teaspoon vanilla extract

Preheat oven to 350°.

Coat bottom of a 9-inch round cake pan with 1 tablespoon melted butter; sprinkle brown sugar over butter. Drain apricots, reserving ⅔ cup liquid; pat apricots dry with paper towels. Arrange apricots, cut sides up, in pan.

Lightly spoon flour into a dry measuring cup; level with a knife. Combine flour and next 3 ingredients; stir well. Beat butter and remaining 4 ingredients with a mixer at medium speed until well blended. Add flour mixture and reserved liquid alternately to butter mixture, beginning and ending with flour mixture.

Pour batter over apricots in pan.

Bake at 350° for 35 minutes or until a wooden pick inserted in center comes out clean. Cool in pan 5 minutes on a wire rack. Loosen cake from sides of pan using a knife or narrow spatula; invert cake onto a plate. Yield: 8 servings (serving size: 1 wedge).

CALORIES 208 (20% from fat); FAT 4.6g (sat 2.7g, mono 0.3g, poly 0.2g); PROTEIN 3.2g; CARB 40.4g; FIBER 0.9g; CHOL 39mg; IRON 1.1mg; SODIUM 178mg; CALC 40mg
EXCHANGES: 1½ Starch, 1 Fruit, 1 Fat

Shortcut Apricot Upside-Down Cake

prep: 10 minutes   cook: 32 minutes

Here's the cake mix version.

 1   tablespoon light butter, melted
¼   cup firmly packed light brown sugar
 2   (8¼-ounce) cans apricot halves in light syrup, undrained
 1   (9-ounce) package yellow cake mix
 1   large egg
 1   teaspoon grated lemon rind
 1   teaspoon vanilla extract

Preheat oven to 350°.

Coat bottom of a 9-inch round cake pan with 1 tablespoon melted butter; sprinkle brown sugar over butter. Drain apricots, reserving ½ cup liquid; pat apricots dry with paper towels. Arrange apricots, cut sides up, in pan.

Combine cake mix, egg, apricot liquid, lemon rind, and vanilla in a bowl. Beat with a mixer at medium speed 2 minutes.

Pour batter over apricots in pan.

Bake at 350° for 32 minutes or until a wooden pick inserted in center comes out clean. Cool in pan 5 minutes on a wire rack. Loosen cake from sides of pan using a knife or narrow spatula; invert cake onto a plate. Yield: 8 servings (serving size: 1 wedge).

CALORIES 193 (19% from fat); FAT 4.2g (sat 1.3g, mono 0.2g, poly 0.1g); PROTEIN 2.3g; CARB 37.3g; FIBER 0.5g; CHOL 29mg; IRON 1mg; SODIUM 233mg; CALC 13mg
EXCHANGES: 1½ Starch, 1 Fruit, 1 Fat

Chocolate-Raspberry Layer Cake

prep: 12 minutes cook: 15 minutes
cool: 5 minutes

Place the remaining half of the cake mix in a heavy duty zip-top plastic bag, and store it in the pantry for up to 3 months. Clip the directions from the back of the box, and attach to the bag. You can make this recipe again, or you can make a half dozen cupcakes from the remaining mix. If you're making 6 cupcakes, just halve the ingredients called for on the package.

1¾ cups chocolate fudge cake mix (about half of an 18.25-ounce package such as Betty Crocker)
1 large egg
1 large egg white
⅔ cup 1% low-fat milk
1½ tablespoons vegetable oil
Cooking spray
¾ cup low-sugar raspberry spread, divided
1½ cups frozen reduced-calorie whipped topping, thawed
½ teaspoon unsweetened cocoa

Preheat oven to 350°.

Combine first 5 ingredients in a large bowl; beat with a mixer at low speed 30 seconds or until moistened. Scrape sides of bowl with a rubber spatula; increase to medium speed, and beat 1 minute or until well blended. Pour batter evenly into 2 (8-inch) square cake pans coated with cooking spray. (Layers will be thin.)

Bake at 350° for 15 minutes or until a wooden pick inserted in center comes out clean. Cool in pans on a wire rack 5 minutes. Remove from pans; cool completely on wire rack.

Place one layer on a plate; top with ½ cup raspberry spread. Top with second cake layer. Cut cake in half, forming two rectangles. Spread remaining ¼ cup raspberry spread over top of one rectangle. Place the other rectangle on top of spread to form 4 layers of cake with raspberry spread between the layers. Spread

whipped topping over top and sides of cake, and sift cocoa lightly over cake. Slice cake crosswise into 8 slices. Yield: 8 servings (serving size: 1 slice).

CALORIES 249 (36% from fat); FAT 10g (sat 3.1g, mono 3.9g, poly 2.5g); PROTEIN 3.8g; CARB 36.8g; FIBER 0.8g; CHOL 27mg; IRON 2.9mg; SODIUM 296mg; CALC 122mg
EXCHANGES: 1½ Starch, 1 Fruit, 1½ Fat

HOW**to**

1. *Top cake with second thin layer, and cut the cake in half, forming two rectangles.*

2. *Place one cake rectangle on top of the other to form one cake with 4 layers.*

Chocolate-Raspberry Layer Cake

nutritional analysis

HOW TO USE IT AND WHY

Glance at the end of any *Superfast Suppers* recipe, and you'll see how committed we are to helping you make the best of today's light cooking. With registered dietitians, chefs, home economists, and a computer system that analyzes every ingredient, we give you the authoritative dietary detail you need for healthful living. We go to such lengths so you can see how our recipes fit into your eating plan. If you're trying to lose weight, the calorie and fat figures may help most. But if you're keeping an eye on carbohydrate, sodium, cholesterol, and saturated fat, we provide those numbers, too. Because many women don't get enough iron or calcium, we give those values. And for those who are trying to increase roughage, we give fiber values. There are also diabetic exchanges for the people who use those values for meal planning.

Below is a helpful guide to put the nutrition analysis numbers into perspective. Remember, one size doesn't fit all, so take your lifestyle, age, and circumstances into consideration when determining your nutrition needs. For example, pregnant or breast-feeding women need more protein, calories, and calcium. And men over 50 need 1,200mg of calcium daily, 200mg more than the amount recommended for younger men.

IN OUR NUTRITIONAL ANALYSIS, WE USE THESE ABBREVIATIONS:

sat	saturated fat	CHOL	cholesterol
mono	monounsaturated fat	CALC	calcium
poly	polyunsaturated fat	g	gram
CARB	carbohydrates	mg	milligram

YOUR DAILY NUTRITION GUIDE

	WOMEN AGES 25 TO 50	WOMEN OVER 50	MEN OVER 24
Calories	2,000	2,000 or less	2,700
Protein	50g	50g or less	63g
Fat	65g or less	65g or less	88g or less
Saturated Fat	20g or less	20g or less	27g or less
Carbohydrates	304g	304g	410g
Fiber	25g to 35g	25g to 35g	25g to 35g
Cholesterol	300mg or less	300mg or less	300mg or less
Iron	18mg	8mg	8mg
Sodium	2,400mg or less	2,400mg or less	2,400mg or less
Calcium	1,000mg	1,200mg	1,000mg

The nutritional values used in our calculations either come from The Food Processor, Version 7.5 (ESHA Research), or are provided by food manufacturers.

microwave cooking chart

Cooking vegetables in the microwave is the best way to preserve nutrients and flavor, and often the quickest way to cook them. Cook all the vegetables at HIGH power in a baking dish covered with wax paper. If you use plastic wrap to cover the dish, be sure to turn back one corner to allow steam to escape.

FOOD	MICROWAVE COOKING TIME	SPECIAL INSTRUCTIONS
Asparagus, 1 pound	6 to 7 minutes	Add ¼ cup water
Beans, green, 1 pound	14 to 15 minutes	Add ½ cup water
Broccoli spears, 1 pound	7 to 8 minutes	Arrange in a circle, spoke-fashion, with florets in center; add ½ cup water
Carrot slices, 1 pound	9 to 10 minutes; stand 2 minutes	Add ¼ cup water
Cauliflower florets, 1 pound	7 to 8 minutes; stand 2 minutes	Add ¼ cup water
Corn on the cob, 2 (large) ears 3 ears 4 ears	5 to 9 minutes 7 to 12 minutes 8 to 15 minutes	Arrange end-to-end in a circle; add ¼ cup water
Onions, 1 pound, peeled and quartered	6 to 8 minutes	Add 2 tablespoons water
Peas, green, shelled, 1 pound (about 1½ cups)	6 to 7 minutes	Add 2 tablespoons water
Potatoes, baking/sweet, medium 1 potato 2 potatoes 4 potatoes	4 to 6 minutes 7 to 8 minutes 12 to 14 minutes	Pierce skins and arrange end-to-end in a circle; let stand 5 minutes after cooking
New potatoes, 1 pound	8 to 10 minutes	Pierce if unpeeled; add 1¼ cup water
Spinach, 10-ounce package fresh leaves	2 to 3 minutes	Wash leaves before cooking
Squash, yellow/zucchini, 1 pound, sliced (4 medium)	7 to 8 minutes	Add ¼ cup water
Squash, acorn, 2 pounds, (2 medium)	9 to 10 minutes	Pierce skins
Turnips, 1¼ pounds, peeled and cubed (4 medium)	10 to 12 minutes	Add ¼ cup water

metric equivalents

The recipes that appear in this cookbook use the standard United States method for measuring liquid and dry or solid ingredients (teaspoons, tablespoons, and cups). The information in the following chart is provided to help cooks outside the U.S. successfully use these recipes. All equivalents are approximate.

EQUIVALENTS FOR DIFFERENT TYPES OF INGREDIENTS

A standard cup measure of a dry or solid ingredient will vary in weight depending on the type of ingredient. A standard cup of liquid is the same volume for any type of liquid. Use the following chart when converting standard cup measures to grams (weight) or milliliters (volume).

Standard Cup	Fine Powder	Grain	Granular	Liquid Solids	Liquid
	(ex. flour)	(ex. rice)	(ex. sugar)	(ex. butter)	(ex. milk)
1	140 g	150 g	190 g	200 g	240 ml
¾	105 g	113 g	143 g	150 g	180 ml
⅔	93 g	100 g	125 g	133 g	160 ml
½	70 g	75 g	95 g	100 g	120 ml
⅓	47 g	50 g	63 g	67 g	80 ml
¼	35 g	38 g	48 g	50 g	60 ml
⅛	18 g	19 g	24 g	25 g	30 ml

DRY INGREDIENTS BY WEIGHT

(To convert ounces to grams, multiply the number of ounces by 30.)

1 oz	=	¹⁄₁₆ lb	=	30 g
4 oz	=	¼ lb	=	120 g
8 oz	=	½ lb	=	240 g
12 oz	=	¾ lb	=	360 g
16 oz	=	1 lb	=	480 g

LENGTH

(To convert inches to centimeters, multiply the number of inches by 2.5.)

1 in				=	2.5 cm	
6 in	=	½ ft		=	15 cm	
12 in	=	1 ft		=	30 cm	
36 in	=	3 ft	= 1 yd	=	90 cm	
40 in				=	100 cm	= 1 meter

LIQUID INGREDIENTS BY VOLUME

¼ tsp					=	1 ml	
½ tsp					=	2 ml	
1 tsp					=	5 ml	
3 tsp	=	1 tbls		= ½ fl oz	=	15 ml	
		2 tbls	= ⅛ cup	= 1 fl oz	=	30 ml	
		4 tbls	= ¼ cup	= 2 fl oz	=	60 ml	
		5⅓ tbls	= ⅓ cup	= 3 fl oz	=	80 ml	
		8 tbls	= ½ cup	= 4 fl oz	=	120 ml	
		10⅔ tbls	= ⅔ cup	= 5 fl oz	=	160 ml	
		12 tbls	= ¾ cup	= 6 fl oz	=	180 ml	
		16 tbls	= 1 cup	= 8 fl oz	=	240 ml	
1 pt	=	2 cups	= 16 fl oz	=	480 ml		
1 qt	=	4 cups	= 32 fl oz	=	960 ml		
				33 fl oz	=	1000 ml	= 1 liter

COOKING/OVEN TEMPERATURES

	Fahrenheit	Celsius	Gas Mark
Freeze Water	32° F	0° C	
Room Temperature	68° F	20° C	
Boil Water	212° F	100° C	
Bake	325° F	160° C	3
	350° F	180° C	4
	375° F	190° C	5
	400° F	200° C	6
	425° F	220° C	7
	450° F	230° C	8
Broil			Grill

recipe index

subject index